Confronting

Many American commentators continue to talk about 9/11 as the day the world changed, but increasingly analysts around the world are concluding that more important than 9/11 have been the ideas that the Bush leadership brought into office in January 2001. George W. Bush's preventive war doctrine, his determination to force "regime change" on adversary nations, and his insistence that America must be absolutely secure have reshaped international relations around the world. Focusing on vital issues including terrorism, missile defense, and nuclear proliferation, analysts from eight countries examine the strategic implications of Bush foreign policy, and the governmental and public responses in their individual countries.

Confronting the Bush Doctrine is the first book to take on the vitally important task of analyzing how the Asia-Pacific region sees and evaluates what the United States is doing. With contributions from an outstanding group of scholars, many of whom are based in the region, this book will prove to be an invaluable resource to all students and scholars of American and Asian politics.

Mel Gurtov is Professor of Political Science and International Studies at Portland State University, USA.

Peter Van Ness is a Visiting Fellow in the Contemporary China Centre and lectures in the Department of International Relations at the Australian National University.

Asia's Transformations

Edited by Mark Selden
Binghamton University and Cornell University, USA

The books in this series explore the political, social, economic and cultural consequences of Asia's transformations in the twentieth and twenty-first centuries. The series emphasizes the tumultuous interplay of local, national, regional, and global forces as Asia bids to become the hub of the world economy. While focusing on the contemporary, it also looks back to analyze the antecedents of Asia's contested rise. This series comprises several strands:

Asia's Transformations aims to address the needs of students and teachers, and the titles will be published in hardback and paperback. Titles include:

Confronting the Bush Doctrine
Critical views from the Asia-Pacific
Edited by Mel Gurtov and Peter Van Ness

Japan's Quiet Transformation
Social change and civil society in the twenty-first century
Jeff Kingston

State and Society in Twenty-first-century China
Edited by Peter Hays Gries and Stanley Rosen

The Battle for Asia
From decolonization to globalization
Mark T. Berger

Ethnicity in Asia
Edited by Colin Mackerras

Chinese Society, second edition
Change, conflict and resistance
Edited by Elizabeth J. Perry and Mark Selden

The Resurgence of East Asia
500, 150 and 50 year perspectives
Edited by Giovanni Arrighi, Takeshi Hamashita and Mark Selden

The Making of Modern Korea
Adrian Buzo

Korean Society
Civil society, democracy and the state
Edited by Charles K. Armstrong

Remaking the Chinese State
Strategies, society and security
Edited by Chien-min Chao and Bruce J. Dickson

Mao's Children in the New China
Voices from the Red Guard generation
Yarong Jiang and David Ashley

Chinese Society
Change, conflict and resistance
Edited by Elizabeth J. Perry and Mark Selden

Opium, Empire and the Global Political Economy
Carl A. Trocki

Japan's Comfort Women
Sexual slavery and prostitution during World War II and the US occupation
Yuki Tanaka

Hong Kong's History
State and society under colonial rule
Edited by Tak-Wing Ngo

Debating Human Rights
Critical essays from the United States and Asia
Edited by Peter Van Ness

Asia's Great Cities
Each volume aims to capture the heartbeat of the contemporary city from multiple perspectives emblematic of the authors' own deep familiarity with the distinctive faces of the city, its history, society, culture, politics and economics, and its evolving position in national, regional and global frameworks. While most volumes emphasize urban developments since the Second World War, some pay close attention to the legacy of the *longue durée* in shaping the contemporary. Thematic and comparative volumes address such themes as urbanization, economic and financial linkages, architecture and space, wealth and power, gendered relationships, planning and anarchy, and ethnographies in national and regional perspective. Titles include:

Hong Kong
Global city
Stephen Chiu and Tai-Lok Lui

Shanghai
Global city
Jeff Wasserstrom

Singapore
Carl Trocki

Beijing in the Modern World
David Strand and Madeline Yue Dong

Bangkok
Place, practice and representation
Marc Askew

Asia.com is a series which focuses on the ways in which new information and communication technologies are influencing politics, society and culture in Asia. Titles include:

Asia.com
Asia encounters the Internet
Edited by K.C. Ho, Randolph Kluver and Kenneth C.C. Yang

Japanese Cybercultures
Edited by Mark McLelland and Nanette Gottlieb

Literature and Society is a series that seeks to demonstrate the ways in which Asian literature is influenced by the politics, society and culture in which it is produced. Titles include:

Chinese Women Writers and the Feminist Imagination (1905–1945)
Haiping Yan

The Body in Postwar Japanese Fiction
Edited by Douglas N. Slaymaker

RoutledgeCurzon Studies in Asia's Transformations is a forum for innovative new research intended for a high-level specialist readership, and the titles will be available in hardback only. Titles include:

1. Japanese Industrial Governance
Protectionism and the licensing state
Yul Sohn

2. Remaking Citizenship in Hong Kong
Community, nation and the global city
Edited by Agnes S. Ku and Ngai Pun

3. Chinese Media, Global Contexts
Edited by Chin-Chuan Lee

4. Imperialism in South East Asia
'A fleeting, passing phase'
Nicholas Tarling

5. Internationalizing the Pacific
The United States, Japan and the Institute of Pacific Relations in war and peace, 1919–1945
Tomoko Akami

6. Koreans in Japan
Critical voices from the margin
Edited by Sonia Ryang

7. The American Occupation of Japan and Okinawa*
Literature and memory
Michael Molasky

* Now available in paperback

Critical Asian Scholarship is a series intended to showcase the most important individual contributions to scholarship in Asian Studies. Each of the volumes presents a leading Asian scholar addressing themes that are central to his or her most significant and lasting contribution to Asian studies. The series is committed to the rich variety of research and writing on Asia, and is not restricted to any particular discipline, theoretical approach, or geographical expertise.

China's Past, China's Future
Energy, food, environment
Vaclav Smil

China Unbound
Evolving perspectives on the Chinese past
Paul A. Cohen

Women and the Family in Chinese History
Patricia Buckley Ebrey

Southeast Asia
A testament
George McT. Kahin

Confronting the Bush Doctrine

Critical views from the Asia-Pacific

Edited by
Mel Gurtov and Peter Van Ness

with contributions by Amitav Acharya, Jong-Yun Bae, Owen Harries, Mel Gurtov, Chung-in Moon, Timothy L. Savage, Chih-yu Shih, Richard Tanter, Peter Van Ness, Nicholas J. Wheeler, Jing-dong Yuan, Alexander Zhebin and cartoons and commentary by Michael Leunig

LONDON AND NEW YORK

First published 2005
by RoutledgeCurzon
2 Park Square, Milton Park, Abingdon, Oxon OX14 4RN

Simultaneously published in the USA and Canada
by RoutledgeCurzon
270 Madison Ave, New York, NY 10016

RoutledgeCurzon is an imprint of the Taylor & Francis Group

© 2005 selection and editorial material, Mel Gurtov and Peter Van Ness;
the chapters, the contributors

Cartoons reprinted with permission from *Strange Creature* by Michael
Leunig, published by Penguin Group Australia, 2003

Typeset in Baskerville by Bookcraft Ltd, Stroud, Gloucestershire
Printed and bound in Great Britain by The Cromwell Press,
Trowbridge, Wiltshire

All rights reserved. No part of this book may be reprinted or reproduced
or utilised in any form or by any electronic, mechanical, or other means,
now known or hereafter invented, including photocopying and recording,
or in any information storage or retrieval system, without permission in
writing from the publishers.

British Library Cataloguing in Publication Data
A catalogue record for this book is available from the British Library

Library of Congress Cataloging in Publication Data
A catalog record for this book has been requested

ISBN 0-415-35533-8 (hbk)
ISBN 0-415-35534-6 (pbk)

For Jodi and Anne

Contents

	List of contributors	xi
	Editors' preface	xiv
1	American crusades: unilateralism, past and present MEL GURTOV	1
2	The Bush Doctrine and the North Korean nuclear crisis CHUNG-IN MOON AND JONG-YUN BAE	39
3	Letting the genie out of the bottle: the Bush nuclear doctrine in Asia TIMOTHY L. SAVAGE	63
4	Talking American, acting Taiwanese: behind Taipei's complete compliance with the Bush Doctrine CHIH-YU SHIH	86
5	Chinese perspectives and responses to the Bush Doctrine JING-DONG YUAN	108
6	The Bush Doctrine, Russia, and Korea ALEXANDER ZHEBIN	130
7	With eyes wide shut: Japan, Heisei militarization, and the Bush Doctrine RICHARD TANTER	153
8	The dangers of American exceptionalism in a revolutionary age NICHOLAS J. WHEELER	181
9	The Bush Doctrine and Asian regional order: the perils and pitfalls of preemption AMITAV ACHARYA	203

10	Australia and the Bush Doctrine: punching above our weight? OWEN HARRIES	227
11	The North Korean nuclear crisis: four-plus-two—an idea whose time has come PETER VAN NESS	242
12	Conclusion PETER VAN NESS	260
	Index	270

Cartoons by Michael Leunig appear between pages 152 and 153

Contributors

Amitav Acharya is Deputy Director and Head of Research at the Institute of Defence and Strategic Studies, Nanyang Technological University, Singapore, where he also holds a professorship. His areas of specialization include regionalism and multilateralism, Asian regional security, and international relations theory. He is the author of the forthcoming book: *The Age of Fear: Power and Principle in the September 11 World* (Singapore: Marshall Cavendish, 2004).

Jong-Yun Bae is a Research Professor of the Institute for Korean Unification Studies at Yonsei University in Seoul. His research interests include Korean foreign policy and decision-making processes. His articles have appeared in edited volumes and in journals such as *Korean Political Science Review, Korean Journal of International Relations,* and *Journal of Economic Policy.*

Mel Gurtov is Professor of Political Science and International Studies in the Hatfield School of Government, Portland State University, Oregon, USA. Among his books are *Pacific Asia? Prospects for Security and Cooperation in East Asia* (Rowman & Littlefield, 2001), *Global Politics in the Human Interest* (4th ed., Rienner, 1999), and *China's Security: The New Roles of the Military* (Rienner, 1999). He is Editor-in-Chief of *Asian Perspective.*

Owen Harries, formerly editor of *The National Interest*, is a Senior Fellow at the Centre for Independent Studies in Sydney, Australia. He served in the Australian government of Malcolm Fraser, was Australia's ambassador to UNESCO, and was chairman of the Committee on Australia's Relations with the Third World.

Michael Leunig's words and pictures were first published in Australia in 1965. He was born in Melbourne and now lives on a farm in north-eastern Victoria. His work has previously appeared in the Melbourne *Age* and *Sydney Morning Herald* newspapers, and in over twenty books. These cartoons are reprinted with permission from Michael Leunig, *Strange Creature* (Penguin Group Australia, 2003).

Chung-in Moon is Professor of Political Science at Yonsei University, Seoul. He is also an adjunct professor of the Asia-Pacific Studies Institute, Duke University. Among his numerous publications are three recent books: *State, Market and Just Growth, Understanding Korean Politics*, and *Ending the Cold War in Korea*. He also serves as an adviser to the National Security Council of the Office of the President, the Ministry of Foreign Affairs and Trade, and the Ministry of National Defense in the Republic of Korea.

Timothy L. Savage is a Visiting Fellow at the Institute for Far Eastern Studies of Kyungnam University. Previously, he was Senior Program Officer for Northeast Asia at the Nautilus Institute for Security and Sustainable Development in Berkeley, California, where he coordinated cooperative engagement programs with North Korea. He is currently working on a biography of Syngman Rhee.

Chih-yu Shih teaches Chinese politics, cultural studies, and political psychology at National Taiwan University. He is the author of numerous books in both Chinese and English, including *The Spirit of Chinese Foreign Policy, Collective Democracy, Negotiating Ethnicity in China, State and Society in China's Political Economy*, and *Navigating Sovereignty*.

Richard Tanter is a Senior Research Associate at the Globalism Institute, RMIT University, Melbourne, Australia. Between 1989 and 2003 he was Professor of International Relations at Kyoto Seika University. He is co-editor of *Bitter Flowers, Sweet Flowers: East Timor, Indonesia and the World Community* (Rowman & Littlefield, 2002). *Masters of Terror: The Indonesian Military in East Timor in 1999*, co-edited with Desmond Ball and Gerry Van Klinken, will be published by Rowman & Littlefield in 2005.

Peter Van Ness is a Visiting Fellow in the Contemporary China Centre and lectures on security in the Department of International Relations, both at Australian National University. His major publications include *Revolution and Chinese Foreign Policy* (University of California Press, 1970) and two edited volumes: *Market Reforms in Socialist Societies: Comparing China and Hungary* (Rienner, 1989), and *Debating Human Rights: Critical Essays from the United States and Asia* (Routledge, 1999).

Nicholas J. Wheeler is a Reader in the Department of International Politics at the University of Wales, Aberystwyth. He is co-author of *The British Origins of Nuclear Strategy 1945–55* (Oxford University Press), co-editor with Tim Dunne of *Human Rights in Global Politics* (Cambridge University Press, 2000), and author of *Saving Strangers: Humanitarian Intervention in International Society* (Oxford University Press, 2000).

Jing-dong Yuan is Director of Research at the East Asia Nonproliferation Program of the Center for Nonproliferation Studies, Monterey Institute of International Studies, where he also teaches Chinese politics and security policy. He is co-author of *China and India: Cooperation or Conflict?* (Lynne Rienner Publishers,

2003), and has published in *Asian Survey*, *Contemporary Security Policy*, *Far Eastern Economic Review*, and the *International Herald Tribune*, among others.

Alexander Zhebin is a Senior Researcher at the Center for Korean Studies of the Institute of Far Eastern Studies in Moscow. He served in North Korea for twelve years as the TASS News Agency Bureau Chief and counselor at the Russian Embassy. He has authored two books and numerous articles on security and unification problems on the Korean peninsula.

Editors' preface

In late 2002, before the US invasion of Iraq, Mel Gurtov, editor-in-chief of the journal *Asian Perspective*, invited Pete Van Ness to guest-edit a special issue of the journal on "The Bush Doctrine in Asia." The idea was to invite scholars from the individual countries of Asia whose views represented as full a geographical range of Asian opinion as possible. We were especially eager to understand how US policy was perceived and understood *on the receiving end*. The two of us had talked together for several years about the need for more critical analysis of US policy in Asia and about how to encourage serious examination of strategic alternatives to existing American policies. The inauguration of George W. Bush as president and the radical initiatives undertaken by the so-called neoconservatives in his administration made that agenda appear even more urgent.

To encourage collaboration among the authors, we organized a workshop for the contributors in June 2003, in Seoul, at the Institute for Far Eastern Studies of Kyungnam University. We are grateful to Dr. Jae Kyu Park, President of Kyungnam University, Dr. B. C. Koh, Director of IFES, Dr. Taik-young Hamm, managing editor of *Asian Perspective*, and their staff for their support and hospitality for the workshop. We asked all contributors to prepare first drafts for the workshop, whether or not they could attend personally, and we discussed each of those drafts together with several Korean colleagues, including Professor Geun Lee, Dr. Sung Han Kim, and Dr. Mikyoung Kim. Thanks to all, we had a lively and productive discussion for two days in Seoul.

In early 2004, we set about transforming the special journal issue into a book, a much more comprehensive study in which all of the original authors were joined by several new contributors. The original articles were updated to serve as chapters in an integrated assessment of the Bush Doctrine. We are delighted that so many distinguished colleagues have written for us.

We chose authors, by and large, whom we knew to be critical of the Bush administration. It was not our intention to provide a balance between positive and critical views of the Bush Doctrine—arguments in support of the Bush administration were readily available on a daily basis from all the major world news media. However, we decided at the outset that we would not attempt to impose a particular conceptual perspective on the contributors. Instead, we asked authors to interpret the Bush Doctrine as they understood it, and to analyze its strategic implications for their particular country or issue area in the way that they believed to be most intellectually appropriate.

In less than four years in office, President George W. Bush and his administration have transformed US foreign policy and reshaped global international relations in profound ways. Many American commentators continue to talk about 9/11 as the day the world changed, but increasing numbers of analysts around the world have concluded that more important than 9/11 have been the ideas that the Bush team brought with it to office in January 2001. These ideas were incorporated in the "war on terror" after the 9/11 terrorist attacks, and they emerged as central components of the Bush Doctrine. The pages that follow comment at length on them: unilateralism, preemptive attack, missile defense, new policies for the use of nuclear weapons, and an apparent contempt for international law, especially for treaties or institutions that might limit or constrain the arbitrary exercise of US power.

The opportunity for the United States to launch such radical initiatives was provided by the collapse of the Soviet Union and the emergence into the "post-cold-war world" of a United States with greater relative power by almost any measure than a single country had ever enjoyed at any time in human history. There no longer existed a challenging state to counter US power. The strategic design that was adopted by George W. Bush, who knew almost nothing about foreign policy when inaugurated, was one that right-wing radicals like Richard Perle and Paul Wolfowitz had been propagating at least since the administration of Ronald Reagan. Presumably one aspect of their ideology that made it attractive to the born-again Bush was its Manichean image of world politics as a struggle between the forces of good versus the forces of evil.

The leading "hardliners" in the Bush administration (Dick Cheney, Donald Rumsfeld, and John Bolton, as well as Wolfowitz and Perle) are often called neoconservatives or "neocons," but such a label is misleading. These men are radicals, not conservatives. Conservative leaders of the most powerful country in the world would ordinarily be determined to protect and sustain that country's immensely privileged global position. But these men are not simply trying to preserve the US position in world affairs; they want to transform it. Some, like Paul Wolfowitz, are visionaries in a nineteenth-century, imperial mold. Dreaming of bringing "civilization" to the non-Western world, Wolfowitz is convinced that the United States can democratize the Middle East in the American image by force. Probably today he is wondering why the Iraqi people are not proving more receptive to the opportunity that the US invasion has given them.

The irony is that these most powerful men in the world have only a limited understanding of power, principally material power and its high-tech, "revolution-in-military-affairs" applications. What they fail to understand are the vital cultural and moral dimensions of power, how authority is won and lost, and what motivates individuals to risk (or even to sacrifice) their lives for a cause that they believe in. The hardliners are convinced their cause is just, but they fail to see how violations of America's own principles (for example, torturing prisoners in Iraq, and holding some 600 prisoners from 48 countries for more than two years without charge or trial in the US concentration camp at Guantanamo Bay) can undermine the legitimacy of their "war on terror," and erode claims that the United States might be held up as a model to other countries.

In his speeches, President Bush projects a naive, dangerously child-like view of the world: a fundamentalist vision of black and white, good and evil, "you are either with us or with the terrorists." His characteristic one-liners fail completely to capture the complex realities of our 21st-century world of contrasting cultures, different religions and ethnicities, and competing identities—of old hostilities, new hopes and dreams, and recurring historical nightmares.[1]

Mel Gurtov's introductory chapter places the Bush administration in historical perspective, and concludes with some thoughts about what US policy might be instead if national security were built around cooperative, humane norms. The essays that follow represent the realities that the American leaders seem least interested to understand: how the rest of the world sees and evaluates what the United States is doing. Seven chapters focus on individual countries or particular sub-regions: Chung-in Moon and Jong-Yun Bae on Korean perspectives, Chih-yu Shih on Taiwan, Jing-dong Yuan on China, Alexander Zhebin on Russia, Richard Tanter on Japan, Amitav Acharya on Southeast Asia, and Owen Harries on Australia. Two others, the chapters by Tim Savage and Nick Wheeler, address key issues in the debate, respectively nuclear weapons and preemption. In the last chapter, Pete Van Ness puts forward the idea of a four-plus-two security consortium for Northeast Asia, another alternative to what the Bush Doctrine thus far has meant for the region. Van Ness closes the study with some thoughts on what we have learned from this collaborative investigation. Michael Leunig's cartoons challenge and amuse us throughout, demonstrating how creative political commentary can be.

Thanks to Anne Gunn and Janelle Caiger for their editorial help.

Note

1 Several recent books, written by or about major figures in the Bush administration, shed new light on the internal workings of the Bush White House and how decisions there are actually made. They are: Bob Woodward, *Bush at War* (New York: Simon & Schuster, 2002); James Moore and Wayne Slater, *Bush's Brain: How Karl Rove Made George W. Bush Presidential* (Hoboken, N.J.: John Wiley & Sons, 2003); David Frum and Richard Perle, *An End to Evil: How to Win the War on Terror* (New York: Random House, 2003); Ron Suskind, *The Price of Loyalty: George W. Bush, the White House, and the Education of Paul O'Neill* (New York: Simon & Schuster, 2004); and Richard Clarke, *Against All Enemies: Inside America's War on Terror* (New York: Free Press, 2004). Woodward had special access to the president and the records of his first 100 days after 9/11 and during the invasion of Afghanistan; he provides the best picture of how Bush sees himself as a war leader. Moore and Slater, two veteran Texas journalists, describe the amoral political genius of Bush's closest political aide, Karl Rove. Frum and Perle, two of the leading neocon ideologists, lay out the grand plan of the hardliners in the administration. Suskind tells the story of Paul O'Neill, appointed Secretary of the Treasury and later sacked by Bush, and O'Neill's despair at just how ideological the administration had become. And, finally, Clarke, the anti-terror czar in the administration and a Clinton holdover, recounts the "war on terror" from inside the White House, where invading Iraq seemed to hold first priority. For readers interested in how the administration *would like to be seen*, Bush's former spin doctor, Karen Hughes, has joined the political-campaign fray with her book, *Ten Minutes from Normal* (New York: Viking, 2004).

1 American crusades
Unilateralism, past and present

Mel Gurtov

Under George W. Bush, anti-terrorism has replaced anti-communism as the dominant motif of foreign policy. But anti-terrorism is not a "new ideology." The ideological center is what it always has been: American primacy, based on self-righteousness, the unilateral pursuit of power, "orderly" (market-based) growth, and other staples of predominance. Terrorism has provided Bush with an extraordinary opportunity at home and abroad to press US primacy. Deterrence has been rejected in favor of preemptive (actually, preventive) attack. This is a dangerous doctrine, one that will undermine rather than strengthen American national security. The chapter proposes an alternative: a foreign policy based on human development and common security.

American exceptionalism, again

American foreign policy, it is often said, moves in cycles: between isolationism and internationalism, bilateralism and multilateralism, generosity and stinginess, involvement in and disengagement from global issues. Viewed this way, American foreign policy appears to be episodic, inconsistent, and therefore immune to prediction. This chapter will argue the opposite: continuity is the leitmotif of US foreign policy, and the unilateral pursuit of national interests, the hallmark of policy in the George W. Bush administration, has strong precedent. What makes today's unilateralism different from that of the past is the international and domestic context in which it is being carried out—the war on terrorism, the absence of a counterweight to US power, and the singlemindedness with which the Bush administration is managing American primacy.

While a full-fledged critique of the current administration's foreign policy is useful in and of itself, the phenomenon of unilateralism deserves some historical interpretation. It derives from American primacy since World War II, the time Henry Luce proclaimed was destined to be the "American Century." Though Stalin's Soviet Union also had pretensions to world domination, only the United States then had the capabilities and the political will to conduct a truly global foreign policy—i.e., to reconstruct the world in conformity with its own interests. Unilateralism was bound to be a recurrent phenomenon in US foreign policy, practiced by liberal and conservative leaderships alike. The construction on a world scale of military alliances and a liberal economic order after the 1944 Bretton Woods Conference reflected the goal of primacy, not a commitment to multilateral partnership or global social and economic equity.

From the Korean War to the Gulf War and beyond, collective security has been a device for furthering US interests. US military and intelligence services have intervened frequently in the internal affairs of other countries, friend and foe alike. Containment was practiced not only against the Soviet Union but also against America's defeated foes-turned-potential rivals, Germany and Japan. Presidential "doctrines" from Harry Truman to George W. Bush have brought whole regions (the Middle East, the Mediterranean, Latin America) and global issues (terrorism, nonproliferation, an open-door trading system) within the scope of vital American interests. The deployment of, threats to use, and actual use of weapons of mass destruction (chemical as well as nuclear) put American diplomacy in a class by itself, as does the extensiveness of US force deployments and basing rights beyond American shores. The practice of selective adherence to international law, and occasional blatant violations of it—as in the Central American conflicts of the 1980s—has long been part and parcel of US foreign policy.

Today's unilateralism is of a particularly muscular sort, arising out of the apparent conviction in official Washington that the war on terrorism has provided the opportunity, not taken in the 1990s, to seize the "unipolar moment." But the argument here is that American unilateralism is not only entirely inappropriate to an increasingly interdependent (and unequal) world; it endangers world peace and further reduces opportunities to promote social justice. The alternative I propose is that the United States exploit its enormous international assets to strengthen human development and common security, especially by working in cooperation with other states and nongovernmental organizations (NGOs). Promoting those global interests will enhance real national security more effectively and decisively than will continued pursuit of unilateral advantage.

Cold-war legacies: Vietnam

The notion that the cold war is over, and—according to Secretary of State Colin Powell—that the post-post-cold-war era is upon us, are at best only partial truths. To be sure, world politics has produced new (though very possibly transitory) realignments of states, and the distance in power between the United States and others is greater than ever. But in other key respects, namely, American leaders' frameworks of beliefs, core values, and patterns of behavior, the cold war remains very much alive. A brief look back at the Vietnam era may be a useful reminder of that other reality.

Two powerful forces affected American decision making in the Vietnam War. Neither was a matter of simple anti-communism. One was the intellectual inability to comprehend the way in which prolonged underdevelopment in a colonized Third World country provided fertile ground for a popular anti-government movement. The Viet Cong were dismissed as terrorists, "scavengers of the modernization process" in Walt W. Rostow's famous line.[1] It seemed that despite an abundance of evidence early on of the Viet Cong's nationalist credentials and of its ability to recruit mainly on that basis, the Americans were mystified by the Viet Cong's staying power.[2] At the same time, the Saigon government's ineptitude, unpopularity, and corruption were privately and frequently acknowledged within US councils.[3] But the chagrin of US leaders over having to work with such an illegitimate partner against a popular foe never translated into a decision to withdraw from Vietnam. In the final analysis, the perceived global and domestic political stakes were judged too high to warrant disengagement—globally, America's reputation if it were humiliated; domestically, Johnson's fear of impeachment. So high, in fact, that the American ambassador felt justified in arguing that the United States had "the right and duty to do certain things with or without the [Saigon] government's approval."[4]

Behind that perception lay a second force: simple and disastrous hubris—the conviction that, come what may, the United States would have to press ahead with the war effort, and take increasing casualties, in order to restore world order. Vietnam was thus addressed as another test of the United States, like the crises over Berlin and Soviet missiles in Cuba. To Rostow, the outcome in Vietnam therefore hinged on "the simple fact that at this stage of history we are the greatest power in the world—if we behave like it."[5] President Johnson, despite growing private doubts about winning, concluded that "national security" required hanging on.[6] Publicly, he would often say to "turn tail and run" would amount to another Munich. The prospect of a humiliating defeat became the argument for "national security."[7] Efforts by doves such as Ambassador John Kenneth Galbraith and Undersecretary of State George Ball to warn (in Ball's words) of impending "national humiliation ... even after we have paid terrible costs," far from prompting consideration of ways to cut losses in Vietnam, were instead met with renewed commitment to fighting on.[8]

After Vietnam

Vietnam is often considered the great divide between the era of the imperial presidency and the era of limitations brought on by a more activist US Congress. Though Congress did reassert its authority in the foreign-policy process during most of the 1970s, with passage of the War Powers Resolution in 1993 the high point, the erosion of that authority was well under way by the end of that decade. Some of the same members of Congress who had been doves during the war led the charge back to the future, driven by events in Iran and Afghanistan but also by the recurrent belief in the necessity to "restore" American primacy. Ronald Reagan's presidency was thus a natural evolution to roll back the clock as much as to roll back "international communism": the modernization of strategic forces, the revived importance of the Central Intelligence Agency, the huge increases in military spending, and interventions in Nicaragua and El Salvador were all premised on the notion that America's defenses had been neglected and that the United States needed to reaffirm its central role in defense of freedom on a world scale. To use Christopher Layne's terminology, America's grand strategy—preponderance—did not change in its essentials between 1945 and 1991: "ambitions, interests, and alliances."[9]

Between the collapse of the USSR and 9/11 there was considerable debate in the United States over policy choices and grand strategy. Here and there could be found critical voices that called for converting the absence of an overriding external threat into an opportunity to withdraw US forces from abroad and refocus foreign policy on human-security interests such as sharply reduced military spending, job creation, and energy conservation.[10] But the prevailing viewpoint was a composite of tactical, not strategic, differences in the political mainstream. There, analysts generally agreed that the United States must protect Israel and the oil-rich states, must maintain its alliances, must prevent the proliferation of weapons of mass destruction (WMD), must promote world trade and foreign investment, must watch out for China, and must maintain large, flexible, high-tech, and dispersed military forces. The great challenge they saw for post-Soviet America was how to avoid isolationism. All the signposts—an inward-looking American public, Congressional budget-watching, suspicions about globalization, wariness of "another Vietnam," nasty communal wars in fragile states, and the lack of a major new enemy ("we have run out of enemies," in General Colin Powell's oft-quoted words)—pointed to difficulty for the US political leadership in trying to arouse support for staying globally engaged.[11] The conventional wisdom was that post-cold-war US foreign policy would have to be much more discriminating than before about when to commit US power and prestige.

"Selective engagement" was the new prescription, but it still amounted to containment. To be sure, there was debate over intervention in the Persian Gulf, Bosnia, Somalia, and Kosovo, just as there was over US participation in the Earth Summit, the North American Free Trade Agreement (NAFTA), and bailout loans for Mexico and the Asian countries during their financial crises in the 1990s. Neo-Realists and neo-Globalists certainly had reason to reexamine fundamental precepts following the unpredicted Soviet demise and China's unpredictably rapid rise. Still, when stripped of rhetorical overlay, the bottom line was consensus about America's role in the world—the lessons presumably learned from the cold war and post-cold-war years. Some of those lessons are:

- Great powers make history; others are condemned to follow it. Francis Fukuyama's famous "end of history" thesis was merely a logical extension of that view.
- Adroitly backing diplomacy with power is what determines historical outcomes. The underlying causes of social, economic, and political change (such as revolutions) are not as important as the decision to enforce one's will on others.
- As the leading hegemonic power, the United States has a responsibility—even a right—to impose and maintain order in an anarchic world. Isolationism and withdrawal from world affairs are unthinkable.[12] Instability of any kind threatens US interests because it means disorder. The United States will work with national leaders who support US objectives. Those who get in the way of US

objectives or who have outlived their usefulness will have to be removed. Democracy and past loyalty have nothing to do with either situation.[13]
- The "free world" depends on the United States for leadership. It is indispensable, the hub of the wheel; there is no one else. The United States is "the sheriff of the posse."[14] Nor should anyone else be allowed to take America's place, pose as a third force, or be in a position to define US goals and strategies. Thus, the US reputation is a critical resource that cannot be allowed to suffer, least of all in distant and seemingly marginal conflicts.
- Hence, "national security" really means global security. Market expansion and access to resources are essential to the US economy and American well-being. Threats to American interests are numerous and come in many forms. To contain if not eliminate them requires maintaining a vast array of capabilities and very high spending levels for national security, including a far-flung network of military bases, partnerships, and access points.
- Domestic support to pursue national-security objectives can be counted on if the threat is appropriately magnified, kept constantly before the public, and demonstrated to bear a close relationship to security at home.

The roots of failure

What lies behind this history of unilateralism? Hegemony, or primacy, in and of itself would not seem to be a sufficient condition for unilateralism, but it is surely a necessary condition. America's uniquely powerful position at the end of World War II thus is the beginning of any discussion of the embrace of unilateralism. Structural issues are also important to an explanation. Robert J. Lieber has proposed that these are "the absence of a plausible challenger" to US leadership, the indispensability of an American role in responding to all urgent international issues, and an external threat sufficient to galvanize public and Congressional support.[15] But beyond those factors may lie deeper impulses. Some critical writers, such as William A. Williams, have found the roots of unilateralism in a history of "open-door" expansionism—a quest for "empire," in a word, that traces its roots to the westward expansion of the United States. Other writers, myself included, see ideology as the fundamental problem: the conflating of global with national security, and the philosophical transformation of "national security" into a set of axioms that have guided Democratic and Republican leaders alike as they sought to make and enforce the rules of world order. Still other critics, such as Richard A. Barnet, have long pointed to the "national security state" as representing the institutionalization of America's global ambitions. Commentators who in their analyses go back to the beginning of the United States emphasize the shared belief of US elites in American exceptionalism—the self-styled vision of the United States as the "City upon a hill," that peculiar (and peculiarly successful) experiment to create "a new nation, conceived in liberty," and henceforth a model for others.

From whichever angle one critically assesses America's rise to global power, two factors seem to be constant: the moral superiority that American leaders have traditionally carried abroad, and the fusion of ideals and self-interest in the pursuit of global primacy.

As Jerel A. Rosati has written, the notion persists among US leaders and publics alike that the United States stands above all other nations in its unique historical advantages and consequently selfless international behavior. Rosati identifies three attributes of that self-image: innocence (the desire merely to be the "City upon a hill"); benevolence (the desire to do good for the world and not merely for oneself); and exceptionalism (a confidence and optimism about the superiority—not merely the distinctiveness—of the American experiment).[16] These beliefs could have led to a turning inward, a determination to perfect the experiment and rely on its successes to inspire the world. Instead, they have translated into a justification of America's destiny to lead—to globalize American ideals and, when faced with resistance, to project American power to enforce those ideals and the practical economic and other interests behind them.[17]

Such a powerful sense of destiny seems born of the conviction that God is on America's side. I can think of no other country whose leaders so frequently invoke the Lord's name to bless its enterprises. For America represents not only material progress but moral purity—civilization itself, as George W. Bush and many who preceded him in office have said. And just as "moral clarity was essential to our victory in the cold war," Bush told West Point cadets in June 2002, it would be essential against terrorism. Fortunately, there is no need to debate issues of right and wrong: "Moral truth is the same in every culture, in every time, and in every place," said Bush. "We are in a conflict between good and evil, and America will call evil by its name."[18] What perhaps so outraged Americans about 9/11, Mark Slouka has dared to suggest, is that

> it had happened here. To us. And, lest we forget, we Americans had been commissioned by God himself to be the light of liberty and religion throughout all the earth. Rwanda? Bosnia? Couldn't help but feel sorry for those folks, but let's face it: Rwanda did not have a covenant with God. And Jesus was not a Sarajevan.[19]

Bestowing the blessings of liberty on others thus comes naturally. But it can lead to destructive decisions. Contrary to American expectations, oppressed peoples may not accept that the United States acts solely for their own good. Faced with angry anti-American demonstrations in the Middle East, Dwight Eisenhower wondered why it was so hard for "people in these down-trodden countries to like us instead of hating us." But that did not stop him from authorizing a CIA operation to overthrow the government of Iran.[20] On the other hand, Lyndon Johnson worried that unless the Vietnamese communists were put in their place, revolutionaries everywhere would "sweep over the US and take what we have."[21] The same fear seems to have colored George W. Bush's interpretation of al-Qaeda's motives for attacking the United States. They hate us, said Bush in his September 20, 2001 address to the US Congress, because of America's freedoms, which they are determined to destroy. Like Johnson, Bush substituted cultural arrogance for fact: most likely, al-Qaeda sought to force Islamic governments and peoples to choose between its extremism and "the idol-worshiping enemies of God," meaning the Americans and their Middle East allies,[22] just as the Vietnamese communists fought to win over patriots who detested the Saigon regime and its US patron. Neither group cared a whit about taking away American freedoms; what both wanted was to keep America out of their internal struggles.

The crusading spirit that animates so many American ventures overseas is leavened by the rationalization that the United States acts abroad only because circumstances force it to do so. It is a break from a traditional isolationism. Liberal critics of American foreign policy such as Henry Kissinger have described an America supposedly torn between its roles as exemplar and crusader, an America whose foreign policies have always "oscillated between isolationism and commitment."[23] The United States has certainly gone through periods of reduced international commitments (such as before 9/11 and in the era of the Nixon Doctrine), and serious efforts by the Congress to constrain presidential power (as in the 1970s). But US leaders have never wavered either in their missionary zeal to make the world hospitable to American values or in their preparedness to project US power to protect or acquire what they wanted. Flagrant interventions in the affairs of other countries and a bullying of governments that stand in America's way are hallmarks of a hegemonic foreign policy. For it is one thing to espouse noble ideals such as self-determination and preach respect for democratic processes. In practice, the US mission has been conceived as sometimes having to "save" those who cannot save (or refuse to save) themselves. Henry Kissinger certainly was not ambivalent about choosing between isolationism and commitment when he determined that the United States could not accept the Chilean people's election of Salvador Allende—a vote he regarded as "irresponsible."[24]

The second fundamental element in US foreign policy is the convergence of "liberal" (Globalist) and Realist interests in doctrines that seek to define world order. The rule of law, democracy, and the virtues of the market (geoeconomics) mesh with the pursuit of strategic advantages and political influence (geopolitics). Neither can stand alone; both are pushed with true belief.[25] Though ideals and self-interest have occasionally clashed, far more often they have been mutually reinforcing, in what has sometimes been called the liberal-conservative consensus, liberal internationalism, or simply the mainstream belief system.[26] Different schools of thought have attributed both very narrow motivations to particular US policies—to promote the military-industrial complex or the profits of multinational corporations, for example—and very grand ones—such as to protect a capitalist world order or democracy. But the thrust behind US foreign policy typically transcends (even if it may in specific cases include) the interests of specific groups and is broader still than either Globalist or Realist interests alone. For what else is at stake, in official Washington's viewpoint, than promoting and protecting "the American way of life"? And that way of life is simultaneously more than capitalism, democratization, or military preponderance alone; it is the sum total of all those professed ideals, material interests, strategic preferences, and acquisitive values that together make us what "we" are—number one, and determined forever to remain so.[27]

The notion that American policy makers are somehow divided in their world view was put to rest most recently by Condoleezza Rice. Writing before her appointment as the Special Assistant for National Security to George W. Bush, she said:

> In fact, there are those who would draw a sharp line between power politics and a principled foreign policy based on values. This polarized view—you are either a realist or devoted to norms and values—may be just fine in academic debate, but it is a disaster for American foreign policy. American values are universal … the triumph of these values is most assuredly easier when the international balance of power favors those who believe in them.[28]

What Rice was really saying was that political will counts. There is no grand contradiction in American attitudes or behavior because in the minds of policy makers, "great powers do not just mind their own business."[29] If America is, as Madeleine Albright famously put it, "the indispensable nation," that is not just a fact of international life but a role US leaders have consciously chosen. In theory, the US government could choose to pursue an entirely different course, such as isolationism or global humanism; but, in practice, the will of American leaders has been to make the world safe for American values and interests.

Unilateralism comes naturally to a country that has been at the top for many years. From Theodore Roosevelt and Woodrow Wilson to Dwight Eisenhower and John F. Kennedy, American leaders historically have been internationalist in their commitment to world order through some form of security cooperation, but nationalist in their determination that no multilateral group would ever have binding authority over US actions.[30] Hence, whether in multilateral or bilateral alliances, in wars (from Korea[31] to the war on terrorism), or in international policies (such as on trade, environment, and immigration), the common and pivotal factor for the United States has been control.[32] This objective has spawned a long-held principle of US policy: the United States should act multilaterally (i.e., in concert with others) where US interests would be well served, but otherwise unilaterally. In the last decade or so, for example, both George H. W. Bush[33] and Bill Clinton[34] endorsed this principle, notwithstanding the seeming differences in their rhetoric—"new world order" for one, "engagement and enlargement" for the other.[35]

The Bush Doctrine

Endless war

America's "unipolar moment," as Charles Krauthammer put it, did not quite happen at the time of the Gulf War.[36] But in reaction to Clinton's emphasis on "engagement and enlargement," a powerful group of neoconservatives emerged in

1997 to propose that the moment for vigorous American leadership of world affairs should not be allowed to pass. This group, the Project for the New American Century,[37] took Ronald Reagan as its hero in advocating substantial increases in US military spending and "moral clarity" about America's right to be the global leader. "He championed American exceptionalism when it was deeply unfashionable," wrote two members of the PNAC, who also argued that the United States, rather than curry favor with authoritarian regimes, should seek to overturn them.[38] Signers of the Project's initial statement included prominent conservative writers, former Reagan and Bush administration officials (including Donald Rumsfeld, Dick Cheney, Elliot Abrams, and Paul Wolfowitz), and Jeb Bush, brother of George W. Bush. To state the obvious, the election of George W. Bush virtually assured that the Project's agenda would be incorporated in US national-security policy. But it would take a triggering event, which came on September 11, 2001, to activate the neocon agenda. At that point a president who had seemed to shy away from an activist internationalism—he had criticized the whole notion of nation-building and proposed during the presidential campaign that the United States be a "humble" nation to gain respect—embraced a new crusade. Like US presidents before him, George W. Bush issued a doctrine: "Either you are with us, or you are with the terrorists."[39]

The point is that a sharp move to the right in US policy was largely preordained. Bush's appointments of hardline senior officials in the Defense and State Departments bear that out. In particular, the authors of the infamous 1992 Defense Planning Guidance draft paper in the first Bush administration—Secretary of Defense Dick Cheney and Paul Wolfowitz, then Undersecretary of Defense for Policy—were now back in power to press their case for a vigorous assertion of primacy. General Colin Powell is said to have been an ardent supporter of that paper's main premise.[40] An unusual number of cabinet and other high-level posts were awarded to corporate leaders and lobbyists; those connected with the major energy corporations dominated the list.[41] Some key policy-making positions went to individuals who were indicted for their actions during the Reagan administration's illegal support and subsequent cover-up of aid to the Nicaraguan contras.[42] Equally indicative of Bush's policy bent were some early policy moves: the elimination of "strategic ambiguity" from US policy toward Taiwan following the April 2001 spy plane incident with China; the upgrading of military and diplomatic ties with Taiwan; the rejection of engagement options for dealing with North Korea and Cuba; and the renewed emphasis on military spending, arms sales, and domestic intelligence-gathering in the name of national security. The overall effect of these policy developments was to show how decisively 9/11 had tilted the balance of influence away from traditional diplomacy and toward the Pentagon, where the disciples of neo-Reaganism were firmly ensconced and, reportedly, where the belief ran strong that the State Department was simply not up to the job of carrying out the president's tough policies in the war on terror.[43]

From this angle, the 9/11 terrorist attacks were a gift to the unilateralists. Without 9/11, they would have had a very difficult time persuading a sufficient number of Congress members that national security required such a dramatic refocusing of policy priorities and budget allocations. After all, this was an administration without a popular mandate, Bush having lost the vote for president. Nor, clearly, would it have been possible to twist the domestic agenda to serve foreign-policy ends—a task that has been welcomed by Attorney General John Ashcroft, whose millenarian views are well suited to a moral crusade.[44] Bush's speech to the nation on September 20, 2001, set the direction, not only by drawing a line in the sand, but also by globalizing the war on terrorism ("civilization's fight," he said then and on later occasions).[45] Realist objectives—defeating al-Qaeda and ousting the Taliban, demonstrating American power and will, controlling the conduct of the war, preventing the spread of weapons of mass destruction, establishing bases and creating alliances against terrorism wherever possible and regardless of the ally's domestic politics—once again were combined with Globalist objectives, such as making the war an ideological crusade ("for a just peace—a peace that favors human liberty," Bush said[46]), rebuilding Afghanistan with pro-US leaders, and securing access to oil. As Vice President Cheney added, using language that also harked back to the cold war, winning the war on terrorism was uniquely America's "responsibility" equally for idealistic and power-political reasons.[47]

One is tempted to conclude from the words and actions of the Bush administration that post-9/11 foreign policy has been an attempt to create the "new world order" that Bush's father failed to achieve. Bush the elder's efforts were undermined by economic troubles at home and the traditional tendency of the American public and the Congress to turn attention away from a distant conflict once victory was in hand. But the younger Bush could credibly claim that the terrorism threat was vastly different from one state's aggression against another—a new kind of war, with no endgame and no clear targets. Such a war lent itself to an open-ended strategy: "The terror that targeted New York and Washington could next strike any center of civilization," Bush intoned. "Against such an enemy, there is no immunity, and there can be no neutrality." Early in 2002 he warned that the war had entered a "second stage," "a sustained campaign to deny sanctuary to terrorists who would threaten our citizens from anywhere in the world."[48] By mid-year it was clear that Afghanistan would be just the beginning, and that the United States reserved the right, in the name of self-defense, to carry the war on terrorism wherever it saw fit.[49]

A war without boundaries gave license to two other elements of the Bush Doctrine: preemptive attack and unilateral action. Deterrence and containment were out as useful strategies; preemptive attack was in. In fact, preemption *was* deterrence. Bush's speech at West Point was crystal clear on this point: "Yet the war on terror will not be won on the defensive. We must take the battle to the enemy, disrupt his plans, and confront the worst threats before they emerge. In the world we have entered, the only path to safety is the path of action." Shortly after, press reports indicated that Bush had directed top officials to formalize the idea, with specific attention going to leaders of the three states—Iraq, North Korea, and Iran—that Bush had already dubbed an "axis of evil."[50] The formal statement appeared as The National Security Strategy of the United States of America in September 2002.[51] It sanctified preemption as being "compelling ... even if uncertainty remains as to the time and place of the enemy's attack." And it backed the case for exercising power with the assumption of global responsibility: to promote what was declared, since the end of the cold war, to be "a single sustainable model for national success"; and to "create a balance of power that favors human freedom."[52] But the cold-war character of preemption could not be missed. Where once it was US policy to "get" Libya's Muammar al-Qaddafi, North Korea's Kim Il-Sung, Iran's Ayatollah Khomeini, Cuba's Fidel Castro, and the Congo's Patrice Lumumba, all of whom were considered illegitimate rulers, it was now perfectly proper to "get" Saddam Hussein, Kim Jong-il, and Iran's clerical leadership. In fact, the only thing that might have saved Kim Jong-il was Bush's preoccupation with Iraq.[53]

Secretary of State Colin Powell was correct to say that "preemption has always been available as a tool of foreign policy or military doctrine." What had changed, he added, was that preemptive attack had risen in importance on Bush's list of options.[54] These remarks glossed over two important points, however. Preemption had never before been used to initiate a full-scale war. Since 1945, the numerous previous uses of force by the United States either were in support of one side in an ongoing civil war (Korea, Vietnam), or were punitive raids carried out against other countries (such as Libya in the Reagan years and Afghanistan and Sudan in Clinton's), or were time-limited interventions (Eisenhower in Lebanon, Johnson in the Dominican Republic, Reagan in Grenada, Bush in Panama). The notion of some Bush advisers that President Kennedy's policy of quarantining Cuba during the 1962 missile crisis was a precedent is entirely misguided.[55] Although Soviet motives at the time were a matter of great uncertainty to the Kennedy administration, it handled the situation by rejecting preemptive attack on the missiles or an invasion of Cuba, and resorted instead to private as well as public diplomacy—precisely the steps the Bush administration did not take when dealing with Iraq.

Moreover, preemptive attack is the wrong term, used—one suspects—for political reasons. A preemptive strike is defensive, undertaken first in reasonable expectation of being attacked almost immediately. What the Bush administration was really touting was preventive war, which is waged offensively to destroy an enemy's war-making assets and its government so as (presumably) to render it unable to become strong enough to attack.[56] The companion concept, limited sovereignty, seeks to rationalize early attack on rogue states. As explained by Richard Haass while he was a member of the State Department, the prevailing view in the Bush administration was that:

> Sovereignty entails obligations. One is not to massacre your own people. Another is not to support terrorism in any way. If a government fails to meet these obligations, then it forfeits some of the normal advantages of sovereignty, including the right to be left alone in your own territory. Other governments, including the United States, gain the right to intervene. In the case of terrorism, this can even lead to a right of preventive, or peremptory, self-defense. You essentially can act in anticipation if you have grounds to think it's a question of when, and not if, you're going to be attacked.[57]

The significance of these aggressive innovations soon became apparent when the administration turned attention to attacking Iraq.

Powell qualified use of the "preemptive" option by insisting that it should be exercised "with great care and judiciousness." And it is true that the Bush National Security Strategy paper cautioned that force would not be used "in all cases to preempt emerging threats ... ," and promised that the United States would rely on other governments and regional organizations "whenever possible." But the paper also was emphatic that "we will not hesitate to act alone, if necessary." Other sources were even less bound by concerns about a public or international outcry. One was Richard Perle, a former assistant secretary of defense under Reagan, director of the advisory Defense Policy Board in the G. W. Bush administration, and a leading Republican voice on national security. Anticipating later public advocacy of attacking Iraq by Cheney and Secretary of Defense Donald H. Rumsfeld, Perle early on pushed hard for preemption as the only way to end Saddam Hussein's rule.[58] In his view, Saddam "has motive and he has means"; he will not be deterred by threat of retaliation; and he's working on a nuclear weapon in hundreds of impossible-to-find locations. Reagan, Perle reported, thought Israel's 1981 surprise attack on the Iraqi nuclear reactor at Osirak was "a terrific piece of bombing," and that was a workable precedent for Perle. The real choice is between waiting for Saddam to act and "tak[ing] some preemptive action," he said. And Iraq should only be the beginning. Once having made clear that other terrorist states will come to the same end—Perle's message would be, "You're next unless you stop the practice of supporting terrorism"—"there's a reasonable prospect ... they will decide to get out of the terrorist business. It seems to me a reasonable gamble in any event."

Preemption became the new arm of unilateralism. As the Bush administration demonstrated in the lead-up to invading Iraq, it was convinced that unilateral attack required only a presidential decision; the United Nations, international law, allies, Congress, and the American public could and should be bypassed. Yet the UN Security Council's resolution (under Chapter 7 of the UN Charter) on cooperating in fighting terrorism, passed unanimously at US initiative in late September 2001, neither defined "terrorist" acts nor endorsed unilateral action by a state against terrorists. The United States rejected Secretary General Kofi Annan's proposal to seek explicit Security Council endorsement, on the grounds that Washington already had it under the resolution.[59] Such a view went well beyond a reasonable understanding of what international law allows when it comes to the use of force.[60] As for allied opinion, the US argument was that since the United States is the chief target of international terrorism, it cannot allow other countries to get in the way of its singleminded pursuit of the culprits.[61] The president and other officials were effusive in expressing their gratitude to the seventeen or so countries that deployed military forces in the war in Afghanistan. As Rumsfeld has written, however, and as preemption implies, surprise is a key element in fighting terrorists. This is no time for making war "by committee."[62]

NATO allies that understood America's commitment to multilateralism to mean genuine collaboration on the basis of equality and in the search for peace were sorely disappointed after 9/11.[63] They saw the Americans take their own road on numerous international issues—the Kyoto Protocol on global warming, nuclear-weapons testing and proliferation, Third World trade, capital punishment, Middle East policy (especially the dismissal of Yasser Arafat as a suitable leader of the Palestinian Authority[64]), and the notion of an "axis of evil," to name just a few. The French foreign minister was moved to say that Europe was "threatened by a new simplistic approach that reduces all the problems in the world to the struggle against terrorism."[65] Such criticisms could be heard around the Middle East as well, even by strong supporters such as Crown Prince Abdullah of Saudi Arabia.[66] Dismayed by Washington's inability to see the big picture and its consequently one-sidedly pro-Israel policies, he proposed a peace plan: Israel would be given full diplomatic recognition and security guarantees by all the Arab states in return for restoration of the pre-June 1967 war borders. (The proposal apparently was never seriously pursued.) The criticisms intensified as US scenarios for an invasion of Iraq became public in mid-2002, as discussed below.

The problem is, how can a superpower that feels itself unconstrained to act alone be stopped?

Capabilities

The US armed forces, like those of other countries, are deeply committed to a "revolution in military affairs" (RMA). But unlike the rest, the American program is global in scope and, thanks to 9/11, little constrained by cost or budgetary politics. Secretary Rumsfeld promised to transform the Pentagon from a threat-based to "a new 'capabilities-based' approach—one that focuses less on who might threaten us, or where, and more on how we might be threatened and what is needed to deter and defend against such threats."[67] Actually, it was Powell and Wolfowitz who had initiated the new approach under George H. W. Bush, before the Gulf War, as they sought to preserve a full-scope military in the face of pressure to cut costs.[68] Prominent features of RMA are the acquisition of vast new response capabilities—for defense against attacks by terrorists, missile attacks, and attacks on space and information assets, for example—and the capacity to deter enemies "from building dangerous new [weapons] in the first place."[69] But this is not old-fashioned deterrence, Rumsfeld has made clear. Deterrence now means "that we take the war to the enemy," which requires high-tech firepower and power-projection capabilities in space, undersea, and everywhere else. Michael Klare did not exaggerate when he argued that Rumsfeld's real intention is to "acquire a capacity to defeat any conceivable type of attack mounted by any imaginable adversary at any point in time ... "[70]

September 11 provided the occasion to finance this agenda. Even before, US military spending and arms sales already far outpaced the rest of the world's. For example, from 1995 to 2000 the US share of world military expenditures was 37 percent, greater than the combined military spending of the next nine countries.[71] US contracts for arms sales, amounting to over $18 billion in 2000, accounted for about one-half the world total.[72] Since 9/11, under officially declared wartime conditions, the Bush administration has had a virtual blank check on military spending. By 2003 official US military spending had soared over $400 billion (including Department of Energy spending on nuclear weapons). Compared with the Clinton years, the differences have less to do with specific programs (such as missile defense) than with cost: $470 billion by 2007, or about $100 billion more for the Bush program than for Clinton's. And only a tiny fraction of that difference is accounted for by the war on terrorism.[73] The difference is therefore better explained by the Bush administration's extraordinary ambitiousness to remake the world and retain, forever, absolute military supremacy—which is precisely what the neocons called for in the 1990s.

Nuclear weapons, discussed at length in Timothy Savage's chapter, have revived in importance under Bush in at least two important ways. First, possible use of nuclear weapons against five "rogue states," as well as China and Russia, remains an option and has been publicly discussed. The strategy was unveiled in a Nuclear Posture Review that was submitted to the Congress in January 2002. Later, US contingency plans were reportedly ordered drawn up to incorporate the use of both strategic and new kinds of tactical nuclear weapons.[74] Second, the number of strategic nuclear weapons will remain at excessive levels. Though the Moscow Treaty of 2002 commits the United States and Russia to reduce strategic warheads to between 1,700 and 2,200, it is full of holes that reflect the unilateralist agenda. Since the treaty calls for the warhead reductions to take place by 2012 but without a particular schedule, and permits withdrawal with three months' notice, actual reductions are highly uncertain. Washington got its way, moreover, by insisting that "reduction" of warheads should not necessarily mean their destruction. The treaty allows them to be put in storage, which the Bush administration has indicated is exactly where most of the warheads will be put.[75] Thus the treaty does not actually require the destruction of a single strategic warhead. Nor are the thousands of Russian and American tactical nuclear weapons, "virtual" (laboratory) and actual nuclear tests, and research and development of more destructive or precise nuclear weapons covered by the treaty. In short, from a global-security point of view, the Moscow Treaty continues a tradition of sacrificing real nuclear-weapons reductions and movement toward nuclear disarmament for national advantage.

The long arm of unilateralism

The globalization of national interests risks strategic overextension, as the classic case of Great Britain two centuries ago shows. "A world order policy based on pacification, reassurance, stability, and economic interdependence expands the frontiers of insecurity for the United States," two writers asserted several years before 9/11.[76] Now those expanded frontiers have come to pass. From Georgia, Yemen, and the Horn of Africa in the west to Indonesia and the Philippines in the east, and across the Pacific to Colombia, the war on terrorism has become global and the US military has dug in.[77] Green Berets trained soldiers in Georgia, for example, and Special Operations forces did the same in Djibouti, Yemen, and Colombia—in the last case, accompanying a shift from drug eradication to counterinsurgency training.[78] About 60,000 US military personnel were stationed in forward bases in the Middle East alone, with Qatar the center of operations in case of war against Iraq. Nearly 1,300 US advisers were based in the Philippines, whose army is fighting the Abu Sayyaf guerrillas. The US military provided funding for police, army, and border-control forces: a $50 million program over two years in Indonesia, a $20 million program in Uzbekistan, and a $200,000 program in Algeria, for instance. Military-to-military relationships were tightened with India and Indonesia, among other countries. US military aid was extended to Nepal, Tajikistan, Yemen, and other countries with serious internal conflicts.[79] Military bases were established or expanded in several countries. Aside from a presence in Afghanistan itself, US forces were encamped in at least three bases in Pakistan, two in Kyrgyzstan (about 1,000 soldiers), one in Uzbekistan (about 2,000), and one in Djibouti (about 800). All these efforts were rationalized as necessary steps to prosecute the war on terrorism; but, in fact, most of them were targets of opportunity with no clear relationship to the pursuit of al-Qaeda or any other international terrorist network.[80]

Manipulation of the war on terrorism to serve other ends was apparent in several places, starting with the former Soviet republics of Central Asia. Without exception, political leadership in these states had passed into the hands of despots who did not show the slightest interest in honest, democratic governance. They learned from the cold war that manipulation is a two-way street; subscribing to "anti-terrorism" enhanced their bargaining power. They were no doubt delighted to cooperate with the United States in return for US aid (and in some cases World Bank loans) and, by implication, political backing in their struggles to quash opposition movements. In return, not only did the United States gain staging areas for its forces and use of these countries' airspace; American corporations acquired a privileged position in the search for new sources of oil and gas, and US arms manufacturers found new markets for their wares, in several instances made possible by presidential waiver of sanctions against the recipient governments.[81] It seems that the closer these governments got to Washington, the freer the hand their leaders believed they had to jail opponents, muzzle the press, salt away aid money and corporate bribes in personal bank accounts, and avoid accountability.[82] Kazakhstan under Nursultan Nazarbayev was a notorious case in point.[83]

In the Philippines, the Abu Sayyaf guerrillas are basically a gang that has been engaged in kidnappings for ransom for about thirty years. Wiping them out would hardly constitute a victory over global terrorism, any more than would eliminating a Mafia operation in, say, Russia. The six-month US military mission ended July 31, 2002, with mixed results. But the real story was Washington's opportunism in pressing for closer military ties with Manila. In August 2002 US and Filipino officials announced that not only would US military aid to the Philippines, in training and equipment sales, be increasing over a five-year period, the two countries would also establish a senior civilian policy-making group, with Filipino communists now the main target.[84]

In Indonesia, until the disco bombing in Bali in October 2002, the case for a direct connection between al-Qaeda and any of the militant Islamic groups operating in that country was not persuasive.[85] Whether that has changed is a matter of opinion. Even before Bali, the Bush administration had quite openly pressured the government of Indonesia to line up against militant Muslim groups such as Jemaah Islamiyah. Bush has clearly been looking for a chance to resume a direct military relationship with Indonesian armed forces, whose human-rights abuses in East Timor and other outlying islands—with the full knowledge and even consent of the United States starting in the Gerald Ford–Henry Kissinger years— have been well documented. Arms sales and other military ties to Indonesia were barred by Congress in 1998 and 1999; but, under Bush, that has not prevented some aid from flowing, using the Pentagon's instead of the State Department's budget to evade Congress' intention. "We are starting down a path to a more normal relationship with respect to military-to-military," Secretary Powell said.[86] (In a perfect illustration of foreign policy at the nexus of Realism and Globalism, at the same time that military ties with Indonesia were being mended, the US State Department intervened on the side of Exxon Mobil in a human-rights case against the company that was filed in the United States by Aceh villagers.[87])

Efforts such as these were clearly part of a larger US strategy for recreating security ties across Southeast Asia, as evidenced by the August 1, 2002 treaty between the ten-member Association of Southeast Asian Nations and the United States to cooperate to "prevent, disrupt and combat" international terrorism.[88] Typically, this development came along with US assurances of no intention to base US troops on Asian soil or to ignore any repression of legitimate dissent. But such assurances ring hollow: there has been no American remonstrating on behalf of human rights and democratic norms in, say, Indonesia or Burma; and the number of US advisers and Special Forces continues to mount. Moreover, the real impact of military cooperation on US security may well be negative. Associating the United States with repressive regimes, making US forces and personnel targets of local opposition forces, undermining the credibility of US efforts to play the role of disinterested third party in international disputes, arousing anti-American nationalism, and becoming party to what are really long-running situations of local violence can hardly be said to enhance America's global position or the attractiveness of American values.[89] Furthermore, as Amitav Acharya's chapter shows, some Southeast Asian officials worry about the possibility that association with the Americans' war on terror might diminish their countries' sovereignty and make them vulnerable to external interference—not from China but from Australia.

The war in Afghanistan also led to major changes in US policy toward India and Pakistan. Washington, needing Pakistan's cooperation to seal off the western border from fleeing Taliban and al-Qaeda soldiers, aligned itself with the military dictatorship of General Pervez Musharraf. Pakistan, whose intelligence service had once been—and, some sources say, still is—an important source of support of the Taliban as well as of pro-Pakistan separatist groups in Kashmir, allowed US Special Forces to roam the borderlands and use at least three of its military bases. Sanctions on Pakistan for its nuclear-weapon tests in 1998 were removed; its government, well known for corruption, received $600 million in aid, an open door to International Monetary Fund (IMF) assistance ($135 million), and access to the F-16 jet fighters that it had bought from the United States but been denied the right to possess. Musharraf, while cracking down on allegedly radical Islamic schools and groups in his country, used the opportunity afforded by the war to cement his rule.[90] Bypassing the parliament, he extended his presidency by five years in a national referendum in April 2002 that was widely condemned as having been rigged. His was the only name on the ballot. Four months later Musharraf gave himself a raft of new powers, including the right to amend the constitution and dissolve the parliament. The State Department politely announced that it still favored "the establishment of democratic civilian rule under constitutional means" in Pakistan.[91] Even the exposure in October 2002 of Pakistani assistance to North Korea's once-secret nuclear-weapons program—providing the DPRK with uranium-enrichment technology in exchange for missile parts—and later of Pakistan as the source of Libya's unsuccessful program to build an atomic bomb, and possibly of Iran's nuclear program, did not dampen US support of Musharraf.[92]

Once having secured Pakistan's loyalty to the larger cause, Washington turned its attention to India. The overt US objective seemed to be to reverse years of mutual disaffection and thus have some leverage over Indo-Pakistani tensions in Kashmir, which by 2002 had again ratcheted up. After September 11 there was a sudden flurry of military activity between the United States and India: exchanges of official visits, joint exercises and patrols, and the resumption of military sales to India that had been suspended because of India's nuclear tests in 1998. Here again was a marriage of convenience that had little if anything to do with the war at hand. For India, the United States represents access to technology and investment, an upgrading of weapon systems, and a source of leverage on Musharraf for stopping "terrorist" attacks on India's portion of Kashmir. For the United States, getting closer to India is probably part of a geopolitical strategy for containing China—the joint sea patrols send just such a message—and yet another potential military staging area in the region.[93]

As discussed below, Russia and China also benefited from pledging to support the war on terrorism. Some analysts have maintained that such a common ground will encourage more cooperative relations between the United States, China, and Russia on issues that divide them. But that seems to be very much a long shot. There is no common enemy; each country defines and deals with terrorism on its own terms. The partnership is skin-deep; and while relations between the United States and Russia and China do involve shared interests—interests, in fact, that are more profound than the war on terror—they cannot hide the deep and numerous sources of division: with China, over its ambitions in Asia, relations with Taiwan,[94] and political reform, for instance; with Russia, over strategic weapons reductions, economic ties with Iran and Iraq, and policies in its "near abroad"; and with both countries over the export of training and equipment for WMD programs.[95]

These shifts in international relationships after 9/11 reveal the impulsiveness of American foreign policy—the sacrifice of a positive, peace-promoting long-term vision, rooted in democratic and humane values, to immediate interests. It is a repetition of a prominent cold-war trend. In every instance today, military opportunities are paving the way for broader political and economic relationships; and those new relationships are feeding the appetite for empire—the chance to extend American "benevolence" across ever-wider regions. Gaining access to all these countries in order to "fight terrorism," "liberate Iraq," and "democratize the Middle East" was never the endgame. The real objective, as in the cold war, was to create a reliable network of international collaborators who gain personally by supporting "the American way of life." In return, the US government was assured of new markets for military as well as ordinary products, new jump-off points for intervention in the Middle East and elsewhere, new foreign-investment opportunities for American companies—in short, all the ingredients believed to be necessary for maintaining the empire.

On to Iraq

It is one thing for Washington to help overthrow a government that does not serve its interests, and quite another to apply hegemonic power directly. Afghanistan seems to have emboldened Bush to make Iraq the next, and most important, test of his doctrine. As the previously quoted speech of Richard Perle in November 2001, among numerous other reports, makes clear, the Bush administration wanted to move on Saddam Hussein well before the summer of 2002. In fact, finding a political basis and a military strategy for eliminating him ("regime change," as it came to be called) was apparently a US objective from the time Bush took office. September 11 meant that other business would have to be taken care of first.[96] But there was no mistaking the administration's priorities, nor what it was prepared to do to enforce them. As Bush's director of counterterrorism, Richard A. Clarke, found the day after the 9/11 attacks, Bush and company had no intention of letting pursuit of Osama bin Laden get in the way of invading Iraq. In fact, they were desperate, despite all evidence to the contrary, to find a link between al-Qaeda and Iraq—a determination that left Clarke feeling "incredulous."[97]

Perle's logic for attacking Iraq—a "reasonable gamble"—is worth noting; it anticipated official US policy. The difficulties of removing Saddam were nothing in comparison with the opportunities, Perle said: "look at what could be created, what could be organized, what could be made cohesive with the power and authority of the United States fresh from a successful campaign to destroy the Taliban in Afghanistan." America, sheriff of the posse; mount up! But when Congressional hearings on Iraq got under way in August 2002, amidst numerous press reports of active war planning by the military, the many unreasonable aspects of such a conflict were on the table: outrage throughout the Middle East and new encouragement for terrorist groups; further alienation of US allies, some of whose leaders (e.g., Germany's Chancellor Gerhard Schröder, who won reelection on an anti-war platform) very publicly disagreed with Bush's aim to overthrow the Iraqi leadership; the possibility that Iraq might use mass-destruction weapons if the regime were on the verge of extinction; the threats to civilian populations; the likelihood that Iraq after Saddam would be unstable, undemocratic, and dependent for security on US forces; and the destabilizing effects of a war on Israel–Palestine relations, the future of the Kurdish people, and other parties in and near Iraq.

Beyond all those considerations lay some crucial matters of fact. Neither at Congressional hearings on Iraq in August 2002 nor for some time afterward did the administration produce evidence that Iraq had any connection to the 9/11 attacks or to al-Qaeda's presumed efforts to acquire weapons of mass destruction.[98] What the administration eventually did produce hardly qualified as evidence— "some" al-Qaeda members had been in Baghdad at one time, and there were signs of "possible chemical- and biological-agent training" of al-Qaeda by Iraq.[99] Nor did the administration produce evidence that Iraq had the means to deliver chemical or biological weapons, was on the verge of achieving a nuclear-weapon capability, or was bent on dominating its neighbors by possessing WMD—all charges that Bush made in a speech to the UN General Assembly on September 12, 2002.[100] As time went on, the rhetoric became increasingly shrill and the charges even more expansive—such as that Iraq might strike the United States first, a charge disputed by the CIA director, who argued that the far greater probability was that Saddam Hussein would use WMD only in response to an attack.[101] The internal challenges to the administration's credibility were so intense that Rumsfeld and Wolfowitz formed their own intelligence team to evaluate the Iraqi threat.[102] It was later revealed that Iraqis in exile with close ties to the Pentagon provided the defectors who became the chief sources of this team's intelligence on Iraq—intelligence that for the most part was worthless as well as self-serving.[103] The case against Iraq thus seemed to be increasingly driven by ideology and timed to election-year politics.

The issue is not that Saddam Hussein had ceased his efforts to acquire and hide WMD capabilities; no doubt such efforts were continuing. Nor is there a question of his regime's systematic human-rights violations, war crimes, and defiance of numerous Security Council resolutions dating from the Gulf War that were designed to ensure constant international access to Iraq's military programs. But such conduct was of long standing, and aside from the periodic US and British bombing of Iraqi missile sites had never been considered the occasion for a war. In short, there was no crisis over Iraq to justify the American demand—for that is what US pronouncements amounted to—that Iraq either prove that it had terminated its WMD programs or face American power, with or without the endorsement of others. As one retired four-star American general said in stating the case for dealing with Iraq within the UN system: "It's a question of what's the sense of urgency here, and how soon would we need to act unilaterally? So far as any of the information has been presented, there is nothing that indicates that in the immediate, next hours, next days, that there's going to be nuclear-tipped missiles put on launch pads to go against our forces or our allies in the region."[104]

One can only conclude from the timing of the presidential decision to go to war and destroy both Iraq's WMD capabilities and its regime that it was motivated not by new information concerning either Iraq's capabilities or its intentions—US intelligence findings had presented a far less threatening and more nuanced picture of Iraq[105]—but, just as Richard Perle proposed, by pure opportunism.[106] In a word, the administration distorted information and lied to the public in order to create the appearance of imminent threat. There were no hidden or deployed weapons of mass destruction (as postwar US surveys determined), there was no close or menacing al-Qaeda–Iraq connection,[107] and there were no Iraqi plans for intimidating its neighbors or attacking the United States. The US–UN bombings during the first Gulf War and subsequent UN inspections of Iraq had destroyed that country's WMD programs and the ability quickly to restore them, just as some former UN inspectors and administration critics had contended.[108]

The administration's hype concerning the Iraq threat was packaged for sale to a public still haunted by Vietnam but outraged by 9/11.[109] Buoyed by the overthrow of the Taliban in Afghanistan and by the establishment of numerous military outposts across Eurasia, the administration probably saw attacking Iraq as a chance to tighten its grip on world politics and economy, specifically including oil supplies.[110] After the war's official end, Bush shifted his rationale for invading Iraq to "liberating" it; but in fact regime change, and not liberating or even disarming Iraq, was always the objective. And it was crucial to achieve it quickly, in light of several considerations: the 2002 elections, which otherwise would favor the Democrats by focusing on poor performance of the economy, corporate scandals, and other domestic issues;[111] the faltering nation-building effort in Afghanistan; the gradual weakening of support in Congress for further military adventures in the absence of new terrorist attacks; the buildup of opposition in foreign capitals. In short, Bush needed to maintain the momentum of the anti-terror war, and the accretion of executive power it had produced. His objective reduced to a simple proposition: to demonstrate the efficacy of a take-charge foreign policy that relied principally on the overpowering use of force.

Opposition in the media and in Congress to attacking Iraq was virtually nonexistent, the legalities of going to war were hardly debated, and possible diplomatic alternatives were dismissed by US officials and key members of Congress. (Among the alternatives were Iraq's invitations in July and August 2002 to the UN to resume discussion on inspections, and to the Congress to send a delegation, with experts, to examine anywhere it wished for evidence of WMD; an Iraqi effort to open back-channel talks with US leaders;[112] and a Canadian-led initiative in the UN that would have required Iraq to meet step-by-step demands for compliance with Security Council resolutions.) The United States' own role in the solidification of Saddam's rule—its "tilt" toward Iraq during the Iran–Iraq war in the 1980s—was ignored, just as it had been in the early 1990s. Other revelations—first, that during that war, the United States (with Saudi cooperation) had shared intelligence information with Iraq's military and knew it would employ chemical weapons against Iran; second, that a US government agency had unwittingly sent Iraq biological samples that found their way into Iraq's germ-warfare program; third, that "the United States has fought aggressively throughout the last decade to purposefully minimize the humanitarian goods that enter" Iraq in order to gain support for "smart sanctions"[113]—got virtually no press attention. Yet both then and later, Washington publicly condemned Iraq's use of poison gas and the threat posed by its biological weapons.[114] And anxieties elsewhere about the terrible human toll in Iraq that US blockages and delays of civilian aid helped exact was diverted by Washington's accusations that Iraq was not using its oil revenues to meet human needs.

Even if members of Congress had wanted to assert their constitutional prerogative and enforce the 1993 War Powers Resolution, their hands were tied. For one thing, the House and Senate had committed the same mistake after 9/11 that they had made early in the Vietnam war, and again in 1991, in approving resolutions on the use of force that were wide open to abuse. The language of the authorizing legislation in September 2001 gave President Bush a virtual blank check to respond to terrorism—first, by authorizing use of "all necessary and appropriate force" to combat terrorism, without any geographical or time limits; second, by resolving that Iraq's refusal to allow full UN inspection of its weapons sites "presents a mounting threat to the United States, its friends and allies, and international peace and security."[115] Some Republican leaders in Congress argued that Bush thus had all the authority he needed to wage war on Iraq.[116] Various Bush administration spokespersons went further, suggesting that even those instruments were unnecessary, since UN Security Council resolutions during the Gulf War and Congressional support at that time still applied in 2002.

Nevertheless, Bush, like his father in 1991, reluctantly accepted the need for Congressional approval of war-making. In late September 2002 he submitted a resolution to Congress that authorized him to

> use all means that he determines to be appropriate, including force, in order to enforce the United Nations Security Council Resolutions [of 1990–1991], defend the national security interests of the United States against the threat posed by Iraq, and restore international peace and security in the region.[117]

The final version closely followed that language.[118] After several days of "debate"—speech-making, in fact—the House of Representatives voted 296–133 in favor and the Senate voted 77–23. (More Democrats favored than opposed the measure in the Senate; the opposite was true in the House.) Once again, Congress allowed a president to define national security in the broadest possible sense, evade the intended restraints of the War Powers Resolution, and have free rein to use military power in the manner and to the extent the president wished. It was, as Senator Patrick J. Leahy of Vermont said, an extraordinary "surrender to the president [of] authority which the Constitution explicitly reserves for the Congress."[119]

The United Nations and allied opinion were the only potential barriers to US war policy. In contrast with Bush's warnings around the first anniversary of the 9/11 attacks—that the United States would act if the UN did not, and (in a speech before the General Assembly) that the UN must either act to disarm Iraq or become "irrelevant"—Secretary General Kofi Annan pointedly criticized countries that chose to act multilaterally only when it was politically convenient to do so. "There is no substitute for the unique legitimacy provided by the United Nations," he said.[120] Iraq responded favorably to Annan's entreaties, offering international inspection "without preconditions." But Bush and his advisers were not merely skeptical; they lobbied hard in the Security Council for a tight one-week deadline for Iraq's agreement to unfettered access. The draft resolution proposed by the United States virtually guaranteed Iraq's rejection and, as the French and others were well aware, made an invasion almost certain.

European Union (EU) leaders and their publics, which in every country were overwhelmingly opposed to war on Iraq, distanced themselves from US policy. Germany's Schröder firmly rejected participating in an attack on Iraq even if the UN Security Council approved it. His defense minister announced that if an attack occurred, Germany would withdraw its counter-WMD force from Afghanistan. French Prime Minister Jacques Chirac said US policy on Iraq was "extraordinarily dangerous" and warned that such unilateralism would, among other consequences, intensify anti-American feelings worldwide.[121] Only Britain's Prime Minister Tony Blair was supportive, even as many in his party were not. Among US Middle East allies, anti-war feelings were just as prominent. "Just open a map," a member of the Kuwaiti royal family described as being close to Washington decision makers said. "Afghanistan is in turmoil, the Middle East is in flames, and you want to open a third front in the region?"[122] If, as Prince Abdullah averred, al-Qaeda's purpose was to drive a wedge between the United States and Saudi Arabia, it was succeeding.[123] Responding to widely reported American comments about using bases in friendly countries for the invasion, King Abdullah II of Jordan vowed that "Jordan will not be used as a launching pad."[124] Even Pakistan's Musharraf, whose government no more welcomed international inspection of its nuclear facilities than did Iraq, said on several occasions that an invasion of Iraq was unwise. Only the Turkish government, beset by economic problems and desperate for debt relief and membership in the European Union, was willing to consider allowing the United States use of air bases (but not deployment of ground forces) in the event of a war with Iraq.[125] All these demurrers proved soft; once the Security Council voted to demand Iraq's compliance with its disarmament resolutions, every Middle East government, including Saudi Arabia and Jordan, acquiesced to US pressure that its territory be available for war on Iraq. All these governments could do was voice their hope that the war would be brief and not result in Iraq's being carved up.

The case for global engagement

Risky business

A post-post-cold-war era it may be, but too many cold-war era practices remain in effect to warrant declaring this "era" all that different from the one it has supposedly replaced. Drawing lines in the sand, waltzing with dictators, putting human rights in the back seat, placing supreme faith in military technology, elevating access to oil and other resources to the top rung of policy objectives, neglecting the root causes of violence directed at the United States and its allies, presuming to have the keys to "nation-building," manipulating an external threat to justify illiberal domestic practices, hyping the enemy's capabilities, preferring punishment to engagement of rivals, interpreting competition for influence as a test of wills, needing to prove that any of the enemy's methods can be defeated, ignoring the UN and allies except when it serves US policy to use them, neutralizing dissent in the name of national security, proclaiming the goal of making the world safe for democracy but acting quite differently, turning foreign policy into a moral crusade—the list goes on and on. When one looks in the mirror of the war on terrorism, one sees the outlines of America's war on communism.

There are differences between the two wars, and one of them is the Bush administration's penchant for going it alone. To its practitioners, unilateralism is relatively cost-free: friends may be discomfited, but they depend on American largesse and have no leverage to do more than protest. Or so it is thought. But alienating America's closest friends does carry risks and costs. The administration's imposition of a tariff (withdrawn after a year) on most steel imports, its rejection of the Kyoto Protocol, and its insistence (as part of its rejection of the Rome Treaty that created the International Criminal Court) that US soldiers be exempt from war-crime prosecution when on UN peacekeeping missions are among the policies that have deeply angered US allies in NATO and other governments, not to mention the UN leadership and international NGOs. Throwing US resources fully into the war on terrorism has led to the neglect of important partnerships, such as with Mexico and much of the rest of Latin America, where the post-9/11 economic downturn worldwide has had profoundly destabilizing consequences.[126] Criticisms of US policy from abroad did not amount to mere carping; they affected the willingness of allies and others to cooperate with Washington, such as on international trade, on the occupation of Iraq, and (in the context of the UN) on international security. (The Spanish public's vote in March 2004, immediately following terrorist bombings in Madrid, to oust a pro-US government in favor of a socialist one is a case in point. The new prime minister announced that he would withdraw the 1,500-member Spanish contingent from Iraq unless the occupation had UN approval.) Coalition politics cuts two ways: Europeans and others may decide to make international policy without the United States, as happened on environmental issues and the International Criminal Court.

Acting alone (or being alone in not acting) risks being left on the sidelines—alone to pay the costs, assume the burdens, add to the interests that might otherwise be shared.[127] John Ruggie's study of US foreign policy in the 1940s and 1950s concludes that unilateralism "opened the door to isolationism" because of failures to act when an overriding human interest demanded it.[128] Particularly for an administration that wants to narrow the range of US interests it is prepared actively to defend, one would think that increased multilateral involvement would be welcome burden-sharing. In humanitarian crises such as Bosnia, Kosovo, and Rwanda, US leadership was found wanting, and hundreds of thousands of needless deaths resulted.[129] Reserving unilateral action for "evil" regimes such as Iraq's, on the other hand, is bound to have devastating consequences, not only (as noted earlier) in the target country and its neighbors, but also for the precedent it sets of preventive attack, for instance, in relations between India and Pakistan, or Russia and Chechnya.

The costs of unilateralism were on display after the US invasion of Iraq officially ended in May 2003. The United States emerged in the position of a colonial authority, exercising power through its military presence and obedient clients throughout the Middle East and Central Asia. Revealing both arrogance and naiveté, Washington proceeded to run Iraq like a protectorate, handpicking its leaders, demobilizing its armed forces, purging its once-ruling party, taking control of its oil, and establishing bases on its territory. But Iraqi resistance, even after the capture of Saddam Hussein, pushed US casualties toward 600 dead. As of the spring of 2004, with a presidential election approaching, Washington was desperately trying to keep the pieces together in Iraq: sustain support of the new constitution by the Shiite majority; meet a mid-year deadline for turning sovereignty over to an Iraqi government not popularly elected; and legally keep US troops in control of Iraq's security at least until the end of 2005. The Bush administration was also seeking financial help from other countries to reduce Iraq's debt. But its unilateral pursuit of war and advantage gravely undermined its postwar search for assistance.

Other American interventions lurk just beyond Iraq. US military leaders apparently envision a long-term policing mission in Central Asia that could make the United States responsible for political "stability" in any number of authoritarian states.[130] As noted, the United States has used the war on terrorism as an opportunity to create a number of bases, training facilities, and political and military partnerships with military-backed governments from Algeria to Indonesia and Colombia. If the cold war is any guide, such partnerships will be manipulated by US partners, human rights and democratization in these countries will suffer, and the US government will be associated with the fate of the regimes whose bed it shares. A decent US foreign policy, genuinely dedicated to "liberty and justice for all," is thus again for sale: the thread that today binds the United States together with partners in the war on terror is purely instrumental and typically has nothing to do with promoting democratic rule, civil liberties, or even free-market capitalism.

In some cases, such alliances undermine other professed (and worthy) objectives. Nonproliferation of WMD is seriously compromised by continued US closeness to Pakistan, whose government's nuclear-weapon establishment sold its secrets and technologies, and by US aid to Yemen, whose government may have helped sell North Korean missiles.[131] America's proclaimed adherence to democratic values loses credibility by association with governments such as Kazakhstan and Azerbaijan, which are irredeemably corrupt and oppressive. Perhaps of greatest consequence for the war on terror is the failure of US efforts to craft an equitable Middle East peace. The generally uncritical US policies toward Israel, which are roundly condemned in Arab and Muslim quarters from North Africa to Southeast Asia, renders the US "road map" for an Israel–Palestine settlement a dead letter. The Israeli government treats its Palestinian citizens in the manner of a colonial occupier: like sub-humans—everyone under suspicion, presumed to be terrorists and prevented by high barriers from freely going about their work. All these governments, and still others that support the Bush Doctrine, consider anti-terrorism a marvelous catchall for suppressing legitimate internal dissent. But so long as they serve US strategic and economic interests, the Bush administration will say nary a word against them—and in fact will see that they are well armed and financially rewarded.

Instead of engaging states that abuse American friendship and flout professed American values, the Bush administration should consider creative ways to reduce tensions with states it says threaten regional security. Its course, however, is to confront so-called rogues. The chapter by Moon and Bae on North Korea brings out the dangers such a course entails. The administration's defenders claim that regime change in Iraq worked to defuse these dangers: fear of US attack, in their view, prompted the North Koreans to agree to multilateral talks concerning their nuclear-weapon program, the Iranians to permit inspectors to view their nuclear facilities, and the Libyans to announce that they were terminating attempts to build a nuclear bomb. This is a very unfortunate interpretation, for it justifies the neocon strategy of relying on force and rejecting diplomatic deals so as not to "reward bad behavior." In fact, there is every reason to think that all three states sought to develop nuclear weapons as defense against attack by the United States or others, in emulation of American deterrence policy, and that their willingness to give up nuclear weapons is negotiable, depending on the removal of US sanctions and the start of American economic aid.[132]

A human-development and common-security agenda

Redefining US foreign and national-security policy requires acknowledging a number of things. One is that what others think about us, and might do to us, is important. The answer to Bush's question "Why do they hate us?" has much to do with the double standards of American policies and the threatening character of a global American culture and economy. It behooves us to change both the reality and the image of America, not (as under Bush) as a matter of public relations, but as a matter of sound internationalism. Secondly, the future reshaping of the planet as the result of declining environmental and ecological trends is a matter of urgent attention. As Jessica Tuchman Mathews has written, among the many changes such declines require of the United States is to make a strong place for multilateral diplomacy—which translates into an international role that "allows leadership without primacy"—and "a planetary sense of shared destiny" in place of indifference to growing North–South cleavages.[133] These are the ingredients of a new internationalism, one that takes grievances, cultural differences, and inequalities seriously.

More specifically, at the heart of human- and common-security approaches to international security is conflict prevention. Global engagement is one form of prevention.[134] Oddly enough, American indispensability can provide a starting point for a strategy that puts engagement back at the center of US foreign policy. Peter Van Ness's chapter in this volume on a "four-plus-two" arrangement to deal with the security dilemma on the Korean peninsula is an example of positive US leadership. For if it is true that the United States, by what it does and by what it chooses not to do, uniquely shapes international politics—in every policy sphere, from trade and environment to peacekeeping and disarmament—then the opportunity is great to influence a large-scale shift of resources to meet global-community needs and provide meaningful security where it matters, in local communities and environments. Global leadership is a precious commodity. It can be used to promote a just peace in the Middle East, Northern Ireland, and Kashmir.[135] It can seek to prevent war by engaging rather than confronting so-called "rogue" states, for if (as the Bush administration has said) weak states are the number-one strategic challenge for the United States, strengthening their human-security conditions makes more sense than bringing them to their knees.[136]

The United States can also provide leadership to abolish nuclear weapons and, in the meantime, to create a powerful global consensus behind drastically reducing nuclear arsenals, ending nuclear-weapon testing and deployment, securing weapons-grade nuclear material and nuclear plants so that the material does not fall into the wrong hands, and halting nuclear proliferation.[137] Instead of squandering the right to lead through engaging in self-righteous, overweening behavior, the United States could set an example—restraint in the use of force and in arms sales and transfers; responsiveness to humanitarian crises; and support of and adherence to international agreements on the environment, human rights, and war crimes.[138]

Preventive steps to promote human development are a second element of a new foreign policy. The United States can direct its own and global institutions' financial, technical, and human resources to programs that will give deserving governments a counterweight to the appeal of terrorist and other dissident groups.[139] Grassroots assistance, funneled through NGOs, can effectively deal with the widely acknowledged structural causes of terrorism: poverty, political and social injustice, corrupt government, unemployment, and consequent despair.[140] Promoting—in fact, subsidizing—foreign investment that creates jobs, debt forgiveness, and microcredit programs that empower the poor are other examples. Instead of pushing for stronger internal security measures, as in Indonesia, the United States would do better to support good governance, since the very forces that people would ordinarily look to for security—the army and police—have the most abominable record when it comes to respect for human rights.[141]

Afghanistan would be a good place to start addressing human-security needs, before it is too late. With the quick removal of the Taliban from power and al-Qaeda from its cells, Afghanistan at first seemed to be an example of the virtues of a hard-hitting military response. But the Afghanistan story has only begun. At the start of 2004, al-Qaeda's top leaders are still at large, and its units have become more audacious in their attacks. Serious internal security problems remain as a consequence of traditional warlordism and terrorist acts. Nation-building in Afghanistan—the very thing the Bush administration had sworn it would never undertake—is going to be exceedingly difficult.[142] National elections scheduled for June 2004 had to be postponed until October for security reasons. The country is cultivating more opium poppy than ever before. Many governments have failed to fulfill their promises of aid, and although new pledges were made at an international donors conference in Berlin in March 2004, it is difficult to imagine that foreign aid will be able to overcome the problems posed by drug lords, the Taliban, and widespread poverty. The government in Kabul was made in America, its leader literally under US (Special Forces) protection and dependent on the support of a Northern Alliance that has an abominable record when it comes to respect for human rights and democratic processes.[143] With American attention and resources shifted to Iraq, Afghanistan looks like it might become an international orphan.

Third, supporting good governance abroad requires setting a positive example of good governance at home. But the Bush administration chose the opposite course—supporting undemocratic government abroad and, in the name of homeland security, undermining civil liberties at home. As happened at the outset of the cold war under Truman, "national security" and patriotic appeals have been exploited to limit the freedoms of American citizens, especially those of Muslim faith and Middle East origins. Mass media have fallen in line, often unquestioningly reporting on the Bush administration's war on terrorism and failing to take note of unlawful detentions, domestic spying, invasions of personal privacy, secretive government, and other official practices that are reminiscent of the Nixon era. Now, however, these practices are occurring with little public debate.

US recognition of the costs of energy dependence is a fourth cornerstone of a new realism in foreign policy. What George Kennan wrote at the time of the Soviet invasion of Afghanistan still applies today: "the greatest real threats to our security ... [are] our self-created dependence on Arab oil and our involvement in a wholly unstable Israeli–Arab relationship," and not any military threat.[144] The United States must substantially reduce its dependence on foreign oil in general (roughly 60 percent of US oil consumption) and Saudi oil in particular (around one-sixth of US imports). The Saudis' demonstrated financial ties to the Taliban and al-Qaeda at various times, their funding and export of an extremist Islamism (Wahhabism), and the fact that fifteen of the nineteen 9/11 terrorists were Saudi citizens, should be sufficient grounds for transforming the tight relationship with the monarchy.[145] The reliable supply of cheap oil has for decades been allowed to overshadow not only the Saudis' toleration of Islamic radicalism but also severe human-rights problems.

Thus far, however, there is no reason to expect that the George W. Bush team will reverse course and work toward establishing a global coalition devoted to human and common security. It fervently believes it has the formula for true international security, namely that all states follow America's example and leadership; and it also believes, like preceding administrations, that the American way is disinterested and selfless. Those who reject US predominance face the full weight of US power. Preventive war then becomes preferable to peace. As Iraq shows, peace can be the nightmare scenario for Bush and company, since it automatically reduces US military options. Finding ways to engage the enemy is a sign of weakness, and recourse to the UN is a waste of time.

The harsh truth of the matter is that these guys simply don't get it—"get" that acting the bully in world affairs comes at a price, though often one that is not apparent until years down the road: the blowback effect that Chalmers Johnson has recently highlighted. September 11 is a tragic case in point, but only the most recent one. Refocusing resources on human needs and embracing common security thus requires much more than different policies and priorities, it also demands a different psychology, one that is sensitive to other cultures and histories, for example, and does not presume that America's destiny is the world's.[146] One of the lessons that Robert S. McNamara drew from the Vietnam years is vital to re-learn today:

> We did not recognize that neither our people nor our leaders are omniscient. Where our own security is not directly at stake, our judgment of what is in another people's or country's best interest should be put to the test of open discussion in international forums. We do not have the God-given right to shape every nation in our own image or as we choose.[147]

The prevailing attitude on the Beltway, however, seems to be that being disliked comes with the territory, with being number one. Such an arrogance of power belongs to imperial rulers, not leaders of a country that holds itself before the world as a model democracy.

As one appraises the costs and benefits of changing course, the objection invariably is made that the United States cannot "afford" to take the risk. Yet, as has recently been argued, the historically unprecedented hegemonic position of the United States today provides a very strong reason why the United States can indeed afford to wait and see: time. The United States can expect to remain number one for many years. It can afford to engage (as well as criticize) China and Russia; it can afford to turn control of Iraq over to the UN; and it can afford to align with other countries on global issues such as the environment and migration.[148] Going it alone and exercising primacy through warfare is always an option; but it should be the last one.

Notes

1. Speech at the US Army Special Warfare School, June 28, 1961; in Michael H. Hunt, ed., *Crises in US Foreign Policy: An International History Reader* (New Haven, Conn.: Yale University Press, 1996), p. 331.
2. "The ability of the Viet-Cong continuously to rebuild their units and to make good their losses is one of the mysteries of this guerrilla war," Ambassador Maxwell Taylor told top US officials in November 1964. Neither forced recruitment nor infiltration of soldiers from North Vietnam provided "plausible explanation of the continued strength of the Viet-Cong ... Not only do the Viet-Cong units have the recuperative powers of the phoenix, but they have an amazing ability to maintain morale." Neil Sheehan et al., eds., *The Pentagon Papers* (New York: Bantam Books, 1971), p. 372. Hereafter cited simply as *Pentagon Papers*.
3. See, for example, the documents in Hunt, ed., *Crises*, pp. 340–41 (a memorandum from Secretary of Defense Robert S. McNamara to President Lyndon Johnson in 1963) and p. 352 (a meeting with Johnson in which the US Ambassador to South Vietnam, Henry Cabot Lodge, declares: "I don't think we ought to take this government seriously"); and in *Pentagon Papers*, pp. 208–9 and 217–18 (two 1963 cables from Lodge).

4 Lodge's comments in meeting with President Johnson and top advisers, July 21–22, 1965; in Hunt, ed., *Crises*, p. 353.
5 Memorandum from Rostow to Secretary of State Dean Rusk, November 23, 1964; in *Pentagon Papers*, p. 422.
6 See the record of his meeting with advisers in July 1965, in Hunt, ed., *Crises*, pp. 351–8. Only George Ball, the Undersecretary of State, among Johnson's closest advisers understood the hopelessness of the situation: "Like giving cobalt treatment to a terminal cancer case," he said of the idea of increasing US aid to the Saigon regime. Ibid., p. 353.
7 As one of McNamara's top aides, John McNaughton, put it, "70%" of the US war effort by early 1965 had come down to "avoiding a humiliating defeat" and only "10%" to "permit the people of SVN [South Vietnam] to enjoy a better, freer way of life." Memorandum of March 24, 1965, in *Pentagon Papers*, p. 432.
8 Ball's comments (italics in original) were made in a memorandum to Johnson of July 1, 1965; in Hunt, ed., *Crises*, p. 348. Galbraith, then ambassador to India, called for a neutral South Vietnam and reduction of the US commitment to its government in a memorandum to President Kennedy of April 4, 1962; ibid., pp. 335–6.
9 Layne, "From Preponderance to Offshore Balancing," in Michael Brown et al., eds., *America's Strategic Choices* (Cambridge, Mass.: MIT Press, 1997), pp. 244–82.
10 See, for example, Eugene Gholz, Daryl G. Press, and Harvey M. Sapolsky, "Come Home, America: The Strategy of Restraint in the Face of Temptation," ibid., pp. 200–43; and Chalmers Johnson, *Blowback: The Costs and Consequences of American Empire* (New York: Metropolitan Books, 2000).
11 Brown et al., eds., *America's Strategic Choices*, is an excellent collection of these views.
12 As the National Security Council's NSC–68, the core American strategic document of the cold war, stated in 1950: "Even if there were no Soviet Union we would face the great problem of the free society, accentuated manifold in this industrial age, of reconciling order, security, the need for participation, with the requirements of freedom. We would face the fact that in a shrinking world the absence of order among nations is becoming less and less tolerable."
13 The point is that "regime change" such as the Bush administration is calling for in Iraq is hardly a novelty in US foreign policy. Whether by coup, subversion, or assassination, and whether to displace an enemy or replace a one-time friend, regime change has always been a policy option. Thus, the United States in past years has played a central role in seeking the overthrow of radical nationalist and leftist leaders such as Patrice Lumumba in Congo, Fidel Castro in Cuba, Salvador Allende in Chile, Arbenz in Guatemala, Sukarno in Indonesia, Mossadegh in Iran, and Muammar al-Qaddafi in Libya; leaders judged unacceptably "soft" on communism such as Archbishop Makarios in Cyprus, João Goulart in Brazil, and Norodom Sihanouk in Cambodia; and friendly but no longer useful leaders such as Ferdinand Marcos in the Philippines, Rafael Trujillo in the Dominican Republic, Mobutu Sese Seko in Zaire, Manuel Noriega in Panama, Anastacio Somoza in Nicaragua, and South Vietnam's trio of presidents: Ngo Dinh Diem, Nguyen Khanh, and Nguyen Van Thieu. Of interest is the comment made by General Paul Harkins, who opposed US support of a coup to oust Diem in 1963: "Leaders of other under-developed countries will take a dim view of our assistance if they too were led to believe the same fate lies in store for them." *Pentagon Papers*, p. 221.
14 See Richard N. Haass, "Beyond Containment: Competing American Foreign Policy Doctrines for the New Era," in Eugene R. Wittkopf and Christopher M. Jones, eds., *The Future of American Foreign Policy* (New York: St. Martin's/Worth, 1999), 3rd ed., pp. 22–38. Haass, later in charge of policy planning in the G.W. Bush administration, concluded: "For now and for the immediate future, the real question hanging over the promise of posses is not so much their utility as it is the willingness and ability of the United States to saddle up and to lead."
15 Lieber, "Foreign Policy and American Primacy," in Lieber, ed., *Eagle Rules? Foreign Policy and American Primacy in the Twenty-First Century* (Upper Saddle River, N.J.: Prentice Hall, 2002), pp. 1–15.
16 Rosati, *The Politics of United States Foreign Policy*, 2nd ed. (Ft. Worth, Tex.: Harcourt Brace, 1999), p. 408.

17 As two writers have said, belief in exceptionalism "can exist without moral arrogance, and pride and patriotism can exist without paternalism." A foreign policy built on expansionism is not preordained. See Tami R. Davis and Seam M. Lyn-Jones, "City Upon a Hill," *Foreign Policy* (Spring, 1987), in Jerel A. Rosati, ed., *Readings in the Politics of United States Foreign Policy* (Fort Worth, Tex.: Harcourt Brace, 1998), pp. 376–86.

18 "Bush's United States Military Academy Graduation Speech," *Washington Post*, June 2, 2002, online at www.washingtonpost.com/ac2/up_dyn/A47940–2002June2?

19 Slouka, "A Year Later: Notes on America's Intimations of Mortality," *Harper's Magazine*, Vol. 305, No. 1828 (September, 2002), p. 39.

20 Eisenhower was speaking in 1953 after his special assistant had told him it would be nice if, for a change, mobs in the Middle East were waving American flags instead of rioting against the United States. See the memorandum of conversation in Hunt, ed., *Crises*, p. 390.

21 Johnson said in 1966: "There are three billion people in the world and we have only 200 million of them. We are outnumbered 15 to 1. If might did make right, they would sweep over the US and take what we have. We have what they want." Quoted in Richard J. Barnet, *Intervention and Revolution: The United States in the Third World* (Cleveland: World Publishing, 1968), p. 25.

22 For this reading of al-Qaeda and Osama bin Laden, see Michael Scott Doran, "Somebody Else's Civil War," *Foreign Affairs*, Vol. 81, No. 1 (January–February, 2002), pp. 22–42.

23 Kissinger, "The New World Order," in Chester A. Crocker and Fen Osler Hampson, eds., *Managing Global Chaos: Sources of and Responses to International Conflict* (Washington, DC: United States Institute of Peace Press, 1996), p. 173.

24 Kissinger's statement, made just before the election of Allende in 1970, was: "I don't see why we need to stand by and watch a country go Communist due to the irresponsibility of its own people." Quoted in James Petras and Morris Morley, *The United States and Chile: Imperialism and the Overthrow of the Allende Government* (New York: Monthly Review Press, 1975), p. vii.

25 As Bush said in his West Point speech (n. 18), "Our nation's cause has always been larger than our nation's defense." Ruggie ("The Past as Prologue?" *International Security*, Vol. 21, No. 4 (Spring 1997), pp. 166–82) seeks to show that, historically, US presidents, whether inclined more toward Realism or toward Globalism–idealism, had to cloak national-interest arguments in world-order garb in order to sell the American public on international engagement. My argument is not about *selling* internationalism but about the convergence of Realist and Globalist interests in the actual *practice* of US foreign policy.

26 The continuity of this dominant belief system has been well established by Ole R. Holsti and James N. Rosenau, "A Leadership Divided: The Foreign Policy Beliefs of American Leaders, 1976–1984," in Charles W. Kegley, Jr. and Eugene R. Wittkopf, eds., *The Domestic Sources of American Foreign Policy: Insights and Evidence* (New York: St. Martin's Press, 1988), pp. 30–44.

27 Benjamin Schwarz, "Why America Thinks It Has to Run the World," *The Atlantic Monthly*, June 1996, pp. 92–102.

28 Rice, "Promoting the National Interest," *Foreign Affairs*, Vol. 79, No. 1 (January–February, 2000), p. 49.

29 Ibid.

30 Ruggie, "The Past as Prologue?" pp. 167–82. Here (ibid., p. 182, n. 74) and in other writings, Ruggie makes the useful distinction between US commitments to a multilateral world order and its resistance to the independent authority of multilateral organizations.

31 During the Korean War, the British government, worried about the possibility that Truman would extend the fighting into China, proposed that the war be directed by a committee in which London would participate. A memorandum noted that Truman "said again that his attitude was that we stay in Korea and fight. If we have support from others, fine; but if not, he said we would stay on anyway." Hunt, ed., *Crises*, p. 222.

32 "Simply put, the US foreign policy establishment does not want international responsibilities to be reallocated because it fears diminished American leadership and a greater—perhaps even equal—German and Japanese voice in international affairs. Better, they say, to bear disproportionate costs than to yield American control." Christopher Layne and Benjamin Schwarz, "American Hegemony—Without an Enemy," *Foreign Policy*, No. 92 (Fall, 1993), p. 6.

33 As Bush once said, "We are the leaders and we must continue to lead." (*New York Times*, March 11, 1992, p. 1. Hereafter, *NYT*.) Bush's statement was in response to questions raised about a leaked Pentagon draft document, entitled the *Defense Planning Guidance for the 1994–1999 Fiscal Years* (see *NYT*, February 17, 1992, p. 1 and February 18, 1992, p. 1). The document called for the United States to maintain the capacity to act unilaterally inasmuch as action through a UN-based coalition was not reliable. The United States, the document said, should "maintain the mechanisms for deterring potential competitors from even aspiring to a larger regional or global role." The key authors of this document would later resurface as top officials in the G. W. Bush administration (see below).

34 "We will act with others when we can, but alone when we must," reads the White House document *A National Security Strategy of Engagement and Enlargement* (Washington, DC: February, 1996). For documentation of Clinton's unilateral actions, see the essays in Lieber, ed., *Eagle Rules?*

35 This is not to ignore important departures from unilateralism, such as Clinton's nuclear-freeze deal with North Korea—the Agreed Framework of October 1994, and the establishment of the Korean Peninsula Energy Development Organization (KEDO)—that ended debate in his administration over using force to squelch North Korea's nuclear-weapons program.

36 "American preeminence [is] based on the fact that it is the only country with the military, diplomatic, political and economic assets to be a decisive player in any conflict in whatever part of the world it chooses to involve itself." Krauthammer, "The Unipolar Moment," *Foreign Affairs*, Vol. 70, No. 1 (1990/91), p. 23.

37 References to this group are based on documents that appear at its Internet site: www.projectforthenewamericancentury.org.

38 William Kristol and Robert Kagan, "Toward a Neo-Reaganite Foreign Policy," *Foreign Affairs*, Vol. 75, no. 4 (July–August, 1996), pp. 18–32.

39 From his speech to the Congress of September 20, 2001; text in *NYT*, September 21, 2001, p. B4. In November, speaking to US soldiers stationed at Fort Campbell, Kentucky, Bush elaborated: "America has a message for the nations of the world. If you harbor terrorists, you are terrorists. If you train or arm a terrorist, you are a terrorist. If you feed a terrorist or fund a terrorist, you're a terrorist, and you will be held accountable by the United States and our friends." *NYT*, November 22, 2001, p. B2.

40 See David Armstrong, "Dick Cheney's Song of America," *Harper's*, October 2002, pp. 76–83.

41 Aside from Bush himself (CEO of Spectrum 7 and a director of Harken Energy), other senior figures who headed energy companies include Richard Cheney (Halliburton), Secretary of the Treasury Paul O'Neill (Alcoa), and Secretary of Commerce Don Evans (Tom Brown). Others who are closely connected with energy companies include National Security Special Assistant Condeleezza Rice (board member of Chevron Oil), Secretary of the Army Thomas White (once vice-chairman of Enron Energy Services, the largest single contributor to the Bush campaign), and White House chief counsel Alberto Gonzales (an attorney for Enron). Several Bush appointees had been lobbyists for energy industries, such as White House Chief of Staff Andrew Card (American Automobile Manufacturers Association). A useful listing is provided in "The Big Book of Bush," *Sierra*, Vol. 87, No. 5 (September–October, 2002), pp. 39, 41.

42 These are Otto J. Reich as assistant secretary of state (and later as special envoy for Western Hemisphere affairs) and John D. Negroponte as ambassador to the UN. Late in 2002, two other indicted former officials joined the administration: John M. Poindexter as Director of Information Awareness in the Pentagon, and Elliott Abrams as Senior Director for Near East and North African Affairs in the National Security Council. In addition, Lino Gutierrez, like Reich, was deeply involved with the Cuban exiles before his State Department appointment in Latin American affairs.

43 Knight Ridder Washington Bureau report, "Rumsfeld, Powell at War for Control of US Foreign Policy," May 4, 2003, online.

44 See Lewis H. Lapham, "Notebook: Deus Lo Volt," *Harper's*, May 2002, pp. 7–9.

45 *NYT*, September 21, 2001, p. B4.

46 "Our nation's cause has always been larger than our nation's defense," he said. Speech at West Point, June 2, 2002, cited earlier.

47 Speech on February 15, 2002, to the Council on Foreign Relations, excerpted in *NYT*, February 16, 2002, p. A6. Cheney said that terrorism had answered the post-cold-war question of where the supreme threat to America lay and what role the United States should play. "Only we can rally the world in a task of this complexity against an enemy so elusive and so resourceful," he said. "The United States and only the United States can see this effort through to victory. This responsibility did not come to us by chance. We are in a unique position because of our unique assets, because of the character of our people, the strength of our ideals, the might of our military, and the enormous economy that supports it."

48 Speech of March 10, 2002; text in *NYT*, March 11, 2002, online ed.

49 See Donald H. Rumsfeld's comments in *NYT*, June 7, 2002, p. A8 and June 10, 2002, p. A8.

50 David E. Sanger, "Bush to Formalize a Defense Policy of Hitting First," *NYT*, June 17, 2002, p. 1. The "axis of evil" phrase appeared in Bush's State of the Union address in January 2002.

51 Text in *NYT*, September 20, 2002, online ed.

52 *The National Security Strategy of the United States*, p. 1.

53 Faced with the North Koreans' decision to abandon its 1994 agreement to freeze its nuclear-weapon program, Washington reacted with moderation. But this was misleading. A "senior [US] administration official" was quoted as saying that "one rogue-state crisis at a time" was Bush's preferred approach, suggesting that North Korea might be next on his hit list after Iraq was subdued. (*NYT*, December 13, 2002, online ed.) Bush, in fact, had made clear his personal distaste for Kim Jong-il. In what was reported as something of a tirade before Republican senators, Bush called Kim a "pygmy" who was in charge of "a gulag half the size of Austin." Howard Fineman, "'I Sniff Some Politics,'" *Newsweek*, May 27, 2002, p. 37.

54 James Dao, "Powell Defends a First Strike As Iraq Option," *NYT*, September 8, 2002, p. 1.

55 As reported by Elisabeth Bumiller and David E. Sanger ("Threat of Terrorism is Shaping the Focus of Bush Presidency," *NYT*, September 11, 2002, online ed.), an unnamed Bush adviser said "it's old-fashioned self-protection—and it comes from the president's gut. The example he refers to from time to time is the Cuban Missile Crisis. In his mind, it's got that urgency." In the missile crisis, the Soviet Union deployed substantial numbers of missiles with atomic warheads in Cuba, close to US shores, prompting a US naval "quarantine" of the island. But Washington and Moscow were able to stop the drift toward war, recognizing the dangers of miscalculation in a crisis environment.

56 David E. Sanger, "Beating Them to the Prewar," *NYT*, September 28, 2002, p. A17.

57 Richard Haass, interviewed by Lemann, "The Next World Order," pp. 45–6.

58 Perle, "Next Stop, Iraq," speech to the Foreign Policy Research Institute, Philadelphia, November 30, 2001; online at www.fpri.org.

59 Elaine Sciolino and Steven Lee Myers, "Bush Says 'Time is Running Out' as Forces Move Into Place," *NYT*, October 7, 2001, online ed. It was just at the time of the resolution that the Bush administration hurried to pay the longstanding US debt to the UN and endorse two UN conventions on terrorism (related to funding and bombings) that the United States previously had ignored. See Serge Schmemann, "Annan Urges New Methods to Fight Terrorism," *NYT*, September 25, 2001, p. B3.

60 See Richard Falk, "The New Bush Doctrine," *The Nation*, July 15, 2002, pp. 9–11.

61 Contrary to Secretary of State Colin Powell's contention that "as a result of 9/11 particularly, he [Bush] sees the value of coalitions and friends." (*International Herald Tribune*, May 23, 2002.) As Richard Perle said, whereas forming a coalition to deal with Saddam Hussein was necessary due to divided views in the United States about going to war, a coalition "today is really not essential ... the price you end up paying for an alliance is collective judgment, collective decision-making. That was a disaster in Kosovo." Perle voiced the suspicion that the real purpose of those who were promoting a coalition was to restrain the United States. "I think we should reject that." (Perle, "Next Stop, Iraq.") Bush may have become more diplomatic after 9/11 when talking about the Russians or the Chinese; but policy toward partners clearly never changed.

62 Today's wars "should not be fought by committee," Rumsfeld has written. "The mission must determine the coalition, the coalition must not determine the mission, or else the mission will be dumbed down to the lowest common denominator." "Transforming the Military," *Foreign Affairs*, Vol. 81, No. 3 (May–June, 2002), p. 31.

63 See, for example, Patrick E. Tyler, "Europeans Split with US on Need for Iraq Attack," *NYT*, July 22, 2002, online ed. An adviser to the German prime minister is quoted as saying: "After September 11, we had the feeling there would be a more multilateral approach" to international affairs by the Bush administration. But more recently, "We have been seeing a very assertive administration on the move in so many areas that people on this side of the Atlantic come to the question whether really there is a new approach." A French official said: "The important thing is to build a coalition for peace in the Middle East, not to build a coalition for war in Iraq."
64 Bush stated in June 2002 that a Middle East peace depended on replacing Yasser Arafat, a classic instance of hegemonic conduct. He showed no qualms about dictating the choice of Palestinian leader, in advance of elections.
65 Suzanne Daley, "French Minister Calls US Policy 'Simplistic,'" *NYT*, February 7, 2002, p. A10.
66 On a visit to Washington, Crown Prince Abdullah was unusually blunt in saying, with reference to US policy toward the Palestinians: "In the current environment, we find it very difficult to defend America, and so we keep our silence." He made clear that the suicide bombings in the West Bank and elsewhere were the result of Israeli repression, and "America has a duty to follow its conscience to reject repression." (Excerpts from an interview in *NYT*, January 29, 2002, p. A12.) Even before the visit, some Pentagon officials and members of Congress were already upset with the Saudis. Senator Carl Levin, chairman of the Senate Armed Services Committee, accused the Saudis of not being sufficiently cooperative in the war on terrorism and suggested that the United States might want to "find a place [for its air bases] where we are much more welcome." James Dao, "Dismay with Saudi Arabia Fuels Pullout Talk," *NYT*, January 16, 2002.
67 Rumsfeld, "Transforming the Military," p. 24.
68 Armstrong, "Dick Cheney's Song of America," pp. 77–8.
69 Rumsfeld, "Transforming the Military," p. 27.
70 Klare, "Endless Military Superiority," *The Nation*, July 15, 2002, pp. 12–16.
71 Based on Stockholm International Peace Research Institute (SIPRI) figures; http://projects.sipri.se/milex/mex_major_spenders.html.
72 Thom Shanker, "Global Arms Sales Rise Again, and the US Leads the Pack," *NYT*, August 20, 2001, online ed.
73 Michael E. O'Hanlon, "A Flawed Masterpiece," *Foreign Affairs*, Vol. 81, No. 3 (May–June, 2002), p. 61.
74 The other countries are North Korea, Iraq, Iran, Libya, and Syria.
75 Michael R. Gordon, "Treaty Offers Pentagon New Flexibility for New Set of Nuclear Priorities," *NYT*, May 14, 2002, p. A8. "'What we have now agreed to do under the treaty is what we wanted to do anyway,' a senior administration official said today. 'That's our kind of treaty.'"
76 Layne and Schwarz, "American Hegemony," p. 4.
77 For a detailed survey, see William D. Hartung, Frida Berrigan, and Michelle Ciarrocca, "Operation Endless Deployment," *The Nation*, October 21, 2002, pp. 21–4. Most of the information that follows comes from various newspaper dispatches.
78 Colombia officially became part of the war on terror at the end of 2002: see *NYT*, December 5, 2002.
79 See reports of the Center for Defense Information at www.cdi.org.
80 Only in Yemen is there a reasonably clear connection to al-Qaeda activities. (See Thom Shanker and Eric Schmitt, "US Moves Commandos to Base in East Africa," *NYT*, September 18, 2002, p. A20.) Singapore has one group, Jemaah Islamiah, also active in Indonesia, that is said to have helped al-Qaeda's communications before the September 11 attacks and planned an attack in January 2002 on the US embassy in Singapore. The connection between al-Qaeda and the Bali bombing has been claimed but not yet proved.
81 Sanctions were waived in the cases of Armenia, Azerbaijan, India, Pakistan, Tajikistan, and Yugoslavia. Rachel Stohl, "Post Sept. 11 Arms Sales and Military Aid Demonstrate Dangerous Trend," Center for Defense Information, June 18, 2003; online at http://www.cdi.org, January 5, 2004.
82 Among the many reports on corruption and misrule in Central Asia that are linked to the war on terrorism, see Edmund L. Andrews, "Spotlight on Central Asia is Finding Repression, Too,"

NYT, April 11, 2002, p. A6; Todd S. Purdum, "Uzbekistan's Leader Doubts Chances for Afghan Peace," *NYT*, March 14, 2002, p. A18; Muhammad Salih, "America's Shady Ally Against Terror," *NYT*, March 11, 2002, p. A25; Ahmed Rashid, "Trouble Ahead," *Far Eastern Economic Review*, May 9, 2002, pp. 14–18.

83 Jeff Gerth, "Bribery Inquiry Involves Kazakh Chief, and He's Unhappy," *NYT*, December 11, 2002, p. A14. At this writing President Nazarbayev faces indictment in the United States in a federal investigation of bribery payments made to him by US oil companies. The oil contracts between Kazakhstan and the companies, also in dispute, were finally settled in 2004.

84 Bradley Graham, "New Defense Ties With Philippines," *Washington Post*, August 13, 2002, p. A10.

85 See the report in the *NYT*, January 23, 2002, p. A1, in which "several American and foreign officials said there was no hard evidence of links between Al Qaeda and Laskar Jihad," the radical Indonesian organization suspected of such links.

86 Todd S. Purdum, "US to Resume Aid to Train Indonesia's Military Forces," *NYT*, August 3, 2002, online ed.

87 Murray Hiebert, "The Era of Responsibility," *Far Eastern Economic Review*, July 11, 2002, pp. 14–16. The administration's letter to the judge in the case mentioned the challenge of Chinese oil companies if Exxon Mobil was forced to withdraw; but its principal—and bizarre—argument was that if Indonesia, "a focal point of US initiatives in the ongoing war against Al Qaeda," were interfered with by virtue of the lawsuit, its "cooperation in response to perceived disrespect for its sovereign interests" would be "imperiled." Jane Perlez, "US Backs Oil Giant on Lawsuit in Indonesia," *NYT*, August 8, 2002, online ed.

88 Associated Press dispatch, in *NYT*, August 1, 2002, online ed.

89 "The US has been criticized [in Southeast Asia] as clumsy, misguided and falling into long-standing local disputes that have festered for years and pose little international threat." Barry Wain, "Wrong Target," *Far Eastern Economic Review*, April 18, 2002, pp. 14–18.

90 Amnesty International was among the international NGOs that charged that the Pakistani government had violated international human-rights standards by deporting or illegally detaining numerous individuals merely on suspicion of being associated with al-Qaeda or the Taliban. Associated Press, "Amnesty Accuses Pakistan on Rights," *NYT*, June 20, 2002, online ed.

91 David Rohde, "Musharraf Redraws Constitution," *NYT*, August 22, 2002, online ed.

92 David E. Sanger, "In North Korea and Pakistan, Deep Roots of Nuclear Barter," *NYT*, November 24, 2002, online ed.

93 Celia W. Dugger, "Wider Military Ties with India Offer US Diplomatic Leverage," *NYT*, June 9, 2002, p. A1; Joanna Slater and Murray Hiebert, "US and India Stage Quiet Rapprochement," *Wall Street Journal*, December 18, 2001, p. A11.

94 See US Department of Defense, *Quadrennial Defense Review Report*, September 30, 2001, online at http://www.defenselink.mil/pubs/qdr2001.pdf and US Department of Defense, *Annual Report on the Military Power of the People's Republic of China*, online at www.nautilus.org/pub/ftp/napsact/special_reports/d20020712china.pdf. The latter document focuses on Taiwan as the "primary driver for China's military modernization."

95 According to testimony by the CIA director, George J. Tenet, before the Senate Armed Services Committee, March 19, 2002.

96 "From the very beginning," said G. W. Bush's one-time Secretary of the Treasury and Alcoa chairman, Paul O'Neill, "there was the conviction that Saddam Hussein was a bad person and that he needed to go." "It was all about finding a way to do it," O'Neill said. No one on the National Security Council questioned the idea. (CBS News, January 10, 2004, based on an interview of O'Neill for the program "60 Minutes"; reported online at www.commondreams.org/headlines04/0110–03.htm.) See also Julia Preston with Todd S. Purdum, "Bush's Push on Iraq at U.N.: Headway, Then New Barriers," *New York Times*, September 22, 2002, online ed.; and Elisabeth Bumiller and David E. Sanger, "Threat of Terrorism is Shaping the Focus of Bush Presidency," *NYT*, September 11, 2002, online ed. According to Bob Woodward's inside account, *Bush at War* (New York: Simon & Schuster, 2002), Paul Wolfowitz was eager to take on Saddam Hussein at the outset of the administration, and Rumsfeld believed the United States "could take

advantage of the opportunity offered by the terrorist attacks to go after Saddam immediately." But Bush was anxious to avoid doing "too many things" at once.
97 Clarke's book, *Against All Enemies: Inside America's War on Terror*, created a political firestorm when it was published in March 2004. See excerpts in *NYT*, March 23, 2004, p. A16.
98 To the contrary: "The Central Intelligence Agency has no evidence that Iraq has engaged in terrorist operations against the United States in nearly a decade, and the agency is also convinced that President Saddam Hussein has not provided chemical or biological weapons to Al Qaeda or related terrorist groups, according to several American intelligence officials." James Risen, "Terror Acts by Baghdad Have Waned, US Aides Say," *NYT*, February 6, 2002, p. A10.
99 Eric Schmitt, "Rumsfeld Says US Has 'Bulletproof' Evidence of Iraq's Links to Al Qaeda," *NYT*, September 28, 2002, p. A8.
100 Text in *NYT*, September 13, 2002, p. A10. The British government did produce a document designed to support these claims (text in *NYT*, September 24, 2002, online ed.); but beyond establishing Iraq's ongoing efforts to build a WMD capability, the document added little that was not already well known.
101 The CIA's analysis concluded that the probability of Saddam Hussein's initiating use of WMD was "low," whereas the likelihood was "pretty high" that he would use WMD *in response to* a US attack on Iraq or in a desperate last act of revenge if attacked. Letter of October 7, 2002, from CIA Director George J. Tenet to Florida's Senator Bob Graham; text in *NYT*, October 9, 2002, p. A12.
102 Eric Schmitt and Thom Shanker, "Pentagon Sets Up Intelligence Unit," *NYT*, October 24, 2002, p. 1.
103 See, for instance, Douglas Jehl, "Stung by Exiles' Role, C.I.A. Orders a Shift in Procedures," *NYT*, February 13, 2004, p. A10.
104 General Wesley K. Clark, former NATO commander and commander of the 1999 Kosovo operation, quoted in Eric Schmitt, "3 Retired Generals Warn of Peril in Attacking Iraq Without Backing of U.N.," *NYT*, September 24, 2002, online ed. Another retired general, the former chairman of the Joint Chiefs of Staff, John M. Shalikashvili, added: "We must continue to persuade the other members of the Security Council of the correctness of our position, and we must not be too quick to take no for an answer."
105 Interviews with analysts in the intelligence community bear out this conclusion. See Spencer Ackerman and John B. Judis, "The First Casualty," *The New Republic*, June 30, 2003, searched online. Later, George J. Tenet, the Director of Central Intelligence, would acknowledge the fragility of the evidence concerning Iraq's WMD and the overestimate of its capabilities to produce them. See his February 5, 2004 speech at Georgetown University, online at www.cia.gov/public_affairs/speeches/2004/tenet_georgetownspeech_02052004.html.
106 Perle's role as one of the key ideologues behind the Bush Doctrine is clear from his most recent book, co-authored with David Frum, *An End to Evil: How to Win the War on Terror* (New York: Random House, 2003).
107 See, for example, Walter Pincus, "Bush Overstated Iraq, al-Qaida Link," *Washington Post*, June 23, 2003; and James Risen, "Iraqi Agent Denies He Met 9/11 Hijacker in Prague Before Attacks on the US," *NYT*, December 13, 2003, p. A8.
108 Among many sources on this point, see the Carnegie Endowment's detailed postwar study, "WMD in Iraq: Evidence and Implications," by Jessica T. Mathews, George Perkovich, and Joseph Cirincione, at http//www.ceip.org (searched January 20, 2004).
109 For a devastating investigation of how the administration deliberately skewed the information available to it on Iraq, see Barton Gellman and Walter Pincus, "Depiction of Threat Outgrew Supporting Evidence," *Washington Post*, August 29, 2003, online ed.
110 There are several reasons why Iraq's oil production and reserves, the second-largest among OPEC states and 11 percent of the world total, surely are a matter of US interest. First, with a friendly regime installed in Baghdad, and production restored to pre-Gulf War levels, the United States could be assured of access to cheaper oil. (The United States already imports over 65 percent of Iraq's oil.) Oil field service companies, including Cheney's former firm, Halliburton Corporation, are reportedly eager to get into Iraq. Rebuilding Iraq's dilapidated facilities would

increase production by about one-third, experts say; and if Saddam Hussein is replaced, American firms stand to gain a clear edge over rival European and other companies. (Neela Banerjee, "Energy Companies Weigh Their Possible Future in Iraq," *NYT*, October 26, 2002, p. B3.) Second, Iraqi production might put a crimp in OPEC's unity; but even if not, it would reduce US dependence on Saudi Arabia, Russia, and other oil producers. In fact, US control of Iraq's oil would also be a blow to Russian oil companies, which expect to be kicked out, and to the Russian government, which is owed about $7.6 billion by Iraq. (See Sabrina Tavernise, "Oil Prize, Past and Present, Ties Russia to Iraq," *NYT*, October 17, 2002, p. A14.) Third, Iraq's revenue from oil production would greatly reduce its reliance on post-conflict US aid. (See Neela Banerjee, "Stable World Oil Prices Are Likely to Become a War Casualty, Experts Say," *NYT*, October 2, 2002, p. A13.) A fourth possible US interest (with reference to previous discussion of American annoyance with the Saudis) might be to sideline Saudi Arabia altogether, since a post-Saddam Iraq would probably play host to the US military as well as become a close oil partner.

111 In a study of Bush's chief political adviser, Karl Rove, the authors specifically charge that Rove favored invading Iraq to preempt these Democratic issues. James Moore and Wayne Slater, *Bush's Brain: How Karl Rove Made George W. Bush Presidential* (Hoboken, N.J.: John Wiley & Sons, 2003).

112 James Risen, "Iraq Said to Have Tried to Reach Last-Minute Deal to Avert War," *NYT*, November 6, 2003, online ed.

113 Joy Gordon, "Cool War," *Harper's*, November 2002, pp. 43–49.

114 Concerning the first revelation, based on interviews with Defense Intelligence Agency officers who were involved in the secret program with Iraq, see Patrick E. Tyler, "Officers Say US Aided Iraq in War Despite Use of Gas," *NYT*, August 18, 2002, online ed. On the second, see Matt Kelley, "US Gave Germs to Iraq in '80s," Associated Press (via AOL), October 1, 2002.

115 Senate Joint Resolution 23 of September 14, 2001, "Authorization for Use of Military Force," authorizes the President "to use all necessary and appropriate force against those nations, organizations, or persons he determines planned, authorized, committed, or aided the terrorist attacks ... in order to prevent any future acts of international terrorism against the United States ..." The resolution acknowledges the War Powers Resolution, but "Congress declares that this [authorization] is intended to constitute specific statutory authorization within the meaning of section 5(b) of the War Powers Resolution." The effect of the latter statement would seem to be that the President does not have to abide by the 60-day stipulation under War Powers for reporting back to the Congress on use of US military forces and gaining Congress' assent. House Joint Resolution 75 of December 20, 2001, provides the President with the quoted support for action against Iraq.

116 For instance, the Republican leader in the Senate, Trent Lott: see James Dao, "Experts Warn of High Risk for American Invasion of Iraq," *NYT*, August 1, 2002, online ed.

117 *NYT*, September 23, 2002, p. A10.

118 The joint House–Senate resolution authorizes use of force "as he [the president] determines to be necessary and appropriate in order to: (1) defend the national security of the United States against the continuing threat posed by Iraq; and (2) enforce all relevant United Nations Security Council resolutions regarding Iraq." Text in *NYT*, October 12, 2002, p. A10.

119 Ibid., p. A11.

120 Excerpts from the speech are in *NYT*, September 12, 2002, online ed.

121 Elaine Sciolino, "French Leader Offers Formula to Tackle Iraq," *NYT*, September 9, 2002, online ed.

122 Quoted in Patrick Tyler and Richard W. Stevenson, "Profound Effect on US Economy Seen in War on Iraq," *NYT*, July 30, 2002, online ed. Jordan's King Abdullah II was even more scornful of US invasion plans. During a visit to Britain he gave an interview with *The Times* in which he said: "In the light of the failure to move the Israeli–Palestinian process forward, military action against Iraq would really open Pandora's box." An invasion would "destabilize American strategic interest even more in the Middle East." Regarding the possibility discussed by US officials of using Jordan as one base for such an attack, Abdullah was clear: "Jordan will not be used as a launching pad." Hoge, "Jordan Says US Attack on Iraq Would Roil Mideast," *NYT*, July 30, 2002, online ed.

123 A briefing by a RAND Corporation analyst on July 10, 2002, to the Defense Policy Board, a Pentagon advisory board headed by Richard Perle, drew considerable press attention. The

briefing was so sharply anti-Saudi—accusing the Saudis of being fully supportive of terrorism and "the most dangerous opponent" in the Middle East—that the Department of Defense had to disavow it. Saudi leaders were incensed. Thomas E. Ricks, "Briefing Depicted Saudis as Enemies," *Washington Post*, August 6, 2002, p. A1.
124 Warren Hoge, "Jordan Says US Attack on Iraq Would Roil Mideast."
125 Turkey's support was surely also contingent on the Americans' not promising the Kurds any form of independence in exchange for their help in fighting Saddam. Turkey badly needed US support for EU membership inasmuch as France and several other EU members strongly objected to Turkish entry on human-rights grounds. In the end, Turkey's parliament rejected sending troops; and after the war, when the Turkish government did decide to send troops, Iraq's interim authority, the Governing Council, rejected them.
126 On Mexico and the disappointment of President Vicente Fox with US priorities, see the interview in *NYT*, September 13, 2002, p. A1.
127 See G. John Ikenberry, "America's Imperial Ambition," *Foreign Affairs*, Vol. 81, No. 5 (September–October, 2002), pp. 44–60.
128 Ruggie, "The Past as Prologue?" p. 171.
129 In those cases, as Bruce W. Jentleson has argued ("Use of Force Dilemmas: Policy and Politics," in Lieber, ed., *Eagle Rules?* pp. 266–81), it was US failure to take the lead in deterring mass violence that became subject to criticism.
130 For instance, General Tommy Franks, head of the US Central Command, has said: "The relationships that we have with surrounding states around Afghanistan will permit us over time to do the work that ... all of us recognize needs to be done. It won't be finished until it's all done." Reuters, "General Suggests Extending US Campaign Against Afghan Neighbors," *NYT*, August 25, 2002, online ed.
131 Yemen, which has never signed the Missile Technology Control Regime agreement that puts limits on sales of longer-range missiles, in December 2002 accepted a shipment of North Korean SCUD missiles, possibly for transshipment elsewhere.
132 See Flynt Leverett, "Why Libya Gave Up on the Bomb," *NYT*, January 23, 2004, p. A25.
133 Mathews, "Redefining Security," *Foreign Affairs*, Vol. 68, No. 2 (Spring, 1989), p. 175.
134 For further comment on the policy changes advocated below, see the concluding remarks in Johnson, *Blowback*, and my own recent work: *Global Politics in the Human Interest*, 4th ed. (Boulder, Colo.: Lynne Rienner, 2000) and, with specific respect to East Asia, *Pacific Asia? Prospects for Security and Cooperation in East Asia* (Lanham, Md.: Rowman & Littlefield, 2002).
135 A good start on the Middle East would be US endorsement of the "Geneva Accord," which was put together by distinguished Israelis and Palestinians over roughly a three-year period and announced December 1, 2003. Text in *Tikkun*, Vol. 19, No. 1 (January–February, 2004), pp. 34–45.
136 On engaging rather than confronting North Korea, for example, see Selig S. Harrison, "Time to Leave Korea?" *Foreign Affairs*, Vol. 80, No. 2 (March–April, 2001), pp. 62–78 and Mel Gurtov, "Common Security in North Korea: Quest for a New Paradigm," *Asian Survey*, Vol. 42, No. 3 (May–June, 2002), pp. 397–418.
137 See the "Urgent Call" on the nuclear danger drafted by Jonathan Schell, Randall Forsberg, and others in *The Nation*, June 24, 2002, p. 12. In recent years the voices of a number of former senior US military, foreign-policy, and intelligence officials have been raised in support of these changes in nuclear-weapons policies. See, for example, the statements of US Air Force General Lee Butler and Army General Andrew Goodpaster, brought together in a Northeast Asia Peace and Security Network (NAPSNet) Special Report, December 6, 1996 (online at http://www.nautilus.org) and the comments of Admiral Stansfield Turner, former CIA director: "Post-Cold War World Demands New Ways to Deal with Warheads," *Los Angeles Times*, January 11, 1999.
138 For more detailed assessment, see the joint publication of the Institute for Energy and Environmental Research and the Lawyers' Committee on Nuclear Policy, *Rule of Power or Rule of Law? An Assessment of US Policies and Actions Regarding Security-Related Treaties* (April, 2002), at www.ieer.org/reports/treaties/index.html.

139 See, in this connection, Ahmed Rashid, "New Wars to Fight," *Far Eastern Economic Review*, September 12, 2002, pp. 14–22.
140 Some of these factors were mentioned by the Director of Central Intelligence, George J. Tenet, in testimony before a Senate committee. Among them he emphasized poor, politically fragile states that "lack the economic institutions or the resources to effectively integrate these youth into their societies." Excerpts from the speech are in *NYT*, February 7, 2002, p. A10.
141 Sidney Jones, "Terror's Aftermath in Indonesia," *NYT*, October 16, 2002, p. A27.
142 For a generally positive portrait of US involvement in Afghanistan's reconstruction, see Michael Ignatieff, "Nation-Building Lite," *The New York Times Magazine*, July 28, 2002, online ed. But this assessment has proven premature.
143 As is well known, the deplorable behavior of Northern Alliance warlords and armies had much to do with the rise of the Taliban in the first place. After Alliance forces helped oust the Taliban, it also became evident that they had engaged in war crimes. Several hundred to perhaps a few thousand prisoners of war died while being transported from the front in closed containers. They were hastily buried in mass graves. US soldiers may have known of such treatment and said nothing. See Babek Dehghanpished, John Barry, and Roy Gutman, "The Death Convoy of Afghanistan," *Newsweek*, August 26, 2002, pp. 20–30.
144 George F. Kennan, "US 'Lack of Balance' in the Afghan Crisis," *San Francisco Chronicle*, February 8, 1980, p. 8.
145 See Ahmed Rashid, *Jihad: The Rise of Militant Islam in Central Asia*, pp. 223–5. It remains unclear how much of the funding of extremist groups comes from Saudi charities as opposed to Saudi government sources. But the point is that the Saudi government has done little to cut off such support for fear of being openly opposed by the radical clergy within.
146 In his September 20, 2001 address, Bush had raised the question of al-Qaeda's motives in attacking the United States. His shallow answer, that they want to take away Americans' freedoms, reveals the low level of cultural (and political) sensitivity that prevails in Washington. Nor does it seem that mainstream foreign-policy groups such as the Council on Foreign Relations do much better. Its 2002 report on foreign criticisms and resentment of the United States treated the matter in the same way as the Bush administration, namely, as a marketing issue: "Today, America has a serious image problem." (In fact, after September 11 a former Madison Avenue advertising executive, Charlotte Beers, was appointed Undersecretary of State for Public Diplomacy to improve the selling of American values in Islamic countries.) The Council got the problem right—the widespread perception of the United States as being "arrogant, self-indulgent, hypocritical, inattentive," culturally insensitive, and out of touch with Third World underdevelopment—but its recommendations consisted mainly of ways to improve American overseas propaganda. The report failed to take a hard look at the US policies that may be responsible for the negative perceptions. See an adaptation of the report by Peter Peterson, "Public Diplomacy and the War on Terrorism," *Foreign Affairs*, Vol. 81, No. 5 (September–October, 2002), pp. 74–94.
147 *In Retrospect: the Tragedy and Lessons of Vietnam* (New York: Times Books, 1995), pp. 323.
148 Stephen G. Brooks and William C. Wohlforth, "American Primacy in Perspective," *Foreign Affairs*, Vol. 81, No. 4 (July–August, 2002), pp. 20–33.

2 The Bush Doctrine and the North Korean nuclear crisis

Chung-in Moon and Jong-Yun Bae

Prospects for a peaceful resolution of the North Korean nuclear problem seem dim. North Korea has undertaken a series of brinksmanship measures in response to the staunch American attitude. Both actors are now locked in a dangerous game of chicken without a clear route to a compromise. Why this collision course? Most critical to the issue has been the advent of the Bush Doctrine, which signals a major paradigmatic change in American foreign and defense policy. Its moral absolutism, hegemonic unilateralism, offensive realism, and focus on weapons of mass destruction and global terrorism have radically changed the terms of US engagement with North Korea. This chapter examines the impact of the Bush Doctrine on the North Korean nuclear problem by showing how it has affected the rise and evolution of the problem. The chapter also delineates future scenarios of the crisis and draws some implications for its peaceful resolution. (The North Korean crisis is a theme that runs through several of the contributions to this volume; see, in particular, Zhebin's Chapter 6 on Russia and the concluding chapter by Van Ness on "four-plus-two.")

Introduction

Ever since North Korea's admission in October 2002 of the existence of a highly enriched uranium (HEU) program, the North Korean nuclear problem has gone from bad to worse. Despite several sessions of the six-party talks hosted by China in Beijing, prospects for a peaceful resolution seem rather dim. Although the Bush administration has said it would seek a peaceful settlement of the North Korean problem through dialogue and diplomacy, its policy initiatives since the Beijing talks show an opposite direction. The United States has sought to apply multilateral pressures to isolate, contain, and transform North Korea through sanctions and related measures. Bilateral coordination with Japan to cut Pyongyang off from cash and technology, close cooperation with China to put additional pressures on North Korea, the Madrid G-10 meeting and enforcement of the Proliferation Security Initiative (PSI), and an American move to penalize North Korea through the UN Security Council all indicate that the Bush administration intends to utilize all possible options, including coercive measures, to resolve the North Korean nuclear issue.

The mounting American pressures notwithstanding, North Korea is still defiant, resorting to the old formula of brinksmanship diplomacy. It has been sending a message to the United States that if Washington removes its hostile intent and assures North Korea's security through a legally binding nonaggression treaty, it is more than willing to resolve all the security concerns, including the nuclear one. But the United States has rejected Pyongyang's offer of simultaneous exchange of its public pledge to verifiable inspection and irreversible dismantling of nuclear weapons for an American security guarantee through bilateral negotiations. The staunch American attitude has made the North undertake a series of brinksmanship measures including the admission of possession of nuclear bombs and reprocessing of spent fuel rods. As a result, the current North Korean nuclear problem has evolved into a dangerous game of chicken without a clear route to a compromise.

Amidst the standoff, new diplomatic efforts have been made in the six-party talks held in Beijing in 2003 and 2004. Considering the collision course that Washington and Pyongyang were on early in 2003, such multilateral diplomatic efforts represented profound progress in the direction of a peaceful resolution of the North Korean nuclear problem. Nevertheless, the United States and North Korea could not narrow the trust gap. Whereas the United States called for a complete, verifiable, and irreversible dismantling (CVID) of North Korea's nuclear programs without any preconditions, the North refused and demanded an exchange of its CVID for American security assurances and compensatory measures. Although the second round of the six-party talks was able to produce some tangible outcomes, as noted below, a rather pessimistic outlook appears to prevail.

What went wrong? North Korea's brinksmanship diplomacy is partly blamed on its inherent insensitivity to changing security parameters since September 11, 2001. But more critical is the advent of the Bush Doctrine, which signals a major paradigmatic change in American foreign and defense policy. Its moral absolutism, hegemonic unilateralism, offensive realism, and focus on weapons of mass destruction and global terrorism have radically changed the terms of American engagement with North Korea. For its proponents, the North Korean nuclear problem cannot be resolved without transforming its regime, which has been portrayed as part of an "axis of evil." American strategic moves to transform the Kim Jong-il regime and North Korea's desperate survival game have profoundly complicated the structure of the nuclear standoff on the Korean peninsula.

This chapter intends to examine the impact of the Bush Doctrine on the North Korean nuclear problem. The first section presents a brief overview of the North Korean nuclear crisis. The second shows how the Bush Doctrine has affected the rise and evolution of the North Korean nuclear problem. The third section attempts to delineate future scenarios of the North Korean nuclear crisis through the angle of the Bush Doctrine. Finally, the chapter draws some implications for the peaceful resolution of the North Korean nuclear crisis.

Understanding the North Korean Crisis: issues and conflicting claims

The North Korean problem is composed of two interrelated issues: nuclear weapons and missiles. The current quasi-crisis on the Korean peninsula has resulted mainly from disputes over North Korea's nuclear-weapons development. There are three dimensions to the disputes. The first is the suspicion concerning the North's past possession of nuclear warheads (one or two) before the signing of the Geneva Agreed Framework in 1994. The second one centers on present nuclear issues related to reprocessing of 8,000 spent fuel rods stored in water ponds, and North Korea's manufacture and export of plutonium, as well as production of additional nuclear warheads, which were previously frozen by the 1994 Agreed Framework. The third dimension is the future nuclear problem associated with the development of an HEU program. The United States claims that North Korea admitted to the program's existence during the visit to Pyongyang of its special envoy, James Kelly, in October 2002.

The current North Korean nuclear standoff started with the problem of the HEU program, a future nuclear issue. James Kelly claimed that Sokjoo Kang, first vice foreign minister of DPRK, admitted to its existence during his visit to Pyongyang. The Korean Peninsula Energy Development Organization (KEDO) thereupon suspended the supply of heavy oil to North Korea under heavy pressure from the United States, which argued that the clandestine development of the HEU program was an outright violation of the Agreed Framework. North Korea officially denied its existence, and accused the United States of fabricating the fact. According to North Korea, Kang did not admit to the existence of an HEU program, but simply emphasized its sovereign entitlement to possess nuclear weapons. The North then began a sequence of reciprocal measures in retaliation. It equated the suspension of supply of heavy oil with the nullification of the 1994 Geneva Agreed Framework. The measures included unsealing the frozen nuclear facilities in Yongbyon, removing monitoring cameras that the International Atomic Energy Agency (IAEA) had installed, expelling three IAEA inspectors, withdrawing from the Nuclear Non-Proliferation Treaty (NPT), and reactivating a 5-megawatt carbon nuclear reactor in Yongbyon.

The situation worsened when North Korea admitted to the possession of nuclear weapons and the near completion of reprocessing of spent fuel rods during three-party talks in Beijing in April 2003. Although the North Korean claims need verification through inspection, premature and imprudent handling of the future nuclear problem aggravated the situation by reviving past and present nuclear issues. If North Korea crosses certain "red lines," such as reprocessing all spent fuel rods, manufacturing and transferring plutonium, possessing additional nuclear weapons, testing them, test-launching medium- and long-range missiles, or engaging in a major military provocation, a devastating escalation of the Korean conflict cannot be ruled out. The downward spiral of the North Korean nuclear problem can be attributed in part to conflicting claims and divergent approaches between North Korea and the United States.

Conflicting perspectives on the origin of the standoff

The United States and North Korea have shown a considerable gap in interpreting the origin of the current standoff. The United States blames North Korea for the current nuclear fiasco. By developing an HEU program clandestinely, the North violated the Geneva Agreed Framework. Moreover, it has failed to comply with international norms and obligations by unsealing and reactivating the frozen Yongbyon facilities, expelling IAEA inspectors, and withdrawing from the Non-Proliferation Treaty. Punishment is the only logical response to the crimes.

But North Korea's position is diametrically opposite. It accuses the United States of violating the Agreed Framework. The United States, says Pyongyang, not only fabricated the charge of its possession of an HEU program, but also violated the letter and spirit of bilateral agreements. The North has therefore been calling for fair treatment as a normal country. North Korea has presented a long list of American wrongdoings: non-delivery of one light-water nuclear reactor by 2003; suspension of the supply of heavy oil; premature demand for obligatory inspection of nuclear facilities that should have taken place only after the delivery of a turbine and generator; failures with respect to relaxation of barriers to trade and investment including telecommunication services and financial and banking settlement within three months of signing the Agreed Framework; violation of the negative security assurance provision in the Agreed Framework as well as of the NPT by positing North Korea as a target for preemptive nuclear attack; nullification of the bilateral agreement on non-hostile intent, mutual respect, and non-interference with domestic affairs by declaring North Korea as a rogue state and axis of evil; attempts to overthrow the regime; and finally US breach of its pledge to support inter-Korean exchanges and cooperation by obstructing North–South economic cooperation.[1]

Divergent approaches to the breakthrough

Pyongyang and Washington differ about how to break through the current stalemate. North Korea has been calling for a simultaneous exchange of its public commitment to give up nuclear weapons for an American security assurance in the form of a legally binding nonaggression treaty. North Korea has made it clear that if the US pledges to implement the agreements embodied in the Albright–Cho joint communiqué of October 13, 2000, namely non-hostile intent, mutual respect, and non-interference with domestic affairs, it is willing to resolve all the American security concerns, including nuclear weapons and missiles. Thus, an immediate North Korean freeze on nuclear reactors and reprocessing of spent fuel rods, as well as verifiable inspection and irreversible dismantling of its nuclear weapons program, are contingent upon an American security assurance.

But the US has rejected the North Korean proposal by adhering to the principle of "dismantle nuclear weapons first, talk later." It justifies the hardline approach by pointing out the previous failure of the Clinton administration. Neoconservative hardliners in the Bush administration believe that the Agreed

Framework was nothing but an act of appeasement that rewarded North Korea's bad behavior. They do not intend to repeat the same mistake of appeasing in response to North Korea's blackmail. Apart from the principle of ABC (Anything But Clinton), they assert that the nonaggression treaty is out of the question since it has to pass through the US Congress.[2] Thus, the difference in handling the current standoff has become another source of contention between Pyongyang and Washington.

Emerging incompatibility in goal-setting

The Bush administration has been advocating the resolution of the current nuclear standoff through dialogue and diplomacy. But its hardliners appear to believe that the North Korean nuclear issue cannot be resolved without a profound regime change in the North. Therefore, they favor isolating, containing, and transforming the North rather than attempting dialogue and diplomacy. The position became much stronger after the American victory in Iraq. Some neoconservative elements in the United States even favor a malign neglect strategy that would let North Korea become a nuclear country. Such a move by the North, they believe, could justify undertaking a more aggressive strategy of isolation, containment, and transformation of North Korea. The Bush administration's recent Proliferation Security Initiative (PSI) and related measures to engage in indirect sanctions and selective naval interdiction underscore this general trend.

The American strategy to isolate, contain, and transform the North has, however, hardened Pyongyang's posture by enhancing domestic cohesiveness and strengthening the hardline position of its military. North Korea has already announced that its official ideology has changed from *juche* to *sungun jungchi* (military first politics). It has also been warning that any overt measures to isolate, contain, and transform the North will result in devastating outcomes. It has been urging that the Bush administration should engage in serious talks on the issues of nuclear weapons and missiles first. Thus, North Korea's position is clear: if the United States removes its nuclear threats, Pyongyang is more than willing to give up nuclear and missiles.

Different modality of dialogue and negotiation

The United States and North Korea have shown a parallel mode in choosing the modality of dialogue and negotiation. North Korea has strongly called for direct bilateral talks with the United States. For North Korea, threats from the United States are real and pressing, and the only way to manage them is to strike a direct deal with the Americans. No other parties but the United States can guarantee the North's security. Moreover, a multilateral approach could be extremely time consuming and high in transaction costs.

However, the Bush administration is firm on this issue and has been pushing for multilateral approaches. It has been trying to utilize the United Nations Security Council as well as other multilateral forums in pressing the North to comply with the American mandate of "dismantle first, talk later." Secretary of State Colin Powell has straightforwardly rejected the idea of direct, bilateral talks with the North by stating: "I think eventually we will be talking to North Korea, but we are not going to simply fall into what I believe is bad practice of saying the only way you can talk to us is directly, when it affects other nations in the region."[3] The Bush administration prefers the multilateral approach not only to save face, but also in order to exert the collective pressure of the international community on North Korea.

Likewise, North Korea and the United States have taken quite opposite views on the origin of the current nuclear crisis and methods of settling it. But recent developments reveal some optimistic signs for a negotiated settlement. Although the April 2003 three-party talks involving the United States, North Korea, and China failed, they paved the way for the six-party talks in August, in which those three countries plus Japan, South Korea, and Russia participated. Its outcome was rather dismal, however, because of the uncompromising postures of the United States and North Korea. North Korea called for a simultaneous exchange of an American security assurance for its public pledge to abandon its nuclear weapons program. But the American position remained firm: unless North Korea undertakes a verifiable dismantling of its nuclear weapons programs, the United States cannot promise any sort of security assurance.

On the occasion of the Bangkok summit of the Asia-Pacific Economic Cooperation (APEC) forum in October 2003, however, the United States began to shift its policy on North Korea. Although President Bush rejected the North Korean demand for "a legally binding bilateral nonaggression treaty," he showed a more flexible attitude by stating:

> And what we have now said is that in return for dismantling the [North Korean nuclear] programs, we're all willing to sign some kind of document, not a treaty, but a piece of paper that says, we won't attack you [Kim Jong-il] ... We haven't worked out the words, but the point is, is that North Korea must hear that in return for the dismantling of their program—in a verifiable way, by the way; I mean, we're going to want to know—that now five nations are willing to say something about his security.[4]

This statement implied that the United States now was willing to give a multinational security assurance to North Korea by amending its earlier position that emphasized a sequential approach of "dismantle first, security assurance later."[5] Moreover, Bush agreed to hold a second round of six-party talks.

North Korea's response was swift and positive. Provided that the United States accepted its position on a simultaneous exchange of non-nuclear possession and security assurances, North Korea was willing to give serious thought to the Bush proposal. North Korean leader Kim Jong-il assured Wu Bangguo, chairman of the Standing Committee of the Chinese National People's Congress, who visited Pyongyang in November, that North Korea would attend the second round of the six-party talks.

Such developments have been conducive to narrowing the gap between North Korea and the United States on two issues: making a breakthrough in the current stalemate and the modality of negotiations. Although there are still sources of contention, differences between the simultaneous action approach of North Korea and the Americans' sequential approach are not likely to remain a major obstacle to negotiations. Moreover, the modality of negotiations has also been resolved. Both North Korea and the United States have accepted the six-party format as a legitimate modality of negotiation. The second round of the six-party talks, which was held in Beijing from Feburary 25 to 28, 2004, was successful in producing some tangible outcomes: agreement on a nuclear-weapons-free Korean peninsula, institutionalization of the six-party talks by setting up a working group, and agreement to resume another round of six-party talks within the second quarter of 2004.

Nevertheless, it seems too early to be optimistic about the outcome of the six-party talks. Different views on the origins of the current nuclear standoff, the ambiguous goals of the United States in dealing with North Korea and its nuclear program (regime transformation versus elimination of nuclear weapons), and more importantly the wide gap in trust between Pyongyang and Washington are likely to impede and even endanger the process of the talks. Even if the six-party talks are able to produce a negotiated outcome comparable to the Ukraine model, subsequent steps such as intrusive inspection and irreversible dismantling of North Korea's nuclear weapons program will be herculean tasks.

The Bush Doctrine and the North Korean nuclear crisis

A careful examination of the nature of the North Korean nuclear crisis clearly indicates that the Bush administration has been taking a much tougher stance on North Korea than ever before. It can be attributed partly to the Bush administration's ABC (Anything But Clinton) policy, since the Clinton administration's policy on North Korea was labeled an appeasement policy during the 2000 presidential election campaign. But what really changed Bush's stance on North Korea was the adoption of the Bush Doctrine after September 11, 2001. The Bush Doctrine is composed of three major tenets: moral absolutism, hegemonic unilateralism, and offensive realism.[6] Let's examine each of these tenets and trace how they have influenced the evolving or devolving nature of the North Korean nuclear crisis.[7]

Moral absolutism and North Korea as an axis of evil

One of the most important factors behind the current nuclear standoff is closely associated with President Bush's perception of the moral foundation of American foreign policy. Bush strongly believes that American foreign policy cannot be detached from moral imperatives. Moral clarity should be its driving force. His speech at the commencement ceremony of the US Military Academy at West Point underscores the centrality of morality, as in the following statement:

> Because the war on terror will require resolve and patience, it will also require firm moral purpose. In this way our struggle is similar to the cold war ... Yet moral clarity was essential to our victory in the cold war ... Different circumstances require different methods, but not different moralities ... There can be no neutrality between justice and cruelty, between the innocent and the guilty. We are in a conflict between good and evil, and Americans will call evil by its name.[8]

This binary classification of good and evil has shaped Bush's perception of North Korea. For Bush, North Korea under the Kim Jong-il leadership, along with Iraq and Iran, is nothing but a rogue state and an axis of evil. There are several reasons for this assessment. First, it is argued that the North Korean leaders brutalize their own people and squander their national resources for their personal gain. Second, the North Korean leaders display no regard for international law, threaten their neighbors, and callously violate international treaties to which they are party. Third, the Bush administration maintains that the North Koreans are determined to acquire weapons of mass destruction, along with other advanced military technology, to be used as threats or offensively to achieve aggressive designs. Fourth, the North Koreans are considered sponsors of terrorism around the globe. Fifth, they are said to reject basic human values and hate the United States and everything for which it stands.[9] President Bush has even gone so far as to display his personal dislike of Kim Jong-il:

> I loathe Kim Jong-il. I've got a visceral reaction to this guy, because he is starving his people. And I have seen intelligence of these prison camps—they're huge—that he uses to break up families, and to torture people ... Yes, it appalls me. It is visceral. Maybe it's my religion, maybe it's me—but I feel passionate about this.[10]

This personal feeling and religious emotion have guided American foreign policy on North Korea, ignoring the country's politics, culture, and history. To Bush hardliners, North Korea is "untouchable"; it cannot be treated as a legitimate negotiating partner. This is all the more so because North Korea is considered a criminal state that has violated the Geneva Agreed Framework and the Non-Proliferation Treaty. In addition, North Korea continues to export complete ballistic missiles and production capabilities along with related raw materials, components, and expertise. Profits from these sales help Pyongyang to support its missile and other WMD development programs, and in turn generate new products to offer to its customers. In the words of US Secretary of Defense Donald Rumsfeld, North Korea is "the greatest proliferator of missile technology," a state that is willing "to sell almost anything."[11]

North Korea also poses problems for the United States in the matter of international terrorism. Although North Korea denounced international terrorism immediately after the September 11, 2001 attacks, signed the UN Convention for the Suppression of the Financing of Terrorism, and joined the UN Convention

Against the Taking of Hostages,[12] North Korea is still considered a terrorist-sponsoring state. *Patterns of Global Terrorism 2002*, issued by the State Department, makes the following statement on North Korea:

> Despite the urging of the international community, however, North Korea did not take substantial steps to cooperate in efforts to combat terrorism. Its initial and supplementary reports to the UN Counterterrorism Committee on actions it had undertaken to comply with its obligations under UNSCR 1373 were largely uninformative and nonresponsive ... North Korea is not known to have sponsored any terrorist acts since 1987. It has sold weapons to several terrorist groups, however, even as it reiterated its opposition to all forms of international terrorism ... Pyongyang continued to sell ballistic missile technology to countries designated by the United States as state sponsors of terrorism, including Syria and Libya.[13]

Based on American moral standards, North Korea is a rogue state and an axis of evil. It not only rejects the core American values such as liberal democracy, free market, and human rights,[14] but also plays a dangerous military game of building and exporting weapons of mass destruction and missiles. The failed state provokes other security concerns such as supplying arms to terrorists, engaging in drug trafficking, and passing counterfeit currencies. Dialogue and negotiations are virtually inconceivable with this evil state. Changing the regime through isolation and containment is the only solution for the United States to pursue.[15]

This moral absolutism embedded in the Bush Doctrine has defined not only the evil nature of North Korea but also the strategic options for dealing with it.

Hegemonic unilateralism and the nuclear standoff

Another striking aspect of the Bush doctrine is hegemonic unilateralism, which can be defined as unilateral US efforts to promote American values and interests worldwide through the projection of its hegemonic power. The *Quadrennial Defense Review* sums it up in the following manner: "US leadership is premised on sustaining an international system that is respectful of the rule of law. America's political, diplomatic, and economic leadership contributes directly to global peace, freedom, and prosperity. US military strength is essential to achieving these goals, as it assures friends and allies of an unwavering US commitment to common interests."[16]

The new American hegemonic unilateralism is framed around several principles. First is the primacy of American values and interests such as freedom, peace, and human rights. Second is unilateral imposition of American leadership through its preponderance of power. Third is a shared understanding that American leadership can prevail over multilateralism. It assumes that, if necessary, the United States as hegemonic leader can override international law, norms, and regimes. Finally, hegemonic unilateralism is based on the new notion of alliance that divides friends and enemies in a binary manner. Listen to George W. Bush: "Every nation, in every region, now has a decision to make. Either you are with us, or you are with the terrorists. From this day forward, any nation that continues to harbor or support terrorism will be regarded by the United States as a hostile regime."[17]

Hegemonic unilateralism has been manifested in several different forms (as other chapters in this book discuss), such as taking the lead in the Senate's refusal to ratify the establishment of the International Criminal Court and unilateral nullification of the Anti-Ballistic Missile Treaty. Initiation of war on Iraq without a resolution of the UN Security Council can be seen as the epitome of American unilateralism.[18] The unilateral US attitude has been applied to its alliance system. As Rumsfeld has suggested, "The mission must determine the coalition; the coalition must not determine the mission. If it does, the mission will be dumbed down to the lowest common denominator, and we can't afford that."[19] Washington's strained relations with France and Germany during the Iraq war reveal precarious discords resulting from the new concept of alliance underlying the Bush Doctrine.

What makes the situation worse is the absence of domestic American checks and balances. There have been numerous domestic critiques of hegemonic unilateralism. Congressional leaders such as Edward M. Kennedy,[20] Robert Byrd,[21] and Chuck Hagel have all emphasized the importance of multilateral cooperation in the conduct of American foreign policy. But the Bush administration has flatly rejected it. Friendly advice from leading Republican figures such as Brent Scowcroft, Lawrence Eagleburger, and James A. Baker III[22] was also ignored. Liberal and conservative commentators alike have all warned of the dangers of unilateral actions that downplay the role of the United Nations.[23] John Ikenberry, for example, criticized such unilateral behavior as demonstrating imperial ambition,[24] and Joseph Nye, in his influential book, *The Paradox of American Power*, warned that no matter how powerful the United States is, it cannot resolve the problems of weapons of mass destruction and global terrorism without forging extensive international cooperation.[25] However, the Bush administration was able to ignore and bypass domestic opposition by resorting to the new public mood in the United States. Liberal critiques of the Bush Doctrine were considered unpatriotic acts. The specter of McCarthyism was revived, silencing domestic opposition. Rumsfeld's powerful appeal that there is no time to make decisions on war through committee meetings prevailed. This deformed domestic check-and-balance system has made the Bush Doctrine all the more unconstrained and powerful.

How has hegemonic unilateralism affected the North Korean nuclear problem? The current nuclear standoff itself is a product of American unilateralism. If the Bush administration had been more attentive to local context and patient in forging international cooperation, the crisis could have been prevented. The current nuclear fiasco was triggered by Sokjoo Kang's admission in October 2002 of the HEU program. Despite North Korea's strategic ambiguity and then denial, the United States established the admission as a solid fact without proper verification and drove the entire situation to the brink of crisis. The United States had sufficient time to consult with South Korea and Japan, and could have undertaken coordinated diplomatic efforts to persuade the North to allow international inspection of the HEU program. The Bush administration did not take these essential steps. Instead, it resorted to an immediate punitive measure of suspending the supply of heavy oil to the North. Such unilateral action invited corresponding reactions from North Korea, aggravating the entire situation. North Korea regarded such action as a unilateral move to nullify the Agreed Framework. For the North, it is the United States that breached the letter and spirit of the Agreed Framework and the Albright–Cho joint communiqué of October 13, 2000, because the United States not only suspended the supply of heavy oil, but also declared the North part of an axis of evil. North Korea further claims that its withdrawal from the NPT is a legitimate act of self-defense in order to cope with American nuclear threats and its strangulation strategy.[26]

American unilateral attitude has also blocked chances for making a breakthrough in the current standoff. Since October 2002, the North has consistently called for peaceful resolution through dialogue. North Korea has argued that since its nuclear development is a logical response to American hostile intent and nuclear threats, it is willing to resolve American security concerns should the United States recognize its sovereignty and assure its security through a legally binding nonaggression treaty.[27] Its preconditions for dialogue and negotiation are not economic assistance but recognition, non-hostile intent, and mutual respect from the United States. What North Korea initially had in mind was simply the Bush administration's public pledge to honor the Albright–Cho joint communiqué on non-hostile intent, mutual respect, and non-interference that was signed in October 2000, which is far short of a nonaggression treaty or an executive agreement.

But the Bush administration rejected the offer, and unilaterally asked North Korea to dismantle its existing nuclear programs completely, verifiably, and irreversibly.[28] Secretary Rumsfeld made this point very clearly by stating that "We will not bargain or offer inducements for North Korea to live up to the treaties and agreements it has signed."[29] For hardliners of the Bush administration, engaging in negotiations with North Korea is seen as an act of appeasement in response to its blackmail, reminiscent of the Clinton administration.[30] Since North Korea has committed a crime by violating international treaties and agreements, it should correct its bad behavior proactively. Otherwise, North Korea should be subject to harsh punishment. Economic assistance and other forms of positive incentives will be considered only after North Korea gives up its nuclear programs. The staunch unilateral American position of "dismantle first, dialogue later" has further complicated the nuclear standoff with North Korea.

The US unilateral posture is not limited to preconditions for dialogue and negotiation; it extends to the modality of dialogue. North Korea has been arguing that its compliance with the IAEA and the NPT is contingent upon the continuing effectiveness of the Agreed Framework that was signed bilaterally with the United States. Thus, it is not obliged to abide by multilateral treaties and agreements when and if the bilateral agreement becomes void. The only way to resolve the current nuclear standoff is through bilateral negotiation between North Korea and the United States, be it restoration or amendment of the Agreed Framework or some other form of bilateral agreement, not only as it is the only viable way to handle the current issues, but also because the current crisis is caused by the unilateral hostile policy of the United States.[31] Moreover, multilateral modalities proposed by the United States cannot be accepted, because to North Korea they represent a subtle move by the United States to evade bilateral responsibility as well as to mount multilateral pressures on North Korea.[32] North Korea still regards the trilateral meeting in Beijing in April 2003 and the subsequent six-party talks simply as preliminary steps toward bilateral talks with Washington.[33]

However, the United States flatly rejects the North Korean proposal for bilateral talks because previous bilateral talks during the Clinton administration failed. The only viable way to root out the North Korea nuclear problem is to mount outside pressures on the North by holding multilateral dialogues. It is not only because North Korea violated international treaties and agreements, and poses major threats to global, regional, and peninsular security, but also because multilateral coordination and cooperation are essential for changing its behavior.[34] It is interesting to note that the United States has taken multilateral rather than unilateral approaches to the North Korean problem. As North Korea perceptively observed, however, the American multilateral approach can be seen as a unilateral offensive in the guise of a multilateral modality to strangulate North Korea.[35]

Offensive realism and North Korea

Offensive realism constitutes the final component of the Bush Doctrine. It is composed of four interrelated strategic elements. The first element is the principle of preemptive action. Departing from the old strategic doctrine of containment during the cold-war era, the Bush administration has emphasized that "we cannot let our enemies strike first,"[36] and that "America will act against emerging threats before they are fully formed."[37] Bush has underscored the value of preemptive action: "Yet the war on terror will not be won on the defensive. We must take the battle to the enemy, disrupt his plans, and confront the worst threats before they emerge ... And our security will require all Americans to be forward-looking and resolute, to be ready for preemptive action when necessary to defend our liberty and to defend our lives."[38]

Condoleezza Rice has justified preemptive action by stating: "Preemption is not a new concept. There has never been a moral or legal requirement that a country wait to be attacked before it can address existential threats ... The United States has long affirmed the right to anticipatory self-defense—from the Cuban Missile Crisis in 1962 to the crisis on the Korean Peninsula in 1994."[39] The paper *National Strategy for Combating Terrorism*, which was submitted to the US Congress, also asserts the relevance of preemptive attack: "If necessary, however, we will not hesitate to act alone, to exercise our right to self-defense, including acting preemptively against terrorists to prevent them from doing harm to our people and our country."[40]

Offensive realism comprises another strategic component. That is the possible use of tactical nuclear weapons in the process of undertaking preemptive action. *The Nuclear Posture Review* (NPR), which was submitted to Congress in January

2002, has pointed out the increasing value of missile defense and use of tactical nuclear weapons in coping with the new security environment of global terrorism and proliferation of weapons of mass destruction. The report suggested adoption of a triad of offensive strike systems (both nuclear and non-nuclear), defenses (both active and passive), and a revitalized defense infrastructure. Central to this new strategic concept are offensive deterrence, namely preemption, and tactical use of nuclear weapons.[41] According to the report, more than seventy countries have constructed underground bunkers, and it is essential to develop new tactical nuclear weapons to destroy HDBT (Hard and Deeply Buried Targets) preemptively.[42]

Use of tactical nuclear weapons has become more feasible than ever before. The US Congress, in the 2003 Defense Authorization Act, appropriated $15 million for the research and development of RNEP (a robust nuclear earth penetrator) in November 2002. Apart from the budgetary appropriation, the Bush administration has been trying to amend or abolish the Spratt-Furse Law of 1993, which prohibits research and development of small-scale nuclear weapons under TNT 5,000 ton.[43] Its amendment or abolition could lift legal obstacles that have impeded research, development, and application of tactical nuclear weapons, making the enforcement of NPR all the more feasible.

The third component of offensive realism is the increasing denial of Westphalian sovereignty. Since 1648, Westphalian sovereignty embodied in the principle of non-interference has served as the most important norm governing patterns of interactions among nations in the international system. But the Bush Doctrine has adopted the new principle of empirical sovereignty by downplaying Westphalian sovereignty.[44] It argues that "the sovereignty of nation-states that commit or sponsor genocide, terrorism, and the spread of weapons of mass destruction should not be respected."[45] The Bush administration's view quoted in Mel Gurtov's introduction—namely, that states that engage in such behavior "forfeit some of the normal advantages of sovereignty, including the right to be left alone" in their territory—deserves our attention.

Finally, offensive realism under the Bush Doctrine is backed up by the primacy of military power. In order to carry out preemptive actions effectively, the United States has been increasing military capability in an unprecedented manner.[46] Condoleezza Rice justifies it by stating that "We will seek to dissuade any potential adversary from pursuing a military buildup in the hope of surpassing, or equaling, the power of the United States and our allies ... But surely clarity is a virtue here. Dissuading military competition can prevent potential conflict and costly global arms races."[47] In connection with this, the United States has been pursuing a preponderance of power in both conventional forces and cutting-edge weapons including intelligence assets.[48] In order to support its massive military buildup, US defense spending reached a record high $396 billion in 2003, and will exceed $400 billion in 2004.[49] US defense spending in 2002 was greater than the total sum of defense spending of the other fifteen largest defense spenders, accounting for more than 45 percent of the world total.[50]

What are the implications of offensive realism for the North Korean nuclear quagmire? Even before the Bush Doctrine was adopted, North Korea was once considered a target for preemptive strike during the first wave of nuclear crisis in 1994.[51] But the Bush Doctrine has made North Korea a target for preemption in all directions. Since George W. Bush designated North Korea as an axis of evil in his January 2002 State of the Union address, the North has become a principal target for American preemptive action. It is more so because North Korea officially admitted the possession of nuclear warheads, the reprocessing of a significant portion of spent fuel rods, and the development of highly enriched uranium. On April 1, 2003, John Bolton suggested that North Korea and Iran would be the next targets after the war with Iraq ended.[52] It was also revealed that the Department of Defense was deliberating on a possible surgical strike on the North Korean leadership just as it had carried out on Iraq's.[53]

Apart from weapons of mass destruction, there are three additional factors that could make American preemptive action all the more likely. First, North Korea is still listed as one of seven terrorist-sponsoring states, along with Iran, Iraq, Syria, Libya, Cuba, and Sudan. *National Strategy for Combating Terrorism* (February 2003) and *Patterns of Global Terrorism 2002* both identified North Korea as a state that sponsors and supports global terrorism.[54] Its missile capability is another factor. It seems too early to make a judgment on whether North Korea has developed intercontinental ballistic missiles sufficient to reach the US mainland. But its possession of Taepodong and Nodong missiles threatening the US mainland and Japan could justify a preemptive action on the part of the United States.[55] Finally, North Korea's superiority in asymmetric forces along the DMZ and the increasing vulnerability of American forces in South Korea could serve as another rationale for American preemptive action.

Congress' appropriation of funds for research and development of RNEP also implies that North Korea could become a US target. Since 1961, North Korea has extensively fortified its military bases as part of four military lines. The Nuclear Posture Review also points out that most nuclear facilities in North Korea have been built underground, as those in Yongbyon and Kumchangri illustrate.[56] North Korea also perceives that the research and development of the bunker buster is designed for it: "The Republic will be the first target of the bunker buster that is being newly developed."[57] Thus, as a result of the Bush Doctrine, North Korea has become a de facto target for American tactical nuclear attack. What is particularly important here is North Korean threat perception. The North justifies its nuclear card as a self-defensive measure against American nuclear attack, making the current standoff all the more difficult to resolve.

The Bush administration is not likely to recognize North Korean sovereignty as long as it resorts to weapons of mass destruction. Moreover, North Korea's alleged involvement in drug trafficking and counterfeit currencies has further tarnished its image as a sovereign state. One of the reasons why the Bush administration has been reluctant to engage in any meaningful dialogues with North Korea lies in its persistent pattern of rogue behavior. Unless North Korea comes up with some drastic measures to revamp its fallen image, the United States could undertake more radical measures to isolate, contain, and transform North Korea through aggressive interference that disregards Westphalian sovereignty. In this context, it cannot be ruled out that North Korea might become another Iraq.

Finally, the United States has been taking some visible measures to restructure its forces in South Korea in order to cope with North Korea's military moves. In anticipation of a major contingency, the United States has announced the War Capability Enforcement Plan. According to the plan, it will be investing $11.3 billion for new weapons and equipment. The United States will also be pushing for missile defense in the East Asian theater. Along with this, the United States has forward-deployed long-range bombers in Guam and reinforced its naval and air capabilities in Japan and South Korea. Whether one regards the Bush Doctrine as being offensive or defensive, it has been instrumental for enhancing US warfighting capability against North Korea.

The Bush Doctrine and prospects for the North Korean nuclear standoff

The Bush Doctrine has led to profound changes in the United States' strategic terms of engagement with North Korea. They involve major paradigmatic transformations in perceptions of North Korea and behavioral style in dealing with it. More importantly, strategic prescriptions for the North Korean nuclear crisis have been radically altered. The Clintonian soft landing has gradually sunk into oblivion, while the brave new world of Bush's moral absolutism, hegemonic unilateralism, and offensive realism have dictated the nature and direction of strategic responses to North Korea. Given the thrust of the Bush Doctrine, two prescriptions are likely to be drawn. One is the military option; the other is malign or hostile neglect and the resolution of the nuclear crisis through regime transformation.

Military options and catastrophe

Neoconservative hardliners have been alluding to the possibility of using military options in dealing with North Korea. Rumsfeld once stated that "We are capable of fighting two major regional conflicts. We're capable of winning decisively in one and swiftly defeating in the case of the other, and let there be no doubt about it."[58] Richard Perle, another leading figure in the neoconservative camp, has also suggested the utility of military actions on nuclear facilities in North Korea as recently as June 2003.[59] In this regard, John Bolton's testimony before Congress draws attention too. He admitted to the possibility of undertaking a three-stage approach of sanctions, interdiction, and preemptive military attack in order to cope with WMD threats from North Korea.[60]

The United States might consider three possible military options. The first is a surgical strike on nuclear facilities in Yongbyon, a move that was debated during the 1994 nuclear crisis. The second is a combination of surgical strike and preemptive all-out attack on North Korea. The final option could involve a sequence of surgical attack, North Korea's retaliation, and counterattack. Regardless of the options, military actions are likely to result in a major catastrophe through conflict escalation. Even a well-planned surgical strike is likely eventually to escalate into a major conflict.

None of these military options seems feasible or desirable. Several factors would deter the United States from undertaking military options.

First is the rather weak rationale for undertaking military action.[61] North Korea is willing to talk with the United States, as well as accept an American request for verifiable inspection and irreversible dismantling of the North's nuclear-weapons program. What Pyongyang wants is a security assurance. There seems to be no reason why the United States should not accept these terms. It would be extremely difficult for the United States to win international support and legitimacy by taking military options while disregarding North Korea's appeal for dialogue and negotiation, even if the North admitted the existence of nuclear weapons.

Second, geopolitics matters. North Korea is different from Iraq. China, Russia, and Japan will strongly oppose American unilateral military actions. The United States cannot win the war with North Korea without winning support from these neighboring countries and utilizing their ground bases. In the worst case, Chinese military involvement in North Korea cannot be ruled out when one recalls the Korean War. The reason is that toleration of aggressive American behavior could bear negative implications for China's own national security.

Third, it seems doubtful whether the United States would be able to achieve its political and military objectives. A surgical strike on the Yongbyon nuclear facilities cannot satisfy the American goal of destroying North Korea's nuclear capabilities. Even though such an attack might be able to resolve the present nuclear problem (i.e., reprocessing of spent fuel rods and manufacturing of plutonium), it cannot eliminate either the past nuclear issue (one or two nuclear bombs) or the future one (highly enriched uranium). Thus, a surgical strike would achieve only a very limited goal, but with devastating potential consequences in terms of a major conflict escalation and massive radioactive fallout over South Korea and Japan. Preemptive all-out attack seems questionable too. No matter how backward and ill-equipped, the North Korean military is the fourth largest in the world. At the same time, the ideology of "military first politics," widespread anti-Americanism deeply embedded in the North Korean people, hostile terrain and fortification of military bases, and asymmetric forces deployed along the Demilitarized Zone would not allow an easy victory for the United States.

Fourth, South Korea's opposition will pose another formidable deterrent. The catastrophic consequences of military actions will make South Koreans deeply opposed to American military actions. Preemptive military actions without full consultation with the South Korean government could instantly jeopardize the ROK–US military alliance, without which the United States cannot undertake effective military operations.

Finally, neither rational calculus nor normative considerations favor military options. North Korea does not possess oil or other valuable natural resources. American economic gains in a war would be minimal, while the costs of war would be prohibitively high. In addition, over a million South Koreans might cross the DMZ and form a human shield against American military attacks.

Malign neglect and protracted military tension

Military options seem less attractive. Cognizant of the constraints and risks associated with the military option, some neoconservative hardliners have shifted their attention to the malign or hostile neglect option.[62] Even Ashton Carter, a liberal who served under Secretary of Defense William Perry during the Clinton administration, has suggested that option, at a congressional hearing on March 6, 2003.[63] The malign neglect option is predicated on several assumptions and related action programs. The most important assumption is "let North Korea go nuclear."[64] There is no other option but to recognize North Korea as a nuclear power, either because of delayed dialogue and negotiation with the North, or because of North Korea's unfailing intention to develop nuclear weapons both for survival and as a bargaining card. But allowing the North to be a nuclear power would not pose any immediate nuclear danger to countries in the region, since it would require more time to emerge as a full-fledged nuclear-weapon state.

Another critical assumption underlying this option is that the North Korean nuclear problem cannot be solved without toppling the regime. As long as Kim Jong-il stays in power, North Korea will want both dialogue and the bomb simultaneously. Removing him from power and creating a new regime in North Korea is the best and surest way to solve the North Korean nuclear dilemma. Thus, the United States and its allies and friends should work together to isolate, contain, and transform North Korea. If they work together, transformation of North Korea will materialize faster than its emergence as a real nuclear power.

The United States has already begun to take a series of actions in this direction. President Bush has already hinted at it by stating that "America is working with the countries of the region to find a peaceful solution, and to show the North Korean government that nuclear weapons will bring only isolation, economic stagnation, and continued hardship."[65] The steps include:

- the Proliferation Security Initiative (PSI), which would allow investigation, interdiction, and confiscation of illicit arms transfers;[66]
- deliberation on extensive measures to isolate and contain North Korea through a ban on arms-related exports and sales, controls over exports of dual use items, prohibitions on economic assistance, and imposition of miscellaneous financial and other restrictions;[67]
- the Japan–US summit in May 2003, at which the possibility was aired of economic sanctions and a naval blockade if the North Korean nuclear problem worsened;
- a sequence of punitive measures comprising economic sanctions, naval blockade and confiscation, and preemptive attack, as happened in the war on Iraq, if North Korea does not show any signs of improvement in its policies

concerning nuclear missiles, conventional weapons, drug trafficking, human rights, and terrorism;[68]
- interdiction of North Korean vessels exporting weapons and drugs, as the United States, Japan, and Australia on June 10, 2003, agreed to do selectively;
- multilateral measures to wipe out North Korea's exports of arms and drugs, discussed in Madrid on June 12, 2003, at a G-10 meeting;[69]
- suspension of construction of a light-water reactor in Shinpo and a UN resolution on economic sanction on North Korea; and
- collective legal efforts to prevent the inflow of materials, parts, and components of weapons of mass destruction into North Korea.[70]

The malign neglect option, leading eventually to transformation of North Korea, does not appear, however, to be a viable way of coping with the current crisis. There are several serious problems.

First, this option would worsen rather than improve the current nuclear standoff, eventually escalating into a major conflict on the Korean peninsula. As Wade Huntley perceptively points out, malign or hostile neglect has become the primary cause of the current crisis and is likely to aggravate rather than ameliorate it.[71] Moreover, the option seems to rely on faulty assumptions concerning the effectiveness of isolation and containment. The option can easily become problematic if the Kim Jong-il regime does not collapse.

Second, its proponents seem to commit the fallacy of underestimating regime durability in North Korea. The North Korean people are well accustomed to hardship under the *juche* system. As Lewis Coser aptly suggests, outside pressures on North Korea will not only strengthen the position of hardliners in the name of "military first politics," but also enhance the regime's internal cohesiveness, undermining the possibility of internal transformation. American efforts to isolate and contain would not bring about a swift demise of the Kim Jong-il regime. The Bush administration should learn from the failure of the Clinton administration. The Geneva Agreed Framework became troublesome because it was based on the faulty assumption of the early demise of the Kim Jong-il regime.

Third, no matter how persuasive and forceful the United States would be, it would be extremely difficult to enforce sanctions against North Korea. China and South Korea are the key players here. Given North Korea's dependence on China and South Korea,[72] sanctions on it will not be successful without the securing of their full cooperation. China, South Korea, and Russia will not lend full cooperation unless the United States exhausts all the possible means for a peaceful and diplomatic solution.

Finally, given North Korea's traditional behavior, the ultimate destination of the malign neglect strategy might be a catastrophic conflict escalation rather than a happy ending through the demise of the Kim Jong-il regime, emancipation of the North Korean people, and final elimination of its nuclear-weapons program. South Korea cannot accept such a development, because its survival and prosperity are at stake.

Conclusion: in defense of engagement and negotiated settlement[73]

The two alternative prescriptions based on the Bush Doctrine appear problematic. Neither the military option nor containment seems to be feasible or desirable.[74] To prevent the Korean peninsula from stumbling along a disastrous path to war, both sides ought to consider in earnest the negotiated-settlement approach of alternating threat and incentive. A nuclear North Korea is unthinkable. It would debilitate South Korea and trigger nuclear proliferation in the region, involving Japan, South Korea, Taiwan, and of course China. The undoing of a nuclear North Korea may require military action, causing enormous collateral damage. Needless to say, neither prospect is desirable. A solution should be found between the twin principles of "no nuclear North Korea" and "no military conflict." The sooner a negotiated settlement is given a chance, the better the prospect of avoiding the two worst consequences. Several steps can be considered in pursuing the negotiated settlement option.

First, utmost attention should be paid to an immediate freeze of North Korea's unruly behavior in the direction of becoming a nuclear power, such as verifiable inspection of nuclear facilities and their irreversible dismantling. Coping with the North Korean threat through isolation, containment, and transformation could be more time consuming and risky.

Second, the six-party talks should be continued and effectively utilized. After a long deliberation on the modality of dialogue (e.g., bilateral, three-party, four-party, five-party, six-party), the United States and North Korea finally accepted the six-party formula and held their first meeting in Beijing in August 2003. The first meeting was not successful, not only because the United States and the DPRK followed their old pattern of bilateral confrontation, but also because the meeting failed to produce any agreed principles, objectives, and procedures for six-party talks. Still, there is no other option but to revive the six-party talks. The breakdown of six-party talks will eventually lead to either unilateral American action or the adoption of a UN Security Council resolution on sanctions against North Korea, both of which could entail catastrophic outcomes. In this regard, the second round of the six-party talks can be seen as a positive step toward the peaceful settlement of the current nuclear standoff. All parties should make every effort to make the six-party talks viable. Despite an array of challenges and obstacles to, for example, verifiable inspection and irreversible dismantling, the six-party talks may not only open an institutionalized channel of communication among the parties, but also serve as a valuable vehicle for confidence building among them.

Third, it should be kept in mind that the six-party talks need to be utilized for dialogue and negotiation rather than for pressure to foster isolation, containment, and transformation of North Korea. What is critical at present is an immediate freeze of North Korea's nuclear activities and their verifiable inspection and dismantling. In so doing, the United States might have to consider relaxing its precondition of "dismantle first, security assurance later." If North Korea does not show a sincere and cooperative attitude in complying with American and international demands for a nuclear freeze and verifiable dismantling, it will be much easier for South Korea, China, and Russia to join the United States in undertaking collective punitive measures against the North, including sanctions. However, it might be difficult for South Korea, China, and Russia to join US-led outright multilateral pressures without there being any meaningful progress in negotiations with North Korea. Thus, the United States needs to relax its rigid position of "CVID without any preconditions."

Fourth, in setting the agenda, the North Korean proposal of a "bold initiative" deserves prudent attention. If North Korea is willing to make a binding public pledge to abandon its nuclear-weapons programs through verifiable dismantling and continue the moratorium on missile-test launching and the export of missile components and technology, its request for a nonaggression assurance, normalization of relations with the United States, non-obstruction of its economic cooperation with Japan and South Korea, and alleviation of its energy situation (including the Shinpo light-water reactor project), will need to be taken seriously. A promising sign was Secretary Powell's hint that the US Congress could endorse a resolution assuring North Korea of America's nonaggressive intent.[75] Although such a resolution is short of a formal nonaggression treaty or pact, it underscores a major policy shift from the previous position of "dismantle first, negotiation later." But opposition from the neoconservative camp is likely to abort the gesture, resulting in another round of rigid confrontation at the six-party talks.

Finally, the process of a negotiated settlement should be tied to engagement for opening and reform in North Korea. Engagement, as opposed to containment or an imposed engagement, should be positively considered for several reasons.

Engagement will entail trust, the most indispensable element for dialogue and negotiation. Given that the current standoff has resulted from mutual distrust, trust-building should be the first step. Engagement will facilitate the process of trust-building between the two.

Engagement is also desirable because it is predicated on the availability of choices for North Korea. While containment forces the North Korean leadership to continue to rely on the status quo and erratic responses of blackmail and brinksmanship, engagement can induce it to deliberate on more practical choices such as Deng Xiaoping's or Park Chung-hee's path to economic opening and reform. Despite suspicion of deception on the part of the North, North Korea has usually shown positive responses to engagement. Thus, engagement can bring about a virtuous, rather than vicious, cycle of interactions in dealing with North Korea.

Along with this, engagement might be the least traumatic, most effective, and fastest way to transform the North, while freezing its risky nuclear ambitions. Korean history demonstrates that regime change by external forces has always been subject to the question of legitimacy. Outside pressures alone, without corresponding formation of domestic civil society, cannot bring about changes in the North. Changes should come from within. In the process, the formation and activation of civil society is essential, something North Korea currently lacks. Engagement, opening and reforms, and creation and expansion of market interests are vital to the shaping of civil society in North Korea.

Ensuing debates notwithstanding, engagement has so far worked in inter-Korean relations. Changes in North Korea are by no means fictional. A little more push for a genuine, not hawkish, engagement by the United States can produce profound changes in a rapid manner. Moreover, South Korea does not want a sudden collapse in the North.

In conclusion, resolving the North Korean nuclear problem through a negotiated settlement and engagement will not be easy. Negotiations with North Korea are inevitably unruly and uncertain. Nevertheless, coercive options such as military actions and isolation, containment, and transformation, which the Bush Doctrine implicitly advocates, can be neither feasible nor desirable. These options should be kept as last resorts until all other alternatives for peaceful resolution have been exhausted. It is time for the United States to step back, take a deep breath, and pursue a prudent policy course.

Notes

1 This list was provided by the DPRK Lawyers Association, *Korea Central News Agency*, February 28, 2003.
2 On this issue, see an exchange of debates between Richard Armitage, Deputy Secretary of State, and Senator Joseph Biden (Democrat) at a Senate Foreign Affairs Committee hearing on the North Korean nuclear issue on February 4, 2003.
3 Ken Guggenheim, "Powell, Rice Reject Talks with N. Korea," *Associated Press*, March 9, 2003.
4 "Roundtable Interview of the President by the Press Pool," aboard Air Force One, October 22, 2003, online at www.whitehouse.gov/news/releases/2003/10/print/20031022-7.html (accessed October 27, 2003).
5 It later became known that what the Bush administration has in mind is the Ukrainian model. Ukraine signed a memorandum of understanding with the United States, Russia, and the United Kingdom in 1994. According to the memorandum, the three countries assured Ukraine's independence, sovereignty, and territory, as well as its security, in return for its complete elimination of nuclear weapons within the framework of the Non-Proliferation Treaty.
6 See George W. Bush, "Address to a Joint Session of Congress and the American People," United States Capitol, Washington, DC, September 20, 2001; online at www.whitehouse.gov/news/releases/2001/09/20010920-8.html (accessed June 8, 2003); George W. Bush, "State of the Union Address," Washington, DC, January 29, 2002, online at www.whitehouse.gov/news/releases/2002/01/20020129-11.html; George W. Bush, "Remarks by the President at 2002 Graduation Exercise of the United States Military Academy," West Point, New York, June 1, 2002, online at www.whitehouse.gov/news/releases/2002/06/20020601-3.html (accessed March 14, 2003).
7 For a more detailed discussion, see Chung-in Moon, "Bush Doctrine and the Prospects for the Relations between North Korea and US," paper presented at the symposium "The North Korean Nuclear Crisis and the Peace of Korean Peninsula," Korean Unification Forum, June 10, 2003 [in Korean].
8 George W. Bush, "Remarks by the President at 2002 Graduation Exercise."
9 George W. Bush, "State of the Union Address."
10 Bob Woodward, *Bush at War* (New York: Simon & Schuster, 2002), p. 340.
11 "Rumsfeld Sees Proliferation as Greatest Threat from North Korea," US Embassy, February 13, 2003, www.usembassy.it/file2003_02/alia/a3021314.htm (accessed June 20, 2003).

12 James Reilly, "The US 'War on Terror' and East Asia," *Foreign Policy in Focus*, Policy Report, February 2002, online at www.pfif.org/papers/asia2002.html (accessed June 4, 2003).
13 Counterterrorism Office, US Department of State, *Patterns of Global Terrorism 2002*, online at www/state.gov/s/ct/rls/pgtrpt/2002/pdf (accessed May 30, 2003), pp. 80–81.
14 Regarding the report of the US State Department on North Korean human rights, see www.state.gov/g/drl/rls/ hrrpt/2003/27775pf.htm (accessed February 27, 2004).
15 Ashton B. Carter, "Alternatives to Letting North Korea Go Nuclear," testimony before the Committee on Foreign Relations, United States Senate, March 6, 2003, at www.cfr.org (accessed May 15, 2003).
16 US Department of Defense, *Quadrennial Defense Review Report 2001*, September 30, 2001, p. 1; Mel Gurtov, "American Crusades: Unilateralism, Past and Present," paper presented on the Annual Convention of International Studies Association, February 26–March 1, 2003, Portland, Oregon, p. 4.
17 George W. Bush, "Address to a Joint Session of Congress"; White House, *National Strategy for Combating Terrorism*, February 2003, at www.whitehouse.gov/news/releases/2003/02/20030214-7.html (accessed June 8, 2003); White House, *The National Security Strategy of the United States of America*, September 2002, www.whitehouse.gov; John J. Mearsheimer, "The False Promise of International Institutions," *International Security*, Vol. 19, No. 3 (Winter 1994/1995), pp. 5–49; Tom Barry, "The US Power Complex: What's New," *Foreign Policy in Focus*, Special Report No. 20, November 2002, online at www.fpif.org/papers/02power/index/html (accessed June 4, 2003); Michael Hirsh, "Bush and the World," *Foreign Affairs*, Vol. 81, No. 5 (September/October 2002), p. 42.
18 Anthony Dworkin, "Interview and Introduction: Iraq and the 'Bush Doctrine' of Pre-Emptive Self-Defense," *Crimes of War Project*, August 20, 2002, online at www.crimesofwar.org/expert/bush-introBush-print.html (accessed May 28, 2003).
19 "Q & A with Donald Rumsfeld," *Chicago Sun-Times*, November 18, 2001.
20 Edward M. Kennedy, "The Bush Doctrine of Pre-emption," statement in the US Senate, October 7, 2002, http://truthout.org/docs-02/10.09A.Kennedy.p.htm (accessed May 28, 2003).
21 Robert Byrd, "The War Debate," *Los Angeles Times*, October 9, 2002.
22 James Baker, "The Right Way to Change a Regime," *New York Times*, August 25, 2002; James Baker, "The Case for Military Action," *Wall Street Journal*, February 4 2003.
23 Richard Deats, "Bush 'Doctrine' Too Narrow," *USA Today*, January 31, 2002; Michael E. O'Hanlon, Susan E. Rice and James Steinberg, *The New National Security Strategy and Preemption Policy*, Brief 113, December 2002; William Galston, "Perils of Preemptive War: Why America's Place in the World Will Shift—For the Worse—If We Attack Iraq," *The American Prospect*, September 23, 2002, pp. 22–5; Stanley Hoffmann, "The High and the Mighty, Bush's National-Security Strategy and the New American Hubris," *The American Prospect*, 13 January, 2003, pp. 28–31; John Steinbrunner, "Confusing Ends and Means: The Doctrine of Coercive Pre-emption," *Arms Control Today*, January/February 2003, online at www.armscontrol.org; Charles Krauthammer, "The Unipolar Moment Revisited," *The National Interest*, Winter 2002/2003; Jonathan Steele, "The Bush Doctrine Makes Nonsense of the UN Charter," *Guardian Unlimited*, June 7, 2002, online at www.guardian.co.uk/bush/story/0,7369,728870,00.html (accessed May 28, 2003).
24 G. John Ikenberry, "America's Imperial Ambition," *Foreign Affairs*, Vol. 81, No. 5 (September/October 2002), pp. 44–60.
25 Joseph S. Nye, Jr., *The Paradox of American Power: Why the World's Only Superpower Can't Go It Alone* (New York: Oxford University Press, 2003).
26 *Rodong Sinmun*, June 11, 2003, at www.kcna.co.jp/calendar/2003/06-06-12/2003-06-12-004.html.
27 *Rodong Sinmun*, June 2, 2003, at www.kcna.co.jp/calendar/2003/06-06-03/2003-06-03-003.html; *Rodong Sinmun*, January 4, 2003, at www.kcna.co.jp/calendar/2003/01/01-06/2003-01-06-002.html; *Rodong Sinmun*, March 5, 2003, at www.kcna.co.jp/calendar/2003/03/03-06/2003-03-06-003.html.

28 "US to Eliminate WMD in All Rogue States, by Force if Necessary," *World-AFP*, June 12, 2003.
29 "Rumsfeld Gets Tough on North Korea," *The Guardian*, December 24, 2002.
30 *Chosun Daily*, April 21, 2003.
31 *Rodong Sinmun*, June 2, 2003, at www.kcna.co.jp/calendar/2003/06/06-03/2003-06-03-003.html.
32 *Rodong Sinmun*, February 8, 2003, at www.kcna.co.jp/calendar/2003/02/02-10/2003-02-10-004.html.
33 *Rodong Sinmun*, June 19, 2003, at www.kcna.co.jp/calendar/2003-06/06-19/2003-06-19-002.html.
34 "Press Conferences with John Bolton, Under Secretary of State for Arms Control and International Security, US State Department," January 24, 2002.
35 *Rodong Sinmun*, June 19, 2003, at www.kcna.co.jp/calendar/2003-06/06-19/2003-06-19-002.html.
36 White House, *The National Security Strategy of the United States of America*, September 2002, p. 15.
37 Ibid.
38 George W. Bush, "Remarks by the President at 2002 Graduation Exercise."
39 "Condoleezza Rice Discusses President's National Security Strategy," Waldorf Astoria Hotel, New York, October 1, 2002, online at www.whitehouse.gov/news/releases/2002/10/20021001-6.html (accessed June 8, 2003).
40 White House, *National Strategy for Combating Terrorism*, February 2003, online at www.whitehouse.gov/news/releases/2003/02/20030214-7.html (accessed June 8, 2003), p. 2.
41 US Department of Defense, *Nuclear Posture Review Report*, submitted to Congress on January 8, 2002, at www.globalsecurity.org/wmd/library/policy/dod/npr.htm (accessed June 4, 2003), p. 7.
42 Ibid., p. 46.
43 See James C. Dao, "Senate Panel Votes to Lift Ban on Small Nuclear Arms," *New York Times*, May 10, 2003; James Dao, "Panel Rejects Nuclear Arms of Small Yield," *New York Times*, May 15, 2003; Charles D. Ferguson and Peter D. Zimmerman, "New Nuclear Weapons?" online at http://cns.miis.edu/pubs/week/030528.htm (accessed June 10, 2003).
44 Stephen Krasner, *Sovereignty* (Princeton, N.J.: Princeton University Press, 1994).
45 White House, *National Strategy for Combating Terrorism*, p. 17.
46 G. John Ikenberry, "America's Imperial Ambition," *Foreign Affairs*, Vol. 81, No. 5 (September/October 2002), pp. 49–50; Tom Barry, "The US Power Complex: What's New," *Foreign Policy in Focus*, Special Report No. 20, November 2002, at www.fpif.org/papers/02power/index.html (accessed June 4, 2003).
47 "Condoleezza Rice Discusses President's National Security Strategy."
48 White House, *The National Security Strategy of the United States of America*, pp. 29–31.
49 United States Senate, Committee on Armed Services, "Senate Armed Services Committee Completes Makeup of National Defense Authorization Bill For Fiscal Year 2004," May 9, 2003, online at www.senate.gov/~armed_services/press/04mark.pdf (accessed June 16, 2003).
50 See Stockholm International Peace Research Institute, Press Release on *SIPRI Yearbook 2003: Armaments, Disarmament and International Security* (Stockholm: SIPRI, 2003).
51 William J. Perry, "The United States and the Future of East Asian Security: Korea—*Quo Vadis*?" in Keun-Min Woo, ed., *Building Common Peace and Prosperity in Northeast Asia* (Seoul: Yonsei University Press, 2002), pp. 121–2.
52 "Iran Next on W's List," *New York Daily News*, April 1, 2003, online at www.nydailynews.com.
53 *New York Times*, May 11, 2003; *JoongAng Ilbo*, May 13, 2003.
54 White House, *National Strategy for Combating Terrorism*, February 2003, p. 18; Counterterrorism Office, US Department of State, *Patterns of Global Terrorism 2002*.
55 George J. Tenet, "The Worldwide Threat in 2003: Evolving Dangers in a Complex World," DCI's Worldwide Threat Briefing to Senate Select Committee on Intelligence, February 11, 2003, at www.cfr.org (accessed May 15, 2003).
56 Department of Defense, *Nuclear Posture Review Report*.

57 *Nodongshinmun*, May 12, 2003 at www.kcna.co.jp/calendar/2003/05/05-12/2003-05-12-001.html.
58 "Rumsfeld Gets Tough on North Korea."
59 *Yonshap News Agency*, June 12, 2003.
60 See the testimony of John Bolton, Under Secretary of State, to the US House of Representatives Committee on International Relations, "US to Eliminate WMD in All Rogue States, By Force if Necessary," *World-AFP*, June 5, 2003.
61 Jeremy Brecher, "Terminating the Bush Juggernaut," *FPIF Discussion Paper*, May 2003, at www.fpif.org/papers/juggernaut/index.html (accessed June 4, 2003); Leon V. Sigal, "North Korea is No Iraq: Pyongyang's Negotiating Strategy," *Arms Control Today*, Vol. 32, No. 10 (December 2002), pp. 11–12.
62 Sonni Efron, "US Said to be Resigned to a Nuclear Korea," *Los Angeles Times*, March 5, 2003; "Bush Shifts Focus to Nuclear Sales by North Korea," *The New York Times*, May 5, 2003.
63 Ashton B. Carter, "Alternatives to Letting North Korea Go Nuclear."
64 Ibid.
65 George W. Bush, "State of the Union Address."
66 *JoongAng Ilbo*, June 2, 2003.
67 Counterterrorism Office, US Department of State, *Patterns of Global Terrorism 2002*, p. 77.
68 As suggested by John Bolton on June 4, 2003, in congressional testimony; see *DongA Ilbo*, June 6, 2003.
69 *JoongAng Ilbo*, June 12, 2003.
70 On October 27, 2003, the United States, China, Japan, South Korea, and four other countries in the Asia-Pacific region held a meeting in Tokyo and agreed to explore such action. *Hankyoreh Shinmum*, October 29, 2003.
71 Wade L. Huntley, "Coping with North Korea," *Foreign Policy in Focus*, February 24, 2003, at www.fpif.org/papers/korea2003.html (accessed June 4, 2003).
72 Institute of Political Education for Unification (IPEU), Department of Unification, *Understanding North Korea, 2003* (Seoul: IPEU, 2003), pp. 149–50.
73 This section draws partly from Chung-in Moon, "Coping with the North Korean Nuclear Quagmire: In Defense of Engagement," paper prepared for presentation at the KEI-Stanford Conference on "The United States and South Korea: Reinvigorating the Partnership," October 23–24, 2003, Stanford University.
74 See Jung-Hoon Lee and Chung-in Moon, "The North Korean Nuclear Crisis Revisited: The Case for a Negotiated Settlement," *Security Dialogue*, Vol. 34, No. 2 (June, 2003), pp.135–51.
75 *Korea Herald*, August 10, 2003.

3 Letting the genie out of the bottle
The Bush nuclear doctrine in Asia

Timothy L. Savage

The end of the cold war held out the hope that the nuclear genie could be put back into the bottle and disarmament achieved. Rather than seizing this historic opportunity, the George W. Bush administration has increased the role of nuclear weapons in US defense policy. In an era when US conventional military power is both unprecedented and unchallenged, US military planners continue to invent new scenarios for possible nuclear-weapons use. Many of the envisioned nuclear contingencies focus on Asia, particularly China and North Korea. In utilizing nuclear weapons to maintain and extend its military dominance, however, the United States ends up encouraging nuclear proliferation in response, while simultaneously undermining US political interests in the region. Instead of looking to build newer, smaller nuclear weapons, the United States should seek to reinvigorate global nonproliferation norms by moving toward nuclear disarmament as required by the Nuclear Non-Proliferation Treaty.

Introduction

The end of the cold-war superpower standoff between the United States and the Soviet Union, which had been characterized by the nuclear terror of Mutually Assured Destruction (MAD), held out the hope that the nuclear genie could be put back into the bottle and disarmament achieved. The early returns were promising. Agreements were concluded that removed nuclear weapons from former Soviet republics, such as Kazakhstan and Ukraine, which had inherited them upon the dissolution of the USSR. US President George H. W. Bush in 1991 announced the removal of tactical nuclear weapons from US military bases and surface ships worldwide. General Lee Butler, who was the head of the US Strategic Command at the time, said later that he saw his role as overseeing the end of his own job.

Rather than seizing this historic opportunity to step back from the nuclear brink, the current administration of George W. Bush has moved to increase the role of nuclear weapons in US defense policy. In an era when US conventional military power is both unprecedented and unchallenged, US military planners continue to invent new scenarios for possible nuclear-weapons use. Many of the envisioned nuclear contingencies focus on Asia, particularly China and North

Korea. In utilizing nuclear weapons to maintain and extend its military dominance, however, the United States ends up encouraging nuclear proliferation in response, while simultaneously undermining US political interests in the region. While the danger of a Dr. Strangelove-type nuclear annihilation has been greatly reduced, the chances that nuclear weapons will be used somewhere in the world are now greater than at any time since the bombings of Hiroshima and Nagasaki in 1945.

The end of arms control

Nonproliferation

From the 1960s to the 1990s, virtually every US administration made some progress in limiting the spread of nuclear weapons. The frightening reality of MAD led all but the most hawkish elements of both major political parties to conclude that, in the words of Ronald Reagan, a nuclear war could never be won and must not be fought. US nuclear policy in both Democratic and Republican administrations thus focused on preventing the spread of nuclear weapons to countries that did not have them, while gradually reducing the size and deadliness of the superpower arsenals. The bipartisan consensus on the desirability of this goal led to a series of successful arms-control agreements, some multilateral—such as the Nuclear Non-Proliferation Treaty (NPT)—others bilateral, such as the Strategic Arms Limitation Talks (SALT) and the Strategic Arms Reduction Talks (START) treaties.

The center of US nonproliferation policy has long been the NPT, the most widely subscribed arms-control treaty in the world, with 187 State Parties as of 2000. Only Israel, India, Pakistan, and Cuba have never signed the agreement. The NPT, which was signed in 1968 and went into effect in 1970, has been widely credited with preventing as many as thirty or forty countries from acquiring nuclear weapons. Increasingly, however, the limitations of the treaty have come into focus. The NPT divided the world into nuclear "haves" and "have-nots." The haves were limited to the five countries that already possessed nuclear weapons at the time of the treaty's signing—the United States, the Soviet Union, Great Britain (which were all among the original signatories), France, and China (both of which joined the treaty in 1992). Under the treaty, the recognized nuclear-weapon states pledged not to transfer nuclear weapons or nuclear weapons technologies to non-nuclear states. In exchange, non-nuclear states were promised cooperation in the peaceful development of nuclear energy.

The terms of the NPT called for a review conference in twenty-five years' time to determine whether the treaty should be extended for a fixed period of time, extended indefinitely, or not extended at all. The administration of President Bill Clinton fought hard and successfully to secure an indefinite extension on May 11, 1995. This highly touted victory, however, masked the underlying fissures in the international community over the direction and pace of nuclear disarmament. Non-nuclear-weapon states complained about the failure of the nuclear-weapon states to implement Article VI, which reads:

Each of the Parties to the Treaty undertakes to pursue negotiations in good faith on effective measures relating to cessation of the nuclear arms race at an early date and to nuclear disarmament, and on a Treaty on general and complete disarmament under strict and effective international control.[1]

Twenty-five years after making this pledge, while the United States and Russia took some steps to reduce the size of their nuclear arsenals, the promised treaty on disarmament was nowhere in sight. India, the largest nuclear-capable country not party to the NPT, frequently cited this inequality as justification for its refusal to join the treaty. After India held nuclear tests on May 11 and 13, 1998, the Clinton administration launched a desperate diplomatic offensive to dissuade Pakistan from following suit. That effort ended in failure when Islamabad conducted its own nuclear tests two weeks later. The South Asian rivals thus became the first new declared nuclear-weapon states since the NPT was first signed.[2]

On the domestic front, there was increasing dissatisfaction in conservative circles with the arms-control agenda. Foreign-policy hawks chafed at the constraints that treaties imposed on American freedom of action, especially with the increasing growth of US power relative to the rest of the world. Why should the world's sole superpower voluntarily give up military options that no one could take from it by force? The first casualty of this assault on arms control was the Comprehensive Test Ban Treaty (CTBT), which aimed to hinder new nuclear developments by outlawing tests of nuclear explosions. The CTBT was designed to strengthen the NPT and nudge the nuclear-weapon states further down the road to disarmament; but critics who had no desire to see Washington give up its nuclear weapons argued that the treaty would harm the ability of the United States to maintain and modernize its nuclear-weapons stockpile. On October 13, 1999, only fifty-one US Senators voted to ratify the CTBT, falling well short of the necessary two-thirds majority. It marked the first time that the US Senate had failed to ratify a security-related treaty since it rejected US membership in the League of Nations in 1919.

The neocon triumph and the new roles of nuclear weapons

The incoming administration of George W. Bush included many of the most ardent opponents of traditional multilateral arms control, such as Vice President Dick Cheney, Secretary of Defense Donald Rumsfeld, Deputy Secretary of Defense Paul Wolfowitz, and Assistant Secretary of State for Nonproliferation and International Security John Bolton. Rumsfeld had led a study on ballistic missile development that claimed that certain so-called "rogue" states, most notably North Korea, would be able to hit the US mainland with nuclear-armed missiles by 2015 unless the United States developed a missile defense.[3] In 1992 Wolfowitz, as Undersecretary of Defense for Policy, supervised the drafting of a Defense Policy Guidance that called for preventing the rise of any state or combination of states that could challenge American dominance. After the draft was leaked to the *New York Times*, domestic and international criticism led then-Secretary of Defense

Cheney to order a revision that used more diplomatic language and gave more lip service to multilateral cooperation mechanisms such as the United Nations.[4]

After Bush Senior was defeated for reelection in 1992, Wolfowitz and Bolton joined other neoconservatives in a study group organized by right-wing columnists William Kristol and Robert Kagan called the Project for a New American Century (PNAC). Many of the ideas that had been dropped from the earlier draft of the Defense Policy Guidance found new life in a report prepared by the project entitled "Rebuilding America's Defenses: Strategy, Forces and Resources for a New Century."[5] The report called for maintaining the "Pax Americana" based on US military, technological, and economic dominance. It urged that the United States "expand the role of democratic peace," and identified East Asia as the primary focus of strategic competition.[6] The report also argued that "raising US military strength in East Asia is the key to coping with the rise of China to great-power status." In particular, it advocated moving the alliance with South Korea beyond its traditional role of protecting against an invasion from North Korea and into a larger regional alliance system designed to contain China. US security guarantees should also be extended to Southeast Asia for the same purpose:

> By guaranteeing the security of our current allies and newly democratic nations in East Asia, the United States can help ensure that the rise of China is a peaceful one. Indeed, in time, American and allied power in the region may provide a spur to the process of democratization in China itself.[7]

Nuclear weapons hold pride of place in this strategy. The report argued that the United States should "maintain nuclear strategic superiority, basing the US nuclear deterrent upon a global, nuclear net assessment that weighs the full range of current and emerging threats, not merely the US–Russia balance."[8] It argued that the most urgent threat was not Russian nuclear power, but a "growing number of small nuclear arsenals—from North Korea to Pakistan to, perhaps soon, Iran and Iraq—and a modernized and expanded Chinese nuclear force." It called for the development of "a new family of nuclear weapons designed to address a new set of military requirements, such as would be required in targeting the very deep underground, hardened bunkers that are being built by many of our potential adversaries." The authors made no bones about their fondness for maintaining the US nuclear force: "US nuclear superiority is nothing to be ashamed of; rather, it will be an essential element in preserving American leadership in a more complex and chaotic world."[9]

The report makes no mention whatsoever of multilateral institutions or treaty commitments as a means to prevent proliferation. Rather, the focus is on counter-proliferation: developing defensive systems to protect US territory and bases against nuclear attack. In public debates, most advocates of missile defense have stressed the need to protect against nuclear missiles being launched either by accident or by "irrational" rogue states or terrorists. The PNAC report, however, made clear that missile defense was needed "to provide a secure basis for US power projection around the world."[10]

> While reconfiguring its nuclear force, the United States also must counteract the effects of proliferation of ballistic missiles and weapons of mass destruction that may allow lesser states to deter US military action by threatening US allies and the American homeland itself. Of all the new and current missions for US armed forces, this must have priority.[11]

Not having to fear a nuclear attack, the United States would be able to act without constraints, particularly against small, weak adversaries like Iraq or North Korea. So while missile defense may be portrayed publicly as a purely defensive measure, it is in fact designed to increase American offensive capabilities by protecting the United States against retaliation by countries that are the targets of American military intervention.

Upon returning to the White House, the neoconservatives moved decisively to turn their agenda into policy. The first order of business was getting rid of the Anti-Ballistic Missile (ABM) Treaty that that United States had negotiated with the Soviet Union in 1972. The ABM Treaty was designed to lock in the terror of mutually assured destruction by assuring that neither side could build a defense against the other's nuclear weapons and take advantage of its new-found security to launch a first strike. The Bush administration argued that the ABM was a dead letter since it had been signed with a country that no longer existed under a vastly different world situation. After months of negotiation failed to persuade Russia to scrap the treaty, President Bush announced on December 13, 2001, that the United States was unilaterally withdrawing from the treaty in six months, as provided by the treaty's escape clause.

The arguments that White House officials used to justify this action echoed those found in the PNAC report, but with a twist. In announcing the withdrawal, Bush stated: "Today, as the events of September 11 make all too clear, the greatest threats to both our countries come not from each other, or from other big powers in the world, but from terrorists who strike without warning or rogue states who seek weapons of mass destruction."[12] Although the September 11 attacks had been carried out with box cutters and commercial airplanes, Bush nonetheless cited them as evidence of the need for a high-tech system to shoot down long-range missiles. While the PNAC had made scant mention of non-state terrorism as a threat that the US military should prepare for, 9/11 provided a powerful pretext for implementing the policies advocated in that report—policies that otherwise would have had little public support.

The Bush administration spelled out its nuclear-weapons policy in the Nuclear Posture Review (NPR) submitted to Congress on December 31, 2001. Not surprisingly, the NPR reads very much like the PNAC report's sections on nuclear weapons.

> Nuclear weapons play a critical role in the defense capabilities of the United States, its allies and friends. They provide credible military options to deter a wide range of threats, including WMD and large-scale conventional military force. These nuclear capabilities possess unique properties that give the

United States options to hold at risk classes of targets [that are] important to achieve strategic and political objectives.[13]

It is worth noting that despite the unchallenged dominance of US conventional forces, and even though recent conflicts have demonstrated that technological superiority trumps numerical advantages in troops, the United States still claims that nuclear weapons are needed to protect against the possibility of being overwhelmed by large numbers of enemy forces. In essence, what the Bush administration seeks is nothing less than total security for the United States, allowing it to act anywhere and anytime in the world free from any constraints. The threat of nuclear attack is Washington's most powerful weapon for trying to coerce hostile countries to act the way that the United States desires.

Like the PNAC, the NPR emphasizes the need to move away from the cold-war logic of Mutual Assured Destruction and toward a leaner, more flexible force that envisions using nuclear weapons in a variety of war-fighting scenarios. In addition to the traditional triad of intercontinental ballistic missiles (ICBM), strategic bombers, and submarine-launched missiles, the NPR calls for a "New Triad" of nuclear and non-nuclear offensive strike systems, active and passive defenses, and "a revitalized defense infrastructure." For the first time, missile defense has been integrated into US nuclear strategy. Missile defense is seen as having the ability "to help provide deterrence and protection against attack, preserve US freedom of action, and strengthen the credibility of US alliance commitments." The effectiveness of the US nuclear umbrella has always been called into question by the uncertainty of whether the United States would really be willing to trade Washington or New York for Paris or Tokyo. By developing missile defenses that could not only protect the United States against long-range missile attack, but also be transferred to willing allies, the United States could continue to pursue an aggressive foreign policy, unconstrained by either domestic fears or the nervousness of more vulnerable allies.

The NPR goes as far as to argue that missile defense technologies can play a role in nonproliferation:

> Defenses can make it more arduous and costly for an adversary to compete militarily with or wage war against the United States. The demonstration of a range of technologies and systems for missile defense can have a dissuasive effect on potential adversaries. The problem of countering missile defenses, especially defensive systems with multiple layers, presents a potential adversary with the prospect of a difficult, time-consuming and expensive undertaking.

In other words, upon seeing US invulnerability, potential proliferators will simply throw up their hands in frustration and instead decide to use their money in more productive ways. This appears to be wishful thinking, especially as it assumes that missile defenses will be 100-percent effective. Richard Garwin, a prominent weapons designer, has shown that the US missile defense system could be breached using relatively low-tech, inexpensive methods such as decoys and small bomblets.[14] When faced with US missile defense, America's enemies, rather than give up their weapons program, are more likely to implement such countermeasures, while simply increasing the size of their WMD arsenals to increase the chances that at least some of the missiles will reach their targets. Furthermore, countries like North Korea that consider their supreme national interest to require resisting American dominance are not going to be dissuaded from attempting to deter US military action regardless of the cost involved. Recently declassified documents demonstrate that in 1968 the United States undertook a major buildup of its nuclear capabilities to counter a limited Soviet missile defense.[15] So even America's own experience in reacting to an opponent's missile defense system belies the neocon analysis.

The NPR tries to justify this renewed emphasis on the role of nuclear weapons in US strategic thinking by claiming that the "New Triad" will allow the United States to reduce the number, if not the importance, of nuclear weapons. With missile defense in place, "the US will no longer be as heavily dependent on offensive strike forces to enforce deterrence as it was during the cold war." In addition, non-nuclear strike forces will make the US less dependent on nuclear weapons for "offensive deterrent capability." This will allow the United States to reduce its nuclear forces to "1,700–2,200 operationally deployed nuclear warheads" as agreed to by President Bush and Russian President Vladimir Putin on November 13, 2001.

The key phrase here is "operationally deployed." While this latest US–Russian agreement may appear on the surface to continue the disarmament process begun with the SALT and START treaties, in reality it does not require either side to destroy a single nuclear warhead. Instead, the weapons scheduled for reduction will simply be removed from active duty, but kept in reserve as a "responsive force" to meet "potential contingencies," defined as "plausible but not immediate dangers." In other words, the United States is going to reduce the number of bullets in its gun to show its peaceful intentions, but carry around a couple of extra magazines just in case.[16] This again demonstrates the neocon agenda to ensure continued US dominance well into the future. Although there is no reason to think that any country will develop a nuclear arsenal large enough to challenge that of the United States in the foreseeable future—especially as the envisioned cuts are supposed to take ten years to implement—the Bush administration wants to hold on to its weapons in perpetuity just to be on the safe side. This kind of hedging goes against the very nature of multilateral arms control, and demonstrates that the United States has no serious intention to fulfill its obligations under Article VI of the NPT.

Mini-nukes

While reducing the total number of deployed nuclear weapons, the Bush administration is seeking to develop a new, more "usable" class of low-yield, ground-penetrating weapons that can destroy deeply buried targets, such as the numerous underground facilities in North Korea. According to the NPR:

With a more effective earth penetrator, many buried targets could be attacked using a weapon with a much lower yield than would be required with a surface burst weapon. This lower yield would achieve the same damage while producing less fallout (by a factor of ten to twenty) than would the much larger yield surface burst. For defeat of very deep or larger underground facilities, penetrating weapons with large yields would be needed to collapse the facility.

On May 20, 2003, the US Congress accommodated the Bush administration's wishes by voting to lift a decade-old ban against research and development into such weapons.[17] In response to criticism from arms-control activists, the US Senate on July 9 voted to cut most of the funding for the program,[18] but on November 18, Congress restored half of Bush's request for earth-penetrating weapons and the full amount for research into low-yield nuclear weapons as part of a catch-all energy bill.[19] The Pentagon is believed to have discussed plans for developing low-yield weapons at a meeting in early March, 2003, that brought together most of the US nuclear establishment.[20]

Critics argue that this program rests on a number of false assumptions on the part of the Bush administration. First is the belief that the radioactive fallout from such weapons can be easily contained. In fact, the sheer size of nuclear weapons means that large radioactive fallout is inevitable in any nuclear explosion. The largest conventional weapon in the US arsenal contains 12,600 pounds of explosives. Even a 100-ton nuclear warhead—150 times smaller than the bomb dropped on Hiroshima—yields a blast equivalent to 200,000 pounds of dynamite.[21] Furthermore, physical limits on how far a bomb can penetrate without cracking the missile's casing mean that any ground-penetrating nuclear weapon would create a massive crater that would spread highly radioactive dirt over a large area.[22]

The second questionable assumption, as articulated in the NPR, is that the mere existence of such weapons would dissuade potential adversaries from even attempting to develop costly countermeasures to the US nuclear arsenal. History shows that technological advances by one country inevitably lead other nations to try to beg, borrow, or steal the technology for their own purposes. The idea that other countries would simply give up trying to develop weapons of mass destruction in shock and awe at the might of the US arsenal flies in the face of both political science theory and historical evidence. Instead, US development of mini-nukes is most likely to spur other nations to develop new weapons systems of their own, and to acquire the ability to target the US mainland in hopes of deterring American action. Experience in everything from compact disc pirating to the hydrogen bomb also shows that once a technology has been developed, preventing it from falling into the "wrong" hands is ultimately a hopeless task. While preventing "rogue states" or terrorist groups from getting their hands on small nuclear weapons that could be snuck into an American city is urgent, perfecting nuclear-weapons miniaturization does not promote the desired outcome.

Zone of strategic competition: Bush nuclear doctrine in Asia

It has been said that the original purpose of the North Atlantic Treaty Organization (NATO) was to keep the Americans in Europe, the Soviets out, and the Germans down. US nuclear policy in Asia also appears to have three goals: defeating North Korea, containing China, and retaining South Korea and Japan within the US alliance system. While NATO was largely successful in achieving all three objectives, there are reasons to doubt whether the new nuclear doctrine espoused by the Bush administration will be able to accomplish its goals.

Defeating North Korea

The most pressing challenge for Bush's nonproliferation strategy remains North Korea. Since George Bush came to office, North Korea has announced the abrogation of the Agreed Framework; removed equipment and expelled inspectors who were monitoring the nuclear freeze; restarted its frozen reactor at Yongbyon; announced its withdrawal from the NPT; declared the 1991 North–South agreement on denuclearization a dead letter; allegedly begun reprocessing spent fuel rods; and claimed possession of nuclear warheads.

A North Korea possessing nuclear weapons poses a threat to US policy in a number of dimensions. The nightmare scenario is that North Korea would use the weapons—against either the United States, South Korea, or Japan—or transfer them to a terrorist group that would. North Korea with nuclear weapons could also become more recalcitrant in its demands and belligerent in its actions, figuring that its adversaries would not risk nuclear war to coerce it into compliance. By becoming the first state to withdraw from the NPT and develop nuclear weapons, North Korea poses a challenge to global nonproliferation norms that could ultimately result in the spread of nuclear weapons throughout the region.

The Bush administration has approached the DPRK nuclear problem less from a pragmatic stance of trying to figure out the most effective means to induce North Korea to get rid of its nuclear weapons, and more from an ideological standpoint that sees the Pyongyang regime as a fundamental evil that should be eradicated from the planet. This is reflected in President Bush's frequent use of personal insults when discussing DPRK leader Kim Jong-il—calling him a "pygmy" and "a spoiled child at the dinner table,"[23] and telling author Bob Woodward that he "loathed" the DPRK leader.[24] Bush's rhetoric was echoed by Undersecretary of State John Bolton during a trip to Seoul, when he referred to Kim as a tyrannical rogue state dictator whose people live in a "hellish nightmare."[25] The message conveyed by such harsh words is clear: the United States, as the sole superpower, should not have to stoop to the level of negotiating with tin-pot dictators such as Kim Jong-il. A negotiated solution that eliminated the DPRK nuclear weapons program but left the regime intact would still be seen by many Washington hawks as rewarding bad behavior, and would stand as a challenge to the goal of building a Pax Americana.

Despite the convening of six-party talks on US–North Korea relations, there is evidence that some hawks in Washington are simply waiting (and perhaps hoping) for what they consider the inevitable failure of dialogue so they can move ahead with their preferred policy of squeezing the life out of the DPRK regime. According to the July 21, 2003 edition of *US News and World Report,* Secretary of Defense Rumsfeld directed Pentagon military planners to develop a new strategy for North Korea, dubbed OP Plan 5030. This plan calls for deliberately increasing tensions on the Korean peninsula short of war, such as by flying surveillance aircraft close to DPRK airspace, or holding large, unannounced military exercises. The idea is that North Korea would be forced to mobilize its military forces in response, using up precious resources and possibly revealing war plans. The hope is that this would put increased stress on the DPRK military and perhaps even provoke a coup against Kim Jong-il.[26]

There is also evidence that members of the Bush administration want to implement an international blockade against North Korea to bring down its government. Knowing that any sanctions regime would require Chinese support to be effective, conservatives in Washington still hold out hope that the PRC can be brought around to a regime-change strategy. As the first round of six-party talks were starting in Beijing, the *Washington Times,* the leading voice of the right wing among US daily newspapers, ran an article claiming that Chinese scholars are increasingly taking to the idea that a collapse of the DPRK regime would be good for China.[27] Richard Perle, former head of the Defense Policy Board, told an ROK newspaper that unless China and other countries went along with an embargo of North Korea, military force would be the only option.[28]

The model for the Bush administration's policy is the collapse of the Soviet Union, which according to neoconservative dogma was a direct result of the military buildup launched by President Ronald Reagan. Putting aside the historical merits of that interpretation, its applicability to North Korea is questionable. For one thing, the DPRK regime bases its legitimacy not on providing its people with a high quality of life, but rather on its ability to safeguard the country against foreign invaders. A common theme in DPRK propaganda is to compare North Korea to a hungry wolf and South Korea to a well-fed dog. The dog might have a full belly and a warm place to sleep, but it is at the whim of the master (the United States) who provides these things, while the wolf remains free and proud. Furthermore, the position that North Korea occupies vis-à-vis the United States is in no way analogous to that of the Soviet Union during the cold war. The Soviet Union was trying to keep together a restive empire while remaining prepared for a possible global confrontation with another superpower. North Korea, on the other hand, is a tiny state fighting only for its own survival. Pyongyang does not need to match every American move; it needs only to maintain a credible deterrent to prevent a preemptive strike on the part of the United States.

While the ultimate effectiveness of Bush's DPRK policy in forcing regime change remains to be seen, there seems little doubt that the administration's actions thus far have increased Pyongyang's interest in nuclear weapons. Back in 1999, former US Defense Secretary William Perry, after completing his review of

US policy toward North Korea, said on the television program *News Hour with Jim Lehrer* that while the United States might not consider itself a threat to North Korea, "I fully believe that they consider us a threat to them."[29] Since coming to office, President Bush has seemingly gone out of his way to reinforce that sense of threat. After lumping North Korea together with Iran and Iraq in an "axis of evil" in his State of the Union Speech on January 23, 2002,[30] Bush went on to enunciate a doctrine of preemption in a graduation ceremony at West Point six months later.[31] Lest anyone fail to take these doctrines seriously, Bush then proceeded to attack Iraq the following year, using questionable intelligence on Baghdad's alleged weapons of mass destruction (WMD) programs as an excuse. The message to Pyongyang was clear: being suspected of developing WMD puts a country in line for a US invasion, but actually having nuclear weapons could make Washington think twice about attacking. It is no coincidence that after the Iraq invasion, North Korea stopped denying that it was developing nuclear weapons, and instead began to claim that its program was further along than previously thought.

The Bush administration's reactions to the DPRK's nuclear development has been to focus primarily on mitigation rather than prevention. Instead of moving aggressively to get North Korea to reinstitute its nuclear freeze and fulfill its obligations under the NPT, the Bush administration's policy goal is to prevent North Korea from transferring nuclear technology to terrorists or other "rogue" states. The focus of this program is the policy of interdiction—stopping DPRK ships suspected of carrying weapons or illegal drugs. To accomplish this, the United States has convened a group of eleven countries under the rubric of the Proliferation Security Initiative (PSI) to seize DPRK ships.[32] The policy was first tested in December 2002, when a Spanish naval vessel operating in the Persian Gulf stopped a DPRK ship laden with missiles bound for Yemen; the ship was soon released as the missile sales violated no international law or agreement that either the DPRK or Yemen had ever signed.[33] Later, Australia seized a DPRK ship loaded with heroin,[34] while Japan made a public display of searching the *Mangyongbong-92*, a DPRK ferry that makes regular visits to Japan to pick up pro-DPRK Korean-Japanese.[35]

The purpose of these interdictions is not only to prevent the possible transfer of WMD technology, but also to deprive the DPRK regime of the foreign currency earnings gained through illicit transactions. Proponents of this strategy justify it as a way to push regime change without increasing the suffering of ordinary North Koreans, arguing that the money from these activities only helps fund the DPRK military. (Official US concern for starving North Koreans has not resulted in the resumption of large-scale food aid shipments, however. The Bush administration has cut food aid to North Korea to about one-third of what it had been under Clinton.) Deputy Secretary of Defense Paul Wolfowitz has referred to the interdiction program as "a major point of leverage" against a country that is "teetering on the edge of economic collapse."[36] Thus the PSI program is an integral part of the US regime-change strategy toward Pyongyang.

Should the Bush administration's policy fail either to convince North Korea to disarm or to trigger its collapse, the United States has not ruled out resorting to military action, which could include the use of nuclear weapons. Indeed, even during the Clinton administration, North Korea continued to play a major role in US nuclear-war-fighting scenarios. For example, in an exercise during the first half of 1998, the 336 Fighter Squadron of the 4th Fighter Wing based in North Carolina used F-15E Strike Eagle fighter-bombers in a simulated nuclear strike against North Korea. The wing commander described the exercise thus:

> We simulated fighting a war in Korea, using a Korean scenario. This included [DPRK] chemical attacks to protect against using full chemical gear [sic]. The scenario ... simulated a decision by the National Command Authority about considering using nuclear weapons ... We identified aircraft, crews, and [weapon] loaders to load up tactical nuclear weapons onto our aircraft ... [The] last phase of the exercise, the employment phase ... required us to fly those airplanes down to a range in Florida and drop [BDU-38s dummy nuclear bombs].[37]

It is important to note that this scenario did *not* involve first use of nuclear weapons by North Korea. The United States has always claimed for itself the right to be first to use nuclear weapons in a conflict on the Korean peninsula, and continues to do so.

A war with North Korea remains an extremely risky proposition, despite US military superiority. If indeed North Korea already does have nuclear weapons, the United States has no way of telling where they are hidden. Since the scuttling of the Agreed Framework led to the expulsion of weapons inspectors, the exact size of the DPRK's nuclear capabilities is becoming increasingly opaque. The more time that passes without solving the nuclear crisis, or at least reinstituting the 1994 freeze, the more nuclear weapons that Pyongyang will be able to develop. Without knowing the exact number or location of DPRK nuclear weapons, it will be impossible for the United States to ensure that it wipes out DPRK retaliatory capability in a first strike, even should the envisioned US arsenal of ground-penetrating "mini-nukes" be in place. A 1998 US Air Force briefing pointed to the difficulty of finding DPRK mobile missile launchers before they have been fired as one of the chief constraints on US preemptive action in Korea.[38]

Given the problems with a regime-change strategy, a negotiated solution to denuclearize the Korean peninsula remains urgent. The six-party talks format is the last, best hope to achieve a peaceful solution. For a solution to be possible, North Korea must be provided with some sort of security guarantee that will give it a sufficient comfort level to forgo the nuclear option. Ultimately, this guarantee could then be expanded into a limited nuclear-weapons-free zone for Northeast Asia, under which the two Koreas and Japan would pledge never to develop or introduce nuclear weapons to their territory, while China and Russia would agree to keep their nuclear deployments outside the zone. While such an arrangement would serve US interests by lowering the specter of a nuclear war that would inevitably involve the United States, it is not compatible with the neoconservative agenda of promoting American dominance. Here, as elsewhere, the Bush administration must decide between truly effective multilateral arms-control pacts or an ideologically driven desire to preserve US freedom of action at all costs.

The second round of the six-party talks, held in late February 2004, showed some degree of progress. North Korea expressed its willingness to freeze and ultimately dismantle its entire nuclear program. The United States for its part offered some hope of improved relations in the long term, holding up the Libyan experience as a model. But lack of trust on both sides continues to hamper a deal. North Korea refuses to admit to possession of a uranium enrichment program, which the United States claims is an undeniable fact. For its part, Washington keeps repeating the mantra of a "complete, verifiable, and irreversible disarmament" (CVID). The problem with this formulation is that no arms-control agreement can possibly reach 100-percent verifiability. By setting the bar so high, the Bush administration is opening the door for regime-change hardliners to renege on the agreement in the future, much in the same way that they rejected determinations by weapons inspectors that Iraq did not have an active weapons program prior to the US invasion.

Containing China

Over the past fifty years, the image of the People's Republic of China in the United States has come full circle. At the beginning of the cold war, China was seen as a threat and a sponsor of Asian communism. After Nixon's visit in 1972, China became a reliable partner in the standoff against the Soviet Union. When the Soviet Union fell, China was transformed into a "strategic competitor" that might challenge American hegemony. These days there is little doubt that China is the primary focus of US strategic military planning outside the Middle East.

Although President Bill Clinton referred to China as a "strategic partner," in fact the concept of a rising China as a threat to the American interests actually originated during the Clinton administration. The US Strategic Command (STRATCOM), in preparing for the 1994 Nuclear Posture Review, conducted a study of possible nuclear-war-fighting scenarios called the Sun City Extended Study. China played a prominent role in these scenarios. In 1998, STRATCOM returned China to the role of a potential adversary in its Standard Integrated Operating Procedures (SIOP), from which status it had been removed in 1982 as part of the US tilt toward China in the Sino-Soviet dispute.[39] Despite these moves, Republicans criticized Clinton for not taking a tougher stance against China, some even going so far as to hint that Clinton was deliberately selling out American interests (such as nuclear secrets or even the Panama Canal) to China in exchange for illegal campaign contributions. The Bush administration came to power pledging to treat China not as a "strategic partner" but rather as a "strategic competitor." Most prominently, Bush moved to raise the level of US relations in Taiwan and to increase arms sales to the island.

The legacy of the United States opening to China in the 1970s remains strong, however, particularly in the economic sphere. While both Democrats (citing human-rights concerns) and Republicans (citing security fears) are quick while out of office to criticize the other party for being too soft on Beijing, both parties rely heavily on campaign contributions from corporations with large stakes in trade with China. This puts US policymakers in the position of wanting to pursue a policy of containing China while needing to avoid the appearance of doing so, lest increased tensions have negative economic consequences. North Korea's continued belligerence provides Washington with a ready-made excuse for its military deployments that avoids focusing on the much larger issue of China. This is particularly clear in discussions of missile defense (MD). Missile defense makes most sense as a means of defending the United States and its allies against China, a declared nuclear state with a small but relatively accurate arsenal of ICBMs. Yet the most oft-cited justification for MD is the still-theoretical threat that North Korea, a technologically backward economic basket case suffering from severe shortages of raw materials, might eventually be able to reach the continental United States with a nuclear-tipped missile. While it is certainly true that North Korea has been trying to extend the range of its missiles, given the state of the DPRK's technology and industry it is highly unlikely that it can build an accurate weapon or one that can carry a heavy payload across the length of the Pacific any time soon. This is to say nothing of the stark reality that launching a nuclear missile at the United States would invite massive retaliation that would constitute the end of the country as we know it. By focusing on North Korea, however, the Bush administration avoids a direct showdown with China that might negatively affect bilateral trade and thus further damage an already weak American economy. The same holds true for US forward deployments in the region, which are well beyond the level of what is required to prevent the impoverished Kim Jong-il regime from attempting an invasion of South Korea or Japan.

China figures prominently in the latest Nuclear Policy Review. China is identified as a country that could be involved in either an "immediate" (well-recognized current danger) or a "potential" (plausible, but not immediate) contingency. In contrast, Russia, which still maintains the only nuclear force sizable enough to rival the US arsenal, is not seen as a potential threat. With the end of the cold-war ideological conflict, "a contingency involving Russia, while plausible, is not expected." Since none of the potential nuclear "rogue" states—the DPRK, Iran, or Pakistan—is going to be able to develop a huge number of weapons in the short term, the US decision to maintain a nuclear arsenal of nearly 2,000 deployed nuclear weapons with thousands more in reserve must have been made with China in mind.

That the United States should focus on China as its main potential nuclear foe after the collapse of the Soviet Union is certainly not surprising. Given China's economic growth, huge population, and vast resources, it is only natural that China should generate some concern in US policy circles. What is disturbing, however, is the apparent lack of interest in Washington for developing arms-control regimes with China, along the lines of the successful SALT and START treaties with the Soviet Union. There is some indication that China would be amenable to such arrangements. Beijing has consistently stated that it will join in nuclear arms reduction talks once the US–Russian disarmament process has reduced their respective nuclear arsenals to a level similar to China's. Some reports suggest that China is on the verge of ratifying the CTBT, while the United States refuses even to send a delegate to the treaty conference.[40]

Instead of taking advantage of the opportunity at least to begin the process of arms control with China, the United States is focusing on countermeasures to Chinese nuclear modernization. Chief among these is the development of missile defense. In addition to National Missile Defense (NMD) to protect US territory, the Bush administration is moving aggressively to implement Theater Missile Defense (TMD) to protect its troops and allies in Asia. Japan has already begun joint research into TMD with the United States. US persistence appears to be breaking through South Korean reluctance to join the TMD program. There are even signs that the United States is pushing to include Taiwan under TMD, despite the obvious problems that would cause in relations with China.[41]

The net effect of all these moves by the United States is to encourage further nuclear developments by China. In the past, China kept its nuclear arsenal at a level sufficient to deter either the United States or the Soviet Union from considering a first strike. Now it needs enough nuclear weapons to be able to deter India, overcome US NMD, and at the same time retain enough of a threat to a TMD-protected Taiwan to discourage moves toward independence. Inevitably, China will seek to increase and modernize its nuclear force, but probably without facing the same kind of economic collapse that the Soviet Union suffered in the 1980s. Whereas the USSR was an overstretched empire with a stagnant command economy, China is a rapidly growing economy, capitalist in all but name, that threatens to overtake the United States in the coming decades. Unlike the United States, China also has no commitments abroad, apart from the problem of patrolling the restive but sparsely populated Tibet and Xinjiang. Given the slower economic growth and vast global commitments of the United States, Washington could well end up being the loser in an arms race with China over the long term.

A policy of containing China through a nuclear-arms buildup threatens to backfire on the United States, by encouraging an arms race without advancing US security. The alternative is to try to bring China into a system of bilateral and multilateral arms control treaties similar to the one that the United States and the Soviet Union used to minimize the danger of nuclear war. Aside from the prickly issue of the status of Taiwan, China has the makings of a status-quo power. It is deeply integrated into the global economy. It is a permanent member of the UN Security Council and has joined the World Trade Organization. China thus has some vested interests in preserving the current world order, albeit not in extending US dominance. Attempting to enforce American unipolarity will push China into a confrontational stance toward the United States, whereas bringing it more deeply into multilateral institutions and treaty arrangements would give it something to lose should the peace be disturbed. Unfortunately, the Bush administration seems determined to move along the former path.

Maintaining the US alliance structure

The American nuclear umbrella has long been viewed as playing a vital role in maintaining the US alliance structure in Northeast Asia. Not only are US nuclear forces seen as providing protection to American allies, it has also been argued that the US nuclear umbrella prevents Japan and South Korea from pursuing independent nuclear capabilities. According to the Nuclear Posture Review:

> US nuclear forces will continue to provide assurance to security partners, particularly in the presence of known or suspected threats of nuclear, biological, or chemical attacks or in the event of surprising military developments. This assurance can serve to reduce the incentives for friendly countries to acquire nuclear weapons of their own to deter such threats and circumstances.

Certainly both South Korea and Japan have the capability to develop robust nuclear weapons programs should they choose to do so. Both have large civilian nuclear-power capacities, to make up for a lack of indigenous oil and natural gas resources. Japan maintains a large stockpile of plutonium, a byproduct of its energy generation that could be easily converted to military use. South Korea pursued a nuclear weapons program in the 1970s, which the United States managed to squash through a combination of military favors to Seoul and pressure on France to halt technology transfers. It is certainly not out of the realm of possibility that a reduction of US security commitments in the region, especially if accompanied by a nuclearized North Korea, could lead either or both of these countries to seek their own *force de frappe*.

The nuclear umbrella has another side, however. The presence of American forces on foreign soil may actually invite attack as much as deter it. North Korea's pursuit of medium-range missile capability has been driven at least in part by the hope of being able to threaten US troops stationed in Japan, which would serve an important rearguard function in case war were to break out on the Korean peninsula. Similarly, neither Japan nor South Korea would have any need to fear that a Chinese attack on Taiwan would spill over into their territories, unless the United States intervened—in which case China might widen the war to include US forces in the region. Inasmuch as US nuclear policy is the spur for DPRK and PRC nuclear developments, alliance with the United States increases the threat that Japan or South Korea could be subject to a nuclear attack. This is particularly the case in regard to China, which unlike the United States has pledged not to be the first country to use nuclear weapons in a conflict.

The US response to fear of nuclear attacks on its allies has been, predictably enough, to push Theater Missile Defense. While Japan has enthusiastically embraced TMD research—at least since the DPRK's 1998 *Taepodong* missile test—South Korea has been much more reluctant. TMD will not protect Seoul against the main threat to it: a large-scale conventional artillery barrage from North Korea. It will, however, anger China, with which South Korea enjoys cordial relations and robust economic ties. Missile defense is also expensive, unproven, and not generally in line with the ROK's long-term defense planning. Increasingly, ROK military planners are chafing at being pushed to purchase weapons programs that reflect American priorities rather than Korean ones.[42] As South Korea moves toward greater political and military self-confidence, basing the alliance structure on US global nuclear strategy rather than on ROK defense needs could well cause a rupture in the relationship.

In the case of Japan, the United States has been encouraging Tokyo to move away from its war-renouncing constitution (ironically enough written under the auspices of an icon of the American right, General Douglas MacArthur) and increase its military power. Some prominent conservatives, such as Senator John McCain, have even gone so far as to suggest that the proper response to DPRK nuclear weapons development is to "remove our objections to Japan developing nuclear weapons."[43] This starkly demonstrates the double standard of US thinking about nuclear weapons: it is perfectly acceptable for US allies like Japan (or Israel) to develop nuclear weapons, but not for "rogue states" like North Korea (or Iran). The argument is that having more nuclear-powered allies will help support US goals and take some of the burden away from the United States to provide a nuclear umbrella.

Advocates of this position, however, misunderstand the Japanese political landscape. The majority of Japanese remain opposed to development of nuclear weapons, a legacy of the atomic bombings of Hiroshima and Nagasaki. The minority that supports a nuclear-weapons program does so for nationalistic reasons. Japanese nationalists, such as Tokyo Governor Ishihara Shintaro, see Japanese dependence on the US military as an extension of the humiliation Japan has suffered since the post-World War II occupation. They want Japan to develop its military capacity so it can throw off the shackles of the US military alliance.[44] A nuclearized Japan would almost assuredly mean that these nationalists had gained power in Japan, which could ultimately spell the end of the US alliance as Tokyo pursued an independent military strategy.

In the long run, it is by no means certain that the US nuclear umbrella can either prevent a nuclear attack on American allies or dissuade them from developing their own nuclear capacity. A more promising way of preventing nuclear war in Northeast Asia is through the establishment of a limited nuclear-weapons-free zone in the region. Under such a plan, the two Koreas and Japan would pledge never to develop, introduce, or use nuclear weapons. The three regional nuclear powers—China, Russia, and the United States—would agree not to deploy nuclear weapons in the region, or use nuclear weapons against any of the three non-nuclear states. Such a zone would replace the vagaries of bilateral nuclear umbrellas with a formal treaty that would bind both nuclear and non-nuclear states.[45] A country that used nuclear weapons against one of the non-nuclear states would be in violation of an international treaty, creating a stronger legal basis for retaliation by that state's nuclear ally. Most importantly, it would remove the incentives for nuclear proliferation in the region, thus fulfilling US nonproliferation goals.

Despite the obvious advantages of such an arrangement, the United States has resisted it for two reasons. One is that it would require Washington to make a no-first-use pledge, something it has consistently refused to do. The second is that a nuclear-weapons-free zone would be problematic for the long-standing US policy to neither confirm nor deny the presence of nuclear weapons on naval vessels (the

NCND policy). Under the NCND policy, the United States on several occasions brought nuclear weapons into Japanese ports in violation of Japan's "three non-nuclear principles."[46] New Zealand's declaration of a nuclear-weapons-free zone and its refusal to respect the NCND policy led to the rupture of ANZUS—the Australia–New Zealand–US alliance that had been a staple of the cold-war order in Oceania. American insistence on its right not only to possess large stocks of nuclear weapons, but to move them around the planet at will, complicates multilateral nonproliferation arrangements even among its own allies.

Nuclear developments in South Asia

While nuclear proliferation in North Asia is a growing threat, the nuclear weaponization of South Asia is already an established fact. Not only have India and Pakistan joined the nuclear club, but Pakistan has become the major source of nuclear technology for other would-be nuclear states. The danger for US policy in South Asia is that the Bush administration's goals in other areas, such as containing China and fighting the war on terrorism, complicate efforts to freeze or even reverse nuclear developments.

The Clinton administration's immediate response to the Indian and Pakistani nuclear tests was to impose sanctions on both parties. When these proved ineffective, however, support in Congress for a sanctions-based approach waned. When the Bush administration came to power, senior officials immediately began discussing the lifting of sanctions based on the nuclear tests, although there was some support for maintaining sanctions against Pakistan related to the overthrow of democracy. To some degree, these moves reflect a decided tilt toward India. Many conservatives hope that improved US–India ties will increase China's strategic encirclement. The United States has authorized Israeli sales of *Phalcon* Airborne Early Warning and Control Systems (AWACS) as well as US-made *Arrow* missiles. Indian Foreign Secretary Kanwal Sibal was quoted as saying that the United States had stopped asking India to join the NPT and was looking for ways to circumvent export restrictions on dual-use items.[47] The Bush administration also attempted, unsuccessfully, to induce India to provide troops to the war effort in Iraq.

While New Delhi has been happy to receive the military assistance that the United States has provided, there are reasons to doubt that India will ever fully embrace a strong military relationship with Washington. India's history of support for the nonaligned movement and the United Nations goes against the Bush administration's unilateralist tendencies. Among India's chattering class, it is easier to find support for a trilateral alliance with Russia and China to counter American hegemony than it is to find people ready to throw their lot in with Washington. While some American observers see a natural affinity between the democracies of India and the United States, cultural and religious differences remain strong. Bush's closeness to the Christian right rankles Hindu nationalists in the ruling Bharatiya Janata Party (BJP) who have been trying to stop Christian proselytizing in India. The importance of domestic politics in India, which tends to be both anti-imperialistic and nationalistic, also should not be underestimated.[48] So by reaching out to India, the Bush administration could well end up undermining nonproliferation norms without making any concrete gains for US strategic interests in the process.

The South Asian situation best illustrates the trickle-down effect of nuclear proliferation. The heavy US dependence on nuclear weapons, and particularly its development of missile defense, is spurring China to increase its nuclear forces. The nuclear threat from China—and the desire to be seen as a strategic equal in Asia—was the motivating factor in India's decision to go nuclear. Once India had played its hand, Pakistan, New Delhi's sworn enemy, could not sit out the nuclear game. As a result, nuclear weapons passed into the hands of an impoverished country with an unstable military regime where radical Islam enjoys widespread support.

In many ways, Pakistan is the ideal place for nuclear proliferation. Weak government control, lack of civilian oversight of the military, and strong support for an anti-status quo ideology make for a volatile mix. Thus the recent revelations that Dr. A. Q. Khan, the father of the Pakistani nuclear bomb, was running a nuclear supply operation that provided weapons technology to states such as North Korea, Libya, and Iran was hardly a shock. While the Bush administration has been touting the revelations as a victory for US intelligence—especially in light of the failure to find any evidence of WMD in Iraq—they also point to the delicate political game that must be played in the region. The United States cannot afford to undermine President Pervez Musharraf, who has already survived numerous assassination attempts that resulted from his support for the US war on terrorism. Thus a conscious decision was made to make Khan the scapegoat for Pakistani proliferation efforts, and to ignore the apparent involvement of the Pakistani military.

Shutting down A. Q. Khan Laboratories will not end the threat of proliferation from Pakistan. Musharraf's position remains tenuous, and the threat of his assassination at the hands of Islamic militants has not dissipated. The Pakistani military contains large segments sympathetic to the cause of radical Islam, especially among the mid-level officers who were trained during the period when the United States was withholding military support. So the Pakistani military cannot be counted on as a bulwark of secularism as in Turkey or Algeria. Furthermore, Pakistan will not be able to sustain its nuclear deterrent without importing fissile material and technology.[49] This leaves the Bush administration with two unpalatable choices: either acknowledge Pakistan as a nuclear state and allow it legally to import what it needs, or watch Pakistan reestablish its nuclear smuggling network to maintain its own weapons capability. Any way you slice it, a nuclear-armed Pakistan is a threat to both global nonproliferation goals and overall US interests.

The future of nonproliferation

This is a crucial time for global nuclear nonproliferation. With the emergence of two more declared nuclear powers, and suspicions of clandestine programs in two others, the Non-Proliferation Treaty, which had successfully prevented nuclear proliferation for over twenty-five years, appears to be fraying at the seams. A statement by the US Senate Republican Policy Committee suggested that it may be necessary to replace the NPT with a new nonproliferation mechanism altogether:

> The actions by North Korea ... and Iran ... as well as actions by Pakistan and India ... demonstrate that the NPT's enforcement mechanism to discipline violators, and its incentives to encourage other states to join, are not working properly. There is no means to enforce the NPT or discipline violators short of preemptive action and military strikes. If a more flexible range of enforcement mechanisms cannot be put in the treaty and the international community cannot summon the will to enforce its terms, the NPT should be scrapped and a new nonproliferation regime created.[50]

This statement underplays the effectiveness of the NPT thus far. The NPT is actually in many ways the most successful arms-control agreement in history. Only three of the five powers that possessed nuclear weapons at the time of the NPT's signing (the United States, the USSR, and Great Britain) were original signatories, but China and France were both induced to join the agreement in 1992. Several other states that began nuclear-weapons programs—such as Brazil, Argentina, and South Korea—and one state that already had nuclear weapons—South Africa—eventually joined the NPT and reversed their developments. This is certainly a far cry from the nightmare of a world awash in nuclear weapons that the satirist Tom Lehrer captured in his 1965 song "Who's Next," which mused about the future acquisition of nuclear weapons by such countries as Luxemburg and Monaco.

It is also worth noting that without the NPT, there would be no legal or institutional basis to challenge the nuclear programs of North Korea or Iran. That being said, there is a need to improve the enforcement mechanisms of the treaty. This should be done by giving more teeth to international arms inspection agencies, such as the International Atomic Energy Agency (IAEA). Currently, the IAEA's only power when dealing with uncooperative would-be proliferators is to report the situation to the UN Security Council. The structure of the UNSC makes it questionable whether this is the best body to deal with violations of the NPT. The veto power of the five permanent UNSC members (the P-5) means that no response is possible without consensus among the great powers, so that more often than not the response to alleged violations is based not on the merits of the case, but on the geopolitical interests of the great powers. Secondly, the P-5 are all enshrined as nuclear-weapon states under the NPT. This reinforces the double standard implicit in the agreement, and turns enforcement of the treaty into a matter of nuclear haves punishing the have-nots for impertinence and insubordination. Unless and until the UNSC is reformed to include non-nuclear states among the permanent members, a separate enforcement body should be created that would be able to make more neutral appraisals of violations and of any punitive actions.

On February 11, 2004, President Bush announced new measures to curb the proliferation of nuclear weapons. The initiative focused on strengthening export controls of dual-use materials and limiting the production of fissile material to the forty nations of the Nuclear Suppliers Group.[51] While these measures may help to make it more difficult for future proliferators to follow the Pakistan model, they are limited by their exclusive focus on preventing states from acquiring the *means* to produce nuclear weapons, while ignoring the *motivation* behind proliferation. As examples from the war on drugs to the war on terrorism show, such an enforcement-based approach can never be wholly effective.

At the heart of the problem of the NPT is that it reinforces the notion that it is all right for certain states to acquire nuclear weapons and unacceptable for others. This argument goes against the very essence of a sovereign right to self-defense enshrined in international law. Either nuclear weapons are perfectly allowable to any country that chooses to include them in its military arsenal, or they are illegal and immoral weapons of terror that should be banned. The international community has already outlawed other forms of weapons that are far less destructive, if equally indiscriminate, such as chemical weapons and land mines. It is time that nuclear weapons are treated the same way under international law. If the NPT is to be salvaged and nuclear proliferation to be averted, the P-5 must reinvigorate the process of leading to complete nuclear disarmament, as they are required to do by Article VI.

The United States does in fact have much to fear from the acquisition of nuclear weapons by countries like Iraq and North Korea. This is especially so as the mobility of US conventional forces makes them largely invulnerable to nuclear attack, forcing nuclear opponents to concentrate on targeting the civilian population centers within the United States instead. But the current policies of the Bush administration are doing more to encourage nuclear proliferation than to prevent it. By refusing to engage in serious efforts at disarmament and moving to develop new classes of nuclear weapons, while at the same time seeking perfect security through the development of missile defenses, the United States is claiming for itself a right to freedom of action that it allows no other country in the world. Such obvious hypocrisy is bound to convince countries opposed to the status quo to seek nuclear weapons as a means of deterring US actions and promoting their own goals. Building more, newer, smaller, or more sophisticated nuclear weapons is not going to prevent nuclear proliferation: it will only encourage it.

Notes

1. The text of the NPT can be found at www.fas.org/nuke/control/npt/text/npt2.htm.
2. It is widely acknowledged that Israel began producing nuclear weapons in the late 1960s, and today probably has between 100 and 200 nuclear weapons. But it has never admitted to their possession nor conducted a nuclear test.
3. "Report of the Commission to Assess the Ballistic Missile Threat to the United States," available at www.fas.org/irp/threat/bm-threat.htm.
4. Patrick Tyler, "Pentagon Drops Goal of Blocking New Superpowers," *New York Times*, May 23, 1992.
5. *Rebuilding America's Defenses: Strategy, Forces, and Resources for a New Century*. Available online at www.newamericancentury.org/RebuildingAmericasDefenses.pdf. The report clearly states in the introduction that it was building on the original draft of the Defense Policy Guidance (p. ii).

6. Ibid., pp. 2–3.
7. Ibid., p. 19.
8. Ibid., p. iv.
9. Ibid., p. 8.
10. Ibid., p. v.
11. Ibid., p. 6.
12. Manuel Perez, "US Quits ABM Treaty," CNN.com, at www.cnn.com/2001/ALLPOLITICS/12/13/rec.bush.abm/?related.
13. Excerpts of the publicly released version of the Nuclear Posture Review are available at www.globalsecurity.org/wmd/library/policy/dod/npr.htm.
14. Richard L. Garwin, "A Defense that Will Not Defend," *Washington Quarterly*, Summer 2000.
15. Hans M. Kristensen, Matthew G. McKinzie, and Robert S. Norris, "The Protection Paradox," *Bulletin of the Atomic Scientists*, Vol. 60, No. 2 (March–April, 2004), pp. 68–77, online at www.thebulletin.org/issues/2004/ma04/ma04kristensen.html.
16. For a critique of the "nuclear hedge," see Hans Kristensen, "Bomb Deal a Dud, Part One," *Bulletin of the Atomic Scientists*, Vol. 58 (January–February, 2002), pp. 25–6, online at www.thebulletin.org/issues/2002/jf02/jf02kristensen.html.
17. "Democrats Troubled by White House Effort to Develop Tactical Nuclear Weapons," *Agence-France Presse*, May 22, 2003, summarized at www.nautilus.org/napsnet/dr/0305/MAY23-03.html#item3.
18. "House Panel Cuts Bush Nuclear Weapons Requests," Reuters, July 8, 2003, summarized at www.nautilus.org/napsnet/dr/0307/JUL09-03.html#item4.
19. "Congress Approves Bush Nuclear Weapons Funds," Reuters, November 18, 2003.
20. Will Dunham, "Pentagon Nuclear Arms Session Worries Critics," Reuters, August 4, 2003.
21. Stephen I. Schwartz, "Build 'em, Test 'em, Use 'em—The Bush Administration Really Loves the Bomb," *Bulletin of the Atomic Scientists*, Vol. 58 (May–June, 2002), pp. 18–19.
22. Robert Nelson, "Low-Yield Earth Penetrating Nuclear Weapons," *Federation of American Scientists Public Interest Report*, Vol. 54, No. 1 (January–February, 2001), available at www.fas.org/faspir/2001/v54n1/weapons.htm.
23. Howard Fineman, "'I Sniff Some Politics,'" *Newsweek*, May 27, 2002.
24. Roland Watson, "Kim is Keeping Kim Jong-il in His Sights," *Times Online*, December 12, 2002.
25. "N. Korea 'Hellish Nightmare': US," CNN.com, July 31, 2003, www.timesonline.co.uk/article/0,,4801-511351,00.html.
26. "Upping the Ante for North Korea," *US News and World Report*, July 21, 2003, p. 7.
27. Joo Yong-Jung, "Optimism in Beijing about Regime Change," *Chosun Ilbo* (Seoul), August 27, 2003, summarized at www.nautilus.org/napsnet/dr/index.html#item12.
28. "Perle Calls for Blockade of N. Korea," *Donga Ilbo* (Seoul), January 13, 2004, online at www.newsmax.com/archives/articles/2003/10/19/232728.shtml.
29. *News Hour with Jim Lehrer*, September 17, 1999, available at www.pbs.org/newshour/bb/asia/july-dec99/perry_9-17.html.
30. "President Delivers State of the Union Address," January 23, 2002, at www.whitehouse.gov/news/releases/2002/01/20020129-11.html.
31. "Remarks by the President at 2002 Graduation Exercise of the United States Military Academy, West Point, New York," June 1, 2002, at www.whitehouse.gov/news/releases/2002/06/20020601-3.html.
32. See www.dfat.gov.au/globalissues/psi.
33. NAPSNet Daily Report, December 16, 2003, online at www.nautilus.org/napsnet/dr/0212/DEC16.html#item1.
34. Jay Solomon and Jason Dean, "Heroin Bust Points to Source of Funds for North Korea," *Wall St. Journal*, April 23, 2003.
35. *NAPSNet Daily Report*, August 25, 2003, online at www.nautilus.org/napsnet/dr/0308/AUG25-03.html#item4.
36. Sang-Hun Choe, "North Korea Sees Sanctions Amid Tough Times," *Associated Press*, June 11, 2003, summarized at www.nautilus.org/napsnet/dr/0306/jun12%2D03.html.

37 "History of the 4th Fighter Wing, January-June 1998," pp. 19–20. Declassified and available online at www.nautilus.org/nukestrat/USA/nsnf/4fw.html.
38 Hans Kristensen, "Preemptive Posturing," *Bulletin of the Atomic Scientists*, Vol. 58, No. 5 (September–October, 2002), pp. 54–9, available at www.thebulletin.org/issues/2002/so02/so02kristensen.html.
39 Hans Kristensen, "The Matrix of Deterrence: US Strategic Command Force Structure Studies," Nautilus Institute, May 2001, available at www.nautilus.org/nukestrat/matrix.pdf.
40 "Signs that China Could Ratify Test Ban, but US, North Korea Snub Treaty," *Agence France-Presse*, September 1, 2003, summarized at www.nautilus.org/napsnet/dr/index.html#item3.
41 "US Pushing for Missile Defense in Taiwan," *Arms Control Today*, June, 2003, online at www.armscontrol.org/act/2003_06/briefs_june03.asp#taiwan.
42 Hamm Taik-young, "Self-Reliance or Arms Buildup? The 2004 Defense Budget Request of the ROK," *IFES Forum*, online at www.armscontrol.org/act/2003_06/briefs_june03.asp#taiwan.
43 Quoted at www.evote.com/weekend_section/01052003/FTNReview.asp.
44 *Northeast Asia Peace and Security Network Daily Report*, April 2, 2003, online at www.nautilus.org/napsnet/dr/0304/apr24.html#item11.
45 For versions of this proposal, see John E. Endicott, "A Limited Nuclear-Weapons-Free Zone in Northeast Asia," *Disarmament Diplomacy*, No. 35, at http://disarm.igc.org/Plnwfznea.html; Lee Samsung, "A Nuclear Weapons Free Zone in Northeast Asia: The Political and Security Context," online at www.peacekorea.org/eng/koreaneyes/samsung01.html.
46 Hans Kristensen, "Japan Under the US Nuclear Umbrella," online at www.nautilus.org/library/security/papers/Nuclear-Umbrella-1.html.
47 "US No Longer Asking India to Sign NPT," *Dawn*, July 4, 2003, online at www.dawn.com/2003/07/04/top18.htm.
48 I am grateful to Zulfiqar Ahmad for the above points.
49 Edward Luce and Farhan Bokhari, "The Dynamics of Being a Nuclear State," *Financial Times*, February 16, 2004.
50 United States Senate Republican Policy Committee, "Iran and North Korea: US Policy toward the 'Axis of Evil,'" available at http://rpc.senate.gov/releases/2003/FOREIGN082503.pdf.
51 Office of the White House Press Secretary, "President Announces New Measures to Counter the Threat of WMD," February 11, 2004, http://www.whitehouse.gov/news/releases/2004/02/20040211-4.html.

4 Talking American, acting Taiwanese

Behind Taipei's complete compliance with the Bush Doctrine

Chih-yu Shih

The Bush Doctrine is about unilateral, preemptive US action to be taken against a potential enemy. For pro-independence forces in Taiwan, China represents this potential enemy. To support the Bush Doctrine means to deter China from using military means to stop Taiwan independence. However, the Bush Doctrine's unilateralism and Taipei's total reliance on the United States taken together destroy the credit that a mediator would need. Taipei has always had its own reasons, from, in the beginning, defiant Chiang Kai-shek's reunification game in Quemoy, through Chiang Ching-kuo's two-handed policy to curb pro-independence pressure, to Lee's use of Washington to promote the cause of independence, and finally to Chen's total reliance on the United States in order to preserve Washington's sympathy in Taiwan's pursuit of independence. Taipei has always tried to sneak its own reasons into its unqualified support for Washington, and Washington has been caught either by surprise or by ignorance each time. The support the Bush Doctrine enjoys in Taipei is no exception.

Taiwan matters, unwittingly

The "Bush Doctrine," now widely circulated, discussed, and practiced, may mean different things to those of different ideology, gender, citizenship, class, ethnicity, occupation, and religion—all of whom may respond in their own particular way. Some of these responses will incur different readings from the Bush administration, and because these interactions cannot be determined in advance, the Bush administration may lose its monopoly over the interpretation of its own strategic design. For example, the Bush Doctrine as implemented in Iraq may suggest to some people in the Middle East the likelihood of an enhanced confrontation between Israelis and Palestinians. Those who would want to see stronger US pressure on Israel may have worried that this would destroy the atmosphere of compromise required for a settlement.[1] On the other hand, they may have wanted to seize the opportunity after the US invasion in Iraq to push the administration to demonstrate its good will toward the Islamic world by making concessions on the Palestinian question. Neither view is directly related to the origin of the Bush Doctrine, which is embedded in the 9/11 tragedy.[2] Both views, however, would distract the Bush Doctrine from its next target: Teheran, Pyongyang, or Damascus.

One of the most noted aspects of the Bush Doctrine is the claimed right of the United States to take unilateral action for the purpose of preempting a potential attack. Ironically, if American unilateralism is interpreted elsewhere out of a motivation unrelated to Bush's war against Saddam Hussein, unilateralism will no longer be just unilateral. How unpredictable the future of the Bush Doctrine actually is depends on how hidden the agendas elsewhere are. In the case of Taiwan, the unreserved support given to the Bush administration by the authorities in Taipei may have more substantial repercussions than can be anticipated today. A Taiwan that the Bush administration can take for granted today is not the same Taiwan that existed in the eyes of earlier American strategic thinkers such as Henry Kissinger, Alexander Haig, and Zbigniew Brzezinski. The earlier authorities in Taipei displayed too strong an agency to be useful to Washington's China policy, embedded first in containment and then in rapprochement. However, the new, useful Taipei that emerged in the 1990s might drag an eager Washington unwillingly into a premature showdown with the People's Republic of China (PRC). Taipei has never been just a passive ally waiting for instructions.

From Washington's point of view, a small player such as Taipei is unimportant, if not totally nonexistent, in considerations of world politics as well as in the determination of US global strategy. Taipei authorities must agree on this, as it is supported by all available information.[3] What is missing in this great-power perspective is an understanding that how the Bush Doctrine is read or misread in Taipei can affect future US strategic thinking on China. Underneath an apparent complete compliance with the US global strategy remains Taipei's little war against China. Along with the evolving politics of identity in Taiwan, the nature of this little war has changed greatly in the past, followed by Washington's reevaluation of Taiwan's strategic value to the United States. Equally important is Taipei's own agenda, which may sometimes catch Washington by surprise. In other words, the full-fledged support from Taipei that Washington enjoys does not mean control over the evolution of the situation in Taiwan. Through some incidental connections, Taiwan's identity politics may lead to a change in US strategy toward China, the result of which cannot be fully anticipated by Washington.

Washington has made the mistake of overlooking Taipei's dual identities, an internal conflict that has almost completely engrossed Taipei's policy thinking. With both Chinese and Japanese postcolonial identities surfacing in Taiwanese politics since the early 1990s, to affirm Taiwan's national identity requires that one be either anti-Chinese or pro-Chinese. In this context, Taipei's attitude toward China as well as its America policy are in essence identity statements. To assert its independence, Taipei views its pro-US gestures as an anti-China demonstration. As a result, Taipei rarely attends to Washington's strategic need to cooperate with Beijing. Ironically, this lack of sensitivity toward Washington's real interests comes with Taipei's claim of total support for the Bush Doctrine. On the other hand, in order to avoid a psychological split, a Taiwanese needs to be alternately Chinese and anti-Chinese in accordance with the situation. The fact that Taiwanese citizens are moving freely between Taiwan and China, in large numbers and without a fixed political loyalty, renders the government's support for the Bush Doctrine almost an irrelevant commitment. The government's national identity strategy together with the people's self-therapeutic response has given the Bush Doctrine meanings that are incomprehensible for Washington.

In this chapter, I will discuss how Taipei's quest for independent statehood has successfully enticed Washington into an assessment about the advantage of supporting the pro-independence authorities in Taipei and how this experience subsequently inspires their responses to the Bush Doctrine. Meanwhile, I will explain why taking Taipei's cooperation at face value may backfire due to other hidden agendas that Taipei authorities refrain from mentioning when dealing with Washington. Lastly, I will suggest a reason why Taipei's total compliance with the Bush Doctrine may create an unwanted burden for Washington. I will specifically dispute the view that Taipei is vulnerable to the US–China relationship, not by arguing that Taipei is sufficiently autonomous, but by uncovering the "weapon of the weak" that is unrecognized by all sides, including Taipei. In the meantime, I will also question the wisdom of Taipei's strategy of total dependence, which I believe will reduce Taipei's agency in reinterpreting the Bush Doctrine. Ironically, Taiwan's agency in coping with high politics may undermine the *realpolitik* assumption shared among Washington, Beijing, and Taipei—that only power and interests matter.

One realism, several interpretations

In Taiwan, the realist approach dominates the official as well as academic literature on Taiwan's America policy. "Triangular relations" game theory particularly attracts writers within the policy circle. There is a good reason for this. Since Taiwan is unable to compete with Beijing globally for diplomatic recognition, the Taiwanese like the triangular perspective which, on the face of it, gives Taiwan nominally equal status.[4] In reality, many recognize that Taiwan is an unequal or asymmetric partner in the triangular formula.[5] Taiwan's policy behavior is a product of the actual triangular relationship, responding to the existing power structure, in which the other two players dominate.[6] There is in fact very little room left for Taipei to maneuver after Beijing and Washington leaders decide their strategy. Taipei is in no position to influence Washington's assessment of Taipei's strategic value at any given moment. Even the literature promoting Taiwan independence and Taiwanese nationalism assigns the agency to Washington, leaving Taiwan with a secondary role, able to decide only the timing and pace in its quest for independence.[7] In other words, the best that Taipei can do is to sneak toward independence as a spinoff, after executing the role that Washington has assigned to it.

If one looks from within Taipei, the story is much more complicated. One critical view sees Washington as a realist actor treating Taipei as no more than a pawn on the chessboard, ready to be sacrificed when necessary. The only question is whether this happens sooner or later. On the other hand, according to the same view, if Taipei should choose to deal with Beijing, it would fare much better, because Beijing would consider Taiwan as part of China and there would be no thought of sacrificing Taiwan. The policy implication of this line of thinking is that Taipei should resolutely oppose the Taiwan independence movement. Only then would Washington stop treating Taiwan as a check on China, leaving Taiwan in peace.[8]

The other side has a completely different assessment, seeing Washington as a realist actor that definitely wants to contain the rise of China. These analysts consider it impossible that Washington would sacrifice Taipei or even allow Taiwan to become part of China;[9] thus Taipei should be a loyal follower of Washington. Obviously, the supporters of the two approaches differ fundamentally in their national identification: the former conceives of Taiwan as a Chinese state, while the latter sees Taiwan as a sovereign state independent of China. Interestingly, both claim to be realists. Decisions about national identity affect how realism is interpreted and practiced. More specifically, whether or not Taiwan is Washington's pawn is a matter of choice for Taipei. If power distribution in the triangle were equal, the change in the Taipei leaders' conceptualization of Taiwan's identity alone could lead to a strategic reappraisal on all sides.

Even during the cold war Taiwan had a choice, though this was not clear until later on in the 1990s when the Taipei authorities decided to transform Taiwan's identity. The cold war in East Asia could have taken a different path if the Taiwanese independence movement had risen forty years earlier. That there was no such movement was probably because Chiang Kai-shek's unification-oriented Kuomintang suppressed it, not because there was no political foundation for it. The political foundations for many post-cold-war developments, including the Taiwan independence movement, existed almost everywhere during the cold war. For example, the Iraqi military threat, to which the Bush Doctrine was supposedly applied, was partly produced by previous US military support for Saddam Hussein during the 1980s. Another example is the fact that the peace movement in 2003 during the war on Iraq recruited supporters largely from the cold-war generation.

In addition, the cold war's international system, let alone the post-cold-war system, was never as monochrome as realists would have us believe.[10] The Middle East often did not fit. Even in Taiwan there could be rebellion, as in the 1958 Quemoy crisis, during which Chiang Kai-shek, against advice from Washington, stationed heavy concentrations of troops in offshore Quemoy to demonstrate his determination to reunite China. When Mao Zedong ordered shelling to cut off Quemoy supplies, Washington came to the rescue, prompting the authors of strategy textbooks to wonder how Chiang had managed to drag an unwilling Washington into such a confrontation.[11]

In 1958, Mao could not prevail over the military superiority of the US superpower. He decided instead to continue the Chinese civil war by symbolically shelling the island of Quemoy. This action of Mao's was exactly what Chiang wanted, as it discouraged the United States from using pressure to persuade him to abandon his dreams of reunification. Thus the legacy of the civil war meant that Washington had to take sides, instead of sitting on the fence. Although it was essential to Chiang's legitimacy in Taiwan, the civil war mentality jeopardized the

Kuomintang (KMT) when Washington was later forced to jettison its commitment to Taiwan's security, switching sides in order to bring about its rapprochement with Beijing. The result was the famous Shanghai Communiqué, whereby Washington complied with the civil war discourse that there is only one China. Accordingly, Washington had to choose sides, jettisoning its former KMT partner. The United States failed the realist test for a superpower: it could not effectively discipline Chiang's desire for reunification, and it found new room to maneuver only after Taipei, on its own initiative, decided to go for independent statehood. Previously, Washington would have had to act against both Taipei and Beijing if it wanted to use an independent Taiwan for its own strategic purposes. By contrast, Washington can intervene with legitimacy today merely by acting as a passive defender on behalf of pro-independence Taiwan. This legitimacy to intervene gives Washington a new leverage in its China policy. Taipei's pro-independence stance entices Washington to use Taiwan as a pawn.

The superpower faces an increasing constraint, since the two societies on opposite sides of the Taiwan Strait remain connected, although indirectly, as they were even during the cold war. This indirect connection was not reported at that time because people in Taiwan who made contact with the mainland risked imprisonment by Chiang's anti-communist regime. Family reunion was such a strong motivation, however, that it reemerged in the 1980s to have a marked influence on the continuing political confrontation between Beijing and Taipei. As Washington increased its pressure on President Chiang Ching-kuo (Chiang Kai-shek's son) to democratize, he formally opened up channels for family reunion to balance the expected surge of pro-independence forces tapped by the process of democratization.[12] Old soldiers among the anti-communist troops were ironically the major beneficiaries of the family reunion policy. Business investment, tourism, and, more recently, the establishment of new families, as well as the migration of college students, followed the wave of family reunions.

If neither the cold-war experience nor civil-war education could prevent new generations from reconnecting, there could hardly be any meaningful superpower influence on these contacts, as they operated beneath the surface of a military deadlock. In other words, some key elements that have shaped superpower realism since the 1950s include at a minimum: Chiang Kai-shek's dedication to reunification, Chiang Ching-kuo's family reunion policy, Taipei's quest for independent statehood, and now Taipei's complete compliance with the Bush Doctrine. All have been motivated by concerns that fall outside the US worldview, but each has affected Washington's evaluation of the situation and its strategic thinking.

From rapprochement to "congagement"

Questionable realism

If not for the Korean War, the United States would not have given its unreserved support to the Chiang Kai-shek regime, and the 7th Fleet might never have been ordered to patrol the Taiwan Strait.[13] Taiwan then was not valuable to the United

States, because it was not even clear that the Chiang Kai-shek regime could survive defeat by the Chinese Communist Party. Later, Taiwan dragged Washington into its reunification game (in 1958), and once Taipei had locked itself into opposition to China, Washington's China policy automatically determined its Taiwan policy. However, after Kissinger introduced the idea of a five-power balance of world politics at the start of the Nixon administration, rapprochement between Washington and Beijing made increasing sense, rendering Taipei insignificant. Indeed from Richard Nixon to Ronald Reagan, realist advisers such as Kissinger, Brzezinski, and Haig saw Taiwan as a burden, ignoring it strategically out of the necessity to facilitate the US–China coalition against the Kremlin. From Taipei's point of view, Jimmy Carter's final decision to de-recognize Taipei in 1979 was treacherous, and Reagan's agreement to reduce arms sales to Taiwan in 1982 was unfaithful. Taipei's spokesman tried in vain to appeal to the old cold-war partnership,[14] which may have inadvertently recalled Dwight Eisenhower's nightmare over the Quemoy crisis. The problem was that the lingering legacy of the civil war for Taipei blocked Washington from treating Taipei as an important player.

Realism appears less rational than expected when one notes Kissinger's failure to consider Taiwan as a check on China. Remember 1954? That was the year that President Eisenhower used Taipei to check Beijing from moving into Vietnam.[15] Taiwan should have been an equally useful strategic check on China, especially during the process of rapprochement. However, Kissinger was convinced that nothing serious would immediately happen to Taiwan. This may or may not have been true, but his insensitivity toward the possibility of using Taiwan as a bargaining chip is an indicator of realism constrained. This insensitivity is particularly conspicuous in light of his obsession with the politics of the balance of power. He preferred to ignore the Taiwan issue rather than cash in on it. After all, Taiwan, as part of China, was of diminished usefulness. Without Taipei's own initiative toward independence, Washington would have no clue as to Taiwan's strategic value under rapprochement. In the end, the Taiwan issue became a moral issue instead of a strategic one, and a realist usually omits the moral issue and does not engage it. In fact, Washington reiterated the civil-war cliché in its acknowledgment of "One China" in its 1979 communiqué on relations with Beijing. As a result, an awareness of Taipei's strategic value did not reemerge until 1995.[16]

In 1995, Lee Tenghui, Taiwan's first popularly elected and native president, successfully planned a homecoming trip to Cornell University, his alma mater. The major rationale for the visit was to break out of Beijing's diplomatic blockade so as to assert Taiwan's independent statehood. Beijing retaliated in the form of missile exercises across the Taiwan Straits.[17] As in 1958, Washington was dragged into the incident to face a potential showdown with Beijing. However, the implications were dramatically different from those in 1958. In the earlier case, the confrontation resulted from the unfinished Chinese civil war, while in 1995–6 the cause was Taiwan's quest for independence. In the latter case, US intervention appeared to be quite legitimately in the pursuit of peace, unlike in the earlier case, in which the issue was to support one party to the civil war in opposition to the other. The US approval of Lee's visit was announced just before a scheduled meeting between Taipei and Beijing, one that carried the expectation of some sort of breakthrough in cross-Strait social and economic exchanges. Some Chinese observers read this as a deliberate move by the United States to manipulate cross-Strait relations for the sake of strategic balance.[18] In other words, Lee's pro-independence policy improved Taiwan's role as a player.[19] From then on, Washington could use its approved level of arms sales to Taiwan and the length of transit stays in US territory that it allowed for Taiwan's presidents as a check on Beijing.

A new "One China"

Since 1996, US officials have made it increasingly clear that the One China policy no longer means support for a united China. Instead, it means that the United States insists that the question of Taiwan's future should be resolved peacefully, and that Taiwan should not unilaterally declare independence.[20] Again and again Washington has conveyed to Beijing that a peaceful resolution is the guiding principle. This principle is the reason why I stated earlier that pro-independence realists believe that Washington is unlikely to give up Taiwan. Taiwan's de facto independence is secure now, from the pro-independence point of view, despite the fact that some pro-independence fundamentalists, former President Lee included, want to establish de jure independence. Lee's offensive realism in 1999, describing the relationship between Taiwan and China as a state-to-state relationship, incurred another strong reaction from China. Washington considered his initiative to be no more than troublemaking. However, pro-independence fundamentalists in Taiwan believe that what Washington did not like was the timing and style of Lee's offensive, not his pursuit of it.[21] Their observations seem accurate judging from the fact that a US delegate in Taiwan openly praised the electoral victory of President Chen Shui-bian in 2000—a person who is widely known for his assertive pro-independence stance.[22]

Unfortunately, President Chen faced a serious political challenge upon taking office. For reasons too complicated to elaborate here, his inauguration witnessed a resurgence of "China Fever" in Taiwan. In 2001, the US State Department sent an analyst to Taiwan to study the nature of this China Fever and concluded that it was a serious phenomenon.[23] In June 2001, President Chen was allowed a transit stay in the United States for a record-breaking three nights on his way both to and from a decoy Central American trip. He was able to meet many politicians during both stays and kept his exposure in the United States technically private. The US support for Chen's leadership was very obvious but not very effective. In 2002, Chen announced a one-side-one-country (OSOC) understanding of the Taiwan–PRC relationship, which was quite similar to Lee's, without any prior notice to Washington. Later on, his aides paid visits to high officials in Washington to explain the statement. This self-belittling gesture actually brought Taipei and Washington closer together than before, because in the past both sides' high officials did not get to meet lest this should give Beijing the impression that Washington had encouraged official contacts with China's renegade province. Although the OSOC statement appeared to be a mistaken move by Chen, there was no talk about troublemaking from the US side. Interestingly, Beijing was satisfied with Washington's disciplining of Taipei and Washington's explanation on behalf of Taipei, apparently failing to notice that Washington, now positioned in between Beijing and Taipei, had adopted a role that blocked reunification.[24]

The US administration, caught between a strategy of both engaging and containing China, implemented a mixed strategy, "congagement." Within this strategic context, Taiwan's pursuit of independent statehood could be used to control the degree of pressure that the United States placed on China. Another divisive issue that could similarly be used was human rights. Lip service on the Taiwan issue was more than enough in trading with China on matters that the US administration perceived to be important, because reiteration of the One-China policy gave the Chinese a feeling of being respected. This feeling compensated for the sense of loss as Beijing cooperated or even conceded on other matters. However, affirming the One-China policy was valuable only if Washington held out the potential threat of deciding not to honor it. Indeed, Washington played around with the wording every time the One-China policy was restated, in order to give the impression that it was Washington's own One-China policy that the United States was committed to, and not the version provided by China. This rhetorical manipulation was possible because of Taipei's drive for independent statehood. Taipei's status as a player was established under the conditions of the congagement policy of the United States and Taipei's pro-independence policy.

From congagement to unilateralism

On America's side

Taipei's self-confidence is increasing over time, even though its two opportunistic declarations of statehood received severe scolding from Washington. It is interesting that Taipei finds these experiences rewarding. This is because Beijing is unable to participate in these behind-closed-doors disciplinary sessions but instead has to listen to the United States' warnings against brinksmanship. In short, being punished can be strategically rewarding. Taiwan's sense of family is so pronounced that Chen Shui-bian once pointed to Clinton's Air Force One aircraft, coincidentally stationed two slots away from his own, to demonstrate how close the two countries are. Chen's administration gives any number of public signals to show how much Taipei depends on the United States for peace and democracy. This terminology is welcomed in Washington, not only because it suits Washington's self-image as the leading democratic country, but also because it serves as a reminder to China that the time is not yet ripe for reunification, and perhaps never will be.[25] Similarly, Chen's wife remarked during a visit to the United States that "Taiwan supports anything the US does."[26] Hers was only one minor show of loyalty. Before and during the US invasion of Iraq, Taipei officials more than once confirmed their total support of the US war plan. Taipei's foreign ministry, for example, supports any plan the United States has for the war and postwar rehabilitation. Chen's spokesman wrote newspaper columns criticizing local anti-war activists for forgetting the US support (its "bequest" or "righteousness") during Taiwan's 1996 missile-test crisis.[27] Chen himself put the question bluntly to the press: "If we do not take the US side, are we not then taking the Iraqi side?"[28] Accordingly, he argued, "supporting the United States is the same as supporting our own country," and is "an act of defending our national security and dignity."[29]

Gradually, however, Washington has lost respect for Chen, not only because of his inability to win respect from his own countrymen, but also because he is not able to mobilize votes in the legislature even to approve the purchase of US submarines. The US representative in Taipei has often been so outspoken that many in Taipei felt insulted.[30] When a news report during the initial stages of the Iraq war mistakenly underestimated the rate of successful interception of attacking missiles by US Patriot missiles—which were on the top of Taipei's weapons purchase list—the US representative's protest came immediately and publicly. The US political attaché personally attended the legislature to mobilize support for the war effort and questioned those anti-war legislators, who then had to explain that they were not anti-American at all. No opposition leader, even one who might normally disagree with anything Chen says, came out on the anti-war side. If reaction to the Iraq war is any guide, there is no doubt that Washington can take Taipei for granted. For the Taipei authorities, Washington is indispensable for Taipei's eventual achievement of independent statehood. All the officials and pro-independence forces in Taipei make this point crystal clear when defending the US invasion of Iraq.

The government's and the pro-independence forces' support extend to the Bush Doctrine. The many and various reasons for this can be found on the Internet, submitted by anonymous writers.[31] First of all, there is the feeling that Taiwan is too weak to make any difference in international politics, so the best thing to do is to follow the United States in whatever it does. However, the supporters of this view do not want to offend the Islamic world either. In the second view, Taiwan has to depend on the United States to cope with the military threat from China. Government officials have often used this argument in their debate with anti-war intellectuals.[32] Since Beijing has reiterated that no military action will be considered unless Taiwan declares independence, government officials must have independence as their ultimate goal in order to justify their worry. The third line of argument is that Beijing does not support the invasion and Taipei must not take the same side that Beijing takes.[33] The fourth view is that the Taiwanese owe Americans a debt for sending two carrier battle groups to protect Taiwan in the 1996 crisis. Thus, now is the time for Taiwan to return the favor and support Washington when support is most needed.[34] Government officials similarly questioned the usefulness of "stripping off clothes" for peace because no one stripped off their clothes when Beijing conducted its threatening missile exercises across the Taiwan Strait in 1996.

The fifth view is that Taiwan must support whatever Washington does so that Washington will be sympathetic toward Taiwan's confrontation with China. Most important is perhaps the view that US unilateralism is the only effective deterrent to Beijing. If the United States defeated Iraq, US unilateralism would become international law. Beijing would then be convinced that it had no hope of taking over Taiwan. That would be the time when Taiwan gained total freedom.

Creating a war atmosphere

An interesting point regarding the aforementioned Internet postings is that most people support Washington not for anti-terrorism, anti-proliferation, or democratic peace reasons, but because of their own little war against China. China in 2003 witnessed the conclusion of the 16th Party Congress and the 9th People's Congress, which endorsed the slogan of stability and development. The new president, Hu Jintao, disclosed his intention to focus on poverty. At the same time, officials in charge of Taiwan affairs have been making peace overtures, beginning in 2001, without even responding to Chen's OSOC provocation. In light of the relaxation of tension on the China side, the enhanced sense of crisis in Taiwan is disproportionate. This suggests that the sense of crisis comes from within Taiwan, not from any heightened war preparation in China. Having observed the unstoppable China Fever, pro-independence fundamentalists in Taiwan launched a series of street demonstrations, but to no avail. Retired President Lee Tenghui is particularly worried about China Fever. Pro-independence forces regard building psychological defenses against Chinese identity as the most important task of the government. The US invasion of Iraq and the Bush Doctrine together provide a hands-on opportunity to improvise, at least discursively, an atmosphere of war with China.

A recalcitrant Taipei is more useful to Washington than a completely dependent Taipei, however. A recalcitrant Taipei receiving periodic discipline from Washington demonstrates to Beijing that Washington is not promoting Taiwan independence. Instead, Washington now appears to be acting on Beijing's behalf to curb this possibility. It is Washington that is standing between Beijing and Taipei to prevent any potential confrontation from breaking out. This mediating position actually protects Taiwan's de facto independence, which in turn enables Taipei to seem to act irresponsibly without worrying that Beijing may retaliate. In this way, Taiwan continues to be a useful pawn that Washington can unleash as it chooses to check Beijing.[35] Since Chen took office, however, and more so since the announcement of the Bush Doctrine, Taipei has acted like a total dependent of Washington's. The political distance between Taipei and Washington has disappeared. This causes problems for the patron, because any recalcitrant move taken by Taipei in the future would be understood by Beijing as an initiative approved by Washington. The loss of agency in Taipei reduces the negotiating space that Washington needs in which to play its role as mediator.

It is this jettisoning of agency that may compel Washington to watch Taipei closely lest another opportunistic move by Taipei should lead to an escalation of tensions between Washington and Beijing. Washington cannot pretend innocence apart from its role as mediator; but Taipei now takes actions independently of Washington, while acting as if it were a dependent puppy. Taipei misinterprets US unilateralism to be total dependence and performs accordingly. This will force a reappraisal of the Bush Doctrine from Beijing's side.

The unnoticeable challenge to the Bush Doctrine

To cope with US–China rapprochement, which completely exposed the absurdity of the two Chiangs' sovereignty claim over the Chinese mainland, Chiang Ching-kuo began a series of changes during the 1980s. First of all, the legitimacy of his leadership could no longer rely on an anti-communist illusion. More importantly, however, he could not simply cut off the linkage between the Chinese mainland and Taiwan, lest this should suggest that the regime his father had moved to Taiwan in 1949 had no reason to continue in power. He had managed a similar crisis during the early 1970s when the Republic of China was expelled from the United Nations, followed by another blow when the Shanghai Communiqué was announced. At that time, Chiang Kai-shek decided to enlarge the scope of democratic elections to win popularity.[36] Chiang Ching-kuo's problem was a matter of life and death for his government, in that he needed to cope, not only with the legitimacy crisis, but also with the rising pro-independence forces inside and outside the island country. In 1987, he opted for a two-handed strategy, legalizing the formation of an opposition political party as well as permitting home visits to the Chinese mainland by those who had migrated to Taiwan with his father's regime.

Most studies of Taiwanese politics note the significance of the lifting of martial law and the subsequent rise of the Democratic Progress Party (DPP), which finally took over the presidency in 2000.[37] Little attention is given to the impact of the early granting of permission to visit the homeland. For Chiang Ching-kuo, the problem was simply using visits to the homeland to balance pro-independence forces. Since the DPP was in the beginning supported by and connected with pro-independence forces, Chiang intended to have his homeland visit policy maintain the Chinese identity of Taiwanese society. For the next thirteen years, Chiang Ching-kuo's plan did not seem successful, both because his successor, Lee Tenghui, turned himself into the most important pro-independence leader and because his regime was taken over by the pro-independence DPP.

Chiang's hope for the China linkage did not actually show any promise until after Chen Shui-bian was elected. As mentioned before, China Fever has been rising since 2000. A harbinger for this development was present in 1996, when President Lee was stunned by how quickly investment and tourism in China by Taiwanese bounced back after the missile crisis. It had been this crisis that had sent angry Taiwanese voters to his side; but their anger evaporated soon after his election.

The reason that Taiwanese businesspeople as well as tourists wanted to go to China after they had just elected a pro-independence president in Taiwan is closely related to Chiang Ching-kuo's home-visit policy, which had encouraged businesspeople as well as tourists to pour into China, however illegally. The 1989 Tiananmen Incident had scared away businesspeople and tourists from all over the world, except those from Taiwan. Since home visits had to transit through Hong

Kong, all other illegal visitors (e.g., businessmen and tourists) took the same route and left their record clean as far as the Taiwanese immigration authorities could tell. Going through Hong Kong, all these trips did not officially exist according to official Taipei. As a result, Taipei had no leverage whatsoever to control travel to China. Indirect trips to China became such a popular activity that the government could develop no effective way to stop it. Statistics show that, up to 2002, over a quarter of the population in Taiwan had been to the mainland. Polls also suggest that people who visit the mainland more often hold a less hostile attitude toward China than people who do not.[38] Since 1992, China's economy has taken off steadily, with a corresponding increase in the number of Taiwanese who have taken up regular residence on the mainland. In other words, the home-visit policy prepared Taiwanese society to be able to go in and out of China freely in both a physical and psychological sense. For the pro-independence leaders who had neither the intention of moving in and out of China nor the chance of doing it, the mind of the people they lead is no longer comprehensible or even friendly.[39]

It is not only the Taiwanese government that finds the China Fever among Taiwanese people incomprehensible: the US government is equally bewildered. Most observers expected that Chen's coming to office would close off any hope for reunification, so the returning or, more precisely, the surfacing of China Fever has puzzled both Taipei and Washington.[40] I believe that only a postcolonial analysis can explain it. Taiwanese have been torn between their Chinese and anti-Chinese identities. The Chinese identity was belittled by the Japanese colonial authorities as a "slave" identity. A further humiliation came in the postcolonial era, after Chiang Kai-shek's regime arrived from the mainland, when Chinese were called *huangmin* (subjects of the emperor). The anti-Chinese identification was well preserved in the name of anti-communism during the cold war. It reemerged in the formation of pro-US or pro-Japanese, as well as pro-independence, attitudes after the cold war. Lee's and Chen's confrontations with China reproduce this feeling from time to time.

On the other hand, people's lives are full of Chinese cultural practices. Reestablishing connections with the mainland through the home-visit route allowed people to cash in on their Chinese identities both culturally and economically. It was the first time in modern Taiwanese history that Chinese identities and anti-Chinese identities did not contradict each other.[41] People could display either one or both, at the time and place of their choosing. But both the pro-independence fundamentalists and the Chinese nationalists are appalled; and, paradoxically, they jointly threaten to take away this ability to move between identities. For the government—and for Washington—Chinese and Taiwanese are not compatible. For Washington, these are two quite different polities, each monopolizing the loyalty of its citizens, especially in Taiwan, where the democratic election process supposedly grants Chen's leadership exclusive legitimacy. Double identities are not comprehensible.

However, the postcolonial strategy of identity in Taiwan has matured. People are very practiced today in shifting sides, socially as well as politically. Voting for pro-independence candidates and residing in China are not necessarily incompatible choices for them. The authorities in Taipei are anxious about this development and continually warn against identity erosion. Since Washington worries about China Fever in Taiwan, too, anxious authorities in Taipei have begun to interpret any deviation in Taiwanese society from Washington's policy as a pro-China move. Taipei wants to make sure that Washington does not doubt Taipei's strategic value, and to this end it goes to great lengths to demonstrate that Taipei is firmly on the US side. For example, when the national-security sector invested heavily in establishing a link with North Korea, the government gave up the whole venture after Washington decided that Pyongyang belonged to the "axis of evil," even though this move indirectly enhanced Beijing's leverage in Pyongyang.[42] The seeming unpredictability of China Fever in Taiwan thus reduces the agency of the government in interpreting and supporting the Bush Doctrine. Consequently, Washington also loses agency in using Taiwan for its own strategic purposes.

Unconstitutional democracy

In addition to its agency in reinterpreting the meaning of the Bush Doctrine, there is similarly an agency in Taipei to redefine democratization in ways unnoticeable to Washington. Indeed, Taiwan is not at all the kind of democracy that many US politicians or academics have wanted to see. When Chen Shui-bian won the presidential election in 2000, the US media reported with optimism that Taiwan could never be a part of China. As the media saw it, the voters' choice signaled their rejection of Beijing's call for unification.[43] Two years after Chen's inauguration, however, few US commentators were still sanguine about Taiwan's separation from China. Taiwan's investors, emigrants, and students poured into China. This forced the White House to reevaluate its Taiwan policy. Beginning in spring 2001, the White House carefully geared up its support for Taipei's independent status by, for example, engineering publicity in the United States while Chen was en route to Central America, probably hoping to curb the levels of China Fever in Taiwan. The result was lukewarm. Nonetheless, Washington seemed to believe that a Taiwan prevented from merging too soon with China would be strategically beneficial.[44]

Washington's reappraisal of Chen's ruling capability has two serious pitfalls. First of all, Taiwan-watchers in the United States fail to recognize that, despite the passage of more than half a century since the end of fifty-one years of colonization by Japan, Taiwanese views of China are *always* ambivalent. Japan's anti-Chinese cultural campaign was so effective that being Chinese Taiwanese was considered inferior during the colonial period. As previously mentioned, identities in contemporary Taiwan are thus both Chinese and anti-Chinese. This is a completely unfamiliar psychology to US analysts, who assume that people must have a consistent self-identity. Taiwanese are protective of their need to preserve alternative Chinese and anti-Chinese identities. When their Chinese side appears too strong, people run to rescue their threatened anti-Chinese element. We witnessed accordingly the rise of an anti-Chinese tide in the 1995–6 missile crisis. The opposite also applies, as we have seen since Chen's election. Washington's rescuing of Chen's proclivity before 9/11 to gain independence has backfired. US support for an independent Taiwan stance gives Taiwanese enough security about their anti-Chinese identities to feel confident in increasing their involvement in China's social life; in fact, Taiwanese are led to insist more on being Chinese by the strength of the anti-Chinese policies.

The second pitfall is that Washington is hurting Taiwan's democracy by using Taiwan as a check on China. To avoid weakening Chen's legitimacy or Taiwan's position as a check on China, some members of the US Congress choose to perceive whatever Chen does as democratic and whoever criticizes him as conservative. This is like a blank check for Chen to resort to *un*democratic and *un*constitutional means in domestic politics. In fact, Chen's government has several times searched, harassed, and sued news reporters for writing on scandals in the intelligence sectors. The government has repeatedly asserted that the premier does not have to abide by the legislature's resolutions.[45] Chen himself has intervened in both policy and personnel decisions that belong exclusively to other branches. He has met military leaders on a regular, but non-constitutional, basis. His cabinet members have refused to accept questioning in the legislature. Having sworn to safeguard democracy and the constitution at his inauguration, Chen now wants to restructure the legislative system and rewrite the constitution. Chen is safe in all this anti-democratic manipulation because his independence gestures are enough for international watchers to regard him as a liberal democrat.[46]

This is why I believe that Washington's support for Taiwan independence only further splits Taiwanese society—now recovering the Chinese element in its identity—as well as Chen's government, which thought it had US support for whatever it took to curb the country's China Fever. This unrestrained mood, together with the widening split between the government and society in its orientation toward China, explains the ban on mainland Chinese books and TV channels. It probably also prompted the racist comment made by Chen's personal secretary that anyone who thinks Taiwanese are Chinese is immoral.[47] When US analysts mistake Taiwan's democracy for Taiwan's independence from China, the hope for democratic consolidation in Taiwan becomes faint.

A recent development in Taiwan suggests how irrelevant Washington's "war on terrorism" has been for Taiwan. As Chen's presidential reelection neared, he decided to hold a referendum on March 20, 2004, that called for the purchase of a US defensive system to protect Taiwan. The referendum fell on the same date as the presidential election. Despite all the constitutional and legal barriers to such a call and the question of the legitimacy of using the referendum in an election campaign, Chen went ahead nonetheless. Washington worried that his move might escalate tensions across the Taiwan Strait; but after repeated calls on Chen to cancel it failed to work, Washington seemed to realize that "democracy in Taiwan" means little more than casting ballots, not to resolve any political disagreements but to achieve national unity.[48] A democracy like this one sounds much closer to Beijing's democratic centrism than the American style democracy—and this has increasingly threatened Washington's strategic need.

Nonetheless, Taipei has been capable of mobilizing sufficient support in the international media to use Washington's "most-favorable-democracy" discourse in Iraq to criticize Washington's reluctance to lend support to Taipei's "war on China."

The war on terrorism—a fiasco

As of this writing, developments in Iraq suggest that the US-led allied forces have been unable to transform Iraq into what they would consider to be a "normal state." As the threat of terrorism continues, the allied invasion has become a fiasco. Terrorist attacks have spread into all corners of the world. In the Middle East, incidents of truck and car bombings have increased sharply in frequency as well as in the publicity they generate, blocking any significant progress on "the road map to peace" that was once considered the solution to Palestinian state-building. From the realist point of view familiar to Washington, the unexpected perpetuation of its adventure in the Middle East calls for a better relationship with Beijing, whose leaders have willingly accommodated Washington's needs in the hope of accumulating credits that can eventually be cashed in on the Taiwan issue. Beijing's cooperation is most clearly demonstrated in its willingness to coopt Pyongyang into multilateral talks concerning the latter's nuclear buildup. These latest developments illustrate Washington's rule of thumb in dealing with Taipei: keep things as they are.

But Taipei leaders do not think like their American counterparts. The political agenda in Taipei concentrates on just two domestic issues: winning reelection for President Chen and creating windows of opportunity for Taiwanese independence. Washington's international concerns are seen differently through their eyes. Consequently, during the six-party talks in Beijing on the nuclear crisis on the Korean peninsula, President Chen, with advice from former President Lee, was concerned not about the rise of Beijing's influence but about how to escalate their own appeals for Taiwan independence. The two presidents held two lengthy private meetings in August 2003, days before the large rally for independence in early September,[49] thus giving the impression of close cooperation despite Chen's denials. Lee calculates that since Beijing is going to host the 2008 Olympics, and has a fast-growing economy that is absorbing Taiwanese investment as well as social interest, China will be content simply to shut down possible windows of opportunity for Taiwan independence, and not take any further action against Taiwan, certainly not military action, at the present time.[50] According to this view, Taiwan must act quickly to gain its total independence before 2008. Naturally, since President Chen faces mounting challenges from the opposition to his run for reelection, the winning strategy is to turn the election into a plebiscite for independence.

In fact, during its first term, beginning in 2000, the ruling pro-independence DPP did not have any convincing achievements. Knowing that most Taiwanese do not want immediate reunification with China, President Chen relies on a strategy to set up a scenario of immediate reunification in order to divide the voting constituency into pro-unification (i.e., Chinese) and anti-unification (i.e., anti-Chinese) camps, with Chen himself on the far side of the anti-unification camp.[51] This strategy aims to overwhelm all other dimensions of the election campaign where Chen is disadvantaged. If he can successfully label the opposition as pro-unification, he still has a chance of staying in office. For this reason, he needs a confrontation across the Taiwan Strait, despite the warnings from the United States against employing any such strategy. In July 2003, his national security adviser had to visit Washington to listen to its very specific and straightforward concerns about escalation in the Taiwan Strait. However, the response to Washington's warning has been cosmetic adjustments at best.

In August 2003, Chen advanced his OSOC position by linking it with a plebiscite, which he calls "the soul of the DPP."[52] In the September rally for independence, Lee announced that the Republic of China never existed on Taiwan. Chen, like his predecessor Lee, adopts the tactic of one giant step forward and an immediate small step back. With Taipei always retreating after each provocation, Beijing is unable to seize the right moment to justify any military action. For Lee, the small step back that he took after announcing his state-to-state theory in 1999 was the promise that there would be no subsequent constitutional amendment. In the same vein, after Chen announced his OSOC in 2002, he sent his minister for mainland Chinese affairs to Washington, promising that his remark would remain unofficial. The further adventurism in August 2003 was similarly followed by Chen's proposal to open direct flights with the Chinese mainland a year after his reelection. This was enough of a step back that Beijing, reluctant to resort to force amidst the atmosphere of domestic reform, responded in a positive fashion, while continuing to insist that any talk of direct flights was meaningless so long as Chen identified Taiwan as a separate state. Both Taiwan presidents seem certain that Beijing is not ready to impose any real sanctions. Little by little, they believe, independence will be realized. If reelection and a plebiscite for independence are conceptually linked and the constituency is effectively divided into Chinese and anti-Chinese camps, their future will certainly look promising both politically and in terms of creating a unitary Taiwanese identity. However, their judgment that Beijing will do no more than bluff will not be appreciated by either Beijing or Washington.[53]

It is doubtful whether Washington can eventually develop a monitoring or a disciplinary system to cope with Taipei. In fact, Washington was unhappy that Chen insisted on holding an anti-China referendum to boost his chances in the 2004 election.[54] Beijing has considered the referendum a provocative move to prepare Taiwan for eventual independence from China. Beijing's reaction prompted Washington to reiterate its opposition to such a referendum in order to prevent a possible escalation of tension across the Taiwan Strait and, at the same time, to exert pressure on Chen to rephrase the referendum in a more subtle tone.[55] However, Chen continued to interpret the referendum to his domestic audience in an anti-China context. As Beijing repeatedly promises not to sit idly by, it is nonetheless ironic that Washington's most faithful ally, which has always claimed it fully supports the Bush Doctrine, is intellectually incapable of comprehending and acting in accordance with Washington's interests. Taipei has failed to become alert to the fiasco of the war on terrorism and the fact that Beijing's significance in Washington's worldview is rising quickly.[56] Taipei is almost completely engrossed in its own pursuit of independence, making its support of the Bush Doctrine at best an instrumental decision.[57] When Taiwan's dependence on the United States becomes no more than a strategic choice, it may raise the question in Washington of Taiwan's reliability.

Conclusion: hidden agencies

There are two kinds of historical agencies hidden in Taiwan's compliance with the Bush Doctrine. The first is the Taipei authorities' change of attitude toward the China mainland, which resulted in Taiwan's rise from a position of no strategic significance to that of a plausible player. As Washington left containment behind and pursued rapprochement with Beijing, Taipei's anti-communism lost value. Only after Lee's new leadership substituted pro-independence for reunification could Washington, by then carrying out "congagement" with Beijing, seriously use Taiwan as a check on Beijing again. Due to the rise of China Fever in Taiwan, the pro-independence Chen administration now reacts with a gesture of total dependence on, and support for, the Bush Doctrine. This gesture damages Washington's role as a mediator between China and Taiwan and, in turn and in time, will reduce Taipei's freedom of action as well as its pursuit of independent statehood. What is missing in the literature on the Washington–Beijing–Taipei triangular relationship is Chiang Ching-kuo's decision to allow home visits by Chinese military migrants in Taiwan. This policy effectively prepared the society for indirect contacts with the mainland and made possible the phenomenon of China Fever ten years later.

The second kind of agency lies in the fluidity of Taiwanese society in being able to change sides socially, politically, and psychologically between China and Taiwan. This is by far the most powerful subversive undercurrent in Taipei's unreserved support of the Bush Doctrine in exchange for Washington's pro-independence policy.

One can imagine a very different history in Taiwan if Washington had not engaged in rapprochement with Beijing. Chiang's reunification policy would not have lost credit, the pro-independence movement would not have incurred serious repression in Taipei, and Chiang Ching-kuo would not have adopted the two-handed policy. Without Chiang Ching-kuo's two-handed policy, an opposition would not have developed as it did overnight in Taiwan, Taiwan would not have installed a democratic election for the presidency as early as it did, and pro-independence forces would not have come to power as quickly. On the other hand, if not for the two-handed policy, Taiwan would not have practiced and normalized an indirect connection with the Chinese mainland, the Taipei authorities would not have been marginalized in the cross-Taiwan Strait exchanges, and China Fever would not have evolved with such unanticipated speed. If the pro-independence forces had not gained power, Washington would not have been attracted again by Taipei's plausible strategic value, Taipei would not have perceived

Washington to be the sole determining factor in its little war against China, and it would not have needed to show its total reliance by supporting the Bush Doctrine so unreservedly. If Taipei had not attracted Washington's attention by taking a pro-independence orientation, Taipei would not have used Washington in its little war against Beijing, Washington would not have gotten involved as a mediator in the first place, and it would not have lost its mediating position because of Taipei's total dependence.

The Bush Doctrine is about unilateral, preemptive American action against a potential enemy. For pro-independence forces in Taiwan, China represents this potential enemy. To support the Bush Doctrine means to deter China's using military means to stop Taiwan independence. Without the Bush Doctrine or Taipei's repeated shows of total loyalty to Washington, it would have been possible for Washington to mediate, or pretend to mediate, between China and Taiwan so as to keep Taiwan from reunification with the Chinese mainland. The Bush Doctrine's unilateralism and Taipei's total reliance together destroy the credit that a mediator would need. Taipei always has had its own interests to protect—from the defiant Chiang Kai-shek's reunification game in Quemoy, to Chiang Ching-kuo's two-handed policy to curb pro-independence, to Lee's use of Washington to promote the cause of independence, and finally to Chen's total reliance to preserve Washington's sympathy for Taiwan's pursuit of independence—and has always been able to sneak those interests into its total support of Washington. Washington has been caught either by surprise or by ignorance each time. The support the Bush Doctrine enjoys in Taipei is no exception. Although the Bush administration has thanked the Chen administration a number of times publicly for supporting Washington, Bush's staff will know eventually that things are not what they seem.

Notes

1. See the discussion of this mood and the counter-mood in Martin Peretz, "Son Shine: The New Bush Doctrine," *The New Republic*, September 9–16, 2002, pp. 21–3.
2. Norman Podhoretz, "In Praise of the Bush Doctrine," *Commentary*, Vol. 114, No. 2 (September, 2002), pp. 19–28.
3. Although never saying that Taiwan is unimportant, some analysts detail how each American commentator speaks on behalf of Taiwan as if all the initiatives must come from the United States; see the summaries of the internal seminar on "The New US Government's Asia-Pacific Policy and Our Adaptation," held by the Taiwan Ministry of Foreign Affairs, March 22, 2001. Accessible at www.mofa.gov.tw/newmofa/faa/faa-5.htm, as of April 7, 2003.
4. Scholars in official positions tend to focus on this equalizing function. See Lin Cheng-yi (now National Security Adviser), *The Triangular Exercise for Taiwan: The Impacts of Communist China and the United States* (in Chinese) (Taipei: Kuikuan, 1989); Wu Yu-shan (now National Science Council Coordinator for Political Science), *Balance or Bandwagon: A New Interpretation of the Cross-Taiwan Straits Relationship* (in Chinese) (Taipei: Chengchung, 1997); Luo Chi-cheng (former Director of Research and Design, Ministry of Foreign Affairs), "The Role of the United States between the Two Sides of the Taiwan Straits—A Balancer" (in Chinese), *America and Europe Quarterly*, Vol. 10, No. 1 (January, 1995), pp. 37–54.
5. Civilian or overseas writers tend to note this; see, for example, Liu Chih-kung, "The Taipei–Washington–Peiping Triangle" (in Chinese), *Issues & Studies*, Vol. 25, No. 5 (1986), pp. 1–15; Hu

Weixing, "China–USA–Taiwan Triangular Interaction and Its Impacts" (in Chinese), in C. Ming, ed., *Win–Win or Lose–Lose?* (Taipei: Chihliang, 1996), pp. 23–42.
6 Ming Chucheng, "The 9/11 Incident and Our Country's Policy of Anti-Terrorism" (in Chinese), paper presented at the Conference on Global Anti-Terrorist Strategy, Ministry of Foreign Affairs, December 12, 2002.
7 See Lin Cheng-yi, "The Meaning of Wolfowitz's Remarks" (in Chinese), Commentary on Current Affairs, The Global Information Net, Kuomintang, online at www.youngkmt.org.tw/Content/HTML/Statement/ShortComment/20020603_14_3861.html.
8 See, for example, Sun Yang-ming, "The One-Side-One-Country Statement Sends Taipei to the Sacrificial Altar" (in Chinese), *Straits Review*, No. 142 (October, 2002), pp. 14–18.
9 See, for example, Lin Chuo-shui (DPP Legislator), "From Clinton to Bush, The US Taiwan Policy under the Framework of Globalization and Post-Cold-War—Responding to the Shaky One-China Policy" (in Chinese), *Policy Notes on National Affairs*, No. 19 (September, 2001), pp. 2–4; Lin Cheng-yi, "Exploring Bush's Taiwan Strait Policy" (in Chinese), *Chinese Affairs Quarterly* No. 7 (January, 2002), pp. 67–81.
10 Jeffrey W. Legro and Andrew Moravcsik, "Faux Realism: Spin versus Substance in the Bush Foreign Policy Doctrine," *Foreign Policy*, No. 125 (July–August, 2001), pp. 80–82.
11 See Thomas Schelling, *Arms and Influence* (New Haven: Yale University Press, 1966), p. 43; Alexander L. George and Richard Smoke, *Deterrence in American Foreign Policy: Theory and Practice* (New York: Columbia University Press, 1974), pp. 363–89; Thomas Stolper, *China, Taiwan, and the Offshore Islands: Together with an Implication for Outer Mongolia and Sino-Soviet Relations* (Armonk, NY: M. E. Sharpe, 1985).
12 For Chiang Ching-kuo's policy rationale, see Yu-shan Wu, "Economic Integration vs. Political Divergence between Taiwan and Mainland China," paper presented at the 1993 annual meeting of the American Political Science Association, Washington, D. C., September 2–5, 1993.
13 See Robert Jervis, "The Impact of the Korean War on the Cold War," *Journal of Conflict Resolution*, Vol. 24, No. 4 (December, 1980).
14 Facing the camera, the government spokesman James Soong asked the American audience in August 1982, "Where do you stand?"—a question reflecting the lingering civil-war perspective.
15 Chen I-Hsin (former New Party legislator), *Sino-US Relations After De-recognition, 1979–1994* (in Chinese) (Taipei: Wunan, 1995), pp. 101–2.
16 Under the China Threat theme, which became popular in the early 1990s, Taiwan's strategic value should have loomed large. Realists' expectations that the dissolution of the Soviet bloc would make Taiwan again relevant were not borne out. Taipei first had to move out of the civil war before Washington could use it without risking direct confrontation with Beijing, and probably also irritating Taipei. For the abortive realist analysis, see Nancy Bernkopf Tucker, "China and America: 1949–1991," *Foreign Affairs*, Vol. 70, No. 5 (1991), p. 75.
17 In addition, there was a propaganda war on Lee.
18 Remarks made by a number of Chinese speakers in August 1995 at a conference, held in Beijing, attended by scholars from both sides of the Taiwan Strait.
19 Lin Chia-lung (a former National Security Adviser, now the government spokesman), "Lee Tenghui and Cross-Strait Relations: A Two-Level Game Perspective," presented at the 29th Sino-American Conference on Contemporary China, May 28–30, 2000.
20 This is the famous US wording with regard to "our one-China policy," as distinguished from China's One-China policy. See Bill Clinton, "I support the One China policy. But part of our One China policy is that the differences between China and Taiwan must be resolved by dialogue, and I feel very strongly about it." President Bill Clinton's Press Conference, March 29, 2000, distributed by the Office of International Information Programs, US Department of State. http://usinfo.state.gov.
21 Lin Chia-lung, "Lee Tenghui and Cross-Strait Relations," p. 29.
22 According to Parris Chang's personal interviews with "the US experts" on Taiwan, the United States is "uncomfortable with the weak position on sovereignty" taken by the opposition leaders and it is very clear in their "mind and bosom" that, underneath its alleged neutrality, the United States will support the candidates of the ruling party during the next presidential campaign. Parris

Chang, "Taiwanese Politics Viewed from Washington, D. C." (in Chinese), *Liberty Times*, April 14, 2003, p. 15. Earlier, in an invitation-only breakfast meeting at Taipei's Lincoln Society, which was held three days after Chen's election in 2000, an official of the American Institute in Taiwan, in an atmosphere of uncertainty, assured his audience that everything would be just fine. A few months later, he confirmed his previous judgment. Ironically, this second statement came at about the same time as the fiasco of the fourth nuclear power plant policy during which Chen sacked his first premier. Apparently, the AIT official meant that China could do nothing to Taiwan's separatist ideology, not that the quality of governing would improve.

23 I was personally interviewed three times by this analyst.
24 See Jacques DeLisle, "US Policy toward Taiwan: Sustaining the Status Quo," *E-notes on "A Catalyst for Ideas"* (Philadelphia: Foreign Policy Research Institute, July 27, 2001).
25 For example, "Political Earthquake in Taiwan," editorial of *The New York Times*, March 20, 2000; "Taiwan's Way of the Future," editorial in the *Washington Times*, March 20, 2000; James H. Anderson, "Tensions Across the Strait," *The Heritage Foundation Backgrounder*, No. 1328 (September 28, 1999); Raymond F. Burghardt, "US–PRC–Taiwan Relations," remarks to the US–ROC (Taiwan) Business Council, 24th Annual Joint Business Conference on US–Taiwan–China Relations Special Seminar, Taipei (June 16, 2000); Murray Weidenbaum, "United States–China–Taiwan a Precarious Triangle," address delivered to the Conference on the Greater China Economy, St. Louis, March 25, 2000.
26 For the remarks of Wu Shu-chen, the First Lady, see "I Support All the Anti-terrorist Activities by the United States," *United Daily* (Taipei), September 21, 2002. See also "Taiwan Will Stand on the American Side Forever," *China Times*, September 27, 2002. Vice President Lu Hsiu-lien was quoted as saying that Taiwan's support of the US war effort in Iraq was the best evidence of Taiwan's loyalty to the United States; see Central News Agency (telegram), "Vice President Lu: The US Should Have Complete Trust in Its Most Loyal Ally, Taiwan" (in Chinese), March 20, 2003.
27 Wu Chao-hsieh (Vice Secretary General of the Presidential Office), "Anti-War Is Not Peace, Anti-US Contradicts Taiwan Interests" (Chinese) *United Daily*, March 18, 2003.
28 Chen made this widely reported and debated remark on March 22, 2003.
29 Central News Agency (telegram), "President Chen Explains the ROC's Reason for Supporting US Anti-terrorism" (in Chinese), April 12, 2003.
30 For the Defense Department's rebuttal of the Ministry of Defense's questioning of the effectiveness of the Patriot missile, see "The US Says the Patriot Interception Rate Is 100%," *United Daily*, March 29, 2003.
31 These comments are accessible at http://udn.com/NEWS/; for similar perspectives, also consult the daily letters to the editor section (called Liberty Bridge) of the *Liberty Times*.
32 Chiu Yi-jen (Secretary General of the Presidential Office) believes that Taiwan is too weak to refuse its support for the Iraqi war. See "Taiwan Has No Room for Not Showing Support," *United Daily*, March 26, 2003.
33 Chen himself took this line of argument in the aforementioned March 22, 2003 remark.
34 Also an argument strongly felt by Wu Chao-hsieh (Secretary of the Presidential Office); see Central News Agency (telegram), "Wu Chao-hsieh: Once the US Launches War on Iraq, Taiwan Should Never Forget Benevolence or Betray Righteousness" (in Chinese), March 17, 2003.
35 See, for example, Lin Chuo-shui (DPP legislator), "China, the United States, and Taiwan Double the Chips" (in Chinese), *Chinese Affairs Quarterly*, No. 2 (January, 2002), pp. 21–33; Chen Long-chih (Adviser to the President), "Breaking through China's Containment of Taiwan—Taiwan's Way of Adaptation After the Clinton-Jiang Summit" (in Chinese), *Forum, New Century Think Tank*, No. 1 (February, 1998), pp. 39–40; Lin Cheng-yi, "The Constraints and the Improvement of Taiwan–US Relations" (in Chinese), *Forum, New Century Think Tank*, No. 9 (April, 2000), pp. 28–31.
36 John P. Copper, "Taiwan's Elections," *Occasional Papers Reprints Series in Contemporary Asian Studies*, No. 5 (School of Law, University of Maryland) (1984), pp. 48–52.
37 Shelly Rigger, *Politics in Taiwan: Voting for Democracy* (London: Routledge, 1999); Alan Wachman, *Taiwan: National Identity and Democratization* (Armonk, NY: M. E. Sharpe, 1994); Linda Chao and Ramon Myers, *The First Chinese Democracy: The Political Life in the Republic of China on Taiwan*

(London: The Johns Hopkins University Press, 1998); Stephen Haggard and Tun-jen Cheng, eds., *Political Change in Taiwan* (Boulder, Colo.: Lynne Rienner, 1991); Christopher Achen, *The Timing of Political Liberalization: Taiwan as the Canonical Case*, APSA Conference Group on Taiwan Studies, 1996.

38 See Yung Wei, "State, Nation, and Autonomy: Conflict Resolution and the 'Linkage Communities,'" paper presented at the International Studies Association Annual Meeting, New Orleans, March 27, 2002.

39 The administration has decided that those whose relatives or who themselves have stayed in China since 1987 for over a year should not be allowed to take certain government positions: "Over One Thousand Officials Must Take Loyalty Check" (in Chinese), *China Times*, March 27, 2003. For another example, Taiwan Solidarity suspects that there is a fifth column hidden in Taiwan's legislature and certain committees; see Central News Agency (telegram), "Taiwan Solidarity: Legislators Studying or Investing in China Are Not Allowed on the Defense Committee" (in Chinese), April 4, 2003.

40 Monique Chu, "Chen Sees Benefit in 'Interim Agreement,'" *Taipei Times*, February 16, 2001; Monique Chu, "Roth Presses Direct Talks with Beijing," *Taipei Times*, February 18, 2001.

41 According to a poll conducted in 2002, 97 percent of the population conceive themselves to be Taiwanese, while 72 percent see themselves as Chinese at the same time. See Yung Wei, "State, Nation, and Autonomy."

42 "Rumors of US Interference Relating to the Abortion of the US$5 Million Trade Project with North Korea," *United Daily*, March 7, 2003.

43 For example, see editorial, "Two Chinas?" *Newsday*, March 21, 2000; Joseph Kahn, "China Indicating Caution on Taiwan," *New York Times*, April 2, 2000; editorial, "China, Taiwan and Democracy," *Chicago Tribune*, March 22, 2000; Thomas L. Friedman, "This Is a Test," *New York Times*, March 21, 2000; editorial, "*L'autre Chine*," *Le Monde* (Paris), March 21, 2000.

44 Ross Terrill, "The One China Fiction and Its Danger," *AEI Online*, September 1, 1999. For an analysis of how Washington should face the possibility of a reunited China, see Nancy Bernkopf Tucker, "If Taiwan Chooses Unification, Should the United States Care?" *Washington Quarterly*, Vol. 25, No. 3 (Summer, 2002), pp. 15–28.

45 Indeed, the executive branch cannot agree that it has to "accept the resolution of the legislature." See Chiu Chinlan, "The Executive Yuan: There Is a Chance to Announce the Reopening of the Construction of the Fourth Nuclear Plant This Week," *Economics Daily*, February 12, 2001.

46 See, for instance, Arthur Waldron, "Taiwan's Democratization Dilemma," *AEI Online*, June 1, 2000.

47 Yang Yuwen, "President Chen: Ethnicity Is Not an Issue," *United Daily*, April 26, 2002.

48 For reflections on the meaning of democracy in Taiwan, see Alan D. Romberg, "No: Bush Rightly Rebuked Taiwan for Recklessly Tilting toward Independence," Insight on the News (posted January 8, 2004), online at www.insightmag.com/news/2004/01/20/Symposium/Symposiumq. Also see Agence France-Presse, Beijing, "Armitage Criticizes Referendum Plan, Questions Motives," Saturday, *Taipei Times*, January 31, 2004. For the purpose of voting according to Chen, see Chen Minfeng, "Chen Wants People to Happily Cast the Ballot," *United Daily*, January 21, 2004.

49 Liu Paochie and Lin Heming, "Three Meetings in Two Days," *United Daily*, August 21, 2003.

50 Lin Heming, "Lee Tenghui Raises the Issue of Establishing the New State in 2008," *United Daily*, July 25, 2002.

51 Li Chaoyang, "How Much Independence Is Enough?" *New News Weekly*, September 4–10, 2003, pp. 28–9.

52 Chen Minfeng, "Bian: OSOC and Plebiscite are the Soul of the Party," *United Daily*, August 13, 2003; Chen Yongshuen, "Bian: There Is Absolutely No Room for Concession concerning OSOC," *United Daily*, August 11, 2003.

53 Chang Tsongchi, "Bian's Move Could Create Troubles for the United States," *United Daily*, August 5, 2002; Lin Paoching, "The American Side Is Worried about Escalation of Tension," *United Daily*, August 5, 2002; Wen Hsianshen, "Tang Jiaxuan: Promoting OSOC Makes Things Difficult," *United Daily*, August 8, 2002.

54 Chen specifically mentioned that anyone against the referendum is siding with China, "Chen: Promoting Absence on Referendum Goes Against Democracy," *United Daily*, January 26, 2004.
55 But he said to the *Los Angeles Times* that the real issue should be independence. Tyler Marshall and Mark Magnier, "Taiwan's Chen Defends Move on Referendum," *Los Angeles Times*, February 8, 2004.
56 Secretary of State Colin L. Powell remarked that Beijing and Washington were in their best relationship in a decade when interviewed by the *Washington Post*'s editorial board on July 22, 2003 (released July 24, 2003 at www.state.gov/secretary/rm/2003/22687.htm).
57 Note the claim by President Chen that Taipei and Washington relations were at their best since the break of diplomatic relations: Liu Paochie, Chang Pofu, Yang Yuwen and Hsu Chinglong, "Taiwan–US Relations Now Best Since 1979," *United Daily*, August 8, 2003.

5 Chinese perspectives and responses to the Bush Doctrine

Jing-dong Yuan

The Bush Doctrine has important implications for China. It challenges principles that Beijing holds dear with respect to state sovereignty, multipolarity, and the role of international organizations. Continued American primacy in international affairs marginalizes China's importance. In addition, key elements of the Bush Doctrine—such as preemption, missile defenses, and a growing US military presence as a result of the war against terrorism—directly affect Chinese national security interests. However, while Beijing has a very negative view of the Bush Doctrine, its responses have been more measured and pragmatic. China recognizes its own limitations and the need to avoid direct confrontation with the United States. Its leaders also believe that the Bush Doctrine will have limited application to only a few exceptional cases, simply because unilateralism cannot be sustained long in the face of domestic and international opposition. Instead, Beijing seized the opportunity provided by 9/11 and the changing focus of US security policy to expand areas of common interest while minimizing the impact of differences. How the Bush Doctrine will affect China's interests in the future will depend on how well the two manage their increasingly complex relationship.

Introduction

The Bush Doctrine has drawn heated debate and criticism at home and from abroad. Widely perceived as departing from the traditional US defense posture of deterrence and retaliation, the new emphasis on preemption raises a series of questions. One is the legality of attacking another sovereign state when the imminence of threats is not clear. Another is its corrosive effect on international norms and institutions. Yet a third is the precedent the US application of preemption sets for other states and regions where the temptation to resort to the use of force to resolve international conflict could arise. While the promulgation of the Bush Doctrine itself can be associated with a series of official documents and statements, some of its key elements, such as the pursuit of US security interests through unilateral means, had already manifested themselves. The September 11 terrorist attacks against the United States only completed this transition.

The Bush Doctrine has important implications for China's security interests. Chinese analysts agree that post-cold-war US national security strategy has remained by and large unchanged. This assessment includes the continuation of US predominance well into the future, the prevention of the rise of regional powers that could challenge US interests, and the promotion of market economies and democratization. But key elements of the Bush Doctrine—such as preemption, missile defense, and growing US military presence as a result of the war against terrorism—directly affect Chinese national security interests. US unilateralism also challenges principles that Beijing holds dear: state sovereignty, multipolarity, and the role of international organizations. Continued American primacy and dominance in international affairs marginalizes China's importance.

The next section briefly discusses the key elements of the Bush Doctrine and the debates between its critics and proponents. This is followed by Chinese analyses that also touch on the broader US post-cold-war national security strategy. The chapter then assesses the implications of the Bush Doctrine for Chinese security interests and Beijing's options. I argue that while Beijing harbors strong negative views of the doctrine, it recognizes that its primary targets remain terrorist groups and rogue states deemed to have close connections with terrorists. For the time being at least, the extent to which the United States can fully exercise its unilateral power is somewhat offset by Washington's need for continued international support and major-power cooperation in dealing with international terrorist threats. China has therefore adopted the more pragmatic approach of not directly confronting US hegemonism. Instead, Beijing has sought to promote a stable Sino-US relationship by expanding areas of common interest and minimizing the negative impact of policy differences.

The Bush Doctrine: charting a new course of preemption

The United States emerged from the end of the cold war as the sole superpower, with historically unprecedented power. The collapse of communism in Eastern Europe and the disintegration of the Soviet Union removed major obstacles to American primacy. The US victory in the first Gulf War (in 1991) further displayed the overwhelming nature of its military prowess and established its unchallenged unipolar position. The focal points of US national security strategy have become the prevention of rising powers from challenging US security interests, the worldwide promotion of the market economy and democratization, and a commitment to deal with emerging threats such as the proliferation of weapons of mass destruction (WMD).

Although the end of the cold war removed major security threats to the United States, new security issues were emerging at the same time. These included regional instability, the growing risk of nuclear proliferation, and the pursuit of WMD capability by a number of states. The Clinton administration sought to consolidate US power by adjusting military alliances (e.g., NATO expansion and new US–Japan defense guidelines), strengthening and consolidating existing international norms and systems dealing with WMD proliferation, and supporting regionally based multilateral security arrangements.

The Bush administration began its term with a different approach to foreign policy. During the 2000 presidential campaign, Bush's foreign policy advisers advocated the use of American power to advance national interests, build and strengthen alliances, and deal firmly with potential US foes.[1] They deplored the Clinton administration's foreign policy as indecisive and overly concerned with multilateralism without sufficient focus on bottom-line results. The Bush administration has reversed foreign-policy direction on a series of foreign-policy issues ranging from dialogue with North Korea to commitments to major international arms control treaties.[2]

Even before the 9/11 terrorist attacks, the Bush administration's approaches to foreign policy had shown signs of unilateralism. The administration (as mentioned elsewhere in this volume) rejected the Kyoto Protocol (on climate change) and the protocol to the Biological and Toxic Weapons Convention, proceeded with missile defense plans, and withdrew from the Anti-Ballistic Missile (ABM) Treaty.[3] The 9/11 attacks further reinforced the notion that traditional approaches to handling security could no longer be relied upon to deal with emerging new threats. In his 2002 State of the Union Address, Bush described North Korea, Iraq, and Iran as constituting the "axis of evil" and asserted that "the United States of America will not permit the world's most dangerous regimes to threaten us with the world's most destructive weapons."[4]

While the philosophical underpinnings of the Bush Doctrine—the neoconservative ideologies of using unrivaled US power to promote its values around the world—were already in place, they were made public after September 11 in a series of presidential speeches and White House documents. Among the most important, cited in previous chapters, were President Bush's graduation speech at West Point in June 2002[5]—in which he called on Americans to be "ready for preemptive action"—and the September 2002 document *The National Security Strategy of the United States of America*, in which Bush warned that "history will judge harshly those who saw this coming danger but failed to act."[6] The new US security vision is shaped by the recognition of emerging threats: a combination of "radicalism and technology," and a danger of terrorist groups armed with WMD and rogue states willing to assist terrorist groups. "To forestall or prevent such hostile acts by our adversaries, the United States will, if necessary, act preemptively."[7]

In addition, the Bush administration has moved beyond—if not completely discarded—traditional arms control and nonproliferation approaches, and now favors (and perhaps already has adopted) what is called a "counter-proliferation" strategy. The Pentagon defines the new strategy as employing the "full range of military preparations and activities to reduce, and protect against, the threat posed by nuclear, biological, and chemical weapons and their associated delivery systems." The strategy is spelled out in the December 2002 White House *National Strategy to Combat Weapons of Mass Destruction* and envisions active homeland defense, including: the development and deployment of ballistic missile defense systems to protect American territories, US troops overseas, and its friends and allies; proactive offensive measures such as preemptive and preventive strikes; and strengthened nonproliferation efforts at home and abroad.[8]

Proponents of the Bush Doctrine argue that the United States should take advantage of the unique opportunity to use its primacy to build a balance of power favoring freedom. Furthermore, given the nature of the threats to its security interests, the US should not hesitate and must be willing to exercise its military power to defend itself and further advance its primacy.[9] However, proponents of the doctrine also suggest that while it is true that preemption has been elevated to a more prominent place in US security policy, the administration is not discarding traditional approaches. Administration officials suggest that preemption will be used "sparingly" and note that "preempting for regime change ought to be a very rare occurrence."[10]

The rationale of the Bush Doctrine lies in the fact that America lives today in a much changed security environment. During the cold war, while both the Soviet Union and the United States possessed huge nuclear arsenals that could destroy the world many times over, the specter of MAD (mutual assured destruction) also induced maximum restraint in Moscow and Washington. However, that same defense posture, relying upon deterrence and massive retaliation, proves less inhibiting to terrorist groups that are stateless and have no assets to protect, and to rogue states seeking weapons of mass destruction whose rationality is hard to determine. To protect American interests calls for the ability and determination to use force preemptively if necessary.

Critics of the Bush Doctrine point out that it could undermine the fabric of the international system and in the end harm US interests. While preemption has always been an element of US national security policy, the context within which it has been announced and reinforced in the aftermath of 9/11 makes it appear to be a more prominent feature of US policy than previously. The reference to the "axis of evil"; the emphasis on the necessity of "regime change"; "either-or" choice; and the actual use of force all send a strong signal. This rather sweeping change has led to serious concerns and incurred strong objections within the United States. These objections relate to the doctrine's open-ended nature, the danger of imitation by others, and the trampling of international laws and norms.[11]

Other analysts doubt whether the United States could carry out its strategy of preemption, due to institutional, moral and practical reasons. James Wirtz and James Russell suggest that "the administration's new doctrine is largely designed for domestic consumption and is unlikely to be fully implemented, because of various normative and practical constraints created by international institutions and politics."[12] The fact of the matter is, "while acting unilaterally might sound good in principle, the political and logistical difficulties of applying force halfway around the world are powerful obstacles to unilateral action."[13] However, while the debates on the Bush Doctrine continue, the perceived negative impact on the international system and indeed its very application in the form of Operation Iraqi Freedom have already raised alarm in the international community and even strained the Atlantic alliance.[14]

The Bush Doctrine: Chinese analyses

Chinese analyses of the Bush Doctrine place it within several broader contexts: the rise of neoconservatism that now dominates US foreign policy, in particular since the Bush administration came into office; the long-term American strategic objective of sustaining its primacy even to the extent of empire building; and the immediate needs and contingencies of combating global terrorism. In their view, the doctrine reinforces the overall post-cold-war objective of sustaining US dominance in international affairs. The "new world order" of the previous Bush administration, introduced right after the close of the first Gulf War and incorporating NATO expansion, promotion of marketization and democratization, and conditional engagement of emerging regional powers, was also designed to help achieve that objective. The September 11 terrorist attacks disrupted that process and necessitated a change of tactics in dealing with the new security threats. The Bush administration seized the opportunity provided by the tragic events to fight international terrorism, but also to legitimize the preemptive use of force and extend its military presence. The doctrine focuses on a number of elements, including: an emphasis on counter-proliferation and military preemption to deal with rogue states and non-state terrorist groups and the imminent threats they pose to US interests; homeland security and missile defenses; the establishment of a new world order via an integration strategy; an elevated role for nuclear weapons and a lowering of the nuclear threshold; regime change; and great-power cooperation.[15]

Chinese analysts also relate the Bush Doctrine to the neoconservative agenda of building the "new empire." They are well aware of the role of new conservatives in the current Bush administration.[16] The core of the group, as represented by the Project for a New American Century and the American Enterprise Institute, are people who have long advocated a resolute approach to foreign policy, the United States' moral responsibility for promoting and spreading democracy, and the need for preemptive action against sources of threats to US security. They are concerned with both terrorism and the rise of China.[17]

In effect, the neoconservatives are suggesting that the collapse of the Soviet Union and the consequent US unipolarity have provided the general environment for the "new empire" concept. The post-cold-war security environment has changed dramatically, and traditional approaches are inadequate in handling current challenges and threats. The United States should take advantage of its unprecedented position in the world to protect its interests and sustain unipolarity, even applying the unilateral and preemptive use of force to root out future threats. The rationales behind such a policy are straightforward: first, deterrence does not work against terrorist groups; second, since terrorist groups do not operate within the bounds of sovereign nations, the concept of sovereignty no longer applies in dealing with them; third, the United States cannot wait for terrorist groups to attack first.[18]

The Bush Doctrine also reflects what Chinese analysts consider to be the strategy of "offensive realism." This in turn is linked to the post-cold-war US global military redeployment to consolidate its continued military superiority through a revolution in military affairs (RMA).[19] The adjustment further highlights the importance of the Asia-Pacific region.[20] People's Liberation Army military analysts point out that the relocation of US military focus to Asia clearly has China as the target. The end of the cold war has left the United States with no comparable rival, and hence China's position has risen.[21] The short-term goals of the United States would be to focus on anti-terrorism and homeland security, including the use of preemption when necessary. A medium-term objective is to seek adjustments in major-power relations. However, for the long term, the goal is to maintain US dominance and promote US values.[22]

Preemption is considered part of an overhaul of post-cold-war US military strategies in the light of the new challenges it faces. Under such circumstances, the cold-war strategy of deterrence may no longer be seen as workable against non-state actors or so-called rogue states; it is natural then that preemption as a military strategy should now be introduced and adopted. The overall approach is a blend of defensive and offensive, conventional and non-conventional, and capability-based defense posture.[23] Three groups of targets stand out prominently: transnational terrorist groups, (rogue) states seeking WMD and long-range ballistic missile capabilities, and states harboring terrorist groups/organizations/activities.[24]

While most Chinese analysts strongly criticize US unilateralism, hegemonism, and preemptive use of force, some point out that such behavior is also—and perhaps mainly—driven by the requirements of anti-terrorism and is not aimed at China. The United States in this view has not given up its traditional strategies of containment and deterrence, and preemption is not aimed at other major powers. Indeed, some of the concerns that drive US policy—such as the Korean nuclear issue and the roots of international terrorism—are also shared by China. In other words, there is a need to differentiate between proposed strategies and actual policy practices.[25] In addition, unilateralism and preemption may encounter both domestic and international criticism, and the fact that Washington needs cooperation with other major powers would seem certain to modify the extent of the execution of the Bush Doctrine.[26]

The Bush Doctrine: implications for China

Arms issues

Chinese reaction to the Bush Doctrine is by and large negative. However, with regard to the exact targets of the doctrine and how it affects China's security interests, there are different views. To some extent, the latter is also predicated on the state of Sino-US relations and their respective foreign-policy agendas at a particular moment. A much improved bilateral relationship since 9/11 provides some cushion against the immediate impact of the Bush Doctrine on China.[27] For the longer term, though, two issues are of relevance. One is the impact of a prolonged US unipolarity and military dominance not only on the international system, but also on international organizations in which China can potentially play a critical role, and on major-power relations. The other is the sustainability of the Bush

Doctrine. The latest developments in Iraq, at the United Nations, and within the US domestic context, all point to growing difficulties in the Bush administration's pursuit of unilateralism and its threatened use of preemption.

Nonetheless, there are serious implications for China in the Bush Doctrine. US nuclear policy and missile defenses could touch off an arms race and directly threaten Chinese security interests. Washington's policy toward the so-called "axis of evil" states creates instability on China's periphery. US unilateralism undermines the prospects for international cooperation, and continued US dominance is an impediment to the establishment of a multipolar world in which China could play an important role.

US nuclear policy is of considerable concern to China. The 2002 US Nuclear Posture Review (NPR), a portion of which was leaked to the media, contains contingency plans to use nuclear weapons against seven countries, including Russia and China.[28] Chinese strategic analysts focus particularly on what they consider as fundamental shifts in the post-cold-war US strategic posture. One is the nuclear threshold. In the past, nuclear weapons were always the weapon of last resort, for deterrence against another state's use of nuclear weapons. However, the new posture suggests the use of nuclear weapons against hardened, difficult-to-penetrate targets, and as retaliation against WMD use by others. Perhaps the most serious concern to Beijing is the potential nuclear use "in the event of surprising military developments," including a war between China and Taiwan.[29]

The NPR calls for a new strategic triad of conventional and unconventional offensive systems, active and passive defenses, and defense industrial infrastructure, aimed at preserving US military dominance and absolute security. Indeed, the US would retain massive retaliatory capabilities against other nuclear powers even after significant cuts in its nuclear arsenals. At the same time, it will also strive for continued conventional superiority, and support the research and development of low-yield "mini-nukes" that would enable it to confront and neutralize threats from the so-called "rogue" states in addition to maintaining credible deterrence against other powers.[30]

With this context, US ballistic missile defenses become even more relevant for Chinese strategic thinking. The bottom line is how US missile defense systems will affect China's core national security interests, in particular the extent to which the US defense posture could undermine the credibility and effectiveness of China's small-size nuclear retaliatory capabilities. How would this affect the outcome of a showdown over Taiwan? Beijing's concerns are obvious. As the PRC has only thirty or so intercontinental ballistic missiles (ICBMs), US missile defense systems, once deployed, could remove China's limited second-strike capabilities. One prominent Chinese missile defense analyst suggests that "China fears that if the USA believes that a first nuclear strike plus a NMD [national missile defense] system could render impotent China's nuclear retaliatory capability, the USA might become less cautious during any crisis involving China."[31] That crisis, in most instances, would be over Taiwan.

Chinese officials and analysts are also concerned about the negative impact that US missile defenses would have on the international security environment and progress in arms control and nonproliferation.[32] The US withdrawal from the ABM Treaty has the potential to undermine the global strategic balance. The ABM Treaty maintained a rough balance between US and Soviet/Russian strategic nuclear forces, reducing the incentives for any preemptive first strike and therefore sustaining stability.[33] For this reason, Hu Xiaodi, the Chinese ambassador for disarmament, argued that the ABM Treaty's "significance is far beyond the scope of the US–Russian bilateral relationship and has a direct bearing on the security of all countries."[34] US missile defenses could touch off a new round of arms race in outer space. A January 2001 report by the Commission to Assess United States National Security Space Management and Organization calls for greater investments in science and technology resources to maintain America's superior space capabilities, which could lead to the development, testing, and deployment of anti-satellite weapons (ASAT) based in space or on earth.[35]

Lessons from Iraq and North Korea

US policy toward the so-called "rogue states" raises at least three concrete issues for China. One is the challenge to state sovereignty. The second is the potentially destabilizing effect such a policy could cause, in turn threatening Chinese security interests. The third is the erosion of international organizations such as the United Nations. The Iraqi and North Korean cases offer good examples. On the Iraqi case, while supporting the return of United Nations weapons inspections without preconditions, China has all along advocated a political settlement of the issue rather than a military solution. Chinese officials emphasize that the Iraqi issue must be resolved within the political framework of the UN system, that Baghdad should comply with all UN resolutions on weapons inspections, and that Iraq's sovereignty must be respected.

Beijing's emphasis on respecting Iraq's sovereignty even as it admonishes Baghdad to comply with all relevant UN resolutions reflects a deeply held principle. Beijing's reservations about providing UN authorization to allow US military actions in Iraq is consistent with its opposition to the use of force to settle international conflict and to interventions in other countries' domestic affairs. Indeed, China has been derided as the "vicar" of state sovereignty at a time when the traditional notion of sovereignty is being challenged and eroded as a result of growing international concerns over human rights abuses and the inevitable demands for "rights beyond borders." For China, one of the key elements in the new international order should be a continued emphasis on state sovereignty and noninterference in domestic affairs. According to one Chinese scholar: "The principle of state sovereignty is a fundamental one in international law. Sovereignty is one of the vital factors for the existence of states and an indispensable feature of the subject of international law. Any theory claiming sovereignty to be outdated is groundless."[36]

China worries about the potential for the United States to use the pretext of humanitarian intervention to challenge its sovereignty over minority regions such as Tibet and Xinjiang. US–NATO intervention in Kosovo sent a chilling warning to policy makers in Beijing that the United Nations could be bypassed and that sovereignty could be ignored and violated. The Bush administration's rhetoric about treating terrorist groups and the states that harbor them alike only heightens China's anxiety. The US military operations that toppled Saddam Hussein—actions clearly beyond the existing UN mandates on inspections—have only heightened China's concerns.

The crisis over North Korea's nuclear weapons program also demonstrates the extent to which US policy toward Pyongyang could affect Beijing's interests. China from the beginning of the crisis stated its positions on the issue: first, peace and stability on the Korean peninsula should be preserved; second, the peninsula should remain nuclear-free; and third, the dispute should be resolved through diplomatic and political methods. These positions form the core of Chinese approaches to the resolution of the nuclear issue. Chinese officials and analysts maintained that the key to resolving the crisis would be direct dialogue between North Korea and the United States. Instead of blaming North Korea for the collapse of the 1994 Agreed Framework, Beijing called for *both* Pyongyang and Washington to return to the agreement and resolve their dispute through dialogue. The Chinese hoped that face-saving ways could be found for Pyongyang and Washington to return to the negotiating table.[37]

Certainly China is wary of North Korea's reckless behavior and does not want the nuclear crisis to get out of control. At the same time, Beijing believes that Pyongyang's nuclear gamble stems from its acute sense of insecurity and vulnerability, and hence any resolution must address this issue. In this context, continued support for North Korea is no longer driven by the need to prop up an ideological bedfellow, but rather impelled by China's long-term strategic interests. China will therefore oppose any measures likely to precipitate the collapse of the North.

Beijing worries that hardline positions maintained by Pyongyang and Washington, and a resultant continued stalemate, could push North Korea to take even riskier steps. A military confrontation on the Korean peninsula would not only cause much destruction but also bring down the North Korean regime, depriving China of a strategically important buffer. The environmental devastation would be severe, and there would be a massive refugee flight into China, where already an estimated 100,000 to 300,000 North Koreans are illegal residents.[38] A hastily unified Korea following the collapse of the North Korean regime would present Beijing with tremendous uncertainty. China could face the prospect of a US military presence right up to the Chinese–Korean border. A united Korea might inherit the North's nuclear and missile capabilities, and rising Korean nationalism could also pose a challenge to Beijing's ability to manage its Korean ethnic minority in Jilin Province. Finally, there is also the specter of a nuclear chain reaction, with concerns over Japan's possible rearmament and nuclearization, using the North Korean nuclear issue as a pretext.[39]

These considerations have led China to adopt a more active diplomacy in order to forestall the potentially negative consequences. Indeed, one could argue that Beijing's efforts played no small part in getting Pyongyang to the April 2003 trilateral meeting in Beijing and in their agreeing to accept the subsequent six-party talks in late August.[40] However, while the process for engaging North Korea has been kept alive, and both China and the United States have found common ground for continued cooperation and consultation, significant differences remain between the two countries over specific approaches and long-term objectives. These differences could in future strain bilateral relations.[41]

International norms and institutions

A third potential consequence of the Bush Doctrine and its unilateral foreign policy is the erosion of international norms and institutions, which would affect China's normative interests in developing a new international order and multipolarity, and strengthening the role of international organizations such as the United Nations. This has clearly been reflected in Chinese ambivalence regarding the US-led anti-terrorism campaigns. While supporting the general goals of combating international terrorism, Beijing has strong reservations about the use of military force. Indeed, prior to US military operations in Afghanistan, Beijing had laid down several conditions to be met before it would endorse US military operations, namely, that actions should be based on "concrete evidence," should strictly observe international law, should not hurt innocent civilians, and should be carried out with authorization from the UN Security Council.[42]

Underlying this ambivalence are Chinese perspectives on the post-cold-war international order and their views on the sources of international terrorism. Chinese perspectives on the post-cold-war world revolve around consistent themes of multipolarity, a greater UN role in world affairs, state sovereignty, and noninterference in domestic affairs. China wants to be consulted on important international issues, and believes key security issues should be handled through the UN Security Council, where Beijing wields veto power as a permanent member. Given China's relatively weak but rising international position, it is natural that it should have repeatedly emphasized the importance of the principles of territorial integrity and sovereignty, and noninterference in internal affairs. Chinese officials and scholars suggest that these principles must form the basis of any new international order.

Finally, the Bush Doctrine, and its application in the name of anti-terrorism, have serious implications for long-term Chinese security interests. Chinese analysts suggest that the United States, taking advantage of the global anti-terrorism campaigns, has been pressing its set strategy of expanding influence and military presence in key regions of the world as part of its global strategy of continuing its dominance and hegemony.[43] Indeed, China is worried about the likely expansion of a US military presence closer to China's doorstep. One legacy of the first Gulf War (that of 1990–1) is an enlarged permanent US military presence in the Persian Gulf and Saudi Arabia. A US military presence along China's periphery could exert further pressure on China.[44] Military operations against Osama bin Laden in Afghanistan have already brought US armed forces to South and Central Asia, with which China shares over 3,000 kilometers of border. China also faces immediate worries about possible backlash and increasing numbers of refugees as a result of US military retaliation. High-ranking Chinese officials also warn that military retaliation could lead to an escalation of revenge begetting revenge, further aggravating terrorism and violence. The Bush administration's rhetoric about the "axis of evil" and the veiled threat to use military means to deal with such regimes only heighten China's anxiety.

China thus faces a serious dilemma in crafting its response to the US war on terrorism. On the one hand, it wants to be seen as resolute and unfailing in its political support for action against terrorism. On the other, it does not want to be closely associated with US military actions that violate state sovereignty and invite retaliation. Beijing wants to join international efforts in the fight against terrorism because international support may help it confront growing terrorist activities in support of separatist movements in Xinjiang. At the same time, China is concerned that prolonged US military operations may set precedents for future interference in domestic affairs and the further erosion of the UN's authority.[45] China wants to seize the opportunity to improve Sino-US relations, but also wants to exploit the opportunity to extract US concessions on Taiwan, missile defense, and its policy toward Xinjiang and Tibetan separatists.[46] These long-term normative and practical concerns are pitted against the more immediate challenges of crafting the right policy in a volatile situation.

Confronting the hegemon: Chinese options

Chinese pragmatism

Clearly, the Bush Doctrine undermines China's broader security interests. How Beijing reacts depends on its interests and objectives, challenges, and resources, and on the options available. However, defining Chinese national interests in an evolving international system has proved no easy task. The first issue to be addressed is the question of China's exact position: is it to be a great power of global reach, or a regional but predominant power, or merely an emerging power with acute regional interests but one that has to share the center stage with other regional, and even extra-regional, contenders?[47] Obviously, a superpower would have different national interests from one with merely regional ambitions. However, the law of uneven development would also suggest that a country's national interests are never static but are changing against the backdrops of the external environment, one's capabilities, technology, and self-evaluation.[48] China stands between being an emerging regional power and one that increasingly sees itself as the natural leader in East Asia, broadly defined.[49] But China's aspirations are obviously constrained, by its own relatively low economic base despite phenomenal growth over the past two decades, the limitation of its power projection capabilities, and, most importantly, by a predominantly Western international system. This being the case, then, Beijing's national interests must remain modest but steadfast on certain critical issues.[50]

The end of the cold war, the transformation of Eastern Europe, and the disintegration of the Soviet Union have affected China's security environment and threat perceptions in important ways. On the one hand, Sino-Soviet normalization and the continuing improvement of the Sino-Russian relationship have removed a major source of threat to China's security; on the other hand, precisely because of the demise of the Soviet Union, the ability of China to exploit its position in the strategic triangle has been greatly reduced. During the cold war, China compensated for its weakness through its alignment and realignment with either of the two superpowers. Chinese foreign policy concentrated on securing a favorable position within the constraints of superpower competition. With the end of the cold war, China finds itself increasingly on the receiving end within the emerging international strategic environment.[51] The difficulties China faced during the Gulf crisis of 1990–91 and afterward are a clear manifestation of the kind of constraints it now must encounter in formulating and implementing foreign policy at both the global and regional levels.[52] Beijing increasingly views post-cold-war uncertainties and security threats as multifaceted, less well defined, and coming from a number of sources.[53]

Obviously, China is faced with not only the opportunities that a post-cold-war environment presents, but also the challenges, some of which will determine the extent to which the opportunities can be exploited. Interestingly, with the exception of a brief period of post-Tiananmen rhetoric of self-strengthening in the aftermath of Western sanctions, the Chinese leadership endorses the China-in-an-interdependent-world line, even if the international political and economic orders are hardly of Beijing's choice. However, challenging the existing system seems out of the question.[54] The lessons drawn from the past five hundred years of struggle for hegemony seem to suggest that challengers have invariably failed; the successful leaders almost without exception have tended to be the partners of their contemporary hegemons. Obviously, given China's current position, a strategy of challenging is doomed to failure; even the perception by others of China as a challenger does more harm than good to its interests, since that would provide a pretext for the current dominating power(s) to turn to containment.[55]

This probably explains why China's foreign-policy approaches remain pragmatic even as it continues to advocate and promote the principles of equality and justice in international affairs and in the construction of a new international order. This goes back to earlier Chinese debates on the post-cold-war international geostrategic environment, and a more realistic assessment of China's own position and the constraints on what it might do. Chinese experts recognized that great powers remain an important factor, and contend that any international order is based on the existing structure of international power distribution and serves its purposes.[56] One Chinese analyst argued:

> It is a reality that countries in the world differ in size. The proposition that all countries, large or small, enjoy sovereign equality and have the right to participate in the settlement of international issues through consultation does not negate the important role big countries play in international affairs. Big countries assume special responsibilities in world affairs.[57]

Indeed, Chinese analysts have viewed the emerging international political order as composed of three pillars: the first represents the five powers (the United States, Russia, the European Union, Japan, and China); the second is the relationships between them; and third is the role of the United Nations.[58] The developments in the late 1990s and China's attempts to forestall US missile defenses also suggest a more realistic foreign-policy stance and the prioritization of diplomacy and use of limited resources.[59]

Managing relations with the United States, and the Taiwan question

Without question, managing its relationship with Washington has always been the highest priority for Beijing. That relationship also affects a number of issues important for China, in particular Taiwan.[60] Chinese scholars have identified a number of characteristics that define post-cold-war Sino-US relations.[61] First, with the end of the cold war, China's weight in the previous strategic triangle has changed, and conflicting views and interests previously concealed or relegated to second-place importance are now assuming greater salience. These contrasting views between Beijing and Washington include differences on issues having to do with the post-cold-war international political and economic order, the role of the United Nations, state sovereignty, humanitarian intervention, and regional security order. At the same time, disputes over trade, human rights, and nonproliferation have increasingly become dominant issues in bilateral relations.[62]

Second, Sino-US relations may be affected by their competing interests in the Asia-Pacific region. At issue are the future regional security architecture, with China promoting its new concept of security cooperation, and the United States continuing to emphasize the importance of military alliances, missile defense, and US–Taiwan ties. Third, ideologies and domestic politics will play a more prominent role in the two countries' foreign-policy decision making.[63] The US debates on the rise of China between the so-called "Blue Team" (which views China's emergence as a great threat to American interests) and the "Red Team" (which sees merit in China's emergence and is confident that an engagement strategy can effectively integrate China into the existing international system) are a clear example. Likewise, the nationalism aroused in the aftermath of the bombing of the Chinese embassy and the EP–3 incident in 2001 also reflect the extent to which Chinese policy makers must heed domestic sentiment in making foreign-policy decisions.[64]

Fourth, there is an imbalance between developments in political and economic relationships. While the post-Tiananmen Sino-US political relationship has remained tenuous and less stable for the reasons discussed above, the bilateral economic ties and interdependence have grown significantly over the same period. In a way, such close economic ties have prevented the occasionally strained bilateral relationship from deteriorating into one of open hostility and confrontation. However, greater economic interdependence has yet to translate into a more stable political relationship. Indeed, at times, it can exacerbate an already fragile political relationship. The pending trade disputes over steel, textiles, and consumer electronics are illustrative of this mix. Finally, despite the changing international politico-strategic environment, the management of bilateral conflicts remains important for the United States, as China is crucial in a number of areas (e.g., the role of the UN, WMD nonproliferation, South Asia, and the Korean peninsula), and Beijing's cooperation is not a foregone conclusion.[65]

Within such a context, the United States remains a major factor in Beijing's threat perception and affects its formulation of security policies. American forces in the Asia-Pacific are increasingly seen as a major obstacle to China's political and diplomatic objectives in the region, in particular its drive for national unification. The US introduction of missile defense systems into the region is also worrisome for China in two respects. It might legitimize Japan's remilitarization, and it could encourage independence elements in Taiwan. For Beijing, the April 1996 US–Japan Joint Declaration on Security and the new US–Japanese Defense Cooperation Guidelines concluded in September 1997 were unwelcome developments in East Asia, with negative effects on Chinese security interests. The continued presence of US military forces in the region, and a resilient US–Japan security alliance at a time of much reduced security threats in the region, only caused the Chinese to ponder on their true intentions and the implications for their own security. While in the past the alliance in Beijing's eyes served a useful purpose of keeping Tokyo from seeking remilitarization, it is now increasingly viewed as a security threat.[66]

Three issues stand out. First, Beijing considers the revitalized US–Japan military alliance to be part of Washington's strategy of containing China. After all, the US–Japan alliance was established during the cold war years with a clearly defined enemy and missions: namely the Soviet Union, and the defense of Japanese territories. With the end of the cold war, the raison d'être (protecting Japan from Soviet attack) no longer holds, and the rationale for its continued existence and even strengthening are unmistakably clear: China is now targeted as a potential adversary.

Second, China is extremely worried about the consequences of a more assertive Japan actively involved in the region's security affairs and seeking to be a "normal" power.[67] The new defense guidelines have in effect shifted the alliance's mission from that of defending Japan to one in which Japan will be actively involved in regional security activities. Japan already has one of the largest defense budgets in the world, and has a military that is but reasonably sized (given its peace constitution) yet is nevertheless the best-equipped one in the region. In addition, Japan's industrial and technological wherewithal will provide it with ready resources should it decide to become a military great power at short notice, including the possible acquisition of nuclear weapons.[68] The new defense cooperation guidelines in effect give Japan the green light to go beyond the original exclusive self-defense to a collective defense function, therefore providing justification for Japan to intervene in regional security affairs.[69] And finally, the guidelines could be interpreted as extending the alliance's defense perimeter to include the Taiwan Strait. China is understandably concerned about the possible intervention of the US–Japan alliance in what it regards as its internal affairs and reunification plans. Tokyo's ambiguity regarding its defense perimeter, based not on geography but on events, only heightens Beijing's anxiety.[70]

Washington's Taiwan policy is the most serious security concern for Beijing. Three trends are particularly disturbing for the Chinese leadership. The first is US deviation from the "One China" principle set forth in the three Sino-US joint communiqués. In recent years, the United States has steadily upgraded its supposedly unofficial ties with Taiwan. High-ranking Taiwanese officials have been granted visas to make transit stops on their way to Central and South America. The second trend is continuing US military sales to Taiwan; these are seen by China as contravening the spirit of the August 17, 1982 Sino-US Communiqué.[71] Over the two decades since the communiqué was issued, the United States has provided Taiwan with a full spectrum of military equipment, including F-16 air superiority fighters, Knox-class frigates, Kidd-class destroyers, anti-submarine S-2T, E-2T "Hawkeye" airborne early-warning aircraft, long-range early-warning radars, attack helicopters, Patriot-derived Modified Air Defense Systems, and "Hawk" and "Chaparral" ground-based air defense systems, among others. The US Department of Defense also runs exchange programs with Taiwan on C4I, air defense, and anti-submarine warfare (ASW).[72]

Third and finally, there have been incessant congressional efforts not only to enhance the US–Taiwan relationship, as is manifest in the Taiwan Relations Act (TRA) of 1979, but also to expand it to include closer security cooperation.[73] The 1999 Taiwan Security Enhancement Act, which was passed in the House of Representatives in a landslide vote, would require even closer defense cooperation between the United States and Taiwan in the areas of defense planning, threat analysis, training programs, and missile defense systems, all of which have been strongly opposed by Beijing.[74] The establishment of the Taiwan caucuses in the US Senate and the House of Representatives are the latest development. In recent years, the United States has steadily upgraded its supposedly unofficial ties with Taiwan. China's strong objections to missile defense coverage of Taiwan therefore are based on the following three reasons: it would encourage Taiwan independence; it would lead to a de facto Taiwan–US security alliance; and it would interfere with China's unification objectives. According to Ambassador Sha Zukang, "TMD in Taiwan will give the pro-independence forces in Taiwan a false sense of security, which may incite them to reckless moves. This can only lead to instability across the Taiwan Strait or even in the entire North-East Asian region."[75]

The Bush administration's evolving China policy hence affects how Beijing assesses the impact of the Bush Doctrine on its security interests.[76] The Bush administration has been critical of the Clinton approaches to US China policy. There are at least three areas of major policy differences. First, instead of viewing China as a "strategic partner," the Bush administration has characterized its relationship with China as more complex, where the two countries can cooperate on certain issues but are likely to compete on others. During the presidential campaigns, candidate Bush on several occasions even referred to China as America's "strategic competitor."[77]

Second, the Bush administration has moved away from a Taiwan policy anchored in "strategic ambiguity." The Clinton administration tilted toward a more explicit "One China" position expressed in the "three no's"—no to Taiwan independence; no to one China, one Taiwan; and no support of Taiwan membership in international organizations where statehood is required. However, Bush administration officials have emphasized American obligations under the Taiwan Relations Act, a strong preference for peaceful resolution of the Taiwan issue, and explicit opposition to coercion and the use of force. Washington has made its commitment to defend Taiwan from an attack by the mainland very clear. In this regard, Bush's controversial statement of "whatever it takes" to help defend Taiwan has deeper philosophical underpinnings shared by a number of high-ranking Bush administration officials.[78] Indeed, the past few years have seen increasing interactions between high-level Taiwanese and US officials, including those between the two militaries. Transit stops granted to Taiwan President Chen Shui-bian and Vice President Annette Lu are also more frequent than during the Clinton administration. Washington has also openly supported Taiwan's bid to join the World Health Organization.[79]

Third, the Bush administration has adopted firmer tactics in dealing with China. The administration will seek Beijing's cooperation where it can, but will also be firm in dealing with China when necessary. Unlike the Clinton administration, the Bush administration will not subordinate concerns over specific issues to the broader goal of preserving the overall bilateral relationship. A good example is in the nonproliferation area. Whereas the Clinton administration sought to use the threat of sanctions as leverage to change Chinese behavior, the Bush administration has used sanctions to penalize Chinese companies and individuals for alleged nonproliferation violations. Indeed, the Clinton administration imposed sanctions against China twice during the entire eight years it was in office, but the Bush administration has already done so nine times.[80] The Bush administration is determined not to allow China to get away with what it considers to be irresponsible behavior.

The 9/11 terrorist attacks on the United States have been a turning point in Sino-US relations. Changes in US priorities following the terrorist attacks provided a "strategic window of opportunity" for rebuilding a tattered bilateral relationship.[81] The Bush administration's international focus is now on the war against terrorism, not on the possibility of a future challenge from China. Washington is seeking cooperation with major powers. Chinese analysts recognize that the challenge for Beijing will be to maximize the benefits and minimize other negative impacts, such as the growing US global military presence and a possible preemptive use of force.[82] How China's security interests will be affected will depend on US domestic politics and foreign policy in the coming years.[83] For the time being at least, common interests in fighting global terrorism and defusing the North Korean nuclear crisis have seen Beijing and Washington enjoy a period of a stable relationship. However, Chinese analysts point out that the new Chinese leadership faces serious challenges in the coming years. Handling these challenges will require that China maintain a stable working relationship with the United

States to advance China's interests. Certainly Beijing should not seek confrontation with Washington. To challenge US unipolarity would only reinforce the position of the "China threat" advocates in the US government.[84] As a result, China's responses to US dominance have remained low-key, and focus on key areas of fundamental security interests such as Taiwan. At the same time, Beijing is seeking opportunities to expand cooperation with the United States to advance its short- to medium-term interests, which are continued economic development and the strengthening of comprehensive national power.[85]

Assuming that unipolarity will remain a fact of life in international politics for some time to come, the primary goals of Chinese foreign policy will be to sustain a benign international environment for the development and strengthening of China's power. China will oppose hegemony but at the same time avoid direct confrontation with the United States. Unilateralism and preemption, while deplorable, are not directly targeted at China, and therefore confronting unipolar hegemonism should not be China's strategic priority. China's security interests are better served by its seeking and developing a strategic dialogue with the United States to reduce mistrust and better address China's security concerns.[86] Beijing's efforts to cooperate with Washington on the North Korean nuclear and anti-terrorism issues, and its participation in the US Container Security Initiative, are guided by such a recognition.[87]

Conclusion

The Bush Doctrine has generated much controversy since its inception and implementation in Iraq. While the underlying rationale for adopting such a unilateralist and confrontational approach is well documented, and indeed administration officials and supporters have gone out of their way in their assurance that the doctrine supplements rather than replaces traditional approaches to security, its impact has been largely negative: it has alienated many members of the international community and deeply concerned others.

Beijing faces a serious challenge. On the one hand, the Bush Doctrine clearly affects Chinese interests in potentially negative ways. US unilateralism erodes and undermines international norms and institutions, and is contrary to principles that China holds dear. These include state sovereignty and multipolarity, and a more prominent role for the United Nations, through which Beijing expects to be consulted and through which it can exert its influence. Unilateral pursuit of absolute US security by abrogating the ABM Treaty and moving forward with ballistic missile defenses directly threatens the credibility of China's limited nuclear deterrence. Missile defenses in East Asia further complicate Beijing's unification agenda and encourage Japanese remilitarization. US handling of the North Korean nuclear crisis creates uncertainty and proliferation risks in China's periphery. Beijing's more active diplomacy in defusing the crisis and jump-starting a dialogue process has been largely driven by the very real concern that Washington's approach to the so-called rogue states may only worsen the situation, which in turn could have a seriously negative impact on Chinese security interests.

While Beijing has a very negative view of the Bush Doctrine, its responses have been more measured, low-key, and pragmatic than some analysts have expected. China recognizes its own limitations and the need to avoid direct confrontation with the United States. At the same time, there is also the recognition that the application of the Bush Doctrine will be limited in scope and will apply to only a few exceptional cases, simply because such a posture cannot be sustained long in the face of domestic and international opposition. Beijing seized the opportunity provided by the changing focus of US security policy in the wake of 9/11 to expand areas of common interest while minimizing the impact of differences. To a significant extent, how the Bush Doctrine affects China's interests in future will depend on how well the two manage their increasingly complex relationship.

Notes

1. Robert B. Zoellick, "A Republican Foreign Policy," *Foreign Affairs*, Vol. 79, No. 1 (January–February, 2000), pp. 63–78.
2. These views are fully explored in Robert Kagan and William Kristol, eds., *Present Dangers: Crisis and Opportunity in American Foreign and Defense Policy* (San Francisco: Encounter Books, 2000). For a general assessment of the Bush administration foreign policy at midterm, see Ivo H. Daalder and James M. Lindsay, *America Unbound: The Bush Revolution in Foreign Policy* (Washington, DC: The Brookings Institution, 2003); "Bush at Midterm," *Foreign Affairs*, Vol. 82, No. 5 (September–October, 2003); "Grading the President," *Foreign Policy*, No. 137 (July–August, 2003), pp. 28–41.
3. Daalder and Lindsay, *America Unbound*.
4. "President Delivers State of the Union Address," January 29, 2002, online at www.whitehouse.gov/news/releases/2002/01/20020129/11.html.
5. The White House, "President Bush Delivers Graduation Speech at West Point," June 1, 2002; emphasis added.
6. President George W. Bush's preface to the *National Security Strategy of the United States of America* (hereafter *NSS*), September 2002.
7. Ibid., pp. 14, 15.
8. Jason D. Ellis, "The Best Defense," *The Washington Quarterly*, Vol. 26, No. 2 (Spring, 2003), pp. 115–33.
9. Thomas Donnelly, "The Underpinnings of the Bush Doctrine," *National Security Outlook*, American Enterprise Institute, January 31, 2003, online at www.aei.org/publications/pubID.15845/pub_detail.asp.
10. "Anticipatory Defense in the War on Terror: Interview with Condoleezza Rice," *New Perspectives Quarterly*, Vol. 19, No. 4 (Fall, 2002), online at www.digitalnpq.org/archive/2002_fall/rice.html.
11. For a strong criticism of the Bush administration foreign policy, see Clyde Prestowitz, *Rogue Nation: American Unilateralism and the Failure of Good Intentions* (New York: Basic Books, 2003).
12. James J. Wirtz and James A. Russell, "US Policy on Preventive War and Preemption," *The Nonproliferation Review*, Vol. 10, No. 1 (Spring, 2003), p. 113. See also Walter Slocomb, "Force, Preemption and Legitimacy," *Survival*, Vol. 45, No. 1 (Spring, 2003), pp. 117–30.
13. Wirtz and Russell, "US Policy on Preventive War and Preemption," p. 118.
14. Ivo H. Daalder, "The End of Atlanticism," *Survival*, Vol. 45, No. 2 (Summer, 2003), pp. 147–66.
15. Zhongguo xiandai guoji guanxi yanjiusuo (China Institute of Contemporary International Relations), *Guoji zhanlüe yu anquan xingshi pinggu: 2002/2003* [Assessment of International Strategic and Security Situations: 2002/2003] (Beijing: Shishi chubanshe [Current Affairs Publishers], 2003), pp. 18–41; Fu Mengzi, "'Yichao' xunmeng: meiguo weilai dazhanlüe ['The Sole Superpower' Pursuing Its Dreams: America's Future Grand Strategy]," *Liaowang* [Outlook Weekly], March 24, 2003, pp. 12–17.

16. Ren Xiao and Shen Dingli, eds., *Baoshou zhuyi linian yu meiguo de waijiao zhengce* [Conservatism and US Foreign Policy] (Shanghai: Sanlian shudian, 2003).
17. Zhang Jianjing, "*Xinbaoshou zhuyi chongji zhongmei guanxi* [The Impact of Neo-Conservatism on Sino-US Relations]," Guangzhou *Nanfeng Chuang*, August 1, 2003, pp. 12–15, FBIS-CPP20030812000028.
18. Zhang Yao, "'*Xindiguo lun' pingxi* [On 'New Empire']," *Shijie jingji yu zhengzhi* [World Economics and Politics], no. 7 (2003), pp. 33–8; Ruan Zongze, "'*Xindiguolun' yu meiguo 'zhenghe waijiao'* [The 'New Empire' and US Policy of 'Integration']," *Meiguo yanjiu* [American Studies], no. 3 (2002), pp. 36–49.
19. Jin Canrong, "*Meiguo: daodi nengzou duoyuan* [The US: How Far Can It Go]?" *Shijie zhishi* [World Affairs], no. 11 (2003), pp. 34–6.
20. *Shijie zhishi* [World Affairs], "*Forum: Meiguo quanqiu junli chongxin bushu* [US Global Military Re-Deployment]," No. 14 (2003), pp. 20–28.
21. Han Xudong and Wei Konghu, "*Tuoshi meiguo junshi zhanlüe datiaozheng* [An Analysis of Major Adjustments in US Military Strategies]," *Liaowang* [Outlook Weekly], May 1, 2001, pp.58–9; Wu Qingli, "*Meiguo yatai zhanlüe maotou zhixiangshui* [To Whom Is US Asia-Pacific Strategy Aimed]?" *Liaowang*, pp. 60–61.
22. Yang Jiemian, "*Meiguo de quanqiu zhanlüe he zhongguo de zhanlüe jiyuqi* [US Global Strategy and China's Strategic Opportunity]," *Guoji wenti yanjiu* [International Studies], March 2003, pp. 11–16.
23. Li Jingzhi, "*Quebao bentu anquan, jiasu zhanlüe tiaozheng* [Ensure Homeland Security, Speed Up Strategic Adjustments]," *Dangdai shijie* [Contemporary World], December 2002, pp. 4–5; Su Bei, "*Bushi weihe na junshizhanlüe kaidao* [Why Does Bush Undertake Surgery on Military Strategy]?" *Jiefangjun bao* [Liberation Army Daily], June 24, 2002.
24. Shen Dingli, "*Meiguo zouxiang 'xian fazhiren' zhanlüe* [The US Embarks on a Strategy of 'Preemption']," *Jiefang ribao* [Liberation Daily], June 28, 2002, p. 22.
25. Yang Jiemian, "*Meiguo guojia anquan zhanlüe*"; Wang Yiwei, "*Zai tuoxie yu jinqu zhijian* [Between Compromises and Advances]," *Zhongguo pinglun* [China Review], August 2003, pp. 16–18.
26. Su Ge, "*Lun meiguo guojia anquan zhanlüe de tiaozheng* [On Adjustments in US National Security Strategy]," *Guoji wenti yanjiu* [International Studies], No. 2 (2003), pp. 5–10, 22.
27. Jia Qingguo, "The Impact of 9/11 on Sino-US Relations: A Preliminary Assessment," *International Relations of the Asia-Pacific*, Vol. 3, No. 2 (August, 2003), pp. 159–77.
28. Paul Richter, "US Works Up Plan for Using Nuclear Arms," *Los Angeles Times*, March 9, 2002, online ed.; William M. Arkin, "Secret Plan Outlines the Unthinkable," *Los Angeles Times*, March 10, 2002, online ed.
29. Zhu Feng, "*Meiguo zhunbei fadong hegongji* [Is the US Prepared to Launch a Nuclear Attack]?" *Zhongguo ribao wangzhan*, March 11, 2002, online at www1.chinadaily.com.cn/worldrep/2002-03-11/20220.html; interviews with Chinese security analysts, March 2002, Beijing and Shanghai.
30. See Zhou Jianshe, "*Meiguo xin anquan zhanlüe*"; Zhu Qiangguo, "*Meiguo heweishe zhanlüe de tiaozheng—hetaishi shenyi baogao pingxi* [Readjustment of US Strategy of Nuclear Deterrence—An Analysis of the Nuclear Posture Review]," *Xiandai guoji guanxi* [Contemporary International Relations], No. 148 (February, 2002), pp. 28–31; Zhu Qiangguo, "US Seeks Absolute Military Superiority," *China Daily*, March 13, 2002; Zhou Jianguo, "Nuclear Strategy of Bush Administration Moving Gradually From Deterrence to Actual Combat," *Jiefangjun bao* [PLA Daily], March 18, 2002.
31. Li Bin, "The Effects of NMD on Chinese Strategy," *Jane's Intelligence Review* (March, 2001).
32. "PRC: Transcript of Sha Zukang's Briefing on Missile Defense on 14 Mar." FBIS-CPP 20010323000025; "*Zhongguo fandui meiguo gao guojia daodan fangyu xitong* [China Opposes US Development of National Missile Defense Systems]," *Renmin ribao* [People's Daily], overseas ed., March 15, 2001, p. 2; author interview with Chinese official, March 2002.
33. Deng Hao, "*Fandao tiaoyue qianjing shenyou* [Dire Prospects for the ABM Treaty]," *Renmin ribao wangluoban* [People's Daily Online], July 7, 2000.
34. "Statement by H.E. Mr. Hu Xiaodi, Ambassador for Disarmament Affairs of China at the Plenary of the Conference on Disarmament," February 15, 2001, Geneva.

35 *Report of the Commission to Assess United States National Security Space Management and Operation.* Executive Summary (January 11, 2001).
36 Wang Jiafu, "International Law and a New International Order," paper presented at the Beijing Symposium on a New International Order, September 2–4, 1991, p. 3; quoted in David Armstrong, "Chinese Perspectives on the New World Order," *Journal of East Asian Affairs*, Vol. 8, No. 2 (Summer–Fall, 1994), p. 471.
37 Bates Gill and Andrew Thompson, "A Test for Beijing: China and the North Korean Nuclear Quandary," *Arms Control Today*, Vol. 33, No. 4 (May, 2003), online at www.armscontrol.org/act/2003_05/gillthompson_may03.asp; Jing-dong Yuan, "China and the North Korean Nuclear Crisis," Center for Nonproliferation Studies, January 22, 2003, at http://cns.miis.edu/research/korea/chidprk.htm.
38 "North Korean Refugees in China: The Current Situation and Strategies for Protection," testimony by Joel R. Charny, Vice President for Policy, Refugees International, to the Senate Committee on Foreign Relations, November 4, 2003, at http://foreign.senate.gov/testimony/2003/CharnyTestimony031104.pdf.
39 Wang Yong and Teng Hongwei, "*Jingti dongya xinlengzhan* [Beware of a New Cold War in East Asia]."
40 Willy Wo-Lap Lam, "Beijing's New Urgency over N Korea," *CNN.com*, July 30, 2003; Jing-dong Yuan, "A Turning Point for Beijing," *International Herald Tribune*, September 2, 2002, p.6, online at www.iht.com/articles/108434.html.
41 Phillip C. Saunders, "US–China Relations in a Changing Nuclear Environment," in Jonathan D. Pollack, ed., *Sino-American Strategic Dynamics in the Early 21st Century: Prospects, Scenarios, and Implications* (Newport: Naval War College Press, 2003), forthcoming.
42 John Pomfret, "China Offers Help—With Conditions," *Washington Post*, September 18, 2001.
43 Liu Jianfei, "Terrorism And Hegemonism Harm World," *China Daily*, March 15, 2003.
44 Liu Jianfei, "*Gouzhu chengshu de zhongmei guanxi* [Developing a Mature Sino-US Relationship]," *Liaowang* [Outlook Weekly], June 2, 2003, pp. 10–11.
45 Denny Roy, "China and the War on Terrorism," *Orbis*, Vol. 46, No. 3 (Summer, 2002), pp. 511–21.
46 Associated Press, "China Hints Its Muslim Separatists Fair Targets in War on Terror," October 10, 2001.
47 Yu Xilai and Wu Zichen, "*Shijie xinchixu yu xinxing daguo de lishi jueze* [The New World Order and the Historical Choice of Rising Powers]," *Zhanlüe yu guanli* [Strategy and Management], No.2 (1998), pp. 1–13.
48 Yan Xuetong, "*Guojia liyi de panduan* [How to Evaluate National Interests]," *Zhanlüe yu guanli*, No. 3 (1996), pp. 35–44.
49 Xin Qi, "'*Zhongguoquan*'—*yige lilun yu xianshi de chuxing* [The 'China Circle'—An Underdeveloped Theory versus Reality]," *Zhanlüe yu guanli*, No. 3 (1996), pp. 1–7.
50 Chu Shulong, "*Quanmian jianshe xiaokang shiqi de zhongguo waijiao zhanlüe* [China's Diplomatic Strategy for the Period of Building a Well-Off Society in an All-Round Way]," *Shijie jingji yu zhengzhi* [World Economics and Politics], No. 8 (August, 2003), pp. 8–13.
51 William T. Tow, "China and the International Strategic System," in Thomas W. Robinson and David Shambaugh, eds., *Chinese Foreign Policy: Theory and Practice* (Oxford: Clarendon Press, 1994), pp. 115–57.
52 Yitzhak Shichor, "China and the Gulf Crisis: Escape from Predicaments," *Problems of Communism*, Vol. 40, No. 6 (November–December, 1991), pp. 80–90.
53 Wang Jisi, "Comparing Chinese and American Conceptions of Security," *NPCSD Working Paper* No.17 (Toronto: North Pacific Cooperative Security Dialogue: Research Programme, York University, September 1992), p.16.
54 Yan Xuetong, "*Zhongguo jueqi de keneng xuanzi* [The Rise of China and Its Choice of Strategies]," *Zhanlüe yu guanli*, No. 6 (1995), pp. 11–14.
55 Shi Yinhong, "*Guoji zhengzhi de shijixing guilu jiqidui zhongguo de qishi* [The Law of Centurial Significance in International Relations and Its Revelance for China]," *Zhanlüe yu guanli*, No. 5 (1995), pp.

1–2. See also Wang Zaibang, "*Shijie lingdaozhe diwei jiaoti de lishi fansi* [Looking into the History of Power Changes in World Leadership]," *Zhanlüe yu guanli*, No. 6 (1995), pp. 1–5.

56 Yu Sui, "*Shijie geju yu daguo guanxi ruogan wenti tantao* [Exploration of Some Issues on the World Configuration and Big-Power Relations]," *Xiandai guoji guanxi* [Contemporary International Relations], No. 2 (February, 1998), pp. 38–44.

57 Wan Guang, "Challenges Facing the World Today and the Establishment of the New International Order," paper presented at the Beijing Symposium on a New International Order, September 2–4, 1991, p.7; quoted in David Armstrong, "Chinese Perspectives on the New World Order," *The Journal of East Asian Affairs*, Vol. 8, No. 2 (Summer–Fall, 1994), pp. 471–2.

58 Hao Runchang, "*Shijie zhengzhi xinggeju de chuxing jiqi qianjing* [The Emerging Structure of New World Political Structure and Its Prospect]," *Heping yu fazhan* [Peace and Development], No. 59 (March, 1997), pp. 1–4.

59 Jing-dong Yuan, "Chinese Responses to US Missile Defenses: Implications for Arms Control and Regional Security," *The Nonproliferation Review*, Vol. 10, No. 1 (Spring, 2003), pp. 75–96.

60 Tang Zhengduan, *Zhongmei qijuzhongde "Taiwan wenti"* [The "Taiwan Issue" on the Sino-US Chessboard] (Shanghai: Shanghai renmin chubanshe, 2000).

61 The following discussion is based on author's interview, Institute of American Studies, China Academy of Social Sciences, August 25, 1998, Beijing; Chu Shulong, *Lengzhan hou zhongmei guanxi de zuoxiang* [Sino-US Relations in the Post-Cold-War Era] (Beijing: Zhongguo shehui kexue chubanshe, 2001); Liu Xuecheng and Li Jidong, eds., *Zhongguo he meiguo: duishou haishi huoban* [China and the United States: Rivals or Partners]? (Beijing: Jingji kexue chubanshe, 2000); Jin Canrong, "*Lengzhanhou zhongmei guanxi de jiben tedian yu kuangjia* [The Basic Characteristics and Framework of Sino-US Relations Following the Cold War]," *Zhongguo Pinglun* [China Review], No. 53 (May, 2002), pp. 14–18.

62 See Bates Gill, *Contrasting Visions: United States, China, and World Order* (Washington, DC: Brookings Institution Press, forthcoming); David M. Lampton, *Same Bed, Different Dreams: Managing US–China Relations 1989–2000* (Berkeley, CA: University of California Press, 2001).

63 Robert L. Suettinger, *Beyond Tiananmen: The Politics of US–China Relations* (Washington, DC: Brookings Institution, 2003).

64 Chinese analysts notice the rise of a new conservatism in American politics and its negative impact on US China policy. See Ren and Shen, *Conservatism and US Foreign Policy*; Yuan Jian, "*Xinbaoshoupai de waijiao sixiang jiqi zai Meiguo de yingxiang* [The New Conservatives: Their Ideas and Impact on American Foreign Policy]," *Guoji wenti yanjiu* [International Studies], No. 2 (April, 1998), pp. 19–28.

65 Chu Shulong, "*Zhongmei hezuo yu fenqi* [Sino-US Relations: Cooperation and Divergence]," *Xiandai guoji guanxi*, No. 6 (June, 1998), pp. 2–6.

66 Thomas J. Christensen, "China, the US–Japan Alliance, and the Security Dilemma in East Asia," *International Security*, Vol. 23, No. 4 (Spring, 1999), pp. 49–80.

67 Lu Zhongwei, "*Riben de guojia zuoxiang yu Ri-Zhong guanxi* [Japan's Course of Direction and Its Relationship With China]," *Xiandai guoji guanxi*, (July, 2001), pp. 2–7.

68 "Opposition Leader Ozawa Says Japan Could Produce Nuclear Weapons," *Kyodo* in English, April 6, 2002. FBIS-JPP20020406000056.

69 Liang Ming, "*Ri-Mei xin fangwei jihua yinren zhumu* [The New US–Japan Defense Guidelines Attract Attention]," *PLA Daily*, December 22, 2000 (internet version).

70 Liu Jiangyong, "*Xin 'Ri-Mei fangwei hezuo zhizhen' heyi lingren youlü* [Why Do the New US–Japanese Defense Cooperation Guidelines Arouse Concern]?" *Xiandai guoji guanxi*, No. 11 (November, 1997), pp. 7–12.

71 Wei-Chin Lee, "US Arms Transfer Policy to Taiwan: from Carter to Clinton," *Journal of Contemporary China*, Vol. 9, No. 23 (March, 2000), pp. 53–75; John P. McClaran, "US Arms Sales to Taiwan: Implications for the Future of the Sino-US Relationship," *Asian Survey*, Vol. 40, No. 4 (July–August, 2000), pp. 622–40.

72 East Asia Nonproliferation Program, Center for Nonproliferation Studies, "Arms Sales to Taiwan: Statements and Developments 1979–2003," online at www.nti.org/db/china/

twnchr.htm. Additional information regarding US arms sales to Taiwan can be found at http://taiwansecurity.org/TSR-Arms.htm.
73 James Mann, "Congress and Taiwan: Understanding the Bond," in Ramon H. Myers, Michel C. Oksenberg, and David Shambaugh, eds., *Making China Policy: Lessons from the Bush and Clinton Administrations* (Lanham, Md.: Rowman & Littlefield Publishers, 2001), pp. 201–19.
74 Julian Baum, "Silent Running," *Far Eastern Economic Review,* July 1, 1999, p. 28; George Gedda, "China Warns Against Sales to Taiwan," Associated Press, October 14, 1999, at www.washingtonpost.com/wp-5…ne/19991014/aponline163839_000.htm.
75 Amb. Sha Zukang, "Some Thoughts on Non-Proliferation," statement to the Seventh Annual Carnegie International Nonproliferation Conference on Repairing the Regime, Washington, DC, January 11–12, 1999, online at www.fmprc.gov.cn/eng/4061.html.
76 Jing-dong Yuan, "Friend or Foe? The Bush Administration and US China Policy in Transition," *East Asian Review*, Vol. 15, No. 3 (Autumn, 2003), pp. 39–64.
77 For a review of candidate Bush's various policy positions regarding China, see the Council on Foreign Relations' website "Campaign 2000: the Candidates, Their Supporters & Experts Debate Foreign Policy," online at http://www.foreignpolicy2000.org/library/index.html.
78 Jane Perlez, "Bush Carries Some Baggage in Developing China Stance," *New York Times*, August 29, 1999.
79 See Robert Sutter, "Bush Administration Policy Toward Beijing and Taipei," *Journal of Contemporary China*, Vol. 12, No. 36 (August, 2003), pp. 477–92.
80 On US sanctions against China, see East Asia Nonproliferation Program, Center for Nonproliferation Studies, "Arms Control and Nonproliferation Sanctions against China," online at www.nti.org/db/china/sanct.htm.
81 Jia, "The Impact of 9/11"; David M. Lampton, "Small Mercies: China and America after 9/11," *The National Interest* (Winter 2001/2002), pp. 106–13.
82 Wang Jisi, "*Xinxingshi de zhuyao tedian he Zhongguo waijiao* [Main Characteristics of the New Situation and China's Diplomacy]," *Xiandai guoji guanxi*, No. 4 (April, 2003), pp. 1–3; Liu Jianfei, "*Zhanlüe jiyuqi yu zhongmei guanxi* [The Period of Strategic Opportunity and Sino-US Ties]," *Liaowang*, January 20, 2003, pp. 56–7; Yuan Peng, "*9.11 shijian yu zhongmei guanxi* [September 11th and Sino-US Relations]," *Xiandai guoji guanxi*, No. 11 (November, 2001), pp. 19–23, 63.
83 Adam Ward, "China and America: Trouble Ahead?" *Survival*, Vol. 45, No. 3 (Autumn, 2003), pp. 35–56.
84 Shi Yinhong, "*Zhongguo de waibu kunnan he xinlingdao jiti miandui de tiaozhan* [China's External Difficulties and Challenges Faced by the New Leadership]," *Zhanlüe yu guanli*, No. 3 (May, 2003), pp. 34–9.
85 Denny Roy, "China's Reaction to American Predominance," *Survival*, Vol. 45, No. 3 (Autumn, 2003), pp. 57–78.
86 Zheng Yu, "*Shijichu zhongguo waijiao shouyao mubiao* [The Key Objectives of China's Diplomacy at the Turn of the Century]," *Renminwang*, September 5, 2003, at www.people.com.cn/GB/paper68/10097/925403.html.
87 "Bonner Says China Will Help with Container Security," *Washington File*, US State Department, August 5, 2003.

6 The Bush Doctrine, Russia, and Korea

Alexander Zhebin

The Bush Doctrine remained almost unnoticed in Russia until the US attack on Iraq. After the war was unleashed, the concept became the object of rather heated discussions, proving the emergence of a new kind of political correctness in Russia, motivated mainly by the drastic turn in President Putin's foreign policy toward the United States and the West after the 9/11 terrorist acts. The Russian expert community and public opinion are divided on questions concerning the United States' true motives, as well as on how Russia should respond to a drastically changed international situation. There are also visible differences between the two countries' approaches to handling the North Korean nuclear crisis. Russia consistently supports preservation of the nonproliferation regime and the denuclearized status of the Korean peninsula. At the same time Moscow is strongly in favor of political and diplomatic methods, and considers any attempt to use force in Korea as an unacceptable challenge to Russia's national security.

The Bush Doctrine and Russia: a great discord

Russia's idea of a new world order

The US decision to proceed with the practical implementation of the Bush Doctrine in Iraq has caused negative reactions from the overwhelming majority of the Russian political elite and the public. That reaction was clearly indicated by President Vladimir Putin's statement on the war, in which he said that there were no formal or international legal bases for the US military action.[1] Clearly, Moscow's greatest concern was not the destiny of the Iraqi regime, but rather the "threat of the disintegration of the established system of international security." As Putin noted, if we allow "international law to be replaced by 'the law of the fist,' whereby the strong is always right and has the right to do anything and, in choosing methods to achieve its goals, is not constrained by anything, then one of the basic principles of international law will be put into question, and that is the principle of the immutable sovereignty of a state. And then no one, not a single country in the world, will feel secure."[2]

Russia realizes that today, when the threat of global nuclear conflict has sunk into the past, other global challenges have assumed center stage: international terrorism, the proliferation of weapons of mass destruction (WMD), drug and human trafficking, organized crime, trade in illegal weapons, financial, economic and other crimes, and threats to the environment and health. At the same time, Russia is firmly convinced that only a multilateral search for solutions to the problems facing the world community can be successful. The 9/11 terrorist acts in the United States demonstrated to the world community most acutely the necessity to meet the new challenges jointly and to give global processes a controlled character.

Russia believes that the new world order should be multipolar, reflecting the existence in the world of different centers of influence. This would require, of course, serious efforts to harmonize interests and work out a common strategy for dealing with international problems. The new world order should be based on the broadest kind of multilateral cooperation. This presupposes the need for a close coordination of the operations of different international structures. There is no reasonable alternative to multilateral cooperation and the strengthening of international law and order, including a central role for the UN. The only question is how to find a practical solution to this problem, which would take into account the legitimate interests of all states.

The long-term objectives of countering these global threats and challenges, which, in particular, were vividly manifested in the setting up of the worldwide antiterrorist coalition, objectively outweigh unilateral approaches, which are frequently based only on ad hoc tactical interests. The building of a new world order is inseparably connected with the necessity of raising the effectiveness of the existing multilateral mechanisms and institutions, in the first place the United Nations.

The same holds for improvements in the international legal order. On the one hand, international law never was nor could it be a frozen compendium of rules, established once and for all. At the same time, it is absolutely necessary that it should develop on the basis of concerted approaches and lead to a strengthening, not an undermining, of international legality. Otherwise we shall encounter attempts by states to ensure their security by way of force, including through the acquisition of WMD.[3]

When Russia speaks of the creation of new WMD nonproliferation and arms-control regimes, this by no means implies the renunciation of the existing regimes and agreements. They are our common protective mechanism, highly reliable and time-tested. An unjustified destruction of the key elements of the international legal structure of nonproliferation can aggravate the military-strategic situation in the world and undermine global security. Moreover, it is necessary to secure the universalizing of the major treaties on the nonproliferation of nuclear weapons and on a comprehensive nuclear test ban.[4]

Russia and the United States

At the same time, Moscow is not at all interested in returning to the old days of confrontation with the United States. Defending the logic of avoiding a new cold war, Russian Foreign Minister Igor Ivanov said:

What does it mean to break up a partnership? Two options are possible: either to expand international legal cooperation and strengthen its legal foundations so that they would be more difficult to violate even for such a powerful state as the United States, or to slide into a confrontation and to divide the world into opposing blocs. And that would be a repeat of the cold war, only still worse. What meets the interests of Russia is the development of multilateral cooperation and the involvement of all the states, even those that are violating international law today, in these processes.[5]

Well before the end of the US military operation in Iraq, Moscow let it be known that Russia intended to continue its strategic partnership with Washington, having declared that Russia is cooperating and will cooperate in the future with the United States in solving any problems, including those of a global character. One of the reasons was the necessity to solve jointly the problem of the nonproliferation of WMD and the means of their delivery. This problem cannot be solved without positive cooperation and interaction between the United States and Russia. The same can be said about the need to strengthen the United Nations and to consider formation of a new architecture of global security in the 21st century. This also concerns the solution of the economic problems facing Russia.[6]

Russia reaffirmed this policy at the Putin–Bush summit meetings in St. Petersburg in June 2003 and at Camp David in September 2003. In a joint statement adopted at St. Petersburg, both leaders pledged to work together to advance stability, security, and prosperity for their people, and to work jointly to counter global challenges and help resolve regional conflicts. They also reaffirmed the two nations' partnership and promised to intensify efforts to confront the global threats of terrorism and the proliferation of WMD and their means of delivery, which threaten their populations and freedom-loving people around the world.[7] President Putin noted with satisfaction that the "fundamental bases of Russian–American relations have proved to be stronger than the complexities with which we have been faced recently." He added that the summit positively confirmed that "there is no alternative to Russian–American cooperation either from the viewpoint of ensuring the national interests of our countries or in terms of the tasks of bolstering international peace and security." Putin believes that the Russian–American partnership may "rally the world community in the face of new threats and challenges."[8]

The course was confirmed during Putin's visit to the United States in September 2003 and his talks with George Bush. The presidents agreed on the next steps in a number of areas to strengthen the existing US–Russia partnership. They issued specific instructions to their respective governments identifying tasks to be undertaken by the appropriate agencies and specifying timelines for doing so, and they underscored their shared intention to monitor fulfillment of these tasks, including strengthening consultation and cooperation in dealing with regional problems such as, as one can conclude from the Joint Statement, the situations in the Middle East and North Korea.[9]

S. Karaganov, the chairman of the influential nongovernmental Council on External and Defense Policy, believes that the Bush administration's overall objective is the modernization—certainly in the American interest and in the American manner—of many of the so-called failed states. He shares an opinion, often expressed in the United States, that in the modern world there is a large group of countries that not only are not capable of providing a normal life for their people but also are the source of threats such as instability, terrorism, religious fundamentalism, and drug trafficking. He describes such states as "political Chernobyls" and calls on Russia to join the American strategy and even to begin to act as, so to speak, the US's regional agent. According to him, Russia's geopolitical position at the frontiers of this huge region of instability makes it a very important power (in partnership with the United States) from the point of view of influencing the region.[10]

Karaganov's ideas and the proposals of other experts with similar views on the matter were presented in a confidential report compiled on the eve of Putin's visit to the United States. The document openly calls for establishing a "strategic alliance" with the United States, and goes as far as advocating Russia's compliance with US military dominance in the world.[11] At the same time, some Russian observers believe that at the press conference that reported on the results of the Bush–Putin negotiations in Camp David, both leaders "exchanged courtesies, but failed to present anything new." Pointing to the fact that the presidents "have not uttered a word about any new steps along the way of strategic rapprochement," these experts started to speak about "stagnation" in Russian–US relations.[12]

They mentioned that three days prior to the talks with Bush, President Putin, while in New York, refused to comment on the Russian position on the future UN Security Council resolution on Iraq, saying only that the two presidents would discuss it at Camp David. However, as was revealed later, they failed to come to an agreement on the matter. Putin declared that "a degree, a level of participation in the restoration of Iraq by Russia will be determined after it becomes clear what will be the parameters of the future possible resolution." The main result of the visit was a confirmation that relations remain friendly and that the parties do not want to spoil them, according to the editor-in-chief of *Russia in Global Politics*, Feodor Luk'janov. "But so far it is impossible to fill partnership with the concrete contents," *Vedomosty* wrote.[13]

Divided views about Russian foreign policy

So it is too early to say that we are beyond the period of Russian–American disagreements, so openly demonstrated in connection with the US attack on Iraq. In Russia, behind a facade of official political correctness, heated arguments proceed concerning the United States' true aims, as well as the policy that Russia should adhere to in the drastically changed international situation. Some observers noted that the discussion conducted on this occasion has shown once again that in Russia there is no national consensus on the fundamentals of the country's foreign policy.[14]

Some researchers believe that the growth of anti-Americanism in Russian society and among the political elite in connection with US actions in Iraq was caused by the fact that Russia's resolute turn toward the United States and the West after 9/11 was not followed by reciprocal steps that could be considered adequate when presented to Russian public opinion. At the same time the former head of the Soviet intelligence service, General L. Shebarshin, has called "an illusion" the hopes of those in Russia who expect any compensation from the United States for Russia's "good behavior."[15]

According to the Chairman of the Defense Committee of the Russian State Duma, General A. Nikolaev, the reliance of the United States and some other countries on the use of force to resolve international problems "will not promote international stability but, on the contrary, will undermine international legal restrictions on arms races."[16] His opinion is supported by Shebarshin, who believes that events in Iraq will result "in acceleration of the development of their own nuclear weapons in Iran, the DPRK, and a number of other countries."[17] Both retired generals pointed out that the United States, when carrying out its new strategy, is ready to act resolutely only against weak opponents when the probability of achieving full success is close to 100 percent. Those states that suspect that they are on the US target list will get the message and will undertake the appropriate measures.[18] General Nikolaev also noted that, under these circumstances, "civilized countries at a regional level" have no option but to follow the US example, thus hinting that Russia reserves the right to resort to the same methods for establishing order on the perimeter of its borders.[19]

The Russian media doubt the Bush Doctrine's official aims—the struggle against the threat of terrorism and WMD proliferation. The influential *Nezavisimaya Gazeta*, commenting on the US decision to relocate troops to bases in a number of East European countries, considers the move as Washington's "cold shower" for Moscow. The newspaper ironically noted that this step was made when Russian politicians had just concluded enthusiastic speeches concerning "constructive cooperation" between Russia and NATO on the occasion of the May session of the Russia–NATO Council. In this connection, the newspaper openly accused Russian Foreign Minister Ivanov and some Russian generals of engaging "in a fruitless fuss about mythical cooperation with the [NATO] alliance in the field of non-strategic WMD" instead of putting on the forum's agenda problems that are really important for Moscow. Regarding as mistakes Russia's decisions to withdraw its peacekeeping contingent from the Balkans and to leave bases in Cuba and Vietnam, the newspaper came to the conclusion that Russian diplomacy was "doomed to hand over one position after another."[20]

Russian observers recognize that nowadays nobody can challenge the United States, whose actions in Iraq have brought to the forefront the concept of a unipolar world. However, estimations of the prospects of the Bush administration's international strategy are rather pessimistic. *Mezhdunarodnaya Zhizn*, a monthly journal that reflects the views of the Russian foreign policy establishment, asserts that US "global responsibility" in the long term will result in America's dispersion of its military and economic forces and an increase of anti-American feelings that will cause "a new wave" of international terrorism against the United States.[21]

When commenting on President Putin's visit to the United States in September

2003, both left- and right-wing politicians in Russia were rather skeptical about statements about the "equal-rights partnership" allegedly reached between Moscow and Washington. Russian communists pointed out that Putin had to make a show, claiming that the partnership existed while Russia was being encircled by US military bases. On the opposite side of the political spectrum, Boris Nemtsov, a leader of the "Union of Right-wing Forces," pointed out that Russia will never be considered an equal partner until it has 40 million poor people and 17 multimillionaires.[22]

Russia in Asia

In Asia, as well as on a global scale, Russia strives to contribute to the shaping of a democratic system of interstate relations, on the basis of joint responsibility and a recognition of the dominant role of the principle of multilateralism, in the name of further strengthening the central, coordinating role of the UN and ensuring priority to the principles of international law. However, whereas when addressing the West, Russia emphasizes its adherence to universally recognized principles of freedom, democracy, law and order, and the observance of fundamental human rights—as well as the identity of Russian and Western approaches to a peaceful resolution of urgent world problems—in the East, it is more inclined to take into account the concrete concerns of countries located in the region. These features of Russian policy were rather explicitly presented during Indonesian President Sukarnoputri's visit to Russia in April 2003 and President Putin's visit to Malaysia in August 2003.[23] Taking into account the negative reaction to the US invasion of Iraq in a number of Asian countries, Moscow did not fail to emphasize that Russia, as well as the majority of the countries of the region, opposed any form of intervention in the internal affairs of sovereign states, and did not accept attempts to undermine their territorial integrity under any pretext.[24]

A number of Russian analysts believe that, despite public US assurances of partnership, Washington deliberately took the course of excluding Russia from the settlement of important military-political and economic problems in the Asia-Pacific region. The media makes comparisons between Russia's policy (e.g., the recent closing of the military base in Cam Ranh Bay in Vietnam) and the US establishment of new bases in Australia and the Philippines and its intention to return to Vietnam. American attempts to hinder Russian military exports to countries in the region (e.g., the US efforts to prevent the sale of Russian fighters to Malaysia) have prompted undisguised irritation in Moscow.[25]

In this context, one can hardly regard as incidental President Putin's decision to meet with Malaysian Prime Minister Mahathir on the sidelines of the G-8 summit in Evian, and his trip to Kuala Lumpur in August 2003. Both leaders declared that the positions of their two countries on many international and regional problems coincided or were close enough, and emphasized their desire to continue close contacts in trade and economic and military-technical cooperation.[26] However, on the eve of his visit to Malaysia, Putin signaled rather clearly who Russia considered to be its main partner in the world arena in an interview with Malaysia's *The New*

Straits Times. He stated that Russia has "many common interests that link us to the United States" and mentioned that Moscow was satisfied with the way relations were developing with the United States in limiting strategic offensive problems, an area he called "the key sphere for both states." He also praised their bilateral relations within the anti-terrorist coalition. The only area in Russian–US relations where he could see difficulties was the sphere of economic cooperation. Nonetheless, he added, here also "as a rule we do find joint and mutually acceptable solutions." According to Putin, "Iraq is a sad exception. I hope that this problem is receding further and further into the past."[27]

On the other hand Russia is making efforts to increase the activity of the organizations of regional cooperation in Asia created on its initiative, such as the Shanghai Cooperation Organization (SCO). At the SCO summit in Moscow on May 29, 2003, Putin called on this organization to respond to terrorism, separatism, and extremism in the region, and to participate actively in building bases of security on the international scene.[28] The Russian leadership also believes that, in the context of new threats to Russia's security, there is an acute need for the creation of organizations in which the military component will apparently have an important place. An example of these efforts is the founding in April, 2003 of the Collective Security Treaty Organization (CSTO), which includes Russia, Belarus, Kazakhstan, Kyrgyzstan, Tajikistan, and Armenia. According to Putin, the CSTO has received the necessary instruments for effective work in ensuring security and fighting against terrorist and narcotics threats.

The CSTO heads of state reiterated their countries' readiness to make a worthy contribution to strengthening regional and international security on the basis of the rules of international law and with the use of the political and organizational resources available to the CSTO. According to Putin, the new body will not duplicate organizations such as the SCO or the Commonwealth of Independent States (CIS), because the other organizations simply do not have the instruments that the CSTO has. Such organizations should not hinder but help each other, the Russian president added.[29] At the same time Russia continues to emphasize that the activity of both the SCO and the CSTO is not directed against any state or group of states.[30]

Russia and the North Korean nuclear problem

The decision of the Democratic People's Republic of Korea (DPRK) to withdraw from the Nuclear Nonproliferation Treaty (NPT) has aroused deep concern in Moscow. The RF Foreign Ministry said in a statement that "such a move can only exacerbate the already tense situation around the Korean peninsula and inflict substantial harm upon the universal international legal instruments for ensuring global and regional security."[31] Since the very outset of the so-called Korean nuclear crisis, Russia has argued consistently in favor of political and diplomatic approaches to solve this acute problem of international relations, which would help, on the one hand, to prevent the acquisition of nuclear weapons in Korea and, on the other hand, to guarantee security and provide conditions for the development of the countries situated in the Northeast Asian region, in particular the DPRK.[32] Russian diplomacy has actively worked for the achievement of these aims with all the parties concerned. Moreover, Russia closely coordinated its actions with the People's Republic of China and always underlined that Moscow would welcome any format for talks and any agreement that would lead to a peaceful settlement of this problem. As before, Russia believes that the most acceptable way to solve the crisis is via a comprehensive solution.

In Putin's opinion, the positions of Russia and the United States on problems of WMD nonproliferation "are closer than they may seem." Taking into consideration his personal contacts with Kim Jong-il, Putin has obviously tried to avoid mentioning North Korea by name. However, since the American list of countries whose actions in this area have caused the greatest concern was limited to Iraq, Iran, and the DPRK, Russia's approach to Iran could be easily extrapolated to embrace the DPRK as well. That holds for the Russian president's remark at the press conference after the meeting with President Bush in St. Petersburg that Russia "doesn't need to be persuaded that WMD must not spread and proliferate across the planet. This concerns not only Iran, but also other regions of the world."[33]

The approach was expressed more explicitly and rigidly in Evian, where Putin promised that Russia "will insist that all Iranian programs in the nuclear field are placed under the control of the IAEA [International Atomic Energy Agency]." He also indicated that Russia will develop its cooperation with all countries "based on how open they are and to what extent they are in a position to place their programs under IAEA control," thus sending a clear message to Pyongyang that relations between Russia and the DPRK henceforth will depend, more than ever before, on North Korean behavior on the nuclear problem.[34]

It is quite possible to assume that comments by a spokesman for the DPRK Foreign Ministry on the declaration adopted at the G-8 summit in Evian, characterizing it as "an expression of mean flattery" of those countries that "favor the US's arbitrary practice," was implicitly referring to Russia's position on the problem, as expressed by Putin after the summit meeting with Bush as well as at the G-8 summit in Evian.[35] Nonetheless, it is worth mentioning that the G-8 Declaration's wording on the Korean problem, to which Russia agreed in Evian, is much tougher than the wording used by Moscow during Putin's summit with Chinese leader Hu Jintao only a week before. Russia and China reaffirmed as their common priority ensuring "a nuclear-free status of the Korean peninsula and observance there of the regime of nonproliferation of WMD." The two leaders signed a joint declaration that emphasized that "the security of the DPRK must be guaranteed and favorable conditions must be established for its socio-economic development." The document rejected as "unacceptable" the scenarios of power politics or the use of force to resolve the problems existing there, and called on the parties concerned to use political and diplomatic methods.[36]

The difference between the approaches of Russia and the United States to possible ways of settling the North Korean nuclear problem was confirmed later in the year during Putin's visit to the United States. According to Bush, the two presidents "strongly urge North Korea to completely, verifiably, and irreversibly end its nuclear programs." However, in his statement, Putin, while promising to continue to work jointly with the United States in resolving the issue, said that appeals to Pyongyang to give up its nuclear ambitions should be accompanied "by extending to North Korea security guarantees," something that Washington flatly rejected as giving in to "nuclear blackmail."[37]

These two traditional aspects of Russia's approach during the current crisis over the North Korean nuclear program have been called into question with increasing frequency. Some Russian observers believe that because of the new priorities facing the international community after 9/11, the hard task of reevaluating Russia's relations with those countries that are included in the list of "rogue states" should be undertaken. A new approach should be applied, it is argued, to contacts both with certain states of the so-called "traditional abroad" (the DPRK falls into this category) and with a number of former Soviet republics.[38]

Commenting on Putin's unusually tough language at Evian toward the "axis of evil" countries, some observers say that these states—both those already named and those which might be added to the list of "rogues"—cannot count on Russia's support because it is weak and cannot protect anybody. Disagreeing with the conclusion some Russian newspapers have hastened to make, these critics claim that Russia as a civilized state should not serve as a "roof" over the heads of those engaged in a "political racket." After Evian, Russia apparently will not sever links with its traditional allies, but at the same time, Moscow will let them know that there will be no "roof" for them either.[39]

Unshared responsibility

Clearly, there are differences in Russian and American approaches to the settlement of the North Korean nuclear problem. First of all, the two sides differ on the question of who bears the responsibility for the crisis. Washington has limited its obligations under the Geneva Agreed Framework of 1994 to two major promises: first, to organize an international consortium (the Korean Peninsula Energy Development Organization, KEDO) for the construction of an atomic power station with two light-water reactors (LWR) in the DPRK; and second, to supply the DPRK with 500 thousand tons of fuel oil annually until the first LWR becomes operational (originally planned for 2003).[40] In return, Pyongyang was supposed to "freeze" its graphite-moderated reactor and other related facilities in Yongbyon where it could produce weapons-grade plutonium, stop construction of two more reactors of the same type, retain NPT membership, and abide by the inter-Korean Declaration of 1991 on the denuclearization of the Korean peninsula.[41]

The United States claims that it carried out its obligations, but that the DPRK has failed to honor its part of the agreement. In fact, North Korea kept the specified facilities "frozen" up to the end of 2002, while the United States actually had not started to build the atomic power station, despite the fact that in President Clinton's letter to Kim Jong-il, the Americans promised to build it by themselves if KEDO failed to undertake the task.[42] The United States was slow to complete the work, because the Clinton administration hoped for an early collapse of the North Korean regime after Kim Il-sung's demise in July 1994, and because the Republicans, after winning the White House in 2000, treated as anathema everything that had earlier been done by the Democratic Party administration, for partisan and ideological reasons.

Nowadays the United States prefers to forget that the Agreed Framework, along with its so-called "nonproliferation clauses," also contains a number of US political obligations to the DPRK, including promises to provide it with "formal guarantees" that the United States will not use nuclear weapons against North Korea and will not threaten it with such weapons, and will move to "full normalization of political and economic relations."[43] The United States has definitely failed to deliver on these pledges. Instead of meeting its commitments, the Bush administration included the DPRK in the "axis of evil" and put it on a list of the countries targeted for preventive, including nuclear, attacks.

According to Washington, the United States stopped deliveries of fuel oil to the DPRK because the North Koreans admitted having a second, alternative uranium-enrichment nuclear program. The formal pretext is that the DPRK promised to observe the 1991 denuclearization declaration in which both Koreas promised to refrain from processing plutonium and enriching uranium.[44] However, the United States prefers "not to notice" the Agreed Framework's similar reference to the necessity of observance of the US–DPRK joint statement signed on June 11, 1993. That document, besides rejecting the "use of force or the threat of force," calls for the United States and the DPRK "to respect sovereignty" and "not to interfere with the internal affairs" of each other, and to continue "dialogue between the governments" of the two countries on the basis of "equality and fairness."[45]

There has been a lot of talk about Pyongyang's "nuclear blackmail" or "extortion" of oil, food, and other aid from "the world community." Events in Iraq proved that it would be a little premature to put an equal sign between the world community and the United States, from which the DPRK demands the fulfillment of the obligations under the Agreed Framework. Washington agreed on deliveries of fuel oil and the construction of the atomic power station in the DPRK because it had no legal grounds to demand the termination of a national nuclear power program in North Korea and was compelled to give something in return. The deal was fixed in the Agreed Framework. The DPRK's demand that the United States meet its obligations under the agreement is not blackmail.

A similar picture involving numerous accusations concerns the DPRK's supposed violations of its "international obligations." One of the basic propositions of international law reflected in the NPT (Article X) says that when a country faces a threat to its existence, it has the right to leave any treaty and to use all means available for protection of its sovereignty and territorial integrity. The North Koreans have taken advantage of this clause. Certainly, an undesirable precedent was created. However, the DPRK has been pushed to exercise this provision by none other than the United States. By putting the DPRK on the list of seven countries that are possible targets for American nuclear attacks, the

United States has broken the letter and the spirit of several international agreements that, together with the NPT, constitute the nonproliferation regime, starting with the obligation of the nuclear states not to threaten non-nuclear countries with nuclear weapons.

The US reproaches addressed to the DPRK and other countries concerning their observance of international obligations and international law are not too convincing, because Washington's record in the field is not faultless. The United States refused to ratify the Comprehensive Nuclear Test Ban Treaty, unilaterally left the Anti-Ballistic Missile (ABM) Treaty, rescinded its signature under the Kyoto Protocol (a major document for mankind's future, intended to counter global warming), refused to join the International Convention on Land Mines, and refused to accept the jurisdiction of the International Criminal Court. Even foreign friends of America concede that such behavior is far from the moral leadership that the United States always claims and that many in the world expect from the United States.

The Bush administration apparently does not wish to recognize any international obligation and prefers to act at its own discretion. At the same time, the United States is inclined to demand from others observance of those international rules that the United States itself is not prepared to respect. The world seems not yet to have caught up with such an "advanced" understanding of international law. Thus there are enough grounds to draw the conclusion that neither side—the United States *or* the DPRK—is without sin. However, on the whole, the list of US violations is much longer than North Korea's list.

Sources of the Korean crisis

Analyzing the sources of the current nuclear crisis in Korea, many observers point out its similarity to one that took place there in 1993–4, but few of them pay sufficient attention to the events that occurred on the peninsula prior to the two confrontations. Both crises were preceded by the Koreas, North and South, taking big strides toward overcoming their chronic enmity, ensuring détente, and establishing cooperation. Shortly before the earlier crisis, the DPRK and the Republic of Korea (ROK) signed and the following year ratified two major documents: the Agreement on Reconciliation, Non-aggression, Exchanges, and Cooperation, and the Declaration on Denuclearization of the Korean Peninsula. Real prospects were unfolding for a major improvement of the situation on the Korean peninsula, a scaling down of the level of military tension, and a promotion of inter-Korean interaction in various areas. Joint inter-Korean bodies started practical implementation of the signed agreements. All this activity came to a halt, however, with the first nuclear crisis of 1993–4.

A decade later, relations between the two Koreas again began to improve, first of all thanks to their own efforts. The beginning was set by the first ever inter-Korean summit in June 2000. Bilateral trade and economic cooperation reached an unprecedented scale. For the first time in history, mine clearing and a relinking of railroads were started in the demilitarized zone that divides the peninsula. Real prospects for the implementation of large bilateral and multilateral economic projects between the two Korean states and their neighbors began to appear.

It is hardly a coincidence that in both cases it was none other than the United States that blocked the way toward further inter-Korean rapprochement. Just as happened a decade earlier, today the United States is trying to force on everybody the impression that North Korea—economically backward, exhausted by famine, freezing from severe shortages of power and heating, and situated at the back of beyond—poses a major threat to world peace and, first of all, to the United States. The US Korean policy today, just as at the beginning of the 1990s, is prompted by the fear that further détente in Korea, started by the inter-Korean summit in 2000, would inevitably call into question the need for a continued US military presence on the peninsula. In the opinion of many experts, a US troop withdrawal from South Korea would remove a cornerstone of the US strategy in Northeast Asia (NEA) and in the Asia-Pacific as a whole, since the strategy is based on bilateral military alliances with Japan and the ROK and the forward deployment of American armed forces in these countries. Besides, final reconciliation between the two Koreas would deprive Washington of the last more-or-less serious argument justifying the creation of both the Theatre Missile Defense (TMD) in Northeast Asia and the US national missile defense (NMD) system. If the so-called "North Korean missile threat" were to be removed, the true plans of the US leadership to neutralize the nuclear-missile means of deterrence of China and Russia would be exposed.

The United States seems to have far-reaching and, for the time being, covert plans concerning the Korean peninsula. These plans received increased urgency in the context of the implementation of the Bush Doctrine, with its talk of preventive strikes using precision conventional armaments of a new generation as well as low-yield nuclear weapons. After the disappearance of the USSR and the collapse of socialism in the East European countries, Washington hoped for an early crash of the North Korean regime. Absorption of the North by the South under the military-political aegis of the United States would have allowed the Americans to establish control over unique strategic vantage points in Asia, located on the common borders of Russia, China, and Japan—the very powers that potentially can still challenge US global dominance. Liquidation of the DPRK not only would conclude the process of a realignment of the results of World War II in Northeast Asia, but also would mean the gutting of the truce that ended the Korean War of 1950–53. The deployment of the US armed forces with their precision weaponry along almost the entire 1400-kilometer-long overland border with China and the 17-kilometer-long border with Russia would result in cardinal changes in the military-political situation in this region and in the Asia-Pacific as a whole.[46]

Some observers are inclined to consider the US attack on Iraq, as well as the Washington-sponsored "anti-terrorist operation" in Afghanistan that resulted in the US acquisition of a number of military bases in Central Asia, as part of a future struggle between the United States and China. General Shebarshin believes that bases in this region are necessary for the United States, "not for fighting terrorism, but for control over the northwest part of China." Moreover, in his opinion, the Americans would be able to encircle not only China but also Russia with military bases.[47]

In view of such plans, Washington's appeals to Moscow and Beijing to take part in certain multilateral efforts with the ultimate aim of liquidating the DPRK look somewhat arrogant. The Russians and the Chinese actually are being called upon to help to create the conditions for bringing American soldiers right up to their own borders. Beijing understands the negative consequences that a possible liquidation of the DPRK has for the PRC. Therefore the Chinese, despite their displeasure with some of Pyongyang's moves, cannot afford to "yield" North Korea. The Americans, in turn, understand that any attempt to take hold of what China has considered its sphere of influence for hundreds of years would mean a major quarrel with the world's largest country, the consequences of which are unpredictable.

The North Koreans have taken advantage of this "draw situation" and, feeling incapable of defending themselves with their obsolete conventional armaments, have started to develop missiles, and probably nuclear weapons, to deter a possible attack. The option was not excluded in the KGB and the SVR (Russian Foreign Intelligence Service) reports published in Russia in the first half of the 1990s.[48] The war against Iraq probably provided the final push for the North Korean leadership to decide to produce nuclear weapons as their only reliable deterrent. After the first round of the six-party talks, held August 27–29, 2003, in Beijing, North Korea openly began to claim that it possessed nuclear weapons, arguing that it "was compelled" by the United States "to build up its nuclear deterrent force."[49]

Citing concrete facts regarding the hostile US policy toward the DPRK (e.g., multinational "naval blockade exercises" and attempts to hinder UN humanitarian assistance to Pyongyang), the North Korean ruling party's newspaper *Rodong Sinmun* asserted that "the DPRK is left with no option but to go its own way now that it has become clearer that the Bush administration does not have any political willingness to drop its hostile policy toward the DPRK and is getting more undisguised in its moves to disarm the DPRK and isolate and stifle it at any cost."[50] Commentaries by the North Korean media left no doubt that this really "bold decision" was also influenced by a "political crisis" that the DPRK saw the United States facing in Iraq, where Washington "can hardly get off the hook." According to *Rodong Sinmun*, the "tragic losses the United States has suffered in Iraq since the end of the war have also put the Bush administration in 'hot water.' The number of American troops who died after the war has already far surpassed the death toll during the war. The colossal military expenditure has seriously affected the US economy, which has been harassed by financial deficit, beclouding the prospects for Bush's reelection."[51] Judging by these evaluations, the North Korean leadership apparently has come to the conclusion that because of "the awkward position of the United States in the international community," Bush's "hawks" will not dare to unleash another major military conflict, at least until diplomacy has been given a real chance. That is why, despite Pyongyang's numerous statements about their lack of interest in the continuation of the six-party talks, one can be almost sure that the DPRK will do its best to keep a negotiating process afloat, though denying in public its vital concern in the continuation of the talks.

Here, too, Pyongyang's behavior so far looks like a bluff. The DPRK's priority remains a dialogue as the only way to get normal relations with the United States, in order to remove an external threat and get access to investments and assistance from the West. The latter is vitally important for Pyongyang, since only then will it be possible to revive the country's economy. Without that, it will be very difficult for the regime to survive.

Future developments on the peninsula and in the region will depend to a great extent on what choice will be made by the United States: whether to limit its demands to the nonproliferation agenda, or to choose a regime-change scenario. If the United States insists on regime change, the emergence of a nuclear-armed DPRK is practically inevitable.

Russia and six-party talks

From the very beginning of the crisis, Russia did not put forward basic objections to a multilateral format for talks, though it considered that the main responsibility for achieving a settlement rested with the United States and the DPRK. Moscow was ready to welcome any format of negotiations and any arrangement so long as it brought about a peaceful settlement of the problem.[52] Russia had proposed the idea of a multilateral forum with the purpose of comprehensive settlement in Korea as early as 1994. However, up until the summer of 2003, nobody was in a hurry to invite Moscow to take part in a multilateral negotiation. At the end of July 2003, the United States declared that it would present a counterproposal for the settlement of the nuclear problem, but only if the DPRK consented to a five-party negotiation (where Russia's participation was not scheduled).

An attempt by some people in the United States—using press reports about US Central Intelligence Agency and SVR collaboration against the DPRK to undermine the Russian special representative's mission to Pyongyang—caused serious doubts in Moscow as to whether the United States actually had the political will to work for a peaceful solution and to take Russian interests into account. The same can be said about a September 2003 Associated Press report alleging, with reference to unnamed US sources, that Russia had been helping the DPRK to develop a long-range ballistic missile capable of reaching US territory. The appearance of this kind of "misleading information does not help the aims of ensuring peace, stability and security on the Korean peninsula," the Russian Federation Foreign Ministry said in a statement, flatly denying such cooperation with other countries, including the DPRK.[53] Some observers considered it a foreign-policy "failure" that Russia was not invited to the trilateral meeting in Beijing in April 2003, so when the DPRK decided to ask Russia to take part in the six-party talks on August 27–29, 2003, in Beijing, this was welcomed in Russia as "a positive step" with a certain feeling of relief.[54]

Partly resulting from Moscow's own diplomatic activity, the North Korean move clearly signaled Pyongyang's frustration with China's position on the nuclear issue. It is hardly coincidental that the invitation to Russia was issued two days after a telephone conversation between Bush and the Chinese leader Hu Jintao, whose position on the North Korean nuclear problem Bush had deliberately praised in public. There are a number of facts testifying to a serious cooling of relations between China and the DPRK. Among the latest are Beijing's decision not to send a Chinese delegation to Pyongyang in July 2003 to participate in the 50th anniversary celebration of the end of the Korean War, and the PRC's jailing for 18 years of the Chinese businessman whom North Korean leader Kim Jong-il had appointed to head a special administrative zone on the border with China. According to some Russian experts, North Korea has indicated that it no longer considers Beijing a reliable partner and a trusted ally. As they say, "a drowning man grasps at a straw." The North Koreans obviously hope to arouse the former rivalry between China and Russia over Korea, or are counting on Moscow's traditional magnanimity and Russian personal contacts with the DPRK's leaders.[55]

Russia proposed a package solution at the six-party talks based on the principles of a stage-by-stage process and a parallel, synchronized implementation of coordinated measures by the concerned parties. Strongly in favor of ensuring a denuclearized status for the Korean peninsula, Russia believes at the same time that the concerns of the DPRK and other participating countries must be taken into account, including the establishment of a favorable environment for economic cooperation and development in the region.[56]

There are different views on Russia's participation in multilateral negotiations. There were warnings that the multilateral format would be meaningful only if it provided for working out a mutually acceptable security formula for all participants. Concerns were raised that a multilateral meeting might turn into a tribunal for "punishment" of the DPRK, which would authorize a US ultimatum in the name of the international community.[57] Russia's attitude to the Beijing talks should, obviously, take into account the need to strengthen peace and security in the strategically important area directly adjoining Russia, the readiness of other participants to give consideration to Russia's legitimate national interests in the region, and also the prospects for a successful negotiation. With respect to this last concern, in the opinion of the majority of observers, there is great uncertainty about the outcome of the negotiations, because of the sharply opposing positions of some of the participants, most of all the United States and the DPRK.

Skeptics point out that the different foreign-policy priorities and domestic political circumstances in each of the six countries involved make it practically impossible to work out a package acceptable to all participants. However, the major obstacle to the reaching of an agreement, if it is to be concluded, will almost certainly be the problem of verification. The issue could prove to be a minefield capable of blowing up the most beautifully designed agreement. In the summer of 2003, detection of Krypton–85 in the atmosphere over the DPRK (its source was never found) demonstrated to the United States the potential problem of having to search some 11–12 thousand North Korean underground sites. The Pentagon's maps are painfully incomplete, and the DPRK might reject such searches. Attempts to impose Iraqi-style inspections on Pyongyang may be unacceptable to

North Korea for a variety of reasons, not least the fact that the DPRK, unlike Iraq, did not lose a war. Moreover, as the North Koreans point out, and not without foundation, Iraq's experience proved that consent to inspections may not save a country from US attack.

A major difficulty that must be dealt with in Beijing will be to work out an agenda for the talks. If the agenda can be quickly worked out, that would be evidence of the six parties' readiness to compromise. Initially, the United States will strive to compel the DPRK first to renounce its military nuclear program and other kinds of WMD and their means of delivery, and second to provide assurances of the liquidation or removal of related equipment and materials, as confirmed by international inspections similar to those carried out in Iraq. In addition, Washington's agenda will include constraints on the DPRK export of missiles and missile technologies, a requirement that North Korean armed forces withdraw from areas adjacent to the DMZ, an end to Pyongyang's alleged support for international terrorism and its export of drugs and counterfeit currency, and the addressing of human rights abuses in North Korea.

The North Koreans have promised to take into account US concerns about WMD, but only in exchange for reliable security guarantees and the removal of obstacles to their economic development. The latter would require, first, the lifting of US economic sanctions that block Pyongyang's access to loans from international financial institutions in order to facilitate the most vital task for the regime's survival, the modernization of the North Korean economy. But the other American demands are likely to be countered with Pyongyang's own demands: the withdrawal of US troops from South Korea, and the establishment of diplomatic relations with the DPRK by the United States and Japan to insure "an equal status" for all participants in the talks.

Another problem for the negotiations is the deep split within the Bush administration concerning how to deal with North Korea. Even former US Defense Secretary William Perry has conceded that some in the Bush administration do not take dialogue with Pyongyang seriously. They expect to impose their demands on the DPRK by employing different types of sanctions and even a blockade. For Bush's "hawks," negotiations are necessary only to demonstrate the impossibility of reaching any agreement with the DPRK and to increase the pressure on Pyongyang.[58] For example, US Undersecretary of State John Bolton's fierce attacks while in Seoul on the DPRK and its leaders, on the day after North Korea announced its consent to the six-party talks, cannot be regarded as anything other than a deliberate provocation with the purpose of disrupting the talks, given diplomatic norms. Presumably, Bolton was aware that North Korea was apt to refuse to continue to dialogue with those who launched personal attacks on the country's top leader. So far, the US attitude suggests that the multilateral negotiations are, at least for the time being, just a screen behind which Washington will attempt to hammer out a new, anti-North Korean "coalition of concerned nations" willing to help, or at least not to prevent, a United States effort to achieve regime change in one more country. It is very important for Russia not to participate in providing this screen, assuming that the United

States would reciprocate, something that we are still waiting for in vain from previous dealings with the Bush administration.

The United States acts in full conformity with its new doctrine: "The mission must determine the coalition; the coalition must not determine the mission." The US administration's reaction to the rather harmless opposition of France and Germany concerning events in Iraq has shown that the hopes of those who expect even a semblance of an equal partnership with the United States are illusory. As is evident from the Iraq case, as well as from the pattern of US relations with some of the former Soviet republics, friends and enemies of America are now defined by their usefulness for the achievement of particular goals in American foreign policy, instead of other considerations like the degree of democracy in those countries. The six-party talks are fraught with another undesirable consequence for Russia. The Beijing forum could be used to replace the role of the United Nations and its Security Council, by creating something like a Northeast Asian regional quasi-council. In contrast with Russia's role in the UN Security Council will be its lack of veto right at the talks, and Russia might end up playing into the Americans' hands by supporting the US intention to ignore the United Nations or push it to the sidelines when and where Washington considers that this might suit its interests.

When we examine the probability of success for the six-party talks, it is also worthwhile to observe the events held at the end of July 2003 in both parts of Korea and in a number of other countries on the occasion of the 50th anniversary of the end of the Korean War. They have shown that half a century after the end of the war, the participants in the war still harbor deep disagreements concerning the war's causes and outcome. In contrast to Russia's consistent regret for its role, as a country that formally did not take part in the conflict, none among those directly involved (the United States, China, the DPRK, and the ROK) has done the same. On the contrary, each of them has asserted and continues to declare that its cause was a "righteous" one. This yawning gap in perception raises a question: if the two sides have failed to move toward reconciliation concerning an event that happened a half century ago, what are the chances that they will be able to find a compromise with respect to such contentious contemporary issues as preventing a new conflict in Korea and maintaining the nuclear nonproliferation regime?

Although Russia officially assessed the first round of the six-party talks as "useful" and pledged its support for a continuation of the talks,[59] Deputy Foreign Minister A. Losyukov, who led the RF delegation at the second round on February 25–28, 2004, in Beijing, was visibly less enthusiastic about the prospects for resolving the problem. After returning to Moscow he conceded that the meeting had produced "no concrete or practical movement toward resolution" of the issue, even warning that the situation could be aggravated and "a military intervention is possible."[60] Several days later, after being appointed as the new ambassador to Japan, Losyukov, in an interview with *Nezavisimaya gazeta*, went as far as to mention the possibility of a "dangerous explosion" in Korea in case there is no progress in the negotiations. The diplomat also said that Moscow maintains bilateral, including top-level, contacts with the North Korean leaders in order to facilitate further talks.[61] However, Moscow should hardly be euphoric about an invitation to join an enterprise in which some of the participants have mutually contradictory objectives, and where the negotiations have been characterized by an unclear mandate, uncertain terms, and an even less certain outcome.

Russia's options

A peaceful solution of the current crisis would suit Russia's national interests best of all. Taking an independent line in searching for mutually acceptable compromises, which would take into account the security interests of all parties involved, could earn Moscow the respect and trust of those participants most interested in peace and stability on the peninsula. First and foremost, it would earn the trust of both Korean states. It would be a mistake for Russia to forget that, according to the Treaty on Friendship, Good Neighborhood, and Cooperation between the Russian Federation and the DPRK that was signed in 2000, and the Joint Russian–Korean Declaration adopted at the Putin–Kim Jong-il summit in Pyongyang the same year, both countries pledged "to abstain from . . . participation in any actions or measures directed against the sovereignty, independence, and territorial integrity of the other party." Ignoring these obligations, and especially the circumstances under which the agreements were concluded, would hardly enhance the influence of Russia's foreign policy or enlarge the number of states that might want to rely on Moscow in time of difficulty.

Alternatively, if Russia were to join a united front with the United States against the DPRK or participate in any sort of coalition against North Korea, that would mean reverting to our diplomacy on the Korean peninsula during the first half of the 1990s. Then, Moscow generally had no particular position of its own, and Russia hastened to impose sanctions on the DPRK almost ahead of Washington. If Russia were to pursue such a line again, it would lose the trust of North Korea and lose influence in South Korea. Moreover, the West would once again cease to take into consideration Russia's position as it related to Korean affairs. Little would be left of Russia's international standing and authority. While ostensibly striving to follow "progressive tendencies" in international relations and to "catch the train" leaving for an unknown destination, some people in Russia totally overlook the main point: it is only a peaceful settlement of the current crisis that is in Russia's national interests. We do not need an arc of instability on the perimeter of our borders throughout the Russian Far East; more important, we want to avoid a "hot war" directly on our borders.

It is also worth keeping in mind that Russia's behavior during the current crisis is being closely watched, and not only by the parties directly involved in Korean affairs. If Russia were to tacitly give in on its position with respect to Korea and indulge those forces in the United States that are trying to establish military-political control over the whole Korean peninsula, this would add nothing to the perception of Russia as a world power—or even of Russia as a regional power capable of defending its own interests. On the contrary, it would result in the most adverse consequences for Moscow's international position, including in countries of the so-called "near abroad."

It is not desirable for Russia to refer the North Korean file to the UN Security Council, where the United States would try to replay the Iraq scenario to achieve regime change in the DPRK. That scenario, as everybody has already seen, calls for passage of a tough resolution in the UN Security Council. Upon its adoption, the resolution is then used to put constant pressure both on the target regime and on fellow UNSC members, and later, if necessary, to declare that the resolution is sufficient authorization for the United States to act unilaterally. Moscow also should bear in mind that the US troops in South Korea are still under the UN flag. One cannot exclude the possibility that an incident might be staged and presented to the world as a clash between the DPRK and the "UN troops." Such an "incident" could be followed by a US invasion of North Korea on behalf of the United Nations, but without the UN's formal consent.

The security of Russia's Far Eastern regions and their populations depends on how events in Korea will develop. In the event of a US–DPRK military conflict, radioactive clouds from Korean Chernobyls (it is necessary to include more than 10 South Korean atomic power plants that might be destroyed) and streams of Korean refugees would possibly not reach America's Pacific coast, but they would surely get to Russia. And perhaps the US maps for targeting their cruise missiles will once again happen to be "out of date," as happened when the Chinese Embassy in Belgrade was bombed during the war over Kosovo. The military option is unacceptable to Moscow, because it would pose a direct threat to Russia's security. Even the low probability that WMD might be used in Korea, a region directly adjoining Russia's borders, would require Russia's air defenses and even its nuclear deterrent forces to be put on high alert. China would be compelled to behave similarly, because in the event of military action, the United States would have mobilized even ahead of Moscow and Beijing, as the United States would be fearful of a DPRK retaliation. Preparing for such a possibility, Russia staged a military exercise in the region in August 2003 under supervision of its Defense Minister.

One can easily imagine what kind of situation might develop, in direct proximity to Russia's borders in the Far East, should the three largest nuclear powers (and also their allies) stand in full readiness for a nuclear conflict—with the US moving in a military force similar to what it brought against Iraq. Any incident could lead to a catastrophe. And the fact that during the last war in Iraq, American bombs and missiles were found on the territory of almost all neighboring countries confirms that it would be impossible to exclude the chance that such incidents might occur. Military conflict might also shatter hopes for the implementation of international oil, gas, transport, and other projects in Northeast Asia that are part of Russian plans for the social and economic development of its Far East. Just the threat of a major conflict would sharply increase the outflow of population from these areas. In case of a war, the demographic situation there could become catastrophic.

For all these reasons, Russia should not hesitate to insist on its own interests on the peninsula. Those interests are no less important than the interests of the states separated from Korea by seas or even by an ocean. Therefore, Russia has the full right to undertake all measures necessary to ensure that other participants in the Korean settlement take Russia's security concerns into consideration, and this is why it is possible that Moscow's reaction to the US attempt to use force in Korea will be much stronger than in the case of Iraq, a country with which neither Russia nor China has a common border. With respect to Korea, Moscow can expect Beijing's support and understanding of its position. In South Korea and even in Japan, there should be a similar understanding, since both countries might also become arenas of military conflict as a result of retaliation by the DPRK.

If the first Korean war finally buried the anti-Hitler coalition, the second large-scale conflict in Korea, which some people are both openly and secretly pushing for, could destroy the anti-terrorist coalition, and present Asia and the world with a new edition of the cold war. Russia realizes that Beijing has a much greater stake in the Korean peninsula than Moscow, for a number of objective reasons. Therefore, it makes sense for Russia to coordinate its reaction to developments on the peninsula with China—all the more so at present, when the basic interests of Moscow and Beijing in Korea coincide. Thus it is not necessary for Moscow to expect serious political losses in the DPRK, since Beijing's sponsorship will make Russian participation even more valuable for Pyongyang.

North Korea's rejection of the Russian offer to provide the DPRK with security guarantees was seemingly met without great concern in Moscow, where quite a few people loathe the idea. Some experts argue that it is necessary to think twice about whether it would be in Russia's national interest to give such guarantees. The issue here is that the RF and the PRC have already promised in their respective bilateral treaties with the DPRK not to participate in any coalition against their neighbor. Let those whose actions have resulted in creating the present situation provide the guarantees, the critics say.[62] Pyongyang is not interested—because, first, it does not feel any threat from China or Russia, and second, the guarantees proposed at this time by Moscow are definitely short of what is desired by North Korea. But the main reason for the DPRK rejection seems to be their worry that consent to Russian–Chinese guarantees would allow the United States to avoid making the kinds of commitments to Pyongyang that the North Koreans are demanding.

Pyongyang's insistence on getting security guarantees from the United States at any cost testifies once more to the consistency of North Korean foreign policy. Pyongyang is convinced that a normalization of relations between the two countries would result in eliminating a major external threat to the regime, which is perceived as coming from the hostile US policy. This attempt to normalize relations was launched as early as 1974, when the DPRK sent a letter to the US Congress urging better relations between the two countries. Moscow has always been suspicious of North Korea's attempts to "change the fundamental nature of the US forces in South Korea from that of aggressor to a neutral or sympathetic, if not friendly, status." Moscow's displeasure was caused mainly by the fact that while calling on the former Soviet Union and later Russia to support the North Korean demand for US troops to withdraw from South Korea, behind the scenes Pyongyang was contemplating another solution. This was the so-called "second-best approach," in which it would settle for a continued but legalized, neutral presence of US troops on the peninsula, instead of demanding their immediate withdrawal.

The revelations in Kim Myong Chol's 1998 essay concerning North Korea's policy did not go unnoticed in Russia. Kim, who used to portray himself as an unofficial spokesman of the DPRK in Japan, wrote that Kim Jong-il and his policy planners believe that a neutralization and legitimization of the US military presence in the South might produce practically the same effect as a US military withdrawal. Neutralized American forces might assume the new role of a peacekeeping force in the Far East. Kim Jong-il might prefer the above-explored alternative of letting the American military presence continue, rather than see a US disengagement from Korea set the stage for a replay of great-power rivalry in the Far East.[63]

Russia also bears in mind that, for well-known reasons, it has lost the place in the DPRK's foreign policy that the Soviet Union had previously held. Even during the Soviet days, Pyongyang tried to develop relations with Washington in disregard of Moscow's interests, as happened during the USS *Pueblo* crisis in 1968.[64] The same situation arises today in connection with the nuclear crisis. Therefore, the level of support from Russia that the DPRK has a right to expect should depend on the degree of Moscow's knowledge about Pyongyang's plans and its readiness to consult Russia, at least on questions affecting Russia's security interests. That is why it is possible that in solving the current crisis in Korea, Russia can take advantage of "Putin's formula," as stated by the Russian president in connection with the events in Iraq. Having reminded everyone that "In recent times—and there have been many crises recently—Russia has not once permitted itself the luxury of being drawn directly into any of these crises," Putin promised to do everything within his power "to prevent Russia being dragged into the Iraq crisis in any form."[65] The North Korean nuclear problem can be resolved satisfactorily only if the legitimate security concerns of all states located in the region, including those of Russia, are taken into account. Any other approach is unlikely to win Russia's support.

Notes

1 Statement by President Putin at a Kremlin meeting, Moscow, March 20, 2003, online at www.mid.ru.
2 Ibid.
3 Speech by Minister of Foreign Affairs of the Russian Federation Igor Ivanov at the Conference on Russia and the New World Pattern, in Moscow, May 12, 2003 (at www.mid.ru).
4 Article by Russian Minister of Foreign Affairs Igor Ivanov, published in Diplomatic Yearbook – 2003 under the heading "On the Road to the Establishment of a System for Counteraction Against Present Day Challenges and Threats," April 22, 2003, online at www.mid.ru.
5 "Transcript of Replies by Minister of Foreign Affairs of the Russian Federation Igor Ivanov to Questions After His Speech to the Federation Council of the Federal Assembly of the Russian Federation," Moscow, March 26, 2003, at www.mid.ru.
6 "The Press Statement of the President of Russia, Vladimir Putin, on the Iraq Problem," Novo-Ogarevo, April 3, 2003, online at www.mid.ru.
7 "Joint Statement by President George W. Bush and President V. Putin on the New Strategic Relationship," St. Petersburg, June 1, 2003, at www.mid.ru.

8 "Russian President Vladimir Putin Joint Press Conference with US President George W. Bush," St. Petersburg, June 1, 2003, at www.mid.ru.
9 "Joint Statement Between the United States of America and the Russian Federation," at www.whitehouse.gov/news/releases/2003/09/20030927–10.html.
10 *Nezavisimaya Gazeta*, May 12, September 29, 2003.
11 Online at www.vvp.ru/20030926.
12 Online at www.gtnews.ru/cgi/news/view.cgi? goto=15702.
13 Ibid.
14 N. Pavlov, "War in Iraq. Some Conclusions for Foreign Policy," *Mezhdunarodnaya zhizn* (Moscow), No. 5 (2003), p. 12.
15 V. Shejnis, "National Interests and Russia's Foreign Policy," *The World Economy and International Relations* (Moscow), No. 4 (2003), p. 46; *Nezavisimaya Gazeta*, March 24, 2003.
16 *Nezavisimaya Gazeta*, May 12, 2003.
17 Ibid., March 24, 2003.
18 Ibid.
19 Ibid., May 12, 2003.
20 Ibid., June 4, 2003.
21 *Mezhdunarodnaya zhizn* (Moscow), No. 5 (2003), p. 5.
22 *Nezavisimaya Gazeta*, September 29, 2003.
23 "Declaration on the Foundations of Friendly and Partner Relations between the Russian Federation and the Republic of Indonesia in the 21st Century," The Kremlin, Moscow, April 21, 2003, at www.mid.ru.
24 "On Results of Indonesian President Megawati Sukarnoputri's Visit to Russia," Moscow, April 24, 2003, at www.mid.ru.
25 A. Boljatko, *The Far East: In Search of Strategic Stability* (Moscow, 2003), p. 41; *Nezavisimaya Gazeta*, June 4, 2003; *Kommersant*, June 4, 2003.
26 "On a Meeting of Russian President V. Putin with Prime Minister of Malaysia Mahathir bin Mohammad," Evian, June 1, 2003, at www.mid.ru.
27 "Interview by President Vladimir Putin of Russia with the Malaysian newspaper *The New Straits Times*," Novo-Ogarevo, July 3, 2003, online at www.mid.ru.
28 "Statement of President of Russia V. Putin at Session of Heads of States of the Shanghai Cooperation Organization," Moscow, The Kremlin, May, 29, 2003, at www.mid.ru.
29 "On Outcomes of Session of Collective Security Council," April 28, 2003, at www.mid.ru.
30 "Statement of Minister of Foreign Affairs of Russia I. Ivanov at Plenary Session of the Council of Foreign Ministers of SCO," Alma-Ata, April 29, 2003, at www.mid.ru.
31 "Statement by the Ministry of Foreign Affairs of the Russian Federation Regarding the DPRK's Intention to Withdraw from the Treaty on the Nonproliferation of Nuclear Weapons," Moscow, January 10, 2003, at www.mid.ru.
32 "Concerning Reports on Possible Talks on Korean Problem in Beijing," Ministry of Foreign Affairs of the RF Report, April 17, 2003, online at www.mid.ru.
33 "Russian President Vladimir Putin Joint Press Conference with US President George W. Bush," St. Petersburg, June 1, 2003, at www.mid.ru.
34 "Russian President Vladimir Putin Remarks at Press Conference Following Group of Eight Heads of State and Government Meeting," Evian, France, June 3, 2003, online at www.mid.ru.
35 "Statement by Spokesman for DPRK Foreign Ministry on the Declaration Adopted at G-8 Summit," KCNA, Pyongyang, June 6, 2003.
36 "Joint Declaration of the Russian Federation and the People's Republic of China," Moscow, May 27, 2003, online at www.mid.ru.
37 "Remarks by President Bush and Russian President Putin in Camp David," at www.whitehouse.gov/news/releases/2003/09/20030927–2.html.
38 N. Pavlov, "War in Iraq: Some Conclusions for Foreign Policy," *Mezhdunarodnaya zhizn* (Moscow), No. 5 (2003), p. 12.
39 *Vremya-MN*, June 5, 2003.
40 See the text of the Agreed Framework in KCNA, Pyongyang, October 22, 1994.

41 Ibid.
42 See the text of the letter in KCNA, Pyongyang, October 22, 1994.
43 See the text of the Agreed Framework in KCNA, Pyongyang, October 22, 1994.
44 "Peace and Cooperation: White Paper on Korean Unification," Seoul, Ministry of National Unification (1996), pp. 208–9.
45 *Rodong Sinmun*, June 12, 1993.
46 Alexander Zhebin, "Some Aspects of Korea's Nuclear Crisis," in V. Tkachenko ed., *Russia and Korea in the Changing World Order* (Moscow, 2003), p. 48.
47 *Nezavisimaya Gazeta*, March 24, 2003.
48 *Izvestiya*, June 24, 1994; "New Challenges after Cold War: Proliferation of Weapons of Mass Destruction," *SVR Report*, Moscow (1993), pp. 92–3; "Nuclear Non-Proliferation Treaty: Problems of Extension," *SVR Report*, Moscow (1995), p. 26.
49 *KCNA*, September 10, 2003.
50 *Rodong Sinmun*, September 25, 2003.
51 Ibid.
52 Ministry of Foreign Affairs of the Russian Federation press statement, "Concerning Reports on Possible Negotiations on the Korean Problem in Beijing," April 17, 2003, online at www.mid.ru.
53 "Russian MFA Information and Press Department Comment in Response to a Media Question Regarding Associated Press Report on Unnamed US Sources' Claim That Russia Helps DPRK Develop a Long-Range Ballistic Missile Capable of Reaching US Territory," September 12, 2003, at www.mid.ru.
54 "Russian Deputy Minister of Foreign Affairs Yuri Fedorov Answers Questions from Japanese NHK Television Company," August 6, 2003, at www.mid.ru.
55 *Rossiiskaya Gazeta*, August 13, 2003.
56 "On the Six-Nation Talks Held in Beijing," Statement by Ministry of Foreign Affairs of the RF, August 29, 2003, at www.mid.ru.
57 *Nezavisimaya Gazeta*, April 11 and 23, 2003.
58 *Washington Post*, July 15, 2003.
59 "Transcript of the Interview Granted by Minister of Foreign Affairs of the Russian Federation Igor Ivanov to Russian and Foreign Media After His Speech at MGIMO(U)," September 1, 2003, at www.mid.ru.
60 ITAR-TASS, February 29, 2004.
61 *Nezavisimaya gazeta*, March 5, 2004.
62 *Rossiiskaya Gazeta*, August 27, 2003.
63 Kim Myong Chol, "Kim Jong-il's Peace Policy," NAPSNET Special Report, January 6, 1998, online at www.nautilus.org.
64 V. Tkachenko, "Lessons of the *Pueblo* Crisis," *The Korean Journal of Defense Analysis*, Vol. 5, No. 2 (Winter, 1993), pp. 224–5.
65 "Press Statement by the President of Russia, V. Putin, on the Iraq Problem," Novo-Ogarevo, April 3, 2003, www.mid.ru.

Men of Steel Q & A

Q. Why steel?
A. Steel will not burst from inner pressure or collapse because of an internal vacuum.
Q. What inner pressure?
A. Murderous rage.
Q. What internal vacuum?
A. Radical shame.
Q. How is shame evident?
A. The pursuit of congratulations and the practice of self-congratulation.
Q. How is murderous anger evident?
A. Excessive 'them and us' talk. Excessive talk of 'military victory' while wearing a lurid grin. Excessive love of power.
Q. Are men of steel immune from war-crimes prosecution?
A. They are already enclosed by steel walls. Punishment enough.

7 With eyes wide shut

Japan, Heisei militarization, and the Bush Doctrine

Richard Tanter

The effects and reception of the Bush Doctrine in Japan have to be seen in the light of a long drawn out and now quickening series of domestic legal, political, legislative, and equipment and force-structure changes in Japanese security policy. The Bush Doctrine has been welcomed for the opportunities it affords to accelerate already existing planning preferences for military expansion and the re-constitution of the Japanese state in a "normal" form—a pattern of "Heisei militarization." Heisei militarization is compatible with both a nuclear and non-nuclear Japan. Both options are consistent with the "normality" that Japanese governments are intent on achieving. Existing Japanese latent nuclear weapons proliferation capacity has been supplemented by both a weakening of domestic cultural and institutional restraints and dramatic changes in the external environment, including security threats from North Korea and an apparent US drift toward acceptance of Japanese nuclear weapons. This raises the possibility of a nuclear-armed Japan within the US alliance, as well as beyond it.

Prologue

In early 2004, two prominent and experienced Japanese Liberal Democratic Party elder statesmen of impeccably conservative credentials spoke out in public in sharp criticism of the dispatch of Ground Self-Defense Forces to Iraq and Japanese support for the ongoing US occupation of that country. Gotoda Masaharu, a former Deputy Prime Minister, told the *Nihon Keizai Shinbun* that the continued US occupation of Iraq is "a new type of colonialism. Imposing one's values on another country also constitutes a kind of imperialism. I don't see how a country [Iraq] can be liberated by bypassing the UN." While the US–Japan security alliance was beneficial for Japan during the cold war, Gotoda argued, it should then have been revised, and should now be replaced with "a bilateral friendship treaty." Gotoda then went to the heart of his warning, characterizing the high degree of risk he saw in the current policy in terms no one familiar with East Asian history could ignore:

> You can call any country a potential enemy if you want to, but it is ill-advised to assume such a posture. The state of things in Japan seems quite precarious, just as it was around 1931 [when Japan invaded Manchuria].[1]

A few days before, former Chief Cabinet Secretary Nonaka Hiromu, just retired from active political life, noted the almost daily release of new military-related policies and initiatives, and criticized what he called Prime Minister Koizumi's "politics of dread":

> This recent business of "[abandoning] the three principles of arms exports," or again, "[sending] the SDF overseas to guard our embassies," it's the same tempo as in the time when the war broke out, when one incredible story after another came tumbling out."

The people, Nonaka said, are "drunk on these words."

> Isn't this just like 1941? While I don't think anything like "war is about to break out," what I'm really becoming afraid of is that it is like that same feeling of a portent that Japan is again taking a mistaken path.[2]

From anyone else, these would be unremarkable comments. From such eminent conservatives they were startling. And the two dates chosen for comparison—1931 and 1941—have deep resonance in any thinking about Japanese foreign policy. To be sure, both men are elderly—and as with many other Japanese of their generation, their conservatism always sat alongside the scars of their wartime experiences. Yet together, Gotoda and Nonaka are pointing to the depth and shock of the changes that have overtaken Japanese security policy in the past few years, and the distance of that previously dominant strain of Japanese conservatism from the new muscular assertiveness under Koizumi. Most importantly, while deeply concerned with the behavior and influence of Japan's alliance partner, they are pointing at the domestically driven character of this shift—and, consequently, at the responsibility of Japanese politicians and those who elect them—for what they fear may be to come.

Frameworks

Before looking directly at the connections between the policies of the Bush administration and Japan, it is important to consider several sets of persistent problems in thinking about Japanese security policy, and about its main focus over the past half-century, Japan's relationship to the United States. Let me start with the cluster of competing frameworks of explanation, in particular the dominant sets of what Kenneth Burke called "the grammar of motives" that Japan is held to have—in discussions both in and outside Japan. There are basically three of these: Japan as Addicted to Militarism, Japan as Victim, and Japan as the Knowing Accomplice. Is Japan basically a would-be revanchist militarist state? Or is it basically a passive victim of American global strategy? Or, with a little more analytical sophistication, is it going along to get along, partially acquiescing in American demands insofar as they are irresistible and might further Japanese goals, but resisting the rush to full-scale remilitarization?

The first framework, Japan as Addicted to Militarism, sees Japan as eternally liable to relapse into militarism, and views virtually any Japanese security policy development through the eyes of East Asian history from the first half of the twentieth century. Japan is seen as being in perpetual danger of relapsing into revanchist militarism. US encouragement of Japanese militarization is thus a thoughtless incitement to this constant danger.

The second framework, Japan as Victim (the inverse of the first view), sees Japanese foreign policy as an almost helpless victim of US policy, with Tokyo weakly acquiescing in any and every US demand. In this view, pressure on Japan from the Clinton administration to integrate the Self-Defense Forces (SDF) with US military East Asian operational planning became the core problem for Japanese foreign policy. In the left-pacifist version, the United States is dragging Japan into war. In the right-nationalist analysis the key problem is the US insistence on maintaining Japan in a dependent, infantile status. Lacking the full panoply of state apparatus, Japan is not yet, in Ozawa Ichiro's now-famous phrase, a "normal country." Or, to paraphrase Ishihara Shintaro's equally famous phrase, in security policy Japan cannot yet "say 'no'" to the United States.

The third framework, commonly heard in elite policy circles in Japan and apparently more sophisticated than the first two, sees Japan as the Knowing Accomplice. This is the image associated with the Yoshida Doctrine. It sees Japan as complying with US demands, but as much as possible limiting its involvements in US global military affairs, and acquiescing only in the face of overwhelming diplomatic pressure and to the extent that Japan can thereby simultaneously realize its own modest goals.

Each of these frameworks is partially correct, depending on the period or aspect examined, but overall they fail to throw light on the character, causes, and consequences of the present shifts in Japanese security policy. Each of these frameworks can be seen in discussions of Japan's response to the Bush Doctrine. In one framework, the dispatch of SDF forces to the Middle East marks the start of a resurgence of imperial Japan implemented by a nationalist prime minister. In another, the United States has bullied Japan into doing its bidding, against Japan's own national interests. Or in the third, the Koizumi cabinet has muddled through, shifting back and forward, giving a little and taking a little, to keep the United States more or less satisfied that its key demands have been met, but also setting boundaries to keep Japan safe from the most extreme demands of the Bush administration.

Each of these frameworks points us to real elements in this conjuncture (the increased salience of certain newer streams of Japanese nationalism, for example; or the high level of US pressure on Japan; or the degree of compromise involved compared to the totality of US demands). However, they each tend to underestimate the most salient feature of the present moment, which is the high degree of utilization of external influences by Japanese politicians for the pursuit of long-held quite radical ends.

The core argument of this chapter is that the effects and reception of the Bush

Doctrine in Japan have to be seen in the light of a long drawn out and now quickening series of domestic legal, political, legislative, and equipment and force-structure changes in Japanese security policy. In essence, the Bush Doctrine has been welcomed for the cover and opportunities it affords to accelerate already existing planning preferences. Gaiatsu or foreign pressure has coincided with—and promoted—domestic elite preferences.

These plans for military expansion and the re-constitution of the Japanese state in a "normal" form long antedate the Bush Doctrine, or even the pressures for closer integration of the US–Japan alliance under the Bill Clinton administration. The powerful currents and tectonic pressures of the Bush Doctrine have intersected with, and been used to further, an existing and essentially domestically generated restructuring of Japanese security policy.

While the slow march toward expansion of Japanese military capacity and removal of obstacles to the use of military force abroad have a long history covering more than five decades, the most distinctive developments have occurred in the last decade and a half, roughly since the end of the cold war. As the reign names of emperors have been used to periodize Japanese history in the modern era, and as the start of the period under consideration almost coincides with the accession of the current, Heisei, emperor of Japan in 1989, it is convenient to refer to a pattern of "Heisei militarization."[3] It is the intersection of the process of Heisei militarization and the Bush Doctrine, together with the pattern of attempted mutual exploitation by the Koizumi and Bush II administrations, that is bringing both heightened uncertainty and magnified security risk to Japan.

Bearing in mind the dominance, in the sets of grammars of motives ascribed to Japan, of the image of Japan as Addicted to Militarism, it is important to stress that this is in no way to argue that Japan is returning, against the trend of the last sixty years, to a militarist-fascist state. While it is certainly true to say that there are very important lines of continuity between the prewar and postwar Japanese state, Japan's military forces by and large are something of an exception.[4] More than in any other area of the Japanese state, there was a severe rupture between Japan's prewar and postwar militaries. Accordingly, fantasies of "resurgent Japanese militarist-fascism" are almost completely incorrect.

More importantly, the emotional fostering of such anachronistic images distracts attention from a much more serious aspect of the present conjuncture of Heisei militarization and the Bush Doctrine, namely the very fact that it is a democratic Japan that is becoming a "normal state." In this world, a normal state is a militarized state. By the new definition, "normal" status for an economic giant in the most militarized region of a highly militarized world is a militarized state with the capacity and predisposition to "the use of force to settle its international disputes." That kind of highly militarized normality under such conditions carries high risks, risks that the Japanese polity may not be well equipped to deal with.

The Bush Doctrine and Japan

Japan has taken up the Bush Doctrine in the following main ways.

- Japan has joined the broad multilateral coalition under the UN and the United States to deal with terrorist groups through increased international police and intelligence cooperation, border and movement controls, and domestic security.[5]
- In 2002 Japan applied the Bush precedent to proclaim a right to regional pre-emptive attack, in particular in relation to North Korean nuclear and missile facilities.
- Following passage of the Anti-Terrorism Special Measures Law, Japan deployed Air Self-Defense Force (ASDF) aircraft and Maritime Self-Defense Force (MSDF) destroyers to support refueling operations in the Indian Ocean region in October 2001 for the US-led invasion of Afghanistan, and extended the deployment repeatedly.[6]
- In September 2003, Japan formally joined eleven countries in the Proliferation Security Initiative, initiated by the United States to establish, through various agreements and partnerships, an effective legal, intelligence, and intervention capacity, to be generated by participating countries' intelligence and naval and coast guard forces in order to detect and interdict the movement of illegal or suspect weapons and missile technologies.[7]
- In December 2003 Japan dispatched 600 heavily armed Ground Self-Defense Forces (GSDF) troops to the south of Iraq to support US occupation and reconstruction activities, as well as expanding its maritime and air presence in the Indian Ocean and Gulf regions.
- Also in December 2003, the Koizumi cabinet announced its intention to deploy US-built lower- and upper-tier missile defenses, allocating 100 billion yen in Fiscal Year 2004.
- Japan joined the United States in its demands that North Korea abandon all aspects of its nuclear weapons programs completely and irreversibly, passed legislation in 2003 to control the very large remittances from Japanese-born Koreans that provide crucial foreign exchange for North Korea, and introduced bills to refuse North Korean ships entry to Japanese ports and to revise the residency rights of Japanese-born North Koreans.[8]

Of these measures in support of the Bush administration's policies, the most politically significant have been the dispatch of military forces to the Indian Ocean and Iraq, the decision to join the US missile defense system and deploy upper- and lower-tier missile defense systems, and the announcement of a regional doctrine that proclaims the right of preemptive attack. All three of these initiatives bring very significant long-term costs and risks (not least, financial in the case of missile defense), as well as increased rather than decreased strategic uncertainty.

SDF deployments to the Afghanistan and Iraq wars

The passage of the Anti-Terrorism Special Measures Law in the immediate aftermath of the September 11, 2001 attacks on New York and Washington was a major victory for both US and Japanese proponents of the use of Japanese military forces outside the country. Although limited to duties in "non-combat zones," two contingents of MSDF ships were sent to the Indian Ocean, with authorization to support US forces in logistical and refueling operations in the sea lanes between Japan and the Persian Gulf, including the US base of Diego Garcia.[9] Although a government preference to include a Kongo-class destroyer equipped with an Aegis air defense system in the flotilla was initially thwarted by public opposition (including from within the ruling coalition parties), SDF ships and aircraft were for the first time engaged thousands of miles from Japan, and in support of US operations outside a United Nations peacekeeping-force structure.[10] Moreover, multiple extensions of the initial, brief, specified period of duty proved politically straightforward in the following year.[11]

Diplomatic activities apart, Prime Minister Koizumi announced three forms of support for the American effort in Iraq. First, Japan would send ground, air, and maritime forces to the Gulf theater, including the deployment of more than 600 GSDF personnel to a "non-combat zone" in southern Iraq to assist with reconstruction. Second, Japan would provide $1.5 billion in direct reconstruction aid to occupied Iraq. Third, Japan would forgive its portion of Iraq's huge foreign debt if other major creditors would follow suit.[12]

A year after the Afghanistan dispatch, the Koizumi cabinet forced the passage of the Iraq Reconstruction Special Measures Law in mid-2003. This was a momentous step in several ways. For the first time since 1945, heavily armed Japanese ground troops were dispatched abroad with rules of engagement that recognized the strong possibility of a requirement for lethal defense. Public opinion was heavily against the Iraq commitment as a whole and the dispatch of the ground troops in particular but, as with other allies of the United States, this fact was ignored by Japanese political leaders. And perhaps most importantly, given the very strong and sustained support at both public and elite levels for a United Nations focus for foreign policy activities, the Iraq dispatch was the first Japanese peacekeeping mission conducted outside UN auspices, being, in effect, part of a system of collective defense with the United States.

There was almost a half-year delay between the passage of the Iraq Reconstruction Special Measures Law and the first deployments of ground troops in late December 2003, principally because of the difficulty in locating an appropriate "combat-free zone" in occupied Iraq.[13] Within ten weeks of the establishment of a GSDF base at Samawah in late 2003, the illusion of a "non-combat zone" dissolved in a mix of farce and horror. Anti-American guerrilla activity in the region escalated soon after the arrival of the GSDF troops. In March and April the Japanese base itself began to be a target for mortar and rocket attacks. These developments led to confining all GSDF troops to base for an extended period, with all off-base reconstruction activities suspended. In early April, the whole Japanese mission in Iraq was thrown into question when guerrillas kidnapped three Japanese civilians (all without any military or even government involvement) and announced that they would be burned alive unless the Japanese government announced the withdrawal of troops forthwith. A confrontation between a hard-line government bent on displaying "resolve," and a population shocked by the consequences of its acquiescence to military adventure, was averted by the release of the hostages through the good offices of a network of Iraqi clerics, reportedly facilitated by what was effectively a ransom payment.[14]

Despite the fortunate outcome of the April kidnapping crisis, it was clear that the Japanese deployment in Iraq was hostage to the Bush administration's capacity and will to hold its imperial line. Whereas the Indian Ocean naval deployment in support of the Afghanistan war had been politically successful, it was clear that the Iraq deployment not only held the possibility of disaster for Koizumi personally but, more importantly, stood a good chance of providing the basis for widespread popular criticism of sending Japanese forces abroad in support of US global intervention strategy.

Moreover, the intentionally high-profile Japanese support of the United States in Iraq could not but change the perception of Japan in the Middle East as a whole. Until the Iraq deployment, Japanese policy in the Middle East had been largely independent of that of the United States, concentrating on commercial access to and investment in sources of oil supply, regardless of alliance politics, and distancing Japan from US support for Israel. Even as the Koizumi administration was searching for a safe haven for GSDF troops in Iraq in late 2003, it defied long-term and strongly expressed US displeasure and signed a major investment deal with Iran to develop the Azadegan oil field. Yet the essentially voluntary Iraq deployment held within it the seeds of the destruction of several decades of relatively independent Japanese foreign policy in the Middle East. The kidnapping crisis aside, would it be possible for Japan to avoid the diplomatic consequences of regional alignment with the United States at a time when US regional credibility was collapsing? The Iraq adventure may have brought kudos for Japan from the Bush administration, but without any doubt it also brought increased uncertainty and precious little expansion of Japan's security.

The missile defense decision

Preoccupation with missile defense has been a characteristic of the Bush administration from its inception, but Japanese involvement with US missile defense planning began long before. A formal decision to support joint research for a Theater Missile Defense (TMD) system was taken by the Hashimoto administration in 1998 in the immediate aftermath of the launching of the North Korean Taepodong missile, which passed through Japanese airspace. In fact, the issue had been on the agenda of numerous consultations between Washington and Tokyo since the administration of Bush the elder.

However, the Cabinet decision in December 2003 to proceed with deployment of upper- and lower-tier missile defense, as well as continuing the joint research and development effort, was an enormous step. The planned deployment between 2007 and 2011 is for four MSDF Aegis-equipped destroyers with Standard-3 missiles to attack enemy missiles in the outer atmosphere, and four air force high-altitude air defense units equipped with Patriot Advanced Capability-3 missiles to attack those which reach the lower atmosphere. The initial announcement put the cost of spending in Fiscal Year 2004 for the upper- and lower-tier systems alone at 100 billion yen, but these figures were almost immediately abandoned. The *Nihon Keizai Shinbun* on December 20 wrote that:

> financial costs are expected to be enormous. In August [2003], the Defense Agency estimated the total cost of purchasing the systems at around 500 billion yen. But on Friday the agency revised up its figure to as much as one trillion yen, including maintenance and repair costs. The new system under development by Japan and the United States is expected to cost "at least double that amount," according to a senior Defense Agency official.

In April 2004 the Defense Agency established a Missile Defense Office to prepare the way for the deployment, and to resolve legal problems—and most likely, the political implications of the technology.[15] Such problems include the question of the legality of exporting missile defense technology if there is a possibility the United States may then pass such technology on to third parties;[16] and, more fundamentally, the question of control over launching—for example, what should be done if another country launches its missiles toward Japan accidentally, and who should make such a decision?[17]

In the context of an alliance where the interests of the alliance partners are not identical, such questions of strategic coordination are always important. However, in the case of US–Japan cooperation in missile defense, the problems are inherent and fundamental. The upper-tier sea-based system by its nature will be dependent on the provision of real-time data concerning target missile launch, trajectory, and identification that will be partly provided by the MSDF Aegis systems, but much more by the still-evolving suite of ground- and satellite-based radar and infrared surveillance systems planned for the US National Missile Defense System.[18] In the case of missile defense, the character of the technology as presently conceived determines the limits of political possibility. The technological integration renders the missile defense system a matter of collective defense, at present regarded as unconstitutional by the interpretation of the government's Cabinet Legislation Office.[19]

The nature of the technology carries further political implications. Not only does it leave Japan dependent on US technological support in time of crisis, but equally, it implicates Japan in the activities of US missile defense systems in relation to Japan's regional neighbors. Like it or not, Japanese technological dependence on the United States for its missile defense system's viability reinforces the perception by China that a Japanese system and an American system are not separate entities. The technology of Japanese missile defense becomes a source of long-term structural antagonism between Japan and China, which can only be obviated by abandoning the technology.

Announcing the cabinet decision in December 2003, Chief Cabinet Secretary Fukuda Yasuo assured the public that such concerns were groundless:

> The introduction of such systems will not contradict the country's defense policy of dedicating its military expenditures solely to defensive purposes, and will not threaten neighboring countries. Nor will it involve any problem related to collective defense.[20]

Both of these claims are implausible, and become more so as the capacities of the developing and necessarily integrated US–Japan missile defense systems unfold. The first stage of the Japanese missile defense system may not in itself be an offensive weapon, but by contributing to the possible negation of the Chinese land-based nuclear deterrence force it would in objective terms facilitate the possibility of a US nuclear offensive against China. There is little doubt that it will provide China with further inducement to hasten and deepen its strategic nuclear modernization program, and set off a regional strategic arms race, with considerable consequences for Japanese defensive and offensive security capacities. Here again, it seems likely that the Koizumi administration decision to support the East Asian application of the Bush Doctrine will increase rather than decrease both strategic uncertainty and the possibilities of compromised Japanese security

Right to preemptive attack

The most direct and least plausible of the echoes of the Bush Doctrine was in the announcement by Defense Agency head Ishiba Shigeru in early 2002 that Japan has, under both its constitution and international law, a right to carry out a preemptive air attack on North Korean missile sites, if the government believes that a missile attack on Japan is imminent.[21] Leaving aside questions of technical military feasibility, Ishiba's announcement immediately escalated the rhetorical framework employed by Japan to that of China's more extreme remarks about Taiwan and North Korea's about South Korea and the United States.[22] Since there was obviously no chance whatsoever of the threat being acted upon, and the gap between apparent aspiration and reality was so great as to be almost delusional, the image of a loose cannon in the tense Northeast Asian security field came to mind. In this field again, the local application of the Bush Doctrine decreased rather than increased the reality of Japanese security.

Interpreting Japan and the Bush Doctrine

How are we to interpret these shifts of Japanese policy in support of the Bush Doctrine? Two characteristics of the application of the doctrine are immediately evident. One is the way in which the American conflation of perceived threats that has evolved into the Global War on Terror (GWOT) has been echoed in the Japanese response. As Jeffrey Record argues in the most sustained and cogent critique of the GWOT:

> the conflation of rogue states, terrorism and WMD [weapons of mass destruction], coupled with the administration's preventive war against Saddam Hussein's Iraq for the purpose of disarming that country, makes the GWOT as much a war on nuclear proliferators—at least the ones the United States does not like—as a war against terrorism itself.[23]

Like an echo across the Pacific lake, Japan has embraced all the rhetorical and policy aspects of the GWOT, with no more discrimination than the original loud voice from Washington, and with even less capacity to achieve the goals without further exacerbating its security vulnerabilities.

The second relevant characteristic, as Peter Van Ness stresses, is this:

> more important than 9/11 have been the ideas that the Bush leadership brought into office in January 2001. Those ideas, which were re-shaped into a "war on terror" after the attacks on the World Trade Centre and the Pentagon, have most profoundly changed the world.[24]

The shapers of security policy in the Bush II administration had been concerned about Japan's place in American security architecture long before they took office. One of those key actors was US Deputy Secretary of State Richard Armitage who, while out of office in March 1999, was principal author of what came to be termed the Armitage Report.[25] In December 2003, almost two years into the application of the Bush Doctrine, Armitage spelled out his own goals for Japan:

> I have been spending 20 some years trying to get in a situation where Japan would again be a great nation, and I think she is . . . We are trying to develop a kind of relationship with Japan that we enjoy with Great Britain, on the other side of the world.[26]

Almost all of the responses of the Koizumi administration to the Bush Doctrine exemplify Armitage's hopes that Japan will assume a place in the US alliance structure comparable to that of Britain—undoubtedly the most loyal and active of US allies. Especially in the case of missile defense and the Iraq expedition, Japan has been aspiring to British status in the US system. While the effects of the September 11 attacks have indeed been striking in Japan, especially coupled with the effects of anxieties about North Korea, all of the crucial initiatives reflect plans drawn up long before 2001.

Armitage's allusion to Britain's role within the system of American hegemony as a model for Japan carries one further implication, intentionally or not. Unlike Japan, Britain is a nuclear-armed American ally—like Israel, and like Pakistan. Armitage's remark raises the thought that the Bush Doctrine could result in a move toward a nuclear-armed Japan within the American alliance—the subject of the penultimate section of this chapter. Long-standing Japanese latent nuclear weapons proliferation capacity has been supplemented by both a weakening of domestic cultural and institutional restraints, including a much diminished peace movement, and dramatic changes in the external environment of both perceived security threats, including from North Korea, and an apparent US drift toward acceptance of Japanese nuclear weapons.

Yet there is a quite different set of analytical problems to be considered in thinking about the responses of the Koizumi administration to the policies of the Bush administration. The first set of questions concerns whether the Japanese responses to the Bush Doctrine are simply a function of well-known and long-standing pressures from the United States or whether they arise from domestic Japanese sources. And either way, what has changed both domestically and externally to permit these and other elements of Japanese military expansion? Or, as it may be more fruitfully understood, what is the connection between the Bush Doctrine and the restructuring of the external aspects of the Japanese state?

The intersection of Heisei militarization and the Bush Doctrine

The Japanese government response to the Bush Doctrine was essentially an acceleration and amplification of changes already under way before Bush came to power, and which have been increasingly the result of Japanese as much as American political initiatives. These had begun in the late 1980s, and especially following the end of the cold war. Despite the reference in the current reign name to peace and tranquillity, it is useful and accurate to group these endogenous changes in Japanese security policy and organization as "Heisei militarization": "Heisei" because the period in question begins just before the end of the cold war, and "militarization" because the dominant characteristics of the security policies from that time onward are an ever-increasing stress on military conceptions of security at the expense of previously well-developed complementary conceptions of security. This includes a continual and growing government-sponsored hollowing-out of the meaning of Article 9 of the Constitution and of the concept of "defensive defense," expanded military budgets, comprehensive upgrading and expansion of military force-structure capacities, legitimation and legalization of use of military force abroad, willingness to rely on military solutions to international problems, and expansion of the domestic coercive powers of the government. There is also a growing promotion of the possibility of the Japanese military's acquiring and using strategic offensive weapons and weapons of mass destruction.

As already argued, these dimensions of militarization are not at all unusual in the contemporary world system: they are, on the contrary, the marks of normality. Equally, they are quite different from the distinctively Japanese model of 1930s militarism best understood as "emperor-fascism."[27] In other words, whatever else the characteristics of Heisei militarization may be, Japan is neither reverting to an earlier form of anti-democratic militarism nor assuming a state form markedly different from those of other militarized advanced capitalist countries with democratic polities. On the contrary, it is becoming a normal country. While it is important not to ignore the acceleration provided by the demands and stresses

164 *Richard Tanter*

emanating from Washington, the key shifts are fundamentally endogenous in character. These shifts can be seen in legislation, in defense plans, and in SDF force-structure and organizational changes.

Legislative changes

An extraordinary amount of security-related legislation has been passed by the Japanese Diet since the early 1990s, and at the time of writing a great deal more was under debate. At least fifteen separate laws dealing with security issues were passed or substantially amended between 1992 and early 2004, and eight major bills were before the Diet in April 2004 (see Table 7.1). The effect of many of the legislative changes in the period of most intense activity after 1999 was cumulative over a short period of time—each law building on and expanding on innovations in its predecessor. The most important of these can be dealt with in three groupings.

In 1992, in the aftermath of the Gulf War, the Miyazawa cabinet achieved passage of the International Peace Cooperation Law (known as the Peace Keeping Operations Law). This permitted the dispatch of lightly armed Japanese SDF personnel overseas under UN peacekeeping auspices for non-combatant duties. For the first time since 1945, under this and related disaster-relief legislation, Japanese military personnel were dispatched abroad, and in the following decade they took part in UN peacekeeping and disaster-relief operations in Cambodia, Mozambique, East Timor, and other countries.

In 1997, the United States and Japan agreed on a new set of guidelines for the implementation of the US–Japan Mutual Security Treaty. The result of US pressure on Japan since the end of the cold war to take a larger share of responsibility for East Asian security under US auspices, the Guidelines were brought into force through a series of new laws and agreements, the most important of which were the Law Concerning Measures to Ensure the Peace and Security of Japan in Situations in Areas Surrounding Japan, the Law to Amend the Self-Defense Law, and the 1999 Agreement to Amend the Acquisition and Cross-Servicing (ACSA) Agreement Between Japan and the United States. Commonly termed a "redefinition" of the alliance, the Guidelines aimed at establishing full coordination and cooperation between the SDF and US forces in Japan, even in times of peace. Under the Emergency System established as a result of the Guidelines, in the event of a government-certified "emergency in the area surrounding Japan," not only the SDF but also Japanese civilian prefectural and local government and infrastructure authorities are required to cooperate in manifold specified ways with US forces. Moreover, the establishment of the Emergency System resulted in a heightening of coordination between the SDF and other parts of the Japanese state, in marked contrast to the previous intentional relative isolation of the SDF—and hence, the prior limitation of its role in both peace and war.

The Japanese side agreed to provide logistical support and intelligence cooperation with US forces in time of crisis, and to prepare for such crisis coordination by prior development of appropriate forms of integration in time of peace. Most important of all, the type of crisis that could invoke such requirements was no longer, as in the original 1976 Guidelines and the Security Treaty itself, one taking place only within the territory of Japan, but rather any security emergency in "the areas surrounding Japan"—a term that was left intentionally undefined in geographical terms.

Clearly, the Guidelines emanated from US pressure and led to a much deeper level of integration between US and Japanese military forces. In retrospect, the implementation of the 1997 Guidelines may come to be seen as the high (or low) point of American acquisition of formally Japanese military capacity. There was certainly great opposition within Japan on precisely these grounds. Yet viewed as a step toward Japanese militarization, the implementation of the Guidelines marked an enormous change, and the beginnings of the application of a systematic rationalization of many aspects of the Japanese state to remove obstacles to the reconstituting of Japan as a "normal state." Together with the associated decisions concerning security planning and force-structure development, they amounted to an enormous change. Moreover, their presentation as stemming from American pressure helped divert attention from the fact that they were greatly welcomed by those in Japan who had been seeking exactly such shifts in attitude.

The 2001 Anti-Terrorism Special Measures Law and the 2003 Iraq Reconstruction Special Measures Law sending troops to support US operations in Afghanistan and Iraq built on many of the characteristics of the earlier legislation, and took them one step further. No longer bound to UN auspices, Japanese troops were allowed to operate under US auspices. No longer tied to "Japan," the definition of "areas surrounding Japan" was stretched and redefined "situationally rather than geographically" to allow deployment in the Persian Gulf and Iraq. Limits on technologies that implied forms of collective defense—such as the electronic intelligence-gathering capacities of Aegis-equipped destroyers—disappeared, to the delight of both the United States and the MSDF. And limits on the type of arms that could be carried almost disappeared as deployment in the "non-combat zone" of southern Iraq was recognized to require substantial autonomous capacity for protection in the event of attack. By the end of 2003, "defensive defense" within the territory of Japan was no longer the actual practice of the SDF. Koizumi, like Hashimoto and Nakasone before him, had long been antagonistic to Article 9 of the Constitution, and sought its destruction—by either revision or erasure. The nationalist wing of the LDP had achieved a major policy goal in 2000 with the establishment of a Diet committee chaired by former Foreign Minister Nakayama Taro to consider and canvass possible revisions to the Constitution, with Article 9 being a core concern of both the committee and most making submissions to it. The committee is to report to the Diet in 2005, whereupon an undoubtedly protracted and tumultuous process of consideration of LDP-initiated proposals for constitutional revision will commence.[28]

Many other changes in government security practice and policy emanated from these and the lesser pieces of legislation passed between 1999 and 2004, and more still will follow if the eight bills before the Diet in the first half of 2004 are passed without great changes. The "Emergency System" established as a result of the

1999 Guidelines legislation is clearly going to continue to evolve and be subject to continual rationalization and deepening. Even if the US alliance were to disappear tomorrow—and, perhaps, particularly if it should do so—this process would continue. American pressures have certainly contributed to these shifts in state structure, but they have an enduring importance beyond American pressures. Especially in the past four years, internal pressures for change and rationalization have been at least as important and effective.

Table 7.1 Japanese security-related legislation, 1992–2004*

1992	International Peace Cooperation Law (Peace Keeping Operations Law)
1992	Law to Amend Part of the Law Concerning the Dispatch of Japan Disaster Relief Teams
1999	Rear-Area Support Act
1999	Agreement to Amend the Acquisition and Cross-Servicing (ACSA) Agreement Between Japan and the United States
1999	Law to Amend the Self-Defense Law
1999	Law Concerning Measures to Ensure the Peace and Security of Japan in Situations in Areas Surrounding Japan
1999	Communications Interception Law
2000	Ship Inspection Operations Law
2001	Anti-Terrorism Special Measures Law
2001	Law to Amend the Maritime Safety Agency Act
2003	Law Concerning Measures to Ensure National Independence and Security in a Situation of Armed Attack (Armed Attack Response Law)
2003	Law to Amend the Self-Defense Forces Law
2003	Law to Amend the Security Council Establishment Law
2003	Iraq Reconstruction Special Measures Law
2004	Revision to the Foreign Exchange and Foreign Trade Law
2004	Bill to refuse port calls by North Korean ships
2004	Bill to protect citizens
2004	Bill on the use of designated public transport and communications facilities
2004	Bill to facilitate smoother operations of US military forces
2004	Bill for revision of the Self-Defense Force Law (revision of ACSA)
2004	Bill to permit the interdiction of military equipment on foreign ships on the high seas
2004	Bill to penalize violations of international humanitarian law
2004	Bill on the treatment of prisoners of war

* Note: as of April 2004. The Cabinet endorsed seven war-contingency bills on March 9, 2004, and a bill to authorize refusal of entry to North Korean ships was submitted to the Diet on April 6.

Security planning framework and force-structure developments

In 1995, the Defense Agency promulgated a new National Defense Program Outline in and after FY 1996 (NDPO), which mapped in general terms the intended development of the Self-Defense Forces for the following decade. Compared to its predecessor almost two decades earlier, the 1995 NDPO was remarkable for its active emphasis on a restructuring of self-defense capacity, with a stress on rationalizing and upgrading the technological base of the SDF, making it more compact and more efficient, and stressing the importance of removing obstacles to smooth cooperation with US forces. In addition to specifying the need to develop capacity to respond to aggression, carry out peacekeeping activities, and participate in disaster-relief operations, the 1995 NDPO emphasized the importance of developing physical and organizational capacity for "high-level intelligence gathering and analysis, including strategic intelligence," as well as "a sophisticated command and communications capability." The strategy paper also required the SDF to "be able to quickly and effectively conduct integrated defense operations from a joint perspective."[29] The geographical framework was "the areas surrounding Japan."

This emphasis on building "more streamlined, effective compact defenses" was heightened further in the guiding principles of the Mid-Term Defense Program (FY 2001–5) adopted in December 2000. The goals for further restructuring of the SDF were to consider: "wider and speedier warfare, higher performance weapons and electronic attacks"; more developed use of communications and information technology; an improved capacity to deal with guerrilla attacks or special operations, as well as nuclear, biological, or chemical weapons; and closer cooperation with the United States "even under normal circumstances."

Under these two plans, a remarkable technical and organizational upgrading of the SDF has taken place, especially in the MSDF and ASDF, and in central command and intelligence structures. The Defense Intelligence Headquarters was established in 1997, integrating and expanding the existing intelligence capacities of the separate forces, and overseeing a major expansion of signals intelligence capacities. In 1998, the decision was made to develop and deploy four military-grade surveillance satellites; two were launched in March 2003, and two more were destroyed in an unsuccessful launch later that year. The 2003 decision to deploy a missile defense system extends that framework, though at the cost of likely severe competition for funds in the future.

It is clear that this process of Heisei militarization is far from complete. In April 2004 a government defense advisory panel commenced formal planning for a long-awaited outline of a new National Defense Program Outline due to be adopted by the Security Council and Cabinet by the end of the year. For the previous two years, speculation had been widespread in the media and policy circles about the possibility of quite fundamental changes in direction and content compared to the two previous NDPOs in 1976 and 1995. Prime Minister Koizumi made it clear that the panel would reconsider the "basic premise of Japan's defense program, which has been to provide basic defense capacity," and should address questions of international terrorism and the proliferation of weapons of mass destruction. Three issues were identified as being the core of the panel's concerns: "building a system to defend against ballistic missile attacks, reducing the existing weaponry line-up, and making international operations one of the core activities of the Self-Defense Forces."[30]

In sum, the Bush Doctrine accelerated certain doctrinal and technological and planning trends that were already under way in Japanese security policy, or had long been planned, whether publicly or not. In many respects, the pressures from America and the framework of responding to "global terror" have provided a degree of cover for this militarization program.

Japanese nationalism and the Bush Doctrine

Not for the first time, when the hot winds of the Bush Doctrine blew through the world system, a nationalist Japanese prime minister found himself faced with the apparently contradictory task of matching his own agenda to that of Washington. The imperial pressure of the Bush Doctrine, demanding a deeper and more active integration of Japan into US global military strategy than even the redefinition of the Japan–US alliance following the 1997 new alliance guidelines, emerged after a decade of rising and multi-faceted Japanese nationalist sentiment. Like his immediate predecessor, Hashimoto Ryutaro, Prime Minister Koizumi in his official capacity frequently and publicly visited the Yasukuni shrine, memorial to those who died in the service of the empire. The most popular political figure in the country throughout the late 1990s had been the former LDP minister and prolific author Ishihara Shintaro, who creatively used his position as mayor of Tokyo to pressure the national government on a range of foreign policy issues, apparently far from immediate urban concerns. Crucial symbolic shifts had taken place with the successful government proclamation that the *hinomaru* and *Kimigayo* should be included in government school ceremonies as the national flag and national anthem respectively, overturning more than four decades of anti-imperial restraint by now-diminished left and pacifist political and intellectual forces. At the level of popular political culture, the manga artist Kobayashi Yoshinori sold millions of books articulating a renovated and emotionally complex anti-American nationalism that appealed in particular to the politically alienated young. Koizumi's own electoral appeal blended a rhetorical deregulationist critique of an apparently moribund "business as usual" LDP–bureaucracy alliance with a new assertiveness of the "commonsense" necessity of further elevating the primacy of security policy.

At first blush, it would seem that the project of pursuing a nationalist agenda is unlikely to be successful while its proponents are caught up in an objectively enhanced subordinate role in an imperial spasm. After all, in certain respects, Koizumi is best compared with Nakasone Yasuhiro who, although he had a firmer hold on power and a far longer tenure than Koizumi has had to date, also came to power with an agenda of domestic reform and nationalist rhetoric. The ardent nationalist Nakasone began his political career as a young member of the Diet writing a direct letter of protest about the humiliations of the American occupation to its proconsul, General Douglas MacArthur, and rose to power on the slogan of "a final settling of postwar accounts." Yet it was Nakasone's fate to come to power just as Ronald Reagan was proclaiming the necessity of allied unity in the fight against the "evil empire" and demanding a greater Japanese role as a bulwark against Soviet Pacific naval expansion. Rather than settling accounts, Nakasone found himself forced to spend his political capital to support the hegemon, much to the disgust of LDP ultra-nationalists such as Ishihara Shintaro. Finding himself second banana in the much-publicized "Ron and Yasu" relationship, Nakasone toned down his habitual nationalist rhetoric, and reached for ways of utilizing the American expansion for his own purposes.

As Koizumi was to do with Bush two decades later, Nakasone swallowed his pride and embraced the sub-imperial role, promising Americans in an interview in the Washington Post that "the whole Japanese archipelago ... should be like an unsinkable aircraft carrier ... against the infiltration of the Backfire bomber."[31] The often quoted simile in fact marked a low point for Japanese nationalists. While promising that Japan would play the role of staunch ally against the Soviets, nothing could hide the fact that the aircraft carrier was equipped with foreign aircraft, not Japanese ones.

Yet while the rhetoric of nationalism had to be set aside, and the symbols of subordination embraced, in the latter part of his five-year period in office, Nakasone was able to begin the movements of security doctrine, budgets, and force structure that were to be completed in the 1990s. The "unsinkable aircraft carrier" remark was coupled to a promise to block the four straits of the Japanese islands to any Soviet submarine, and to "defend the sea lanes between Guam and Tokyo and between the Strait of Taiwan and Osaka."[32] Moreover, through the 1986–90 Mid-Term Defense Program, Nakasone not only finally broke the 1 percent of GNP defense spending limit, but also expanded spending to modernize all three Self-Defense Forces.

Two decades later, confronted by the Bush Doctrine and the rhetoric of the Global War on Terror, Koizumi has pursued a similar strategy of apparent alliance accommodation, but has obtained greater freedom of action than Nakasone. Certainly, the changes in Japanese security policy initiated under the GWOT rubric evoked less challenge in Japan than the 1997 new alliance guidelines, which very visibly integrated US and Japanese forces. In part this is because of the universal aspects of the appeal of the GWOT after 9/11: up until the invasion of Iraq, all of the changes could be presented as a Japanese response to a global problem of undoubted relevance to Japan. But there were also at least three specifically Japanese perceptions of threat that merged with the global structure of threat to which the GWOT was presented as a response: the Aum Shinrikyo sarin attacks in Tokyo; North Korea's launch of the Taepodong missile and its parallel nuclear weapons development; and the North Korean confirmation in 2002 of the kidnapping two decades previously of large numbers of Japanese citizens. With this combination of global and local sources of threat, presented without any effective opposition or countervailing interpretation or alternative security perspective,

Koizumi was able, even more than leaders of other US allies, to blur the distinction between the US-led war on terror and the completion of the autonomous project of Heisei militarization.

Nationalism in subordinate alliance partners is not singular in its makeup. As the Australian and British cases show, right up until certain points of unavoidable conflicts of national versus imperial interest, nationalism of a particular kind can coexist with—and be presented as—loyalty to the empire. Flattery, to the effect of the enormous value to the imperial or global project of the subordinate's role, can assuage what would otherwise be experienced as humiliating:[33] Japan can be presented as the "most important US ally outside NATO." The difficulty comes when national and imperial interests too evidently diverge. For Japan, as for other US allies, the deployment of troops to Iraq is likely to be one such point of strain. The politics of military production are a perennial point of contention, and the techno-nationalist politics of very large military-related projects such as missile defense, surveillance satellites, rockets, aircraft, and warships and their associated electronics and weapons systems have been and will continue to be very sharp, though not highly visible in the Japanese case.[34] The Iraq adventure aside, perhaps the most vulnerable point for Koizumi the nationalist would be if the issue of the US bases in Japan were to become effectively linked to his support for the Bush Doctrine—either from the much-diminished pacifist left or from the anti-American nationalist right.

The nuclear options and the normal state

Amidst all of these marked shifts in security policy emanating from Tokyo and Washington, the most contentious and difficult question to assess is whether there is any imminent change in the Japanese government's attitude toward acquiring nuclear weapons. For the past four decades and more, Japanese nuclear policy has been bound by the three "non-nuclear principles": Japan will not possess, manufacture, or allow the deployment or transit of nuclear weapons within or across its territory.[35] To anticipate the conclusion of the argument, Heisei militarization is compatible with both a nuclear and non-nuclear Japan. Both options are consistent with the "normality" that Japanese governments are intent on achieving. However, the road to the more dangerous nuclear option is now more open and more attractive than ever before. Moreover, there is a real possibility that a nuclear-armed Japan could emerge not only within the US alliance, but even with US assistance. Four aspects will be only briefly noted here: recent developments in Japanese political elite attitudes, recent developments in US policy and attitudes, developments in the strategic environment, and developments in Japanese technological capacity.

Contemporary Japanese attitudes and policy

Powerful domestic institutional and cultural constraints on Japanese militarization in general and nuclear weapons acquisition in particular, in the form of a highly organized and mobilized peace movement backed by cross-generational public opinion, have weakened dramatically.[36] One of the most visible reflections of the decline of the peace movement and the "peace generations" in Japan is that the climate of mainstream public discussion—what is sayable in "respectable" political circles—has widened dramatically in the past decade. Whereas public calls for nuclear armaments were once deeply shocking to the great majority of Japanese citizens, they are now almost commonplace.[37]

A slew of public comments and alleged "slips of the tongue" and "misquotations" by senior Japanese politicians, all of them current or former ministers, have opened the way. While government policy on nuclear weapons remained formally unchanged, the accumulation of such elite public remarks had a distinct effect on the range of policy debate.

In 1999, Nishimura Shingo, Liberal Party MP and then Deputy Director-General of the Defense Agency, argued in an interview with the Japanese version of *Playboy* magazine that the SDF should be turned into a "proper army," and went on to call for the question of nuclear weapons to be placed on the agenda of the Diet.[38] In April 2002, Ozawa Ichiro, former Secretary-General of the Liberal-Democratic Party and then leader of the Liberal Party, criticized what he regarded as the arrogance of Chinese criticism of and opposition to Japan, and warned China that "it's possible for us to produce 3,000 to 4,000 nuclear warheads."[39]

The Nishimura and Ozawa comments do not represent government policy. Nishimura was immediately dismissed. Ozawa, powerful figure that he has been both in and out of government over two decades, was in opposition at the time he made his statement, and no government figure supported his comments. However, this was the first time that the leader of a major political party had taken such a stand publicly. In doing so, Ozawa facilitated the legitimation of advocacy of nuclear weapons as a respectable topic for mainstream debate.

On May 31, 2002, just a month after Ozawa's outburst, Chief Cabinet Secretary Fukuda Yasuo repeated the earlier assertion that there are no constitutional barriers to acquiring nuclear weapons, and that Japan should be able to do so. Not only are the non-nuclear principles subject to change, he said, but "as the time has come to amend the Constitution, the Japanese people may also now believe that the time has come for this country to have nuclear weapons . . . Japan, too, could possess nuclear weapons."[40]

Following an uproar, Prime Minister Koizumi issued a clarification, saying that Japan had no intention of changing the principles or acquiring nuclear weapons. Yet Fukuda's inflammatory comments, which were quite possibly intentionally so, were also entirely correct.[41]

While none of these statements can be said to express government policy, the very fact that they were uttered into the highly symbolically charged Japanese political force field altered the shape of the sayable in Japanese politics, and worked to legitimize discussion of nuclear weapons in the mainstream of Japanese politics.

Contemporary US attitudes and policy

Intersecting and influencing this shift in the domestic Japanese climate of discussion of a previously taboo subject was a separate stream of comments from across the Pacific—all of which were closely noted in Japan. Once again, the very structure of the discourse—its overt character, its speculative discussion of "inevitable" consequences of conceivable contingencies, and the political eminence of those involved—all added to its consequences, whether wholly intended or not. Four types of sources were involved.

First, Vice President Dick Cheney raised the possibility of a nuclear-armed Japan as one consequence of a nuclear-armed North Korea.[42] Second, in a visit to Tokyo the immediate past Secretary of Defense, William Cohen, asked Japanese politicians if they would consider taking that path if North Korea did in fact get nuclear weapons.[43] Third, Senator John McCain went one step further and directly warned China that if it did not prevent North Korean nuclear armament, then it was inevitable that Japan would acquire its own nuclear weapons.[44]

Prominent journalists and academics took the next step. The darling of the Bush establishment, Charles Krauthammer, argued in January 2003 that the United States should warn a "recalcitrant" China that unless it blocked a nuclear North Korea, the United States would not only allow Japan to go nuclear but give it the missiles to do so. "If our nightmare is a nuclear North Korea, China's is a nuclear Japan. It's time to share nightmares."[45] Charles Pena argued for replacing the US nuclear umbrella over Japan with "two nuclear-armed democratic nations (both with vibrant economies)": Japan and South Korea.[46]

While none of these statements represented government policy, they reflected a major reversal of the certainties of the climate of US policy toward Japanese nuclear weapons of the previous four decades. Nonproliferation among America's East Asian allies was moving from being a constant of US policy toward being a dead letter—as in other regions in the cases of Britain, Israel, and Pakistan. The climate of debate on both sides of the Pacific had changed forever.[47]

Strategic incentives to nuclear weapons acquisition

Three shifts in the strategic environment of Japan in recent years have made it more likely that a Japanese cabinet will make the decision to acquire its own nuclear weapons: the North Korean drive to nuclear armament, the US commitment to deploy a global missile defense system, and the Bush administration's commitment both to upgrade and expand the US nuclear arsenal, and to consider the use of new forms of nuclear weapons in its "Global War on Terror."

The North Korean nuclear crisis has had the most direct effect on the Japanese nuclear debate, especially following the August 1998 launch of the three-stage Taepodong missile. This factor has been influential in a number of different ways. Japanese attitudes toward the US promise of extended nuclear deterrence have always been ambivalent, and the North Korean development has revived fears that the long-proffered US nuclear umbrella may either leak or simply be taken away.

China's quantitative and qualitative missile and nuclear weapons development is an almost inevitable consequence of the US decision to deploy a global missile defense system. China believes itself to be the real long-term target of what it sees as a threat to its nuclear deterrence capability. Japan's decision in December 2003 to join with the United States and deploy sea- and ground-based missile defense systems places Japan in a position of long-term structural antagonism to China. Leaving aside the quite separate matter of nuclear developments in regard to Taiwan, a visible expansion of the Chinese strategic nuclear force would strengthen the hand of Japanese supporters of an independent nuclear capacity, and those within Japanese elite policy circles who hold fundamental suspicions of China that have long driven US neoconservatives.

Finally, US nuclear policy itself has, under the Bush administration, influenced the Japanese nuclear debate. High-level discussion of deploying low-yield battlefield weapons (so-called "mini-nukes" or nuclear "bunker-busters") during the US invasions of Afghanistan and Iraq palpably contributed to the erosion of the post-Nagasaki taboo on the use of nuclear weapons. And the particularly Japanese sense of anxiety on this issue was compounded by other Bush administration nuclear policies, such as the abandonment of any attempt to secure Congressional ratification of the Comprehensive Test Ban Treaty, and the leaked 2002 Nuclear Posture Review.

Developments in Japanese technological nuclear capacity

Finally, the country's technical capacity to develop and deploy an effective nuclear armament has itself rapidly grown in the 1990s. There are three core requirements for a usable nuclear weapon: a weaponized nuclear device, a sufficiently accurate targeting system, and at least one adequate delivery system. Japan now has the undoubted capacity to satisfy all three requirements.

There has been little doubt for more than a decade that Japan could build a sophisticated nuclear device rapidly, possibly in less than a year—at the very least, a tritium-boosted plutonium fission weapon, and quite possibly a thermonuclear weapon.[48]

This Japanese capacity to build a plutonium weapon in short order has long been known—and discreetly advertised. The fact that this situation is well known in itself constitutes a latent nuclear capacity—by letting other countries know that while it does not possess nuclear weapons, it could acquire them quickly and easily, Japan marks its being a step away from actual possession, which status carries its own strategic value short of actual possession. The very ambiguity of apparently inconsistent policy statements like Fukuda's helps to reinforce the value of that latent nuclear capacity.[49]

Japan's visible latent nuclear capacities continue to evolve. By 2004 Japan's combination of fission and breeder reactors and reprocessing facilities was described as an "already massive latent nuclear capability."[50] Gsponer and Hurni in particular have emphasized Japan's long-standing and "ambitious" inertial confinement fusion program, and an ambitious magnetic confinement fusion program. These facilities allow high-level research into the physics of thermonuclear weapons, simulation of tests of such weapons, and the production of tritium, the crucial element in boosted fission weapons. More importantly, they also make possible the production of "fourth generation nuclear weapons in which fusion materials (i.e. deuterium, tritium, and lithium) will be used instead of fissile materials as the main explosive."[51]

In this context, US policy to support Japan as the preferred host country for the planned huge International Thermonuclear Reactor (ITER) became a matter of great concern, since such a fusion research facility would permit the legal production of large amounts of tritium. Given the small amounts required for fusion bomb production, the danger of undetected diversion rises accordingly. Gsponer and Hurni conclude that "building ITER at the Rokkasho site will turn Japan into a virtual thermonuclear superpower."[52]

The US decision to press so strongly for the location of the ITER in Japan does raise the question of whether the current administration is fully committed to a non-nuclear-armed Japan—and adds to the grounds for considering the possibility of a nuclear-armed Japan either within the US alliance or beyond it.

The second important shift in Japanese potential nuclear-weapons capacity is a direct consequence of the wider pattern of Heisei militarization: the development of adequate targeting systems. A capacity to locate and monitor potential military targets—especially targets smaller than cities, such as weapons factories or missile sites—is crucial to an effective nuclear capacity. In 2003 Japan launched two of an intended set of four military-grade visual and synthetic aperture radar surveillance satellites, as the result of plans announced in the aftermath of the launching of the Taepodong missile.[53] This was followed by the establishment of imagery intelligence analytical units within the Cabinet Information Office and Defense Intelligence Headquarters, in a dramatic expansion of imagery intelligence interpretation capacity.[54] Even without relying on imaging intelligence supplied by the United States under the UKUSA Agreement, to which Japan is a Third Party signatory, Japan has the most advanced imagery intelligence capacity in Asia after that of China.[55] Indeed, one of the factors cited as behind the Hashimoto cabinet's decision to develop the surveillance satellite was an alleged delay by the United States in providing Japan with timely data on the Taepodong launch.

The third requirement for an effective nuclear weapons capacity is an adequate delivery system—at least one, if not more. In the secret 1993 Defense Agency study of a Japanese capacity to attack North Korean military sites, it was concluded that a lack of an aerial refueling capacity would mean that ASDF F-1 and F-4EJ fighters carrying 500-pound (conventional) bombs could not reach their targets and safely return to home base.[56] Following the decision in 2001 to acquire Boeing 767 refueling aircraft, this limitation was largely, if not completely, removed.[57]

A much more effective and less vulnerable delivery system became available in the late 1990s in the form of the giant H-IIA liquid-fueled rocket. It is in principle a highly capable delivery system for a payload as heavy as 17 tons—more than enough for a nuclear weapon. Liquid-fueled rockets are susceptible to satellite monitoring in the hours before they are launched, as they must be loaded with extremely cold liquid hydrogen. However, only the United States, Russia, and China presently have the capacity to monitor such preparations for launch (the United States and the Soviet Union relied on such behemoths for much of the cold war).

In sum, compared to the situation at the end of the cold war, Japan has a comprehensive latent nuclear weapons technical capacity. At the same time, elite attitudes to positive consideration of Japanese nuclear weapons in both Japan and the United States have shifted dramatically. This in turn has validated public discussion of the nuclear option in ways unheard of in the decades prior to the end of the cold war. At the same time, powerful domestic institutional and cultural constraints on Japanese militarization in general and nuclear weapons acquisition in particular (in the form of a highly organized and mobilized peace movement backed by cross-generational public opinion) have weakened dramatically.

Nuclear-armed states are "normal countries" in the contemporary world, and the extension of Heisei militarization in the nuclear direction does not in itself indicate any politically sinister new turn. However, the strategic costs and risks for both Japan and its region would be considerable. The intersection of Heisei militarization and the Bush Doctrine has contributed to the lowering of the nuclear bar for Japan.

Conclusion: with eyes wide shut

The intersection of Heisei militarization and the Bush Doctrine was a contingent event, greatly accelerating and solidifying the processes of restructuring of external aspects of the Japanese state that were already under way in the years after the end of the cold war. It is likely that a continuation of the policies of the Clinton administration would have facilitated the continuation of those processes, as they did in the second half of the last decade, but at a smaller, less intense, and less comprehensive level than did in fact take place (and is still continuing). Japan is proceeding toward full normalization, moving closer to throwing off all the external and self-imposed restraints that for half a century produced a disjuncture between its economic status as the world's second largest national economy and its restricted status in global security activities.

In the existing world system, normalization of this kind necessarily means militarization, and that is precisely what Japan has undertaken, a process accelerated, but not caused, by the demands of the Bush Doctrine. Indeed, all of the political, legal, and military-technical processes of Heisei militarization that have developed within the US alliance also greatly increase the basis of an autonomous foreign and security policy beyond that alliance. The chances of Japan's soon becoming involved in further militarization on the basis of meeting its own perceived security needs, irrespective of the consequences of further demands from the US imperium, are now very high, as with all such normal states, especially when they are economic superpowers. As with France and Britain, this will very likely involve Japan in military interventions abroad—to protect citizens and crucial economic interests deemed threatened by existing conflicts. The Malacca

Straits, Aceh (Indonesia), and the Philippines come to mind as possibilities under certain circumstances. Similarly, the likelihood of Japan's moving from latent nuclear power to actual nuclear power is now considerably greater than a decade ago. For all that such developments would be highly undesirable, such an outcome of Heisei militarization would not be a reversion to the old stereotype of Japan as addicted to militarism, but rather would mirror the common and dangerous behavior of a normal state in a militarized world.

Not surprisingly, given the degree of incoherence and even irrationality of imperial US policy under the Bush administration, the acceleration of the process of Heisei militarization provided by the Bush Doctrine has also diminished rather than increased Japanese security. Japan has allowed itself to become technologically bound to an ongoing conflict with China through missile defense. And the enthusiastic participation of the Koizumi cabinet in the ongoing war of occupation in Iraq will lead inevitably, not only to the first Japanese deaths in a foreign war since 1945, but also to the first killing of foreigners by Japanese troops in five decades. And with that will come an inevitable reassessment of Japan by all countries.

Notes

1. "SDF Dispatch (2): Former Vice Premier Gotoda Doubts Cause of Iraq War," *Nihon Keizai Shinbun*, February 9, 2004, on *NikkeiNet Interactive* at www.nni.nikkei.co.jp. Interviewer's explanatory note.
2. "Nonaka Hiromu talks about 'Dangerous Japan'" (Japanese), *Asahi Web News*, January 29, 2004, at webnews.asahi.co.jp/you/special/2004/.
3. This term is used only to refer to a period of Japanese history. It does not suggest any particular relationship to the current emperor or any activities by him.
4. The most striking area of continuity is in economic policy and in the economic ministries. See, for example, Chalmers Johnson's classic exposition of the links between the prewar Ministry of Munitions and the famed postwar Ministry of International Trade and Industry in his *MITI and the Japanese Miracle* (Stanford, CA: Stanford University Press, 1982). A comparable argument could be made in the area of communications policy.
5. For details of Japanese actions regarding UN and other recommendations on financing, visas, and other forms of cooperation regarding terrorism after September 11, see the Ministry of Foreign Affairs, *Japanese Report on Implementation of the APEC Leaders Statement on Counter-terrorism*, May, 2002, at www.mofa.go.jp.
6. Gavan McCormack, "Japan's Afghan Expedition," *Japan in the World*, December 2001, at www.iwanami.co.jp/jpworld.
7. "A statement of interdiction principles was released in Paris September 4, 2003 by eleven nations that are participating in the Proliferation Security Initiative. 'PSI participants are committed to the following interdiction principles to establish a more coordinated and effective basis through which to impede and stop shipments of WMD, delivery systems, and related materials flowing to and from states and non-state actors of proliferation concern, consistent with national legal authorities and relevant international law and frameworks, including the United Nations Security Council.'" See "Proliferation Security Initiative," *Global Security*, at www.globalsecurity.org. As of March 2004, the total number of participating countries was fifteen. Both participating and non-participating countries, especially China, raised serious and substantive questions about the legality of the proposed interdiction regime under current international and national law. In March 2004 the Japanese government introduced a bill into the Diet that would authorize marine

Self-Defense Force vessels to halt and attack on the high seas foreign ships suspected of carrying military equipment to an enemy country.

8   In addition to the legislative changes, existing regulations were utilized to harass North Korean ships entering Japanese ports. In June 2003 "nearly 2,000 inspectors went to the port of Niigata to check for customs and immigration violations, infectious diseases, and safety violations on the North Korean vessel Man Gyong Bong–92." *Korea Crisis—Blockade* at www.globalsecurity.org.

9   The Anti-Terrorism Special Measures Law also authorized such SDF activities within "Australian territory," presumably referring to the Australian Exclusive Economic Zone (EEZ) around Christmas and Cocos Islands. See *Basic Plan Regarding Response Measures Based on the Anti-Terrorism Special Measures Law, Cabinet Decision of November 16, 2001*, at www.kantei.go.jp/foreign.

10 The Aegis-equipped *Kirishima* was eventually dispatched in December 2002, after the government dismissed concerns that the capacities of its 500-kilometer radius air defense system would mean that the MSDF would effectively participate in collective defense with the US. "Aegis ship leaves on security mission," *Japan Times*, December 17, 2002.

11 For a detailed review of the first MSDF dispatch, see *Special Report: Japan Maritime Self Defense Force Support to the War in Afghanistan*, US Pacific Command, Virtual Information Center, November 27, 2001, at www.apan-info.net/terrorism.

12 This would involve Japan, the largest creditor, abandoning its previous long-held policy of opposition to large-scale debt forgiveness, which was always accompanied by warnings concerning the folly of such "moral hazards."

13 This difficulty was exemplified early on by the killing of two senior Foreign Ministry officials in November 2003.

14 The Japanese government strongly denied money was involved in the release, but the tabloid and magazine press in Japan continued to maintain that a ransom had been paid. Given the endemic lack of transparency in Japanese Foreign Ministry overseas operations, it is not possible to dismiss the media claims out of hand. See, for example, *Shukan Posuto*, April 19–25, 2004 (at www.weeklypost.com), and "Aisawa Denies Govt Paid Ransom To End Hostage Crisis," *NikkeiNet*, April 20, 2004, at www.nni.nikkei.co.jp.

15 *Daily Yomiuri*, December 23, 2003.

16 One Japanese system of interest is the new FPS-XX radar system, under development for deployment in the Sea of Japan region from 2008. According to JDA sources, "the new radar will use electronic scanning to control the orientation of electro-magnetic waves, and is expected to have high capabilities for detecting ballistic missiles, which move faster and have a smaller reflective surface compared to airplanes." *NikkeiNet Interactive*, September 14, 2003, at www.nni.nikkei.co.jp.

17 The *Nihon Keizai Shinbun* reported on March 28, 2004, that the Defense Agency would seek a revision of the Self Defense Law that would allow "the mobilization of the Self Defense Forces for counter-missile action solely on the order of the Prime Minister." At present, this requires a decision by the Security Council and the Cabinet that a threat of attack exists, and then a Diet decision to deploy the SDF. "Agency Seeks to Mobilize Missile Defense System on PM's Order Alone," *NikkeiNet Interactive*, March 28, 2004, at www.nni.nikkei.co.jp.

18 The precise ways in which the sensor and command and control elements of the National Missile Defense System (which will include Battle Management Command, Control and Communications [BMC3], Ground Based Radar [GBR], Upgraded Early Warning Radar [UEWR], Forward Based X-Band Radar [FBXB], and the Space Based Infrared Sensor [SBIRS-Low] system) will be connected to the regional sea-based missile defense systems deployed on US Navy and Japanese MSDF Aegis-equipped destroyers are still unclear. See GlobalSecurity.com, *National Missile Defense*, and *Aegis Ballistic Missile Defense (BMD) Navy Theater Wide [LEAP]*, at www.globalsecurity.org/space/systems.

19 Richard J. Samuels, *Politics, Security Policy, and Japan's Cabinet Legislation Bureau: Who Elected These Guys, Anyway?* Japan Policy Research Institute (JPRI) Working Paper No. 99 (March 2004), at www.jpri.org.

20 *NikkeiNet Interactive*, December 19, 2003 at www.nni.nikkei.co.jp. See also the *Statement by the Chief Cabinet Secretary, 19 December 2003*, at www.kantei.go.jp/foreign.

21 *Mainichi Shinbun* (Tokyo), January 24, 2003, at www.mainichi.co.jp. There was an earlier but less assertive claim to the right to a preemptive attack by one of Ishiba's predecessors, Norota Hosei, in March 1999. See the explanation by the Ministry of Foreign Affairs, *Press Conference by the Press Secretary, 5 March, 1999*, at www.mofa.go.jp.

22 One of the crucial issues is that of aircraft range. Per existing government interpretations, under Article 9 of the Constitution, offensive weapons are not permitted in the SDF. Therefore, the ASDF has no long-range bombers. A secret Defense Agency study in 1995 had considered the technical feasibility of such action, and determined that at that time, it was beyond the capacity of ASDF F-1 and F-15 aircraft to carry 500-pound bombs to North Korea and return safely. (See *NAPSNet Daily Report*, August 27, 1999, at www.nautilus.org.) Boeing B-767 refueling aircraft have since been acquired. There are, however, other unanswered technical obstacles, most importantly limitations on Japan's intelligence capacities, which remain dependent on access to US material until such time as all four Japanese imagery intelligence satellites are launched (two were launched in 2003, but two were destroyed when an H-IIA missile launch failed in November 2003) and are functioning adequately, and the Defense Intelligence Headquarters imagery analytical office and the Cabinet Satellite Intelligence Center are fully staffed and functioning.

23 Jeffrey Record, *Bounding the Global War on Terrorism* (Carlisle, PA: Strategic Studies Institute, US Army War College, December 2003), p. 21.

24 Peter Van Ness, "The Bush Doctrine in Asia: A Brief Introduction," *Asian Perspective*, Vol. 27, No. 4 (2003), p. 6.

25 Richard L. Armitage, Paul Wolfowitz, et al., *A Comprehensive Approach to North Korea* (National Defense University, Strategic Forum), at www.globalsecurity.org.

26 "Excerpts from Armitage Interview with Nikkei," *NikkeiNet Interactive*, December 25, 2003, at www.nni.nikkei.co.jp.

27 On the concept of emperor-fascism, see Herbert P. Bix, "Rethinking 'Emperor-system Fascism': Ruptures and Continuities in Modern Japanese History," *Bulletin of Concerned Asian Scholars*, Vol. 14, No. 2 (1982).

28 Under Article 96 of the present constitution, amendments shall be initiated by the Diet "through a concurring vote of two-thirds or more of all the members of each house, and shall thereupon be submitted to the people for ratification, which shall require the affirmative vote of a majority of all votes cast thereupon." Details of the committee's work can be found in its November 2002 interim report, available in English at www.shugiin.go.jp/itdb_english.nsf/html/kenpou/english.

29 *National Defense Program Outline in and after FY 1996*.

30 "Govt to Revise Defense Outlines to Address New Threats," *Nihon Keizai Shinbun*, April 28, 2004, at www.nni.nikkei.co.jp.

31 Euan Graham, *The Security of Japan's Sea Lanes 1940–2003: "A Matter of Life and Death"?* (PhD dissertation, Australian National University), March 2003, p. 194.

32 Ibid.

33 "Excerpts from Armitage Interview with Nikkei," *NikkeiNet Interactive*, December 25, 2003, at www.nni.nikkei.co.jp.

34 For a history of Japan's postwar arms industry, see Kihara Masao, *Nihon no Gunji Sangyo* (Tokyo: Shin Nihon Shuppansha, 1994); Richard J. Samuels, *"Rich Nation, Strong Army": National Security and the Technological Transformation of Japan* (Ithaca, NY: Cornell University Press, 1996); and Michael J. Green, *Arming Japan* (New York: Columbia University Press, 1998). On the history of Japan's rocket development, see Matsuura Shinya, *H-II Rokketo Josho* (Tokyo: Nikkei BP, 1997).

35 Announced by Prime Minister Sato Eisaku in 1967, and confirmed in a parliamentary resolution of January 24, 1971. For comprehensive reviews of the situation concerning Japanese nuclear weapons in the latter half of the 1990s, see Andrew Mack, *Proliferation in Northeast Asia* (Washington, DC: Henry L. Stimson Center, Occasional Paper No. 28, July 1996), and Morton H. Halperin, *The Nuclear Dimension of the US–Japan Alliance*, July 1999, at www.nautilus.org.

36 This decline in the capacity of the Japanese peace movement has a number of sources. The first is the general collapse of the organized left based on the power of trade unions allied with the former Socialist Party and the Communist Party. A second is the worldwide decline in a sense of imminent nuclear crisis that accompanied the end of the cold war, which led to comparable collapses in

the peace movements of other advanced capitalist countries. The third source is simply the demographics of the population—the aging of the World War II generation that provided the emotional underpinning of the once very large peace movements of Japan.

37 For example, the furor that followed Shimizu Ikutaro's early 1970s essay *Nippon, kokka tareyo!* or Ishihara Shintaro's Diet speech in 1969. On Ishihara's early position on nuclear weapons, see John Welfield, *An Empire in Eclipse: Japan in the Postwar Alliance System* (London and Atlantic Highlands, N.J.: Athlone Press, 1988), p. 260.

38 Referring to possession of nuclear weapons as "a power of control" over the behavior of states, Nishimura revealed what is in fact a widespread masculine sexualization of public political thinking in Japanese elite male political circles. He likened states to rapists: "If a rapist were not punished, everyone, including us, would be a rapist. Since we have some power of restraint in terms of punishment, we will not become rapists." But see "Japanese Apology for Nuclear Call," *Guardian* (London), October 21, 1999, at www.guardian.co.uk.

39 *Japan Times* (Tokyo), April 7, 2002. Ozawa subsequently maintained that he was not advocating the acquisition of nuclear weapons, but merely pointing to a danger that may result from Chinese policy. Ozawa merged his Liberal Party into the main opposition Democratic Party of Japan in 2003.

40 Tokyo Governor Ishihara Shintaro, the most popular politician in the country, phoned Fukuda immediately to support him, saying: "Japan can possess nuclear weapons. Go for it!"

41 The three "non-nuclear principles" are not a matter of law; rather, they are just an expression of opinion by the Cabinet and the Parliament, and in no way legally bind future government actions. Equally, Article 2 in the Atomic Energy Basic Law abjures Japanese nuclear proliferation, but is not legally binding without further concrete legislation, and that has never been forthcoming. See Japan Nuclear Cycle Development Council, *Non-Proliferation Policies in Japan: The Atomic Energy Basic Law*, at www.jnc.go.jp/kaihatu/hukaku.

42 *Kyodo News*, March 17, 2003.

43 Ayako Doi, "Unforeseen Consequences: Japan's Emerging Nuclear Debate," *PacNet Newsletter*, No. 12 (March 13, 2003), at www.csis.org.

44 "Japan Arming Itself with Nuclear Weapons Inevitable: McCain," *Kyodo News*, February 17, 2003, at www.japantoday.com.

45 Charles Krauthammer, "The Japan Card," *Washington Post*, January 3, 2003.

46 Charles V. Pena, "World or Homeland? US National Security Strategy in the 21 Century," *Open Democracy*, May 29, 2003, at www.opendemocracy.net/debates.

47 Defense Agency head Ishiba Shigeru rejected Cheney's and similar remarks, saying that "As the victim of nuclear attacks in 1945, Japan is opposed to nuclear proliferation and it does not consider possessing [sic] nuclear weapons." Repurted in "Japanese Defense Chief Rules Out Nuclear Arms Race," *Yahoo! Japan News*, March 28, 2003.

48 Gsponer and Hurni note that all the declared nuclear powers, including India and Pakistan, have successfully tested boosted nuclear weapons without failure on their first try, which they interpret as meaning that the required design is now very well known to such governments. See André Gsponer and Jean Pierre Hurni, *ITER: The International Thermonuclear Experimental Reactor and the Nuclear Weapons Proliferation Implications of Thermonuclear Fusion Energy Systems* (Geneva: Independent Scientific Research Institute, 2004). The most likely immediate route to a nuclear device would be using the small amounts of weapons-grade plutonium derived from the Monju and Fugen fast breeder reactors, or failing that, reverting to using the mountain of reactor-grade plutonium. (Both Monju and Fugen have ceased functioning, Monju possibly permanently, as a result of accidents.) The next most likely route to nuclear weapons would be to utilize the huge amounts of reactor-grade plutonium presently stored at Rokkasho or in Britain and France. The troubled reprocessing plant under construction at Rokkasho—the largest industrial project ever undertaken in Japan—if completed, will simply magnify this capacity.

49 Early in 2003, the administration announced that the United States would reenter the long-running project to build an International Experimental Thermonuclear Reactor. Five years earlier, the Clinton administration had withdrawn the United States from further participation in this long-term nuclear fusion research project. Impelled partly by its close political association

with the depressed nuclear power industry, and in part by the logistical and production requirements of its policy of expanding and upgrading US nuclear weapons stockpiles, the Bush administration committed a large budget to the project.

50 Gsponer and Hurni, *ITER*, p. 12.

51 Ibid., pp. 27–53, 62.

52 Ibid., p. 12.

53 One of the two satellites was a synthetic aperture radar satellite, and the other carried an optical sensor. *Mainichi Shinbun*, March 28, 2003, at www.mainichi.go.jp.

54 It is true that the reported resolution of the visual satellites at one meter is far less than the reported resolution of current US military surveillance satellites. However, this resolution is in itself sufficient for the purpose at hand—and in any case, the actual resolution achieved by the satellites may well be much higher than has been reported.

55 On Japan and the UKUSA Agreement, see Jeffrey T. Richelson and Desmond Ball, *The Ties That Bind* (Boston: Allen and Unwin, 1985), pp. 171 ff.

56 The F-1s would have to ditch in the Sea of Japan, and the F-4EJs would have only one possible Japanese base at which they could land—and then with difficulty.

57 "Defense Budget Covers Purchases of First Refueling Plane," *Japan Times*, December 21, 2001.

8 The dangers of American exceptionalism in a revolutionary age

Nicholas J. Wheeler[1]

This chapter considers whether the Bush Doctrine seeks to establish a new rule for the preventive use of force against states and terrorist groups armed with weapons of mass destruction. Alternatively, does the Doctrine aim to carve out an exceptional right of intervention that is restricted to America alone? After emphasizing the dangers of changing the general rules on the use of force, I argue that the Bush Doctrine is not seeking such a modification. Instead, the new strategy should be viewed in the context of American exceptionalism. This has two sources: the long-standing belief of successive American governments that it is a carrier of universal values, which the United States has a historic responsibility to protect; and the administration's belief that the United States is uniquely threatened after 9/11, and thus is justified in exempting itself from the ordinary legal rules. The chapter highlights the dangers of this type of thinking. It also considers whether it is possible to ameliorate US unilateralism by devising new collective approaches to the threat posed by the spread of weapons of mass destruction to terrorist groups.

Introduction

In a landmark speech to the United States Military Academy at West Point on June 1, 2002, President George W. Bush declared that America could not rely on a strategy of deterrence for its security after 9/11. Instead, he claimed that faced with the perils posed by terrorist networks and "rogue states" acquiring weapons of mass destruction (WMD), the United States might have to strike first before the danger had materialized.[2] No American government had ever advanced such a justification for the use of force, and it has profound implications for the existing international legal framework regulating the recourse to violence. The US decision, in conjunction with its British and Australian allies, to militarily overthrow the regime of Saddam Hussein in March 2003 has been viewed by many as the first test of the so-called "Bush Doctrine." In the eyes of the majority of states in international society, America's new strategy posed a fundamental challenge to the principles underpinning the UN Charter.

The central question guiding this chapter is to explore whether the administration is seeking to create a new legal basis for the use of force that would be available to all states. Or, is the new US policy an attempt to carve out an exception to the existing legal rules that applies only to America?

The first part of the chapter examines the strategic rationale behind the Bush Doctrine, clarifying the conceptual ambiguities that have crept into the debate over whether it is a strategy of preemption or of preventive war. Next, I explore the efforts made by the State Department's Policy Planning Director, Richard Haass, to justify preventive military action as being in conformity with new understandings of sovereignty that emphasize responsibilities as well as rights. I argue that this ingenious attempt fails to meet the criticism that the Bush Doctrine issues a general license for intervention. This is because Haass, and other administration officials who argue in a similar vein, refuse to specify who should decide when a state has behaved so irresponsibly that it becomes a legitimate target for intervention. The final part of the chapter argues that far from establishing new rules for the use of force, the Bush Doctrine is best understood as a product of a moral and legal exceptionalism that claims to exempt America from existing rules. This revolutionary response to the threat from global terrorism establishes the United States as the sovereign that decides when the sovereignty of others can be infringed.

Beyond preemption and toward preventive war

Historians will have to judge whether the Bush Doctrine would have seen the light of day without the attacks against the United States on September 11, 2001. What can be said with greater certainty is that 9/11 gave the Bush administration a clear focus for defining America's national interest given the prior demise of Soviet power. The "war on terrorism" has become the legitimating standard against which to defend US foreign policy in the same way that the Soviet threat played this role in justifying containment in the late 1940s. What is different about the current situation is two-fold: first, America finds itself in a hegemonic position where it can exercise overwhelming power against any putative foe. But second, the United States faces a situation where for all its awesome firepower, it remains vulnerable to attack by hidden terrorist networks possessing WMD.[3] Washington's nightmare scenario is that groups like al-Qaeda will acquire these weapons, and the Bush Doctrine is the administration's response to this danger.

There are two routes that could facilitate such a transfer of weapons. The first is that governments that already possess these weapons or, crucially, are in the process of developing them, could sell them or hand them over to groups like al-Qaeda. The second is that state actors could lose control of these weapons and they could inadvertently fall into terrorists' hands. Either way, the Bush Doctrine proceeds from the premise that the threat posed by global terrorism is beyond traditional strategies of deterrence and containment. In his speech at West Point, the President highlighted the limits of deterrence in meeting this new danger. He stated, "Deterrence—the promise of massive retaliation against nations—means nothing against shadowy terrorist networks with no nation or citizens to defend."[4] There is no reason to dissent from this conclusion: terrorists like al-Qaeda are stateless and hence have no homeland to retaliate against. Moreover, being committed to martyrdom, they are impervious to the traditional cost–benefit calculations so central to effective deterrence.[5] What remains much more controversial, and deeply problematic, is the administration's claim that the only effective way to meet this challenge is to remove those governments—by diplomatic or military means—that are viewed as potential conduits of WMD to the terrorists.

Bush's identification of Iraq, Iran, and North Korea as specific sponsors of terrorism in his January 2002 State of the Union Address would have been more persuasive if evidence had been adduced of direct links between these states and al-Qaeda. Rather, what motivated the administration was the conviction that such links either must exist—however covertly—given the evil nature of these regimes, or would develop in the future. Benjamin R. Barber captures the way in which the war on terror became focused on state actors against whom there was no direct evidence of culpability for the attacks against the United States on September 11. He writes that the new

> doctrine is designed to apply to known terrorist perpetrators who have committed aggressive and destructive acts but whose location and origins remain uncertain; it has been applied however, to states whose location is known and identity obvious even though their connection to actual aggression is far less certain.[6]

Barber's contention overlooks how far the Bush administration has identified a specific threat emanating from "rogue states" armed with or developing WMD. Even without the link to global terrorism, Bush and his advisers believe that the very nature of these regimes poses a fundamental threat to both America's values and its security.

In his West Point speech, Bush had not explicitly rejected deterrence in relation to Iraq, Iran and North Korea—those he had labeled an "axis of evil" in his 2002 State of the Union Address. However, the *National Security Strategy* (NSS) document of September 2002 explicitly identified the development of WMD by "rogue states"[7] as a challenge to both America and the world. The NSS stated that the pursuit of, and global trade in, such weapons by these states has become a looming threat to all nations.[8] Moreover, it argued that deterrence was just as ineffective in meeting the long-term danger posed by "rogue states" armed with WMD as it was in meeting the peril posed by non-state actors equipped with such weapons. The NSS considered that the regimes governing these states were extreme risk-takers, prepared to gamble all in the pursuit of their fanatical objectives. The NSS drew a comparison between the risk-averse character of the Soviet Union during the cold war, and the propensity for risk-taking on the part of today's "rogue states." It declared that "deterrence based only upon the threat of retaliation is less likely to work against leaders of rogue states more willing to take risks, gambling with the lives of their people, and the wealth of their nations."[9] Given the administration's prognosis that both "rogue states" and terrorist groups were beyond deterrence, the only effective strategy was to ensure that the danger posed by these entities could not materialize in the first place.

Preemption or prevention?

In his 2002 State of the Union Address, Bush had warned that "I will not wait on events while dangers gather. I will not stand by as peril draws closer and closer. The United States of America will not permit the world's most dangerous regimes to threaten us with the world's most destructive weapons."[10] Five months later at West Point, the President underscored his determination to go on the offensive against America's enemies. Bush stated that, "If we wait for threats to fully materialize, we will have waited too long ... We must take the battle to the enemy, disrupt his plans, and confront the worst threats before they emerge."[11] This commitment to taking the offensive against America's enemies was center-stage in the NSS. "*To forestall or prevent* such hostile acts by our adversaries, the United States will act preemptively."[12] The drafters of the NSS employed the language of preemption to describe the new strategy. Yet what was actually being unveiled stretched this concept well beyond its normal usage, leading to the charge that what was actually being declared was a policy of preventive war.[13]

Understanding the distinction between preemptive and preventive action is crucial to understanding the extent of the shift in American policy, and to realizing the dangers that such a strategy poses to world order. A preemptive strike is one where a state, or group of states, uses force in response to an imminent threat. Michael Walzer is uncomfortable with this language of imminence if it is invoked to refer only to "the immediate moment" and thereby does away with the category of cases where there is room for deliberation about how to respond. It is Walzer's contention that it is possible to distinguish between justifiable preemption and unjustified aggression by judging whether the following criteria are met: "a manifest intent to injure, a degree of active preparation that makes that intent a positive danger, and a general situation in which waiting, or doing anything other than fighting, greatly magnifies the risk."[14] He maintains that Israel's first strike against the Egyptian air force in 1967 met this threshold of "sufficient threat."[15]

International law is ambiguous on whether states have a right of preemptive self-defense in cases where a failure to act might lead to the loss of territorial integrity or political independence. Article 51 of the UN Charter requires that an "armed attack" take place before the right of self-defense is triggered. State practice and *opinio juris*[16] appear to support such a strict interpretation of the law.[17] However, some international lawyers argue that a right of anticipatory self-defense exists in customary international law.[18] It is maintained that this right to preempt in times of crisis is not extinguished by Article 51, and that since the *Caroline* case of 1837, there has been a restricted right of preemptive action. The *Caroline* was a US vessel that was allegedly preparing to transport guerrilla forces and ammunition to assist rebels who were challenging British rule in Upper Canada. The British attacked the ship before it could put to sea, sending it over Niagara Falls. The criteria for exercising a right of anticipatory self-defense emerged during the treaty negotiations a few years later in an exchange of letters between the British and American governments. The British Foreign Secretary, Lord Ashburton, defended attacking the *Caroline* on grounds of self-defense. But the American Secretary of State, Daniel Webster, replied that for the plea of self-defense to be accepted, the British government would have "to show a necessity of self-defense, instant, overwhelming, leaving no choice of means, and no moment for deliberation."[19] The NSS seeks to justify its conception of preemption by representing it as being in conformity with a legal right. Condoleezza Rice, the President's National Security Special Assistant, and a key figure in the drafting of the NSS, contended that the case for preemption should be seen as a continuation of a long tradition in which "the United States has long affirmed the right to anticipatory self-defense."[20] But it is evident that what is being proposed in the NSS is a radical departure from anything that Webster envisaged as justifiable self-defense.

The NSS agues that the existing legal right of preemption rests "on the existence of an imminent threat—most often a visible mobilization of armies, navies, and air forces preparing to attack."[21] It calls for a broadening of "the concept of imminent threat to the capabilities and objectives of today's adversaries. Rogue states and terrorists do not seek to attack us using conventional means."[22] Groups like al-Qaeda armed with WMD could kill millions of civilians from secret bases, and without warning. The location of "rogue states" is known, but the NSS worries that the leaders of these states will also attack the United States covertly, employing the most destructive weapons known to humankind. The strategy document points out that given the enormous costs of inaction in the face of such terrifying weapons, there is a "compelling case for taking anticipatory action to defend ourselves, *even if uncertainty remains as to the time and place of the enemy's attack.*"[23] This formulation is very different from the criteria established by the *Caroline* case, and it is this which leads to the charge that it represents a new American policy of preventive war. The latter is one that is fought with a view to warding off a potential danger before it materializes into a specific intention and preparations to attack.

There is nothing new about this idea, and Walzer's cited case of the War of the Spanish Succession illustrates this.[24] The war was fought against France in the belief that it was necessary to prevent the balance of power from tipping dangerously in Louis XIV's favor. Here, war was justified by the fear that if Europe failed to act against France, it would eventually succumb to its hegemony. Walzer criticizes this type of thinking on the grounds that "war is justified ... by fear alone and not by anything other states actually do."[25] For the architects of the Bush Doctrine, the "fear" that WMD might find their way into American cities provides sufficient justification for anticipatory strikes. The contention in the NSS that such attacks are permissible, even in the absence of a specific threat, reflects the administration's conviction that the traditional distinction between preemptive and preventive war has broken down as a useful category after 9/11.

This is not the first time in American history that momentous technological and political developments have made such reasoning attractive. At the dawn of the nuclear age, some in the US defense establishment advocated a policy of preventive war as the only response to the threat that would be posed by the Soviet acquisition of nuclear capabilities. Fortunately, Presidents Truman and Eisenhower rejected such proposals.[26] Truman opposed the whole idea on moral grounds, and his publicly stated justification is worth reiterating in a context where the current administration in Washington claims the moral high ground. In a public address to the nation in 1950, Truman declared: "We do not believe in aggression or preventive war. Such a war is the weapon of dictators, not of free democratic countries like the United States."[27] What motivated the enthusiasts of preventive nuclear war in the first decade of the nuclear age was the belief that America faced a new and unparalleled danger. Moreover, they considered this emergency to justify an American exemption from ordinary moral and legal restraints. Senator Edward M. Kennedy drew attention to this parallel with the Bush Doctrine in a speech he gave to the Senate on October 7, 2002. He pointed out that the argument of those who wanted to launch preventive war against the Soviet Union was that the "uniquely destructive power of nuclear weapons required us to rethink traditional international rules."[28] Kennedy is a strong critic of the Bush Doctrine, and is very worried about what he sees as the attempt in the NSS to rewrite the rules governing the use of force.

Israel's attack in 1981 on the Iraqi nuclear reactor at Osirak is a model of what the Bush administration has in mind by its policy of "anticipatory action"[29] against rogue states and terrorist groups. The reactor was not operational and it was under full-scope International Atomic Energy Authority (IAEA) safeguards. Israel was determined that it would not allow its enemy to develop nuclear weapons that might be used against it. Speaking before the US Congress in late 2002, former Israeli Prime Minister Benjamin Netanyahu reflected that his country had acted in 1981 "because we understood that a nuclear-armed Saddam Hussein would place our very survival at risk."[30] But Israel's action was almost universally condemned as an act of aggression, and even the United States voted in the Security Council to support a resolution censuring the action.[31] The unanimous view in the Council was that Iraq's fledgling nuclear energy program did not pose a threat to Israel that could possibly justify its plea of anticipatory self-defense. Certainly, the Iraqi reactor, even when switched on, could not possibly be seen as posing an imminent threat in Webster's term. If we move along the spectrum and consider Walzer's criteria of "sufficient threat," this judgment becomes more complex. The government of Saddam Hussein viewed Israel as a major foe. Moreover, had Iraq broken out of its NPT obligations, its nuclear ambitions would have been accelerated by having a reactor operational at Osirak. The question as to whether the Israeli strike was a legitimate one turns on how far delaying such an action would have exposed it to unacceptably high risks.[32]

The current administration in Washington has rendered a very different interpretation of Osirak than that which prevailed at the time.[33] For example, Vice President Richard Cheney, in a speech to US war veterans in August 2002, hailed the Israeli strike for setting back Iraq's nuclear ambitions.[34] It was clear from Cheney's speech that he viewed the Israeli attack as entirely legitimate, and he put America's enemies on notice that "We under no circumstances will allow an enemy to develop against our people weapons of mass destruction."[35] According to Lawrence F. Kaplan and William Kristol, two prominent advocates of the Bush Doctrine, Osirak "stands as the very model for preemptive action, undertaken in the face of a clear, though hardly imminent, threat and despite howls of international protest."[36]

The logic of the Bush Doctrine is that it could justify actions taken anywhere on a spectrum spanning the restrictive criteria of the *Caroline* case on the one hand, to full-blown preventive war on the other. This assessment raises two fundamental questions. First, is the Bush administration seeking to establish a new right of anticipatory action that would be available to other states? Second, who should decide when this doctrine is to be applied? Richard Haass, former Director of the State Department's Policy Planning Staff, began in 2002 and early 2003 to set out a rationale that would justify states' resorting to preventive military intervention. Haass' arguments were specifically aimed at securing international legitimacy for an attack against Iraq. But they rested on an appeal to a changed understanding of sovereignty that created a new basis for the use of force—a basis that, at least in principle, was applicable to all states.

Anticipatory intervention and the "limits of sovereignty" thesis

The "limits of sovereignty" thesis is underpinned by the contention that state sovereignty is a responsibility and not a right. This changed understanding of the principle of sovereignty gained ground in international society during the 1990s in response to debates over the legitimacy and legality of humanitarian intervention.[37] The Special Representative to the UN Secretary General for Internally Displaced Persons, Francis M. Deng, labeled this approach "sovereignty as responsibility."[38] The Secretary General himself is a great enthusiast for this doctrine. Speaking in 1998 before NATO's intervention in Kosovo, Kofi Annan emphasized that the UN Charter belongs to the peoples of the world and not to the states that are their representatives at the UN. He asserted that "The [UN] Charter protects the sovereignty of peoples. It was never meant as a license for governments to trample on human rights and human dignity. Sovereignty implies responsibility, not just power."[39] This is not a rejection of the core principles of sovereignty and nonintervention; rather, states that claim these rights must recognize responsibilities for the protection of citizens inside their jurisdictions.[40]

Taking this change of normative context as his point of departure, Haass sought to argue that the Bush Doctrine was in conformity with this new conception of sovereignty. He argued in a series of speeches that there should be three exceptions to the norm of nonintervention. He set these out clearly in an address to the International Institute for Strategic Studies (IISS) on September 13, 2002. The first limit to sovereignty arises in cases where a state fails to uphold "basic, minimum standards of domestic conduct and human rights." Haass cited NATO's intervention in Kosovo as being guided by this new understanding of sovereignty. The second exception to the nonintervention principle, according to Haass, arises in cases where states act as safe havens for terrorist groups. Haass suggested that the US intervention against the Taliban in October 2001 represented a good example of this principle in practice. There was widespread international support, he said, for the idea that "sovereignty can provide no protection for governments that carry out or abet such terrorism." It was not the Taliban who had executed the attacks against the United States on September 11, but "virtually everyone agreed it was legitimate for the United States to intervene in Afghanistan and target the Taliban."[41]

The above limitations on the exercise of sovereign rights are relatively uncontroversial. However, Haass' third claim for a limit to sovereignty is much more readily disputed. He reiterated the administration's developing position that deterrence was inadequate to cope with the threat posed by terrorist groups like al-Qaeda, and in relation to rogue states governed by leaders like Saddam Hussein. Haass argued that "today, we are on the cusp of a third adjustment to our thinking about sovereignty ... in this new international environment where terrorism and WMD are intersecting ... [and where] the dangers of inaction outweigh the costs of action. In these extreme circumstances, a strong case can be made for preventive military action."[42] He followed up this speech with another in January 2003, in which he developed the view that certain states developing WMD risk exposing themselves to legitimate intervention by others. He declared:

> When certain regimes with a history of aggression and support for terrorism pursue weapons of mass destruction, thereby endangering the international community, they jeopardize their sovereign immunity from intervention, including anticipatory action to destroy this developing capability.[43]

Haass did not explicitly address the crucial question of who should decide when such intervention was justified. But an important clue to his position can be seen from the fact that at no point did he seek to restrict a right of "anticipatory action" to the United States, recognizing no doubt that such a double standard would be unacceptable.

It is evident from an interview he gave a few months earlier to Nicholas Lemann of *The New Yorker* that the Director of the State Department's Policy Planning Staff accepted that a right of preventive military intervention should be available to other states. Haass reportedly claimed that "if a government fails to meet [its] obligations, then it forfeits some of the normal advantages of sovereignty ... [and] ... *other governments, including the United States, gain the right to intervene*."[44] This proposition finds support in Rice's statement that "preemption ... does not give a green light—to the United States or any other nation—to act first without exhausting other means, including diplomacy."[45]

A flawed logic

Haass' attempt to justify the Bush Doctrine by locating it as both a logical and necessary development of the idea of "sovereignty as responsibility" was an ingenious one. However, there was a fundamental flaw at the heart of his position. This stemmed from his concern to ensure that the principle of sovereignty remained the cornerstone of the contemporary world order. He recognized that sovereignty enabled states holding different conceptions of justice to develop an ethic of coexistence that upheld interstate order. "We do not want to return to a world," he said, "in which governments routinely intervene in one another's internal affairs. In an age of advanced conventional weapons and new instruments of mass destruction, this would be a recipe for catastrophe." This led him to argue for "a general presumption in favor of respecting sovereignty."[46] The problem that Haass failed to address was how this commitment could be reconciled with a doctrine of "preventive military action" that ceded to individual states enormous discretion over the use of force.

The NSS had tried to anticipate this criticism by arguing that "nations [should not] use preemption as a pretext for aggression."[47] But critics argued that in failing to establish clear criteria for distinguishing between "legitimate anticipation"[48] and illegitimate aggression, the Bush Doctrine issued a general license for intervention. In fairness to the administration, some officials did try to establish limits to the operation of the preemption doctrine. From these statements and comments, it is possible to identify four criteria that the administration viewed as crucial in determining whether an anticipatory strike was justifiable. The first is a past history of aggression, both against neighboring states, and against that government's own citizens. Second, as Rice put it in her 2002 Wriston lecture, "the threat must be very grave."[49] Unfortunately she supplied no elaboration of how this should be determined. Neither did Haass, who was content to leave it as a situation where "it's a question of when, and not if, you're going to be attacked."[50] Next, administration officials stressed, in Rice's words, "that the risks of waiting must far outweigh the risks of action."[51] Finally, the National Security Adviser emphasized in a number of speeches and interviews that no state should use force preemptively before exhausting diplomatic efforts. The problem with this attempt to limit the applicability of the preemption concept is that it does not address the thorny issue of who is to decide when these indicators for triggering anticipatory action have been met.

It is no surprise, then, to discover that the administration has been accused of legitimating a doctrine of anticipatory war. In his speech to the Senate, Kennedy charged that the Bush Doctrine "would also send a signal to governments the world over that the rules of aggression have changed for them too, which could increase the risk of conflict between countries."[52] From the opposite end of the US political spectrum, that doyen of realism, Henry Kissinger, cautioned that it was "not in the American national interest to establish preemption as a universal principle available to every nation."[53] This criticism has been echoed in foreign ministries across the world, and received an eloquent expression in Annan's speech to the General Assembly in September 2003. The Secretary General expressed his deep unease with a policy that "represents a fundamental challenge to the principles on which, however imperfectly, world peace and stability have rested for the last fifty-eight years ... if it were to be adopted, it could set precedents that resulted in a proliferation of the unilateral and lawless use of force."[54]

The Bush administration has stubbornly resisted these warnings about the dangers of the preemptive policy set out in the NSS. I will argue later in the chapter that this reflects the legal and moral exceptionalism driving current American policy. However, an alternative argument is that senior officials like Rice and Haass were not persuaded that the assertion of a new legal rule by the United States would lead others to emulate it. This thinking is well captured in Robert Kagan's comment: "I don't think we're moving into the age of preemption ... I don't think other nations are being restrained from taking action by the fact that no one has set the precedent of preemption. That's not why China is not attacking Taiwan. That's not why India is not attacking Pakistan."[55] Kagan is right that the world will not suddenly find itself in an age of anticipatory intervention because of the strategy enunciated in the NSS. Few states find themselves in situations where such policy choices are forced upon them. However, some do, and it is in these cases—two of which Kagan actually cites—where there is good reason to feel concerned that governments might seek to defend their actions by appealing to the rationale underpinning the Bush Doctrine.[56] The case of India and Pakistan provides a very good illustration of the dangers here.

India's belief, for example, that Pakistan is complicit in terrorist attacks against Indian forces in Kashmir might lead it to attack the bases of Islamic extremists inside Pakistan, leading to a war that has the potential to go nuclear. The worry is that in a future crisis between the two countries, such as erupted in Spring 2002 over Kashmir, "a US policy of preemption may provide hawks in India the added ammunition they need to justify a strike against Pakistan in the eyes of their fellow Indian decision-makers."[57] India's Finance Minister Jaswant Singh, visiting Washington at the end of September 2002, lost no time in lending his support to the Bush administration's policy of preemption. In doing so, he offered a very different reading of Article 51 from the one held by the majority of international society. Singh declared that, "where there is deterrence there is preemption. The same thing is there in Article 51 of the United Nations Charter." Moreover, he asserted that preemption was a policy that should be available for all states: "it is not the prerogative of any one country," he said, adding that "preemption is the right of any nation to prevent injury to itself."[58] The likelihood that others would invoke the US language of preemption to serve their own ends was underlined by North Korea's statement on February 6, 2003, that "preemptive attacks are not the exclusive right of the US"[59] One further adverse consequence of the US self-identification with a policy of preemption is that it significantly reduces US diplomatic leverage in counseling restraint in cases where governments are deliberating over the merits of launching an anticipatory attack.[60]

The need for a new international legal framework

Modifying international law to permit a right of anticipatory action beyond the restrictive definition established by the *Caroline* case clearly poses considerable dangers to the fabric of interstate order. Yet the specter of outlaw states facilitating terrorist groups to acquire WMD, and the fact that once armed in this way such groups would be beyond deterrence, demonstrates the patent inadequacy of the existing UN framework regulating the use of force. The Bush Doctrine is a revolutionary response to revolutionary times. The UN Secretary General recognized as much when he appealed to the General Assembly to empathize with the fears that make some states feel "uniquely vulnerable since it is those concerns that drive them to take unilateral action."[61] Annan did not mention the United States by name, but his message was clear: a key challenge facing the UN was to persuade Washington that the vulnerabilities driving the Bush Doctrine could be effectively addressed through UN collective action.

Annan's radical prescription for meeting the disease of global terrorism without succumbing to the ills of unilateralism was for the Security Council to devise new rules governing the preemptive use of force. The Secretary General posited that the Council urgently

> needs to consider how it will deal with the possibility that individual states may use force preemptively against perceived threats. Its members may need to begin a discussion on the criteria for an early authorization of coercive measures to address certain types of threats, for instance, terrorist groups armed with weapons of mass destruction.[62]

Two important implications follow from Annan's position: first, states should secure Council authorization before undertaking anticipatory action, and, second, the Council should arrive at such judgments based on the application of agreed criteria. Even if it proves possible to reach a consensus on the substantive principles that should determine the use of force, Annan's formulation sidesteps the troubling issue of what should happen if the Council fails to agree that such conditions have been met in a particular case. This was the problem that divided the five permanent members of the Security Council (Perm-5) over military intervention in Kosovo. And disagreements of this kind arise most acutely in such cases of anticipatory intervention.

In the case of Kosovo, there was no disagreement in the Council that the Milosevic government in Yugoslavia was in violation of its international humanitarian responsibilities. Instead, controversy centered on whether all peaceful means had been exhausted, whether the humanitarian crisis was so grave that it warranted recourse to force, and whether violent means would do more harm than good. On all these questions, there was plenty of room for reasonable disagreement. Russia and China strongly opposed intervention, and the former made clear it would veto any resolution seeking authority for NATO to intervene. Faced with deadlock in the Council, and believing classified intelligence reports that predicted a humanitarian catastrophe if no action was taken, NATO made the decision to bypass the Security Council. This was condemned by Russia, China, and India (which, as a non-member, requested to participate in the Council's debates over NATO's action).

Set against this, the wider membership of the Council showed by their rejection of a Russian resolution condemning NATO's action that they sympathized with the moral reasoning behind NATO's action. In justifying the votes they cast against the Russian position, some of these governments implicitly blamed Russia for unreasonably preventing the Council from acting to discharge its humanitarian and security responsibilities under the Charter.[63] While many members of the Council castigated Russia for its behavior over Kosovo, they overlooked the legitimate grounds for contesting whether the human rights situation in Kosovo had reached the threshold that justified military intervention. What this case highlights is the fundamental problem of reaching a consensus on intervention when evidence is ambiguous, as it is always going to be when the merits of anticipatory action are being deliberated.

The difficulties that bedeviled the Council over Kosovo reappeared in its deliberations over the legitimacy of attacking Iraq. In this case, the United States and the United Kingdom sought Council approval for a strike against a member of the UN so as to prevent it from acquiring WMD that could be used against other states and/or transferred to terrorist groups. There were attempts by these governments to portray the Iraqi threat as an urgent danger, but the case for war did not rest on this premise. Rather, both the Bush administration and the Blair government were convinced that the regime of Saddam Hussein clearly met the conditions for what Walzer defined as a "sufficient threat." It will be recalled that these are malign intent, active preparations that make that threat a real danger, and a situation where the costs of waiting far outweigh the costs of action. However, in a reverse of the Kosovo case, the United States and the United Kingdom found themselves holding a minority position in the Council.

The majority of states, led by France and Russia, were not persuaded that Iraq's development of WMD constituted a "sufficient threat" to justify forcible regime change. They did recognize that Iraq was in violation of a host of Security Council resolutions, dating back to 1991, demanding disarmament of its WMD. However, rather than employ the military instrument to neutralize this threat, most members looked to Hans Blix, and his team of UN weapons inspectors, to contain the danger. Under Resolution 1441, adopted unanimously on November 8, 2002, Blix was required to report back to the Council on whether Iraq was in "material breach" of Resolution 1441. The latter had given Iraq "a final opportunity to comply" with its disarmament obligations under successive Council resolutions.[64] Had Blix in his reports to the Council on January 27, February 14, and March 7, 2003, found incontrovertible evidence of Iraq's development of WMD, this would have changed the dynamics in the Council in favor of a new UN resolution authorizing the use of force. Instead, it was evident that had the United States and the United Kingdom (and Spain, which supported the Anglo-American position) proposed such a resolution, this would have failed to secure the necessary nine votes, leaving aside the issue as to whether France and Russia would have vetoed it.

The lesson of Iraq is a clear if troubling one: even if the Security Council were to follow up Annan's recommendation and arrive at criteria to decide when anticipatory intervention was justified, this would not resolve the thorny problem of agreeing in particular cases whether they had been met. Few would argue that intervention should be prohibited in all cases where the Council is paralyzed by the threat of the veto, and intervention to prevent or end genocide is often cited as a justifiable exception to the rule of Council authorization. In such situations, the

Council performs the role of what Thomas Franck calls "a global jury,"[65] in which it judges the legality and legitimacy of such actions. In this regard, Kosovo and Iraq were both undertaken without explicit Council authorization, but the reactions of other Council members varied enormously in the two cases. NATO's action was generally excused as a technical breach of Charter rules that was justifiable on moral grounds. By contrast, the action of the United States and the United Kingdom in invading Iraq was interpreted as a fundamental breach of Charter principles that challenged the very pillars of UN authority.

In suggesting that a right of anticipatory intervention should be open to other states, Rice and Haass did not make this conditional on Council approval. Yet in failing to do so, they laid themselves open to the charge, in Joseph Nye's words, that "any state could set itself up as judge, jury and executioner."[66] This was the concern that had motivated Annan to call upon the General Assembly to devise new collective rules for the use of force. But this criticism of the Bush Doctrine misinterprets the real intention behind it: to ensure that a right of anticipatory intervention is restricted to the United States alone. This reflects the explosive cocktail of legal and moral exceptionalism that shapes the mindset of the current administration in Washington.

America as the exceptional hegemon

The idea of the United States as an exceptional nation is deeply rooted in the psyche of the American people. This belief in the special character of that republic can be traced back to the vision of the Founding Fathers. Historically, the notion that America has a special mission in the world has manifested itself in two contradictory foreign policy impulses. On the one hand, it generates an isolationist ethos in which the United States seeks to distance itself from overseas entanglements, lest these corrupt and damage the democratic project at home. On the other hand, this belief in America as "a city upon a hill" has led it to expand and to strike out against foreign foes in the belief that it has a "manifest destiny" to universalize American values. In 1917, President Woodrow Wilson made the fateful decision to commit American forces to support Britain and the Commonwealth against Germany. He believed that the German threat imperiled both American values and its long-term security. In his declaration to Congress on April 2, 1917, Wilson declared that "the world must be made safe for democracy ... civilization itself seeming to be in the balance."[67] In keeping with America's exceptionalist vision, the President held that the United States was the only agent of global salvation, and that if America acted in defense of its principles, then this would assure its and the world's safety.

The "new mandarins of American power"[68] believe that the threat from global terrorism and rogue states makes this an equally momentous moment in US history. The President and his closest advisers deem that American values are endangered on a worldwide scale, and that only the final triumph of these over the forces of terror will assure America's survival. In his 2003 State of the Union Address, Bush expressed this Manichean struggle between good and evil in the following terms: "Once again, this nation and all our friends are all that stand between a world at peace, and a world of chaos and constant alarm ... we are called to defend the safety of our people, and the hopes of all mankind. And we accept this responsibility."[69] Even before 9/11, the administration had perceived a dangerous world in which national security depended upon military strength. After the vulnerability of American cities to suicide bombing attacks was so brutally revealed on September 11, Bush, Cheney, and Rice stated repeatedly their belief that the United States faced a new and deadly menace to its very survival. Wilson defended America's intervention in the First World War on the grounds that the United States had both a moral mission and a compelling security interest in protecting liberal democratic values. The Bush administration argues that faced with the threat from global terrorism, the continuation of this project is indispensable to national survival: if the world is not made safe for democracy, there will be no safety for America in the world.

In her *Foreign Affairs* article in 2000, Rice asserted that "American values are universal."[70] The logical corollary is that humanity should recognize that American interests and global interests are indivisible. The disturbing implication of this messianic worldview is that the United States can only be secure if it recreates the world in its own image. In describing Iraq, Iran, and North Korea as an "axis of evil," Bush made clear that there could be no lasting coexistence between the United States and "rogue states" that develop WMD. This commitment to regime change stems importantly from the moral compass guiding the administration, and especially the President. But it is also driven by the strong conviction that as long as these regimes remain in power, the intolerable risk exists that they could develop nuclear weapons. Through either deliberate design or inadvertence, these deadly instruments could find their way into terrorist hands. Consequently, the Bush Doctrine is predicated on the belief that eliminating dangerous weapons in the hands of "rogue states" requires nothing short of their removal from power.

Against this background, it becomes evident that from Washington's perspective, the Security Council's commitment to disarming Iraq through the route of UN weapons inspectors was fatally flawed. The UN route relied on the premise that the United States could accept Saddam's remaining in power provided that his military ambitions were effectively halted. However, Bush and the other neoconservatives driving American policy believed that there could be no long-term guarantee against Iraq's developing nuclear weapons if the Baathist regime was not overthrown. Thus, the discussions in the Council as to whether the UN inspectors should be given more time failed to address the core security problem posed by Iraq: the combination of Saddam's malign intent and Iraq's long-term military potential created a future peril to American security that had to be neutralized. Hans Blix might have talked in his reports to the Council about the need for the Council to put in place a long-term system for verifying that Iraq was not developing WMD. But this aspiration ran up against the deep-rooted conviction among the neoconservatives that America should not rely on other states, or international institutions, for its security.[71]

The new administration had put the world on notice before the attacks on September 11 that it would privilege American values and interests over fidelity to the rules of multilateral bodies.[72] What changed after 9/11 was the belief that America confronted a state of emergency that could only end when the threat from global terrorism had been finally eradicated. In his foreword to the NSS, Bush declared that "the war against terrorists of global reach is a global enterprise of uncertain duration."[73] What defines this emergency is the administration's belief that the existing international legal framework is inadequate to meet the new threat. Given the unique character of the threat posed by terrorist groups armed with WMD, and the indispensable need for American power in meeting it, the administration looks to the rest of the world to recognize that the United States should be accorded special rights and privileges. The NSS affirmed the administration's commitment to working through the UN and other international institutions. But as Iraq showed, this does not extend to accepting real constraints on America's freedom of action, especially where this involves decisions on the use of force. An important clue to the mindset guiding Bush, Cheney, Rice, Secretary of Defense Donald H. Rumsfeld, and his deputy Paul D. Wolfowitz can be gleaned from a comment by Richard Perle (a member of Rumsfeld's Defense Policy Advisory Board) that US unilateralism over Iraq marks the death of the "fantasy of the UN as the foundation of a new world order." What is noteworthy about this statement is Perle's characterization of this "fantasy" as being grounded in the belief in security's power to be delivered "through international law administered by international institutions."[74]

The administration's rationale for America's exiting the ordinary legal rules has striking parallels with Carl Schmitt's justification of the Nazis' dismantling of the rule of law in Germany in the 1930s. Schmitt argued that all law is radically indeterminate, and that "the primary and most important question is not [the always easily disputable and dubious] content of the norm, but rather the question of *quis judicabit?*"[75] What was crucial for Schmitt was that it is the sovereign, by virtue of its power, that decides the *exception*. In the case of the Nazis, Hitler declared a state of emergency and then enacted new laws to justify actions that destroyed the rights that had existed under the previous legal order. In terms of international law, a favorite example cited by Schmitt was how the United States had fashioned a legal system in the Americas based on the nonintervention treaty while using the same device to justify actions that contradicted its basic premise. Reflecting on the Monroe Doctrine, he wrote that it "is a very general, very broad 'Doctrine' which provides grounds for altogether contrary forms of action ... Only the United States determines what the Monroe Doctrine means in the concrete case."[76] A similar logic can be seen at work in the Bush Doctrine: it is America, the global sovereign, that determines who has abused sovereign rights and should be intervened against. And this exceptional right to act outside the framework of the UN Charter is restricted to America alone. The administration would seek to justify this special right by pointing out that the United States is the only power that is in a position to save humanity, and that others should welcome it carrying this burden.[77] A Schmittian reply would be that America gets to decide the exception because no one else is in a position to challenge it.

The latter perception has characterized the dominant response to the Bush

Doctrine from governments and peoples around the world. Millions across the globe demonstrated against going to war in Iraq, and the administration's policies are frequently characterized as both imperialist and dangerous. No one denies that the United States faces a legitimate danger from terrorists who are prepared to die for their cause and who can escape retaliation. But what is strongly contested is that the new American strategy of "anticipatory attack" and regime change will make it more secure. Indeed, as David Hendrickson has argued, the "depiction of the malady of the *revolutionary power* increasingly fits the United States."[78] The defining feature of a revolutionary power, as Kissinger brilliantly argued in his classic *A World Restored*, is not that a state feels insecure—since this condition is endemic to a system of sovereign states—*but that nothing can reassure it.*[79] As a consequence it seeks the will-o'-the-wisp of absolute security, fermenting insecurity for all. In a post-9/11 world this requires that the United States create a world in which WMD and terrorism can never come together. Yet as Pierre Hassner chillingly points out, since "there will always be some terrorists and some weapons of mass destruction ... the only end in sight to such a war would be total ... control by the United States."[80]

One response to America's exceptionalist claim would be to embrace it, the moral justification being that the Bush Doctrine—wielded by a state with America's virtue and power—offers the only hope of defeating the terrorists. However, the problem with this line of argument is that others—allies and enemies alike—are not persuaded that the threat from global terrorism and rogue states warrants abandoning the UN Charter framework. The Bush Doctrine seeks nothing less than the elimination of the risk that terrorist states or groups could use WMD against US targets. But one perverse consequence of the new policy is that it is likely to accelerate the proliferation of WMD as potential targets of US intervention seek to acquire nuclear weapons as a deterrent against being attacked. Moreover, if the United States threatens military action against those developing such weapons, this might be the one action that would induce those states to do the one thing the United States is desperate to avoid, namely, supply terrorist groups like al-Qaeda with access to these weapons.

The more America tries to defend the Bush Doctrine by appealing to exceptionalist arguments, the more it will be robbed of international legitimacy. The architects of the NSS exhibit a curious naiveté about power, in failing to understand that it cannot last unless it is grounded in a wider consensus about norms and values that goes beyond calculations of narrow military capabilities.[81] Intriguingly, the normally opposed schools of classical realism and liberal internationalism have made common cause in critiquing the administration for its dismissive attitude to international law and international institutions.[82]

The Bush administration stands at a crossroads, and which way it turns will have a decisive impact on the future world order. One direction lies in continuing along the revolutionary path mapped out in the NSS. Iraq was the first test of the new doctrine, and the risks and costs associated with that operation have been far higher than the administration anticipated. Beyond Iraq, there remain the questions of how to deal with states like Iran, Syria, and—most troubling given its acquisition of a few nuclear devices—North Korea. If the administration should seek to apply its remedy of "anticipatory attack" to these cases, the consequences would be even more far-reaching and dangerous than has been the case with Iraq, especially in relation to North Korea. But there is another road that can be taken, one that recognizes the wisdom of moderation in statecraft and that recognizes that even hegemons need a law-governed order in which to secure their interests and values.

Conclusion

In assessing the moral, legal, political, and strategic issues raised by the Bush Doctrine, it is important to bear in mind that it is open to two fundamentally different interpretations. On the one hand, the new US policy of "anticipatory action" can be conceived of as an attempt to alter the Charter-based rules governing the use of force. Such a legal change, if widely accepted in international society, would represent a radical shift in the legitimate bases for using force. The UN Charter was aimed at severely restricting the recourse to war on the part of individual states. The Bush Doctrine relaxes these restraints by issuing a general license for intervention in cases where a state judges that others are developing WMD that will pose a future threat to its very existence. It does not require the existence of an imminent threat to be triggered, and it does not depend upon the authority of the Security Council. On the other hand, I have argued for a different reading of the Bush revolution in national security policy. This alternative explains the Bush Doctrine in terms of American exceptionalism. Far from seeking to change the general rules on the use of force, America seeks to exempt itself from these, whilst simultaneously claiming a special right to intervene to protect the United States from the dangers of global terrorism. In either manifestation, it is evident that the Bush Doctrine represents a radical assault on the principles of the UN Charter.

The question raised by the Bush administration's challenge to the UN is whether the rules in the Charter can safeguard collective security in a post-9/11 world. The American answer is that it will not rely for its security on international law and international institutions: the stakes are too high to wait for multilateral security mechanisms to respond to the challenge. The UN Secretary General's response to this unilateralist approach was to appeal to the General Assembly to devise new rules on the use of force that would persuade the United States that its security anxieties could be effectively addressed through UN action.[83] Annan is rightly prepared to cross the Rubicon of preventive military action against terrorist groups armed with WMD, though he was silent on whether this extended to regime change in states harboring terrorists. The Council's difficulties in reaching agreement over anticipatory intervention in the cases of both Kosovo and Iraq underline the importance of trying to establish criteria for deciding when such actions are permissible. But it would be exceedingly optimistic to think that such criteria would have produced a consensus in either of these cases, even if it might have clarified the points of disagreement more concretely.

Annan agrees with Haass that sovereignty brings with it concomitant responsibilities in relation to WMD. But where the State Department official had evaded the central question of who should authorize armed action, Annan believes that this authority must be given to the Council. Yet what happens if the Council is judged by particular states to be unwilling or unable to sanction the use of force, as happened over Kosovo and Iraq? Franck would argue that unilateral action of this kind is always open to the "jurying" function performed by UN political organs.[84] The case of Kosovo is illustrative, since while NATO acted without express Council authorization, its breach of Charter authority was treated with considerable leniency by a Security Council and General Assembly sympathetic to the moral claims behind NATO's use of force. By contrast, the United States' and the United Kingdom's reasoning over war against Iraq failed to elicit a similar response.

The disagreement over Iraq turned on the question of whether it constituted such a threat to regional and global security that it justified regime change in Baghdad. Annan's hope for bringing the United States back into the UN fold rests on the contention that it is possible to devise new collective mechanisms that will persuade the United States to eschew unilateralism. The problem is that while the United States acts like a revolutionary power, it is beyond the reassurance of existing or new UN institutional mechanisms. What worries the administration after 9/11 is not the 99-percent near-certainty that "rogue states" armed with WMD would be deterred from threatening US interests or aiding terrorists, but the 1-percent uncertainty that they might act. It is the elimination of this type of risk that drives current US policy. Yet the United States will never be able to build an international consensus around this proposition, because it sanctions going to war against hypothetical dangers that have not yet materialized. The administration would reply that the costs of delaying action in such cases are too high to risk. But if other states were to employ the same logic, the principles of sovereignty and nonintervention upon which the existing international order rests would come crashing down.

Given that the administration is well aware of this, it must be laying claim to special rights that it wishes to deny to others. This is rooted in the related convictions that America is uniquely threatened after 9/11, has a responsibility to use its position of military superiority to promote a world safe for democratic values, and is thus justified in deciding when other states should forfeit their sovereign rights. Few if any states, friend or foe, would accept America's taking on this mantle of global Leviathan. And if this cannot be resisted in conventional military terms because of America's overwhelming strength, it will be challenged by other means. One highly probable and dangerous form of resistance is the spur it will give others to acquire nuclear weapons. Such a development would, paradoxically, magnify the risks that the Bush Doctrine is aimed at eliminating. It would also create the very crises that might lead the United States, or those it seeks to forcibly disarm, to use force preventively. The second counterproductive effect of the strategy is that future American military adventurism beyond Iraq is likely to further increase support for extremist groups like al-Qaeda. What is missing from the Bush Doctrine is recognition of the poverty, violence, despair, and anger that lead some individuals to seek salvation in terrorist acts of religious martyrdom. In espousing the principle that sovereign states have specific responsibilities related to fighting terrorism and the spread of WMD, the United States should not overlook its own responsibilities in addressing the causes, as well as the symptoms, of global terrorism.

The Bush administration's militarized approach to the "war on terror" stems from the belief that America is threatened on an unprecedented scale. It also leads to the axiom that the emergency is too great to rely on existing multilateral mechanisms of security, crucially the UN. America has often paid lip service to international law while breaking it. But it has never issued as direct an assault on the rules determining the use of force as it has done with the Bush Doctrine. Unless the current or future administrations adjust their attitude to the UN, there is little hope that the Council will be able to devise new rules to cope with the threat posed by global terrorism. Despite all its limitations, the UN remains the best hope of building a collective security system that can regulate state and non-state violence in world politics. Bush claimed in his West Point speech that deterrence and containment were outmoded in coping with the new threats; American actions in the coming years will determine whether we should add the UN to that list.

Notes

1 This chapter was first presented as "The Bush Doctrine: the Responsibilities of Sovereignty or a Revolutionary Challenge to the Principles of International Order," Social Science Research Council workshop on "International Law and Terrorism," Washington, DC, November 14–15, 2002. I am grateful to all the participants for their contributions. I would like to thank Michael Byers, Anne Harris, Peter Van Ness, and especially Toni Erskine for their comments on earlier versions of this chapter.
2 "Remarks by the President at the 2002 Graduation Exercise of the United States Military Academy," June 1, 2002, online at www.whitehouse.gov/news/releases/2002…/20020601-3.htm.
3 David Rieff, "Hope is Not Enough," *Prospect*, October 2003, p. 32.
4 "Remarks by the President."
5 John Ikenberry encapsulates this problem by noting that terrorist groups like al-Qaeda "cannot be deterred because they are either willing to die for their cause or able to escape retaliation." Ikenberry, "The Lures of Preemption," *Foreign Affairs*, September–October 2002, p. 51.
6 Benjamin R. Barber, *Fear's Empire: War, Terrorism, and Democracy* (New York: Norton, 2003), p. 105.
7 The NSS identified the following characteristics that it claimed "rogue states" shared in common: "These states: brutalize their own people and squander their national resources for the personal gain of the rulers; display no regard for international law, threaten their neighbors, and callously violate international treaties to which they are party; are determined to acquire weapons of mass destruction, along with other advanced military technology, to be used as threats or offensively to achieve the aggressive designs of these regimes; sponsor terrorism around the globe; and reject basic human values and hate the United States and everything for which it stands." *The National Security Strategy of the United States*, September 20, 2002.
8 Ibid.
9 Ibid.
10 George W. Bush, State of the Union Address, January 29, 2002.
11 "Remarks by the President."
12 *The National Security Strategy of the United States*, emphasis added.

13 David C. Hendrickson, "Toward Universal Empire: The Dangerous Quest for Absolute Security," *World Policy Journal*, Fall 2002; and Barber, *Fear's Empire*.
14 Michael Walzer, *Just and Unjust Wars: A Moral Argument with Historical Illustrations* (London: Allen Lane, 1977), p. 81.
15 However, as Michael Byers points out, Israel claimed that Egypt's blocking of the Straits of Tiran was a prior act of aggression thereby justifying self-defense under Article 51 of the Charter. Michael Byers, "Preemptive Self-defense: Hegemony, Equality and Strategies of Legal Change," *The Journal of Political Philosophy*, Vol. 11, No. 2 (November, 2003), p. 180.
16 *Opinio juris* refers to that subjective or intersubjective element of the law that accompanies the practices of states. If states engage in a practice and claim that this is permitted or required by the law, then over time, this practice will acquire the status of a new customary law. For a fuller discussion, see Anthony C. Arend and Robert J. Beck, *International Law and the Use of Force: Beyond the UN Charter Paradigm* (London: Routledge, 1993), p. 6.
17 Byers, "Preemptive Self-defense," p. 180.
18 For a good overview of these debates, see ibid. and Neta C. Crawford, "The Best Defense," *Boston Review*, Vol. 28, No. 1 (February–March, 2003).
19 J.S. Davidson, *Grenada: A Study in Politics and the Limits of International Law* (Aldershot: Gower, 1987), p. 101.
20 Condoleezza Rice, 2002 Wriston Lecture, New York, October 1, 2002.
21 *The National Security Strategy of the United States*.
22 Ibid.
23 Ibid. (emphasis added).
24 Walzer, *Just and Unjust Wars*, pp. 78–80.
25 Ibid., p. 77.
26 For a discussion of preventive war thinking in the United States in the early cold-war period, see Scott D. Sagan, "More Will be Worse," in Scott D. Sagan and Kenneth Waltz, *The Spread of Nuclear Weapons: A Debate Renewed*, 2d ed. (New York: Norton, 2003), pp. 55–9.
27 Quoted ibid., p. 56.
28 Senator Edward M. Kennedy, "The Bush Doctrine of Pre-Emption," October 7, 2002, at www.truthout.com/docs_02/10.09A.kennedy.p.htm.
29 This phrase is the one employed in the NSS; from the administration's point of view, it nicely evades the question of whether the Bush Doctrine is a strategy of preemptive or preventive war.
30 Quoted in Lawrence F. Kaplan and William Kristol, *The War over Iraq: Saddam's Tyranny and America's Mission* (San Francisco: Encounter Books, 2003), p. 89.
31 For a discussion of the international response see Christine Gray, *International Law and the Use of Force* (Oxford: Oxford University Press, 2000), pp. 114–15.
32 This calculation of risks is complicated by the fact that had Israel delayed striking in 1981, but subsequently felt compelled to eliminate the reactor at Osirak, it would by this stage have become operational. An attack of this kind would have significantly increased the risks of civilian casualties, given the dangers of radioactive fallout.
33 This partly reflected the fact that after the 1991 Gulf War, the UN weapons inspectors who went into Iraq under Resolution 687 discovered that Iraq was much closer to having a nuclear weapon than had previously been believed.
34 Richard Cheney, "Remarks by the Vice President to the Veterans of Foreign Wars 103rd National Convention," August 26, 2002. This is a controversial claim, because many commentators argue that the Israeli strike simply forced Saddam Hussein to develop a covert nuclear weapons program, the scale of which was revealed by the UN weapons inspectors who went into Iraq after the 1991 war.
35 Ibid.
36 Kaplan and Kristol, *The War over Iraq*, p. 89. Both of these neoconservative writers, through the newspaper *The Weekly Standard* and the *Project for a New American Century*, have been influential voices in the philosophy behind the Bush administration's foreign policy.
37 For a detailed discussion of this development, see Nicholas J. Wheeler, *Saving Strangers: Humanitarian Intervention in International Society* (Oxford: Oxford University Press, 2000).

The dangers of American exceptionalism in a revolutionary age   201

38 Francis M. Deng, *Protecting the Dispossessed: A Challenge for the International Community* (Washington, DC: Brookings, 1993); Francis M. Deng et al., *Sovereignty as Responsibility* (Washington, DC: Brookings, 1995); and Francis M. Deng, "Frontiers of Sovereignty," *Leiden Journal of International Law*, Vol. 8, No. 2 (1995), pp. 249–86.

39 Kofi. A. Annan, "Reflections on Intervention," 35th annual Ditchley Foundation Lecture, June 26, 1998, reprinted in *The Question of Intervention: Statements by the Secretary General* (New York: United Nations, 1999), p. 6.

40 This idea of sovereignty as a responsibility and not an inherent right was given its most thoughtful and extensive elaboration in the report of the International Commission on Intervention and State Sovereignty (ICISS). See *The Responsibility to Protect: Report of the International Commission on Intervention and State Sovereignty* (Ottawa, 2001). The ICISS was an independent commission set up by former Canadian Foreign Minister Lloyd Axworthy. It reported to the UN Secretary General in September 2001.

41 Richard Haass, address to the 2002 IISS Annual Conference, London, September 13, 2002.

42 Ibid.

43 Richard Haass, "Existing Rights, Evolving Responsibilities," remarks by Ambassador Haass to the School of Foreign Service and the Mortara Center for International Studies, Georgetown University, Washington DC, January 15, 2003.

44 Quoted (emphasis added) in Nicholas Lemann, "The Next World Order," *The New Yorker*, March 25, 2002, online at www.eco.utexas.edu/facstaff/Cleaver/bushDoctrine.htm.

45 Condoleezza Rice, Wriston Lecture.

46 Haass, "Existing Rights, Evolving Responsibilities."

47 *The National Security Strategy of the United States.*

48 This is Walzer's term in his *Just and Unjust Wars*, p. 85.

49 Rice, Wriston Lecture.

50 Quoted in Lemann, "The Next World Order."

51 Rice, Wriston Lecture.

52 Kennedy, "The Bush Doctrine of Pre-Emption."

53 Henry Kissinger, "Preemptive Strike on Iraq to Improve Peace Prospects," *The Sunday Times*, August 11, 2002.

54 Kofi A. Annan, speech to the UN General Assembly, September 23, 2003, reprinted in *The New York Times*, same date.

55 Peter Slevin, "New Strategy Courts Unforeseen Dangers," September 22, 2002, online at www.reutlinger-friedensgruppe.de/new%20strategy.htm.

56 Barber, *Fear's Empire*, p. 99.

57 Michael E. O'Hanlon, Susan E. Rice, and James B. Steinberg, "The National Security Strategy and Preemption," Policy Brief No. 113, The Brookings Institution, December 2002, p. 7.

58 Ramtanu Maitra, "US–India Ties: An Adept Adaptation," *Asia Times*, October 8, 2002, online at www.atimes.com/atimes/South_Asia/DJ08Df07.html.

59 This statement was specifically aimed at warning Washington not to launch a preemptive attack against North Korea's fledging nuclear capabilities. The Deputy Director of the North Korean Foreign Ministry, Ri Pyong-gap, declared that "the United States says that after Iraq, we are next ... but we have our own countermeasures." (Jonathan Watts, *The Guardian*, February 6, 2003). Benjamin Barber argues that the Bush Doctrine establishes "a significant precedent ... North Korea can justify a strike against South Korea, anticipating an American action (based on American rhetoric) against North Korea; or for that matter, Iraq could have rationalized a preventive strike against the United States or its allies, anticipating what was after all, a well-advertised American intention to launch a war against Baghdad (Barber, *Fear's Empire*), p. 99.

60 O'Hanlon, Rice, and Steinberg, "The National Security Strategy and Preemption," p. 7.

61 Speech by Kofi A. Annan to the General Assembly, September 23, 2003; *The New York Times*, September 24, 2003, p. A11.

62 Ibid. Writing in a personal capacity, Edward Mortimer, director of communications in the office of the UN Secretary General, argues that "the challenge is very clear. Either in a relatively short space of time (2005 has been suggested as a deadline) the international community agrees on

credible rules about the use of force, giving a reasonable assurance that it will not be used arbitrarily and unilaterally but collectively ... or we must resign ourselves to going back to a world uncomfortably like that of the 1930s." Mortimer, "Got A Better Idea," *Prospect*, November 2003, p.11.

63 For a detailed discussion of Security Council decision making over Kosovo see Wheeler, *Saving Strangers*, pp. 275–84; and Ian Johnstone, "Security Council Deliberations: The Power of the Better Argument," *European Journal of International Law*, Vol. 14, No. 3 (June, 2003), pp. 437–81.

64 SCR 1441, adopted November 8, 2002.

65 Thomas Franck, *Recourse to Force: State Action Against Threats and Armed Attacks* (Cambridge: Cambridge University Press, 2002), p. 186.

66 Joseph S. Nye, "Before War," *Washington Post*, March 14, 2003.

67 Woodrow Wilson, *War Messages*, 65th Cong., 1st Sess., Senate Doc. No. 5, Serial No. 7264, Washington, DC, 1917, pp. 3–8.

68 This phrase is taken from the title of Alex Callinicos' book, *The New Mandarins of American Power* (Cambridge: Polity Press, 2003).

69 George W. Bush, State of the Union Address, January 28, 2003.

70 Condoleezza Rice, "Promoting the National Interest," *Foreign Affairs*, Vol. 79, No. 1 (January–February, 2000), p. 49.

71 Kaplan and Kristol, *The War Over Iraq*, pp. 91–4.

72 Rice, "Promoting the National Interest."

73 *The National Security Strategy of the United States*.

74 Quoted in Nehal Bhuta, *Constellations*, Vol. 10, No. 3 (2003), p. 17.

75 William E. Scheuerman, *Carl Schmitt: The End of the Law* (Oxford: Rowman and Littlefield, 1999), p. 145.

76 Ibid., p. 150.

77 Barber, *Fear's Empire*, pp. 98–101.

78 Hendrickson, "Toward Universal Empire," p. 9.

79 Kissinger argues that "only absolute security—the neutralization of the opponent—is considered a sufficient guarantee, and thus the desire of one power for absolute security means absolute insecurity for all the others." Henry Kissinger, *A World Restored: The Politics of Conservatism in a Revolutionary Era* (London: Victor Gollancz, 1977), p. 2.

80 Pierre Hassner, "Friendly Questions to America the Powerful," *The National Interest* (Fall 2002).

81 An excellent criticism of the Bush administration's understanding of power is developed in Christian Reus-Smit's forthcoming book, *American Power and World Order* (Cambridge: Polity Press, 2004).

82 On the classical realist side, there is Hendrickson's comment that "the more powerful the state, the more important that it submit to widely held norms and consensual methods" (Hendrickson, "Toward Universal Empire," p. 4). Compare this to G. John Ikenberry's argument that "Unchecked US power, shorn of legitimacy and disentangled from the postwar norms and institutions of the international order, will usher in a more hostile international system, making it far harder to achieve American interests" (Ikenberry, "The Lures of Preemption," p. 78).

83 For an argument that the United States should take the lead in devising new UN based rules on the use of force, see Michael Ignatieff, "Why Are We in Iraq?" *New York Times*, September 7, 2003.

84 Franck, *Recourse to Force*, p. 181.

9 The Bush Doctrine and Asian regional order

The perils and pitfalls of preemption

Amitav Acharya

This chapter offers a critical perspective on the Bush Doctrine's impact on the Asian, especially Southeast Asian, security order. It proceeds in five parts. The first examines the problematic nature of the Bush Doctrine, such as its deliberate conflation of preemptive and preventive war and its expansive scope as a "grand strategy of transformation." This is followed by an analysis of the responses of Southeast Asian states to the doctrine. The third part looks at the "imitation" effects of the Bush Doctrine in Asia-Pacific, where it may be reshaping national security strategies of some states such as Australia and Japan. Next comes consideration of the consequences of the war in Iraq. The last part of the chapter evaluates how the Bush Doctrine, with its underlying basis in US power dominance in a unipolar global setting, affects the Asian security architecture, particularly the balance between bilateral and multilateral security approaches to regional order.

The Bush Doctrine and Asia

For centuries, international law recognized that nations need not suffer an attack before they can lawfully take action to defend themselves against forces that present an imminent danger of attack. Legal scholars and international jurists often conditioned the legitimacy of preemption on the existence of an imminent threat—most often a visible mobilization of armies, navies and air forces preparing to attack. We must adapt the concept of imminent threat to the capabilities and objectives of today's adversaries. Rogue states and terrorists do not seek to attack us using conventional means. They know such attacks would fail. Instead, they rely on acts of terror and, potentially, the use of weapons of mass destruction—weapons that can be easily concealed, delivered covertly, and used without warning ... The United States has long maintained the option of preemptive actions to counter a sufficient threat to our national security. The greater the threat, the greater is the risk of inaction—and the more compelling the case for taking anticipatory action to defend ourselves, even if uncertainty remains as to the time and place of the enemy's attack. To forestall or prevent such hostile acts by our adversaries, the United

States will, if necessary, act preemptively. The United States will not use force in all cases to preempt emerging threats, nor should nations use preemption as a pretext for aggression. Yet in an age where the enemies of civilization openly and actively seek the world's most destructive technologies, the United States cannot remain idle while dangers gather.

The National Security Strategy of the United States of America,
September 2002

The American presidential doctrine outlined in *The National Security Strategy of the United States of America* (hereafter referred to as the NSS document) has significant implications for the Asian security order.[1] Unlike some past presidential doctrines, such as the Nixon Doctrine, the Bush Doctrine is not specifically oriented toward Asia. Its target is a global threat, although this threat is very much present in Asia. But three factors make the Bush Doctrine important to the Asian security order. First, the Bush Doctrine is an outgrowth of the administration's "axis of evil" formulation, which implicated North Korea. Hence it is of direct relevance to the US approach to the conflict on the Korean peninsula, especially in the wake of North Korea's disclosure about its nuclear-weapons program. Second, the idea of preemption that forms the core of the Bush Doctrine has found its own adherents in the Asia-Pacific region, especially in Australia, and possibly in Japan and India. Hence one of the more significant implications of the Bush Doctrine may also be the way it reshapes national security strategies in the region. Third, the Bush Doctrine, and its underlying basis in the US power dominance in a unipolar global setting, will affect the Asian security architecture, particularly the balance between bilateral and multilateral security approaches to regional order.

What shapes Asian responses to the Bush Doctrine? It should be noted that the Bush Doctrine is about much more than preemption; the latter is but one of the means through which what John Lewis Gaddis has described as "a grand strategy of transformation" is being pursued.[2] But preemption lies at the core of its agenda and is of particular importance to Asia and the international community at large. The Bush Doctrine has a simple premise: the United States will use force, preemptively if necessary, to deal with regimes that pose a threat to US strategic interests, especially by sponsoring terrorism or acquiring weapons of mass destruction. The logic of preemption rests on the argument that the United States now faces "undeterrable non-state enemies." Deterrence (which requires a clear target) and containment worked during the cold war because the adversary was clearly identifiable. In the case of terrorist threats, however, the targets are elusive. Terrorists cannot be deterred also because they are willing to commit suicide. Deterrence would not work "against shadowy terrorist networks with no nation or citizens to defend."

Thus measures that go beyond deterrence must be sought. Neither does containment appear as effective any more. Containment allows a dictator to remain in power, and build weapons of mass destruction. Containment will not work "when unbalanced dictators with weapons of mass destruction can deliver those weapons on missiles or secretly provide them to terrorist allies." Hence, the United States has to respond differently: "If we wait for threats to fully materialize, we will have waited too long."[3]

Since it was announced, the doctrine of preemption has been the subject of much debate and controversy. Before turning to the specific Asian responses to the doctrine, it would be useful to summarize the main points of criticism coming from the international community. At least two sets of criticisms may be noted here.

The first is the conflation, perhaps deliberate, of preemption and prevention.[4] The Bush Doctrine is really about preventive war. Preemptive war is defined as "an attack initiated on the basis of incontrovertible evidence that an enemy attack is imminent."[5] In contrast, a preventive war is defined as "a war initiated in the belief that military conflict, while not imminent, is inevitable, and that to delay would involve great risk."[6] There are two key differences between these two concepts: timing and evidence. Graham Allison of Harvard University describes the logic of preventive war as follows: "I may someday have a war with you, and right now I'm strong and you're not. So I am going to go to war now." This logic, Allison argues, was what prompted the Japanese decision to attack Pearl Harbor—except some say Japan waited too long. By comparison, Daniel Webster's criteria for preemption, which he formulated as US Secretary of State in the first half of the 19th century but which even today remain the US legal standard, outline the justification for launching a preemptive war in the following manner: the threat must be "instant, overwhelming, leaving no choice of means, and no moment for deliberation." This is what gives preemptive war some legal and moral justification. In contrast, preventive war has less or no such legal standing, because by definition the line separating preventive war and outright aggression becomes blurred. According to Jeffrey Record, this may be part of the reason that the Bush administration deliberately used the term "preemption" rather than "prevention" in the NSS document.[7]

A second set of concerns about the Bush Doctrine brings together a variety of political views against having a grand strategic presidential doctrine.[8] As a Brookings Institution analysis of the NSS points out:

> Elevating the preemptive option to a policy doctrine has serious negative consequences. For one, it reinforces the image of the United States as too quick to use military force and to do so outside the bounds of international law and legitimacy. This will make it more difficult for the United States to gain international support for its use of force, and over the long term, may lead others to resist US foreign policy goals more broadly, including efforts to fight terrorism. Elevating preemption to the level of a formal doctrine may also increase the Administration's inclination to reach for the military lever quickly, when other tools still have a good chance of working. Advocating preemption warns potential enemies to hide the very assets we might wish to take preemptive action against, or to otherwise prepare responses and defenses. In this tactical sense, talking too openly about preemption reduces its likely utility, if and when it is employed. Finally, advocating preemption may

well embolden other countries that would like to justify attacks on their enemies as preemptive in nature.[9]

Asian responses to the Bush Doctrine mirror many of the critiques advanced by the Brookings Institution paper[10] and by Mel Gurtov in his introduction to this volume. In general, responses from the region have been influenced by reservations and misgivings about the wider political aspects of the Bush Doctrine. In Asia, the doctrine has been perceived as being expansive and all-encompassing. As an outgrowth of the "axis of evil" formulation, the Bush Doctrine is not just a military response to a military threat. Its underlying premise that getting rid of weapons of mass destruction and defeating the terrorist threat might require "regime change" is especially unnerving to Third World states, particularly when that regime change may also necessitate the physical occupation of the target state. The doctrine's equating of tyrants with terrorists is also important in the Asian context.

Moreover, the Bush Doctrine advocates a proactive policy of promoting democracy, unlike the Clinton administration, which assumed democratization as a result of the end of the cold war. This adds to the nervousness in some parts of Asia about the doctrine. It is this expansive ambit of the Bush Doctrine, and its use of language such as "regime change,"[11] that forms the basis of a good deal of concern in a highly sovereignty-minded region where national security and regional order are often a fig leaf for regime security and survival.

Another important factor that has shaped the perception of the Bush Doctrine in Asia is its close identification with overwhelming US power. Preemption and prevention go hand in hand with preeminence. These are credible options only for the world's only superpower. As Gaddis points out, preemption "requires hegemony because of the need [for the United States] to operate in several different theaters."[12] Hence, while the NSS talks about forsaking America's "unilateral advantage" and creating "a balance of power that favors human freedom," it also makes clear that "our forces will be strong enough to dissuade potential adversaries from pursuing a military build-up in hopes of surpassing, or equalling, the power of the United States." It argues that "US hegemony is also acceptable because it is linked with certain values that all states and cultures—if not all terrorists and tyrants—share." In his speech at West Point that presaged the NSS, President Bush declared bluntly: "America has, and intends to keep, military strengths beyond challenge."[13] This echoed the now infamous Defense Planning Guidance authored in 1992 by Paul Wolfowitz, a key architect of the Bush Doctrine.

Finally, most Asian critics share the general concern of the international community about US unilateralism and the lack of accountability that has accompanied US power dominance. The limits of the Bush Doctrine are set not by international norms or allied reactions but by America's dubious capacity for self-restraint. One of the main objections to the Bush Doctrine in Asia is the prospect of Washington securing for itself a blank check to strike any regime that runs afoul of it by acquiring weapons of mass destruction or by bringing on some other pretext.[14] Given the Bush administration's tendency toward unilateralism,

America's assurances of maintaining a high threshold and its promises not to act casually or irresponsibly are not enough.

The Bush Doctrine has shown a clear pattern of disregard for multilateralism, as was also evident in its opposition to the International Criminal Court, its rejection of the Kyoto Protocol, and its abrogation of the Anti-Ballistic Missile (ABM) Treaty. The Bush Doctrine is part of a pattern of unilateralist behavior by the current administration, which raises several concerns. What is the threshold of preemption? What sort of evidence would be needed to justify a military strike? What is the limit to such strikes? Will it be proportional? Will it involve political control of the target country? (The administration's decision to occupy and rule Iraq provided a definitive answer to this question.) Asian reactions to the Bush Doctrine have also been shaped by the concern that it might lead to hasty military action, without exhausting all possible diplomatic means.

Many of the misgivings about the Bush Doctrine in Asia were evident before the war in Iraq; but this war, and the terrorist attacks on Bali in October 2002, have had a major impact on Asian debates and attitudes toward the concept and policy of preemption. On the one hand, these events seem to have given preemption a new respectability and even legitimacy. While it cannot be said to have had a snowballing or imitation effect, the Bush Doctrine nevertheless did encourage similar reformulations from other states in the region. In turn, this has generated a considerable amount of debate and reaction from other regional actors. Hence, a good way to assess the implications of the Bush Doctrine for Asian security order is to look at how it has resonated in the region and has been debated there.

Southeast Asian responses to the Bush Doctrine

Until 9/11, Southeast Asia had occupied a marginal place in US strategy. The end of the cold war further contributed to the erosion of US interest in the region. Domestic pressure in the Philippines resulted in the removal of US military bases from the country in 1991. The loss of these bases was partially offset by Singapore's offer of military facilities to US naval and air forces, but this could hardly replace the gigantic Subic Bay naval base and Clark Field air base in the Philippines. Despite repeated US assurances of continued strategic engagement and the "revitalization" of the US–Japan alliance, Southeast Asia remained secondary to other theaters, while US involvement in regional security organizations, though not insignificant, was secondary to its bilateral commitments and defense linkages in the region.[15] Moreover, in 1992, the US Congress restricted US military aid to Indonesia through the International Military Education and Training program (IMET), because of the military's poor human-rights record. While the United States continued to sell arms to Indonesia, Singapore, Malaysia, and Thailand, and maintained military exercises with Thailand, there was no combined exercise with the Philippines between 1995 and 2000. Despite Southeast Asia's problems with diffuse transnational dangers such as drug trafficking, illegal migration, and piracy, these were not considered to be significant threats to US national security comparable to the problem of terrorism a decade later.

The September 11 terrorist attacks led to a major shift in US policy toward Southeast Asia. Terrorism brought about the "re-engagement" of the United States in Southeast Asian security. As one analyst puts it, Southeast Asia now has a "more prominent place in US foreign policy than at any time since the end of the cold war."[16] The Bush administration sees terrorism, especially al-Qaeda, as a transnational operation with a global reach, with the Middle East, South Asia, and Southeast Asia (the last through the al-Qaeda "affiliate" Jemmah Islamiah) as its main breeding grounds. The threat of terrorism in Southeast Asia, and, more importantly, the extent of official acknowledgment of it, varies significantly from country to country, and this shapes attitudes toward the US-led war on terror and the Bush Doctrine more generally.

Terrorism has dominated the national-security concerns of Singapore and the Philippines. These two countries are also closest to the Bush administration's position on the challenge posed by terrorism and the types of comprehensive counter-terrorism strategies (including homeland security) required to deal with it. The Philippines has emerged as Southeast Asia's frontline state in the war on terror. Since September 2001 it has developed the closest military links with the United States.[17] President Arroyo, visiting Washington in November 2001, issued a strong statement of support for US actions, declaring that "the American and Filipino people stand together in the global campaign against terrorism."[18] A flow of US military assistance to Manila totaling more than $100 million ensued, including equipment such as a C-130 transport plane, eight UH-1 helicopters, several fast patrol boats, trucks, and more than 30,000 M-16 rifles. Later, in early 2003, Washington offered another US $78 million to train and equip Philippine troops. Manila also received trade benefits such as trade credits, tariff reductions, and debt write-offs that are potentially worth more than $1 billion.[19] In November 2002, the two countries signed a Mutual Logistics Support Agreement (MLSA) that allows the United States to stockpile essential equipment and supplies in the country.

US–Philippines counter-terrorism cooperation includes joint "exercises" between their troops against the Abu Sayyaf group. After the southern Philippines was designated as a target suitable for immediate retaliation against the terrorist network responsible for September 11, 2001,[20] the United States in January 2002 deployed a Joint Task Force there composed of some 1,200 troops, including 160 US Special Forces advisers.[21] They were backed by aircraft and surveillance technology for use by the Armed Forces of the Philippines (AFP) against the Abu Sayyaf group. Though described as engaged in "training exercises," US Special Forces troops in June 2002 were actively involved in combat operations against Abu Sayyaf.[22] In February 2003, the Bush administration announced its intention to deploy 3,000 "combat troops" (as opposed to trainers) to the Philippines, sparking a major controversy in the Philippines and forcing the United States to back down. Washington issued a clarification that training would remain the sole purpose of the new deployment.

Several factors drive the US–Philippines military cooperation. For Manila, an increased American presence and strategic links with the United States not only help its resource-starved military to gain access to vital US equipment, they also mitigate Manila's immediate and long-term concerns about the rise of Chinese power. The new logistics agreement with the United States negotiated in the context of the war on terror could also be a strategic asset to Manila in countering future Chinese encroachments in the territories that it disputes with China in the South China Sea. But the Arroyo government's support for the Bush Doctrine has not gone unchallenged domestically. A strong criticism came from Vice President Teofisto Guingona, who had disagreed publicly with President Arroyo's policy of seeking US military help in counterterrorism campaigns in the southern Philippines. "The main premise of a first-strike policy," he said, "is to make the world a safer place, but many fear it could only generate the opposite and breed animosities. Might does not make right."[23]

Singapore's close defense ties with the United States antedate the Bush Doctrine. In November 1990, the two sides signed a Memorandum of Understanding. This and an accompanying addendum grant the United States access to the Sembawang port, the Paya Lebar air base, and the new Changi naval base. The first foreign warships to berth at the latter were three US naval vessels, including an aircraft carrier, in March 2001.[24] When the Subic Bay base in the Philippines closed, Singapore invited the United States to establish a small logistical presence in the country. Following 9/11 and the subsequent war in Afghanistan, Singapore provided logistics and support facilities for a number of transits made by US military aircraft and naval vessels. A major milestone in US–Singapore security ties is the decision to work toward a "Framework Agreement for the Promotion of a Strategic Cooperation Partnership in Defense and Security." This was announced on October 21, 2003, by President Bush and Prime Minister Goh Chok Tong during the former's visit to Singapore. The Bush visit, in the words of a joint statement, reflected "the strong and multi-faceted US–Singapore partnership, which saw the signing of the US–Singapore Free Trade Agreement earlier this year, [as part of] a history of cooperation, congruent interests, and shared perspectives." The proposed Framework Agreement, to be concluded "as soon as possible," would expand bilateral cooperation in counterterrorism, counterproliferation of weapons of mass destruction, joint military exercises and training, policy dialogues, and defense technology.[25] Singapore, while cautious about the domestic and regional fallout of its close ties with the United States, due partly to a realization that such ties make Singapore a terrorist target, has been an ardent supporter of the Bush administration's war on terror. Like Washington, it believes terrorism backed by fundamentalist Islam to be the most significant threat to regional and global security.

The discourse on terrorism in Indonesia and Malaysia is quite different. Until the Bali bombings of October 12, 2002, Indonesia refused to acknowledge the presence of al-Qaeda or Jemmah Islamiah on its territory. Even after the Bali tragedy, it has not embraced the kind of expansive notion of terrorism and terrorist groups that the Bush administration proposes. Although it acknowledges the threat of domestic terrorism, Malaysia has rejected any link between Islam and terrorism. (Singapore is less reticent about acknowledging such a link.)

Terrorism is not a dominant security issue for Vietnam. Although terrorist incidents or links have been found in Laos (difficult though it is to separate terrorism from existing domestic insurgencies) and Cambodia (the latter as a transit point of terrorist groups), neither has made an overt issue of it. In the case of Myanmar, the junta has found it convenient to label the Rohingyas Muslims as terrorist groups, but otherwise remains preoccupied with suppressing the democratic opposition and ensuring regime survival.

It is important to distinguish between Southeast Asian attitudes toward the United States after September 11, 2001, and their response to the Bush Doctrine of preemption and the US invasion of Iraq. Misgivings about the justification for the Iraq war did not prevent three Southeast Asian countries—Thailand, the Philippines, and Singapore—from officially joining the "coalition of the willing" in the Iraq war. While Singapore was the only country among the three not to get "major non-NATO ally" status, it nonetheless justified its support for the attack on Iraq by citing the threat posed by Saddam's development of weapons of mass destruction. Goh Chok Tong himself stressed the dangers posed by Iraq's attempt to acquire weapons of mass destruction as the basis for Singapore's support for regime change in Iraq. During a trip to Japan, Goh stated: "It is clear to everyone, unless that person wears blinkers, that this is a war to remove the weapons of mass destruction from Saddam Hussein."[26] Singapore had to support the United States, because "If weapons of mass destruction were to fall into the hands of terrorists, they could also become a threat to Singapore, which two years ago was targeted by a terrorist group."[27] The government also cited Iraqi violations of UN resolutions. Another Singapore argument concerned US credibility: a retreat from military confrontation at a late stage would have undermined US credibility and encouraged other dictators to challenge US power and international order. Since Singapore signed a free trade agreement (FTA) with the United States soon after the Saddam regime was toppled, speculation was rife that Singapore's support of the war was partly a way of ensuring that the FTA was not disrupted. The Singapore government, however, has denied such a link.

While most Southeast Asian governments and elite circles showed sympathy for the US after the 9/11 attacks, they have been far more critical of the Bush administration's conduct of the war on terror, particularly its unilateralism and its doctrine of preemption. The latter doctrine has been viewed with misgiving in the region because it smacks of a new US interventionism and a threat to the principle of sovereignty that remains salient in the Association of Southeast Asian Nations (ASEAN). To be sure, ASEAN does not speak with one voice when it comes to relations with the United States. In Islamic Southeast Asia, popular reactions to the Bush Doctrine have been especially hostile, thereby affecting government responses. For example, soon after the 9/11 attacks, President Megawati of Indonesia made a much-publicized visit to the White House to show solidarity with the United States; but domestic disapproval of this stance soon forced her to criticize the US attack on Afghanistan.

While domestic concerns have led some Southeast Asian governments, especially Malaysia and Indonesia, to criticize the Bush Doctrine and the war on Iraq, this has not prevented them from seeking US support in the regional war on terror. This reflects a belief that the war on terror does not require a preemptive doctrine per se, and that the war on Iraq might have been a major distraction from it. Singapore, Thailand, and especially the Philippines have all stepped up their security cooperation with the United States, with Thailand and the Philippines accorded major "non-NATO ally" status by the United States, and Singapore having signed a security cooperation agreement with Washington.

At the grassroots level, Southeast Asia has seen a marked rise in anti-US sentiments. The resentment against specific aspects of the war on terror and the war in Iraq has aggravated the lingering sense of resentment against the United States for its perceived lack of support for Southeast Asian states when a severe currency crisis hit the region in mid-1997. The problems encountered by the United States in pacifying Iraq after a quick and "decisive" military victory, and its failure to advance the Israeli–Palestinian peace process, have caused doubts throughout the region about the US approach to the war on terror, which favors military over diplomatic and political instruments. Anti-American sentiment has been on the rise, especially in Indonesia. There, according to a Pew Foundation opinion survey, the number of people who had an unfavorable opinion of the United States rose to 83 percent, compared to 75 percent in 2000. Indonesia was among the five Muslim countries—along with Jordan, Morocco, Pakistan, and the Palestinian Authority—where Osama bin Laden was chosen as one of the three political leaders people would most trust to "do the right thing" in world affairs.[28]

For Southeast Asian governments, support for the US-led war on terror can be a double-edged sword. While helping them to secure access to US resources, military and economic, and to conduct their own war on terror, reliance on US help is also costly on the domestic front. Hence, regional governments have to maintain a delicate balance in supporting the United States while maintaining domestic cohesion. Both public opinion and elite opinion throughout Southeast Asia continue to regard US support for Israel as the "root cause" of terrorism, with Malaysia going the farthest with this view. As then Malaysian Deputy Prime Minister (now Prime Minister) Badawi told a conference in Kuala Lumpur in June 2002, "Muslim anger is ... fueled by the impunity with which Israel ignores and flouts UN resolutions, and the protection it receives in the world body from friends that prevent any enforceable sanctions' being imposed upon Israel ... International terrorism ... cannot be quelled without resolving the Palestinian–Israeli issue."[29]

"Imitation," resistance, and controversy

The Australian position

Attitudes in Southeast Asia toward the Bush Doctrine should be assessed against this backdrop. No Southeast Asian country, Singapore included, has imitated the United States in proclaiming a doctrine of preemptive strikes, although Singapore clearly has the military wherewithal. But they have responded critically to other Asia-Pacific countries that have followed Bush's lead. Of particular importance is the regional reaction to Australia's own doctrine of preemption. The Australian posture is all the more pertinent because it occurred before the Iraq war and was in response to the terrorist bombings in Bali on October 12, 2002, which saw the killing of about 190 people, almost half of them Australian.[30]

Not long after the tragedy, on December 1, 2002, Prime Minister John Howard stated: "Let me make it perfectly clear: if I were presented with evidence that Australia was about to be attacked and I were told by our military people that by launching a preemptive hit we could prevent that attack from occurring, I would authorize that preemptive hit and expect the opposition to support me in the process." From his standpoint, the principle that a country "is entitled to take preemptive action" when it faces the prospect of being attacked is "a self-evidently defensible and valid" one.[31] As part of his pathway to preemption, Howard advocated a revision of international law and the UN Charter. He stressed that since the most likely threat to a nation's security was non-state terrorism, the present body of international law could no longer cope with the changed circumstances confronting the world.

The exact nature of the Howard policy remains somewhat murky, especially regarding whether the military action it envisaged would be unilateral or in cooperation with governments of the states concerned.[32] If unilateralism were an option, then Howard's corollary to the Bush Doctrine would actually go a step further than Bush's preemptive strategy. The latter targets "rogue" states accused of developing weapons of mass destruction and exporting terror. Howard's targets are Southeast Asian states that have no plans for such weapons and that are not willing exporters of terror to Australia or elsewhere.[33]

There were several underlying reasons for the Howard posture. One obvious factor was the perceived terrorist threat to Australia, starkly underscored by the Bali tragedy. Howard believed that domestic political considerations would prevent Asian governments, especially Indonesia, from accepting Australia's help in rooting out terrorists on their soil who were plotting against Australian interests. Hence Australia needed its own preemptive strategy. But as Australia's long-serving leader, Howard is known in Asia for his staunchly pro-US stance, which included referring to Australia's role as a "deputy sheriff" to the United States in the region.[34] After taking over the reins of power, Howard downgraded Australia's engagement with Asia from the closeness under his Labor predecessor Paul Keating, instead enhancing the country's defense links with the United States, in keeping with its traditional security strategy of defending its interests in Asia and beyond in close collaboration with "great and powerful friends." Southeast Asians would obviously be neither great nor powerful enough to be courted as strategic partners as Howard moved Australia from forward defense to forward preemption. In the wake of the Bali tragedy, preemptive regional strikes could also be expected to appeal to a domestic audience that questioned the government's preparedness against terror and demanded stern action against the al-Qaeda network. Furthermore, Howard has never been known to be unduly sensitive to Asian opinion.

The link between Howard's statement and the Bush Doctrine, to some Asian minds at least, became quite clear when, on the eve of a visit to the Asia-Pacific region, US Deputy Secretary of State Richard Armitage stated: "I very much appreciate and support the Prime Minister's statement." He added: "It was also a wake-up call to some neighbors that they need to better police themselves and rid themselves of the scourge of terrorism ... because then there is no need for anyone to preempt any threats."[35] White House spokesman Ari Fleischer also commented that "[t]he President of course supports preemptive action. September 11 changed everything, and nations must respond and change their doctrines to face new and different threats."[36]

Reactions around the region

Given the opposition from Malaysia and other Southeast Asian nations, Japan was a surprising supporter of the Howard statement. Its Counter-Terrorism Ambassador, Shigeta Hiroshi, said he was "comfortable" with Australia's position, which he said had originally been misrepresented by journalists. Speaking in Tokyo, Shigeta said that after reading a full transcript of Howard's remarks, he considered that Australia was "in favor of respecting international law."[37]

Although his Southeast Asian neighbors did recognize that Howard was by no means riding on a national consensus (some of his severest critics had been the Australian media and his Labor opponents at home), this did not prevent a harsh reaction against his statement from the region. Howard's statement drew severe criticism from many Southeast Asian leaders, especially in Malaysia, and to a lesser extent in the Philippines and Indonesia.[38]

Malaysia has led the opposition to Howard's statement on preemption. Although many analysts put it down to Malaysia's long-standing feud under the Mahathir government with Australia, it must be recognized that Malaysia has also been a firm opponent of the Bush Doctrine of preemption. Malaysia backed the US strike against the Taliban, providing access and overflight rights to the US forces engaged in that operation. But it took a different stand on preemption, especially as the concept applied to Iraq. Prime Minister Mahathir articulated and echoed many of the same concerns as the critics of the preemptive doctrine: its questionable basis in international law, its flouting of UN authority, and the risk of giving the United States a pretext for unilateral strikes on any country that opposes US policies. But he also added another dimension: that the Bush Doctrine was part of an overall counterterrorism strategy driven by "paranoia" and arrogance and was tinged with an anti-Muslim bias.[39] He faulted the United States for failing to address the root cause of the conflict: the Palestinian issue. Mahathir accused Israel of sponsoring state terrorism in the occupied territories.

Against this backdrop, the Howard statement was seen in Malaysia as an extension of the Bush Doctrine. In an editorial titled "Uncle Sam's Foremost Flunkey," the Malaysian newspaper *New Straits Times* alleged that Howard's statement was meant to create "an international legal environment that affords freedom and legitimacy of action for the US and its satellite states such as Australia in the prosecution of the war on terrorism."[40] Criticizing the Howard statement, Malaysian Defense Minister Datuk Sri Najib stated: "The armed forces of a nation cannot intervene in another country without permission. Malaysia does not allow such meddling in internal affairs because our own armed forces are quite capable of dealing with terrorism. We do not welcome intervention from any country." The minister stressed that Malaysia would also not agree to Australia's proposal to amend the UN Charter to empower a country to launch such strikes, because it violates the sovereignty of an independent country.

Mahathir himself took a stronger stand against Howard, saying that Malaysia would consider it "an act of aggression" if Australia or any other nation intruded into the country to fight purported terrorism, and it would take action under its laws. To him, Howard's remarks were not only disappointing but also arrogant. In a stinging attack on Australia, he said: "There are many countries in East Asia, all of which are Asian countries. This country [Australia] stands out like a sore thumb trying to impose its European values on Asia."[41] Rafidah Aziz, Malaysia's Minister of Trade, criticized both Australia and those countries, such as Japan and the United States, that appeared to back Howard. She told reporters that her country "did not need alarm bells or wake-up calls from anyone" and that Japan should not be "too comfortable unnecessarily." She added, "I hope they don't have to face an Australian attack one day, if they know that in Japan there is terrorism ... As you know, Japan has its own share of terrorist activity."[42] Defense Minister Najib also made clear that preemption was not an option for Malaysia. Its government had no plans to seek approval from the UN to carry out preemptive strikes. "We have made our position on the matter very clear. Even if the UN gives us permission ... we will refuse."[43]

In Indonesia, a *Jakarta Post* editorial ("Howard Strikes Again") deplored "Howard's arrogance and insensitive remarks" and suggested that it "would not improve existing regional cooperation in the fight against terrorism."[44] Foreign Minister Hassan Wirayuda argued that "[t]he majority of the United Nations members would find it difficult to accept. And the 115 nonaligned countries would have the same [stance]."[45] He did not hesitate to state that "in facing the problem of terrorism, an important principle that prevails and that we respect is international cooperation." Any move "toward unilateralism as contained in Prime Minister Howard's discourse, I think, will be hard for other countries to accept."[46] Indonesian military chief General Endriartono Starto viewed "such an action ... [as] an act of aggression against another sovereign country ... [and Indonesia] will not stand by."[47]

The Philippines government's specific reaction to the Howard statement was far more critical and reflected greater consensus within the political system. Foreign Secretary Blas Ople opined: "We cannot allow the fundamental doctrine of sovereignty to be set aside in the name [of combating] terrorism."[48] Philippines National Security Adviser Roilo Golez said he would call for reconsideration of an antiterrorism agreement now being negotiated with Australia. He called Howard's statement "quite arrogant and because of this I have recommended that we review and go slow on the proposed anti-terror pact with Australia because they might use this for their preemptive strike agenda."[49]

Thailand offered a more moderate critique of Howard. Prime Minister Thaksin Shinawatra did not "want to make a comment on Mr. Howard's remark," because "Thailand and Australia have a close relationship. I am confident that if the Australian prime minister has some questions about Thailand he will telephone me."[50] But a Thai government spokesman, Ratthakit Manathat, was less reticent: "Nobody does anything like this. Each country has its own sovereignty that must be protected."[51] Foreign Minister Surakiart Sathirathai cautioned that Thailand was capable of handling the regional terrorism issue and was willing to cooperate with other countries. "But cooperation should be based on international law and the United Nations Charter."[52]

Responding to the criticisms, Howard maintained that his initial remark had not been directed at Australia's immediate neighbors. His statement had "related to the determination of this government to take legitimate measures if other alternatives were not available—if there [were] a clear, precise, identifiable threat."[53] He further insisted, "I made those remarks very carefully, in a very low-key fashion. They were quite accurate, they were not directed at any of our friends."[54] This has tempered negative reactions to Australia's preemption doctrine somewhat, although the main reason for this might be the realization that Australia lacks the capacity for unilateral preemption in Southeast Asia.

The ripples of Iraq

Debating the consequences of preemption

As the controversy over the Howard statement died down, the US attack on Iraq became the other major occasion for debate and dissent over the Bush Doctrine in Asia.[55]

India became one of the first Asian countries to speak the language of preemption in a somewhat self-serving manner. In early April 2003, soon after the United States went to war in Iraq, India's Foreign Minister Yashwant Sinha told parliament that India had "a much better case to go for preemptive action against Pakistan than the US has in Iraq." In his view, Pakistan's nuclear capability and its support for the Kashmir groups make it a "fitter case" for intervention than Iraq.[56] Moreover, Pakistan fulfilled the third criterion laid down by the Bush Doctrine on preemption: being ruled by an authoritarian regime. Ignoring US objections to this viewpoint, Defense Minister George Fernandes supported Sinha, although he somewhat qualified his support by making a distinction between intention and reality: "No, we are not talking about any intention here. There is no intention as such, but whatever he has said is correct."[57]

Pakistan, which opposed the Bush Doctrine, reacted to the Indian statement strongly.[58] Prime Minister Zafarullah Khan Jamali and Foreign Minister Khurshid Mahmood Kasuri called Sinha's argument "ridiculous." In a statement, the Pakistani Foreign Minister said: "India should not harbor any illusions of launching preemptive strikes against Pakistan, as it would constitute a major miscalculation on its part." Jamali added at a cabinet meeting, "We know how to defend ourselves."[59]

216 *Amitav Acharya*

The United States has argued that while preemptive attacks were permissible in the case of Iraq, the same logic does not hold for India, which is fighting Pakistani-sponsored terrorism, or for China, which wants to reunify with Taiwan. As White House Press Secretary Ari Fleischer put it: "What is different is the unique history of Iraq. Different policies work in different parts of the world, and different doctrines work at different times and in different regions, because of local circumstances."[60] China too rejected India's right of preemption. Its Foreign Ministry spokesman Liu Jianchao stated: "China has always held that conflicts or disputes between states should be solved peacefully through dialogue instead of resorting to force or the threat of use of force." He added, "India and Pakistan are countries of importance in South Asia and have great responsibility in maintaining peace and stability in the region."[61]

Subsequently, India toned down its position on preemption. Kanwal Sibal, India's Foreign Secretary, said that comparisons between Pakistan and Iraq were rhetorical in nature and were not intended as "advance indication for any kind of imminent action" against Pakistan.[62] Fernandes described the talk about preemption as a "casual statement and not any policy decision of the government or a considered view of some section."[63]

China has taken a firm stance against the Bush Doctrine. According to Chinese Foreign Ministry spokesman Liu Jianchao, while China is a staunch supporter of the fight against all forms of terrorism, it is also of the opinion that strikes must be based on "conclusive evidence, [have] clear-cut targets and [be] in accordance with the Charter of the United Nations and international codes of conduct."[64] Some analysts have speculated whether the US strike on Iraq might lead China to consider developing its own preemptive strategy to deal with its "rogue" province, Taiwan. According to one report, China may be

> calculating how successful use of preemption by the US in Iraq can be applied to Taiwan ... any action that moves Taiwan further from China or closer to de jure independence—for example increasing US arms sales or including Taiwan in a regional missile defense system—will trigger a strong reaction from Beijing. Having set the precedent of preemption where vital national interests are at stake, the US can expect China to follow suit. China has always framed the Taiwan question as one of vital national interest and territorial integrity.[65]

But there is a potential for misreading Chinese thinking here. To be sure, faced with the imminent prospect of Taiwanese independence, should Beijing decide to exercise its military option it would want to move quickly before American forces could come to Taiwan's rescue. In this sense, Beijing may want to "preempt" an American reinforcement of Taiwan. But this does not equate to the Bush Doctrine's approach; Beijing generally appears to prefer a strategy of deterrence in handling the Taiwan issue.

Given North Korea's status as a charter member of the "axis of evil," it is only natural that it would be at the center of questions about "after Iraq, what?" South

Korea's new president Roh Moo Hyun, who has a declaratory commitment to his predecessor's policy of closer engagement with North Korea (albeit complicated by allegations of corruption and payment to the North Korean regime to persuade it to agree to its summit with President Kim Dae Jung in pursuit of his "Sunshine policy"[66]), has been especially nervous about the extension of the Bush Doctrine to the Korean peninsula. In his words: "I would like to discuss with President Bush that the circumstances on the Korean Peninsula may not be appropriate for applying this principle [of preemption] from the very beginning. The mere thought of a military conflict with North Korea is a calamity for us."[67] As Roh sees it, the answer to the inter-Korean situation is not preemption but dialogue: "Trust will be established among parties, and the door to peaceful resolution will open if the parties involved engage in dialogue with sincerity."[68]

But whether North Korea is a ripe target for preemption is a matter of some debate. "What the cases of North Korea and Iraq show is that if the threat is genuinely serious, the preemption doctrine is not pursued," said Zbigniew Brzezinski, who was National Security Adviser to President Jimmy Carter. "If the threat is not immediate but, as the president said, grave and gathering, then you rely on preemption. It is less risky and more satisfying to beat up someone who is less threatening than more threatening."[69] Another skeptic, Philip Bowring, a former editor of the *Far Eastern Economic Review*, points out that "[t]he pre-war shift of US policy from deterrence to preemption had aroused plenty of concern in the region, but only in South Korea did discussion of its consequences get beyond the academic. On North Korea, the United States seems to have little option but dialogue other than a preemptive strike, the thought of which horrifies all of East Asia."[70]

Other critics have based their doubts about the Bush Doctrine on the grounds that the situation in North Korea may be too late for preemption. As one of them wrote:

> American power may be unchallengeable for now, but using that power for preemption is optional and controversial. Maybe it has succeeded in Iraq, although what Saddam Hussein could have done with whatever nasty weapons he had is in doubt. In any case, the world still contains probable North Korean and potential Iranian nuclear weapons, and other weapons of mass destruction may be in the hands of other parties including terrorists. But the Korean dilemma has already proven it is too late for preemption—as it is for nonproliferation, the dovish approach to the same objective.[71]

On the other side are those who believe that preemption in the Korean peninsula is quite doable, especially with some adjustments to US military deployments in South Korea. According to arch-conservative *New York Times* columnist William Safire, "While defeating Saddam Hussein, the United States let it be known that it was prepared to pull its 37,000 tripwire troops out of harm's way along the Demilitarized Zone, opening the possibility of an air assault on plutonium production."[72] Safire and others argued that the Iraqi example prompted

North Korea to take a more moderate posture: a shift from brinksmanship to diplomacy. The subsequent hints from the United States suggesting a withdrawal from the DMZ area to a less frontline position lends some credence to this perspective.

While the Bush team's aim to make the United States safe from weapons of mass destruction and international terrorists will remain operative, the goal of regime change will face several reality checks. For example, regime change in North Korea through military intervention may not be worth the risk or may need an approach different from that used in Iraq. One has to be careful about generalizing from the Iraq episode to how the United States will respond to other apparently similar challenges. Likewise, for political and economic reasons, the United States will not reject international cooperation in every instance, although the appeal of the UN to a serving US president is clearly at its lowest point in memory.

Japan's own turn to preemption has been most clearly led by Defense Minister Ishiba Shigeru. Ishiba believes that a preemptive strike would be a logical response to an impending North Korea missile attack: "it is too late if [a missile] flies toward Japan. Our nation will use military force as a self-defense measure if [North Korea] starts to resort to arms against Japan." Ishiba added that, if necessary, Japanese preemption could be independent of the United States, since there was no such thing as "a free ride in the post-cold-war era."[73] He also downplayed possible constitutional barriers: "Japan's constitution doesn't intend that we just wait and be attacked. This is not just what I think. It should be decided according to popular opinion and from listening to the Japanese people."[74] In comments clearly directed at North Korea, Japanese Prime Minister Koizumi Junichiro told the Diet that if the Japanese government believed that a foreign country had a clear intention or plan to invade Japan, "we could not just let the Japanese people be harmed by doing nothing."[75] The Japanese parliament's approval of war-preparation legislation heralds the possibility of Japanese preemptive military action overseas, the Chinese Communist Party's newspaper has reported.[76] Although Koizumi has said that Japan will not alter its "exclusively defensive defense," Ishiba has indicated that should the United States launch a preemptive attack in the Pacific like that in the Iraq war, "it is by no means impossible" that Japan would invoke "emergency legislation" to help the US military, so the possibility of launching a preemptive attack actually exists.[77] In this sense, the Bush Doctrine has become the rationale and spur for Japan's own preemptive strategy.

Given the range of responses in Asia to the Bush Doctrine, it is important to ask: have Asian criticisms of the Bush Doctrine had any impact on the US administration's policy? At the second annual Shangri-la Dialogue held in Singapore from May 31 to June 1, 2003, US Deputy Secretary of Defense Paul Wolfowitz made a surprising statement that "the preemptive part of the NSS is a bit overstated." He also took care to describe the action in Iraq as "preventive" action, rather than "preemptive." Moreover, Wolfowitz insisted that preemption would be used with discrimination between cases, although it was now part of the vocabulary and remained firmly within the "menu of choice."[78]

Table 9.1 Asian participants in the "coalition of the willing," 2003

Country	Per capita GDP[79] (US$)	Military expenditure as percent of GDP[80]	Troops in coalition[81]	Additional contributions/other forms of non-combat support[82]
Japan	27,200	1.00	0	
South Korea	18,000	2.80	700[a]	
Mongolia	1,770	2.50	0	
Philippines	4,000	1.50	PW[b]	
Singapore	24,700	4.90	0	Possible PW Troops

Source: available from Council on Foreign Relations, online at www.whitehouse.gov/infocus/iraq/news/20030327-10.html and www.areporter.com/sys-tmpl/thecoalitionofthewilling/
a Non-combat troops
b Undisclosed number of troops pledged for post-war (PW) deployment

Asian responses: a summing up

In considering what has determined Asian governments' responses to the Bush Doctrine, particularly since the beginning of the war in Iraq, three factors appear especially noteworthy. First, domestic considerations have played an important role in several states. Such concerns were especially salient in the case of the Roh administration in South Korea, which had come into power on a platform that stressed the engagement of North Korea and a politically acceptable redeployment of US forces in South Korea. In Southeast Asia, governments in the Islamic majority states, especially Malaysia and Indonesia, were particularly worried that public endorsement of the Bush Doctrine would invite popular backlash. While these states were willing partners of the United States in the war against terrorism, they wished to keep security collaboration with Washington as low-key and covert as possible (see Table 9.1). Even Thailand, a member of America's San Francisco system of bilateral alliances, was constrained by its southern Muslim population from joining the "coalition of the willing" against Iraq.[83] In contrast, the Howard government in Australia played to a domestic audience in a climate of heightened nationalism generated by the Bali bombings, in advancing its own doctrine of preemption.

A second factor shaping Asian attitudes toward the Bush Doctrine is normative. The extent to which the doctrine proved to presage military action to bring about regime change has conflicted all along with not just the widespread appeal of Westphalian sovereignty but also the noninterference norms in Asia in particular.

Third, Asian governments have been genuinely concerned about the Bush administration's scant regard for multilateralism, especially at the global level. While many Asian states support, or can at least live with, the US preference for bilateralism, they also regard the UN system as of vital importance to their security network of small and weak states. Even Singapore's Lee Kuan Yew, an otherwise staunch ally of the United States, warned the Bush administration of the consequences of unilateralism: "Throughout history, every force has generated a counterforce. For the present, Russia, China and many countries in the European Union want to maintain good or friendly relations with the US There is reason to hope that tending to these relations can prolong US pre-eminence. Not to do so may persuade more nations that the way to restrain American unilateralism is to join a group of all those opposed to it."[84]

Lee's comments reflected misgivings about the Bush Doctrine from a *realpolitik* perspective. Other criticisms of the doctrine from Asia, as noted, have been normative. The divergent and divided Asian reactions to the Bush Doctrine mean that it will not have a single or uniform impact on the national-security strategies of the Asian states. This division was further underscored in the reactions to the Iraq war. Japan, the Philippines, South Korea, and Singapore officially joined the US-led "coalition of the willing," although none provided combat troops to the operation as Australia did. Malaysia and Indonesia remained critical, sometimes harshly so, about the US attack.

This division is neither unexpected nor unexceptional. Europe experienced a more bitter division that introduced grave uncertainties about the future of NATO and the transatlantic relationship. Nor are such divisions, which reflect the pursuit of national interests, necessarily destabilizing. Moreover, Asian leaders have shown understanding and acceptance of their differences, thereby precluding immediate damage to bilateral and intra-regional relations. But to keep the region from being polarized into pro-US and anti-US camps, these intra-Asian differences need to be managed. Otherwise, a casualty could be Asia-Pacific regional institutions involving the United States and its close ally, Australia (whose image had already taken a beating before its strong support for the US invasion, due to the Howard government's talk about preemption against terrorist targets in neighboring countries). The decline of Asia-Pacific multilateralism might give a boost to East Asian cooperation, but there could be a fallout here as well if China perceives Japan's and the Philippines' backing for the United States to be part of a long-term strategy to constrain Chinese power.[85]

Implications for Asian security architecture

Against this backdrop, the Bush Doctrine's impact on the Asian security order could be divided into two areas. First, it has contributed to a significant strengthening of America's bilateral alliances in the region. Among its traditional allies, Japan, South Korea, and Australia joined the "coalition of the willing" in Iraq, although only Australia explicitly endorsed the preemptive strategy. Japan maintains a characteristic ambivalence, while South Korea has been noticeably reticent to see the doctrine applied on the Korean peninsula. Although not part of the original San Francisco system, Singapore has emerged as an ally of equal importance, while the Philippines has been brought back into the fold. Thailand, despite its decision formally to stay out of the "coalition of the willing," maintains its close strategic alignment with the United States.

But domestic constraints will temper the close identification of the Asian allies with Washington's more grandiose schemes for Asian security. The strengthening of bilateralism does not ensure the legitimacy of the United States as the chief regional security actor. Neither does it ensure that the Asian allies will have a greater role in the management of regional security issues. The gap between US power and that of its allies as well as adversaries has increased dramatically. Sections of the Bush administration view alliances as messy and unnecessarily constraining when it comes to military operations. Even where the United States seeks the help of allies, their role and influence over joint operations would be limited because they cannot keep up with US technical prowess. America's Asian alliances, always unequal entities, are more so now than they have been since the end of World War II.[86]

To be sure, the NSS document does mention the salience of alliances and the need for multilateral action. But no one takes this seriously. Here Asia's skepticism is similar to that elsewhere, but the scale of reaction varies. In Europe, the Bush Doctrine produced the most serious rift in US–German relations since World War II. German opposition to the planned US attack on Iraq might have been prompted by domestic compulsions, but Germany is not alone in Europe in opposing US policy toward Iraq. Europeans generally complain about US "instrumental" multilateralism, which they contrast with the "principled" multilateralism (based on rule of law and diplomacy) of European states and regional institutions.

Asian countries, whose approach to multilateralism may be more pragmatic than principled, have in the main chosen to remain passive about their discomfort with the Bush Doctrine so as not to complicate their ties with Washington. However, there is also an underlying concern that Asia, like Europe, has much to lose from an assertive American unilateralism. While discreet silence at the implications of the Bush Doctrine might serve the short-term interests of Asian countries that need American backing against the terrorist threat, in the long run they might well find the consequences of US unilateralism to be negative. The situation is all the more acute because of underlying concerns that North Korea could become the next target of the Bush Doctrine.

Against this backdrop, one might note a second major implication of the Bush Doctrine for Asia: that it has undermined, if not destroyed, hopes for a more robust multilateral security order in Asia. This is not to say that the United States would choose a unilateral stance on Asian security issues in every instance and against every potential adversary in Asia. Indeed, a major irony of the current wave of US unilateralism is its explicit call for multilateral approaches to the North Korean crisis. As the White House stated during the latter part of 2003, it saw the issue as a regional rather than a bilateral one and would for that reason be operating multilaterally. Yet it is also important to bear in mind that the multilateral approach that the United States seeks in the Korean crisis is that of a small and ad hoc group, not the larger and more institutionalized ASEAN Regional Forum. While not disengaging from such institutions, the United States is unlikely to allow itself to be constrained by their normative framework unless it can actively shape and dominate them. There is diminished prospect for a binding institutional framework emerging from the post-Iraq regional security order, in which the US accepts restraints on its strategic policy and behavior, whereas its regional preeminence and preferred policy frameworks (such as the "axis of evil" and the Bush Doctrine) are recognized and institutionalized. The Bush administration's policy preferences are too controversial for such an institutional bargain.

Selected references

Amitav Acharya, *The Age of Fear: Power and Principle in the September 11 World* (Singapore: Marshall Cavendish, 2004).

John Lewis Gaddis, "A Grand Strategy of Transformation," *Foreign Policy* (November–December, 2002).

John Lewis Gaddis, "Frontline: the War Behind Closed Doors; Interviews, John Lewis Gaddis," Public Broadcast System program online at www.pbs.org./wgbh/pages/frontline/shows/iraq/interviews/gaddis.html.

John Gershman, "Is Southeast Asia the Second Front?" *Foreign Affairs*, Vol. 81, No. 4 (2002), pp. 60–74.

"Iraq and the 'Bush Doctrine' of Pre-emptive Self-Defense," Crimes of War Project, Expert Analysis, online at www.crimesofwar.org/expert/bush-intro.html.

J. Robert Kerrey and Robert A. Manning, *The United States and Southeast Asia: A Policy Agenda for the New Administration* (New York: Council on Foreign Relations Press, 2001).

The National Security Strategy of the United States of America (September, 2002). Online at www.whitehouse.gov/nsc/nss.pdf.

Michael E. O'Hanlon, Susan E. Rice, and James B. Steinberg. "The New National Security Strategy and Preemption," Working Paper, Brookings Institution (accessed 13/12/02), at http://www.brookings.edu/dybdocroot/views/papers/ohanlon/20021114.pdf.

"President Bush Delivers Graduation Speech at West Point," The White House, Office of the Press Secretary, June 1, 2002. Online at www.whitehouse.gov/news/releases/2002/06/20020601-3.html.

Jeffrey Record, "The Bush Doctrine and War with Iraq," *Parameters* (Spring, 2003), pp. 4–21.

Rizal Sukma, "US–Southeast Asia Relations After the Crisis: The Security Dimension," Background Paper prepared for the Asia Foundation's Workshop on America's Role in Asia, Bangkok, March 22–24, 2000.

Notes

1 *The National Security Strategy of the United States of America* (September, 2002), online at www.whitehouse.gov/nsc/nss.pdf. For an earlier statement of the Bush Doctrine, see: "President Bush Delivers Graduation Speech at West Point," The White House, Office of the Press Secretary, June 1, 2002, online at www.whitehouse.gov/news/releases/ 2002/06/20020601-3.html.

2 John Lewis Gaddis, "A Grand Strategy of Transformation," *Foreign Policy* (November–December, 2002), pp. 50–57.

3 For analysis of the Bush Doctrine, see Michael E. O'Hanlon, Susan E. Rice, and James B. Steinberg, "The New National Security Strategy and Preemption," Working Paper, Brookings Institution, online at www.brookings.edu/dybdocroot/views/papers/ohanlon/20021114.pdf;

"Iraq and the 'Bush Doctrine' of Pre-emptive Self-Defense," Crimes of War Project: Expert Analysis, online at www.crimesofwar.org/expert.bush-intro.html.
4 This paragraph draws heavily from Jeffrey Record, "The Bush Doctrine and War with Iraq," *Parameters* (Spring, 2003), pp. 4–21.
5 US Department of Defense, *Dictionary of Military and Associated Terms* (Washington, DC: 2001), p. 333.
6 Ibid., p. 336.
7 Record, "The Bush Doctrine and War with Iraq."
8 John Lewis Gaddis argues that the Bush Doctrine may be called a grand strategy for three reasons. First, it responds to a crisis. Crises do generate grand strategies, as in 1941 at Pearl Harbor and the British attack on the White House in 1814. Crises show that old strategies have failed and new ones are necessary. Second, the doctrine is comprehensive, and global (not regionally specific) in scope, with the global and regional aspects closely interconnected. Third, it has both short-term and long-term objectives. It is not about crisis management or what to do tomorrow and next week, but what we would expect to see at the end of it. In this context, the doctrine espouses a variety of goals: a world safe for democracy, peace and democracy in the Middle East. In this respect, the Bush Doctrine, according to Gaddis, has more in common with the Truman administration's approach to the cold war: "we will win it at the end." Hence Gaddis found it reasonable to argue that the Bush Doctrine is the "most fundamental reshaping of American grand strategy ... since containment." John Lewis Gaddis, "Frontline: the War Behind Closed Doors: Interviews, John Lewis Gaddis," PBS Program available online at www.pbs.org/wgbh/pages/frontline/shows/iraq/interviews.gaddis.html, p. 2.
9 O'Hanlon, Rice, and Steinberg, "The New National Security Strategy and Preemption."
10 See, for an overview, Amitav Acharya, "Dubya's Dangerous and Divisive Doctrine," *Straits Times*, October 16, 2002.
11 See for example the views of Mahathir Mohamed, the outgoing Prime Minister of Malaysia, and Asia's strongest critic of the Bush Doctrine. Brendan Pereira, "Mahathir Makes a Stinging Attack on West," *Straits Times*, June 20, 2003, p. 3.
12 Gaddis, "A Grand Strategy of Transformation," p. 2; Gaddis, "Interviews, John Lewis Gaddis," PBS Program, p. 7.
13 "President Bush Delivers Graduation Speech at West Point," The White House, Office of the Press Secretary, June 1, 2002, online at www.whitehouse.gov/news/releases/ 2002/06/20020601-3.html.
14 This concern has been heightened by the subsequent furor over the administration's manipulation of intelligence related to Iraqi WMD capability, which has suggested that the administration is not above manufacturing a pretext where none exists.
15 For background to US–Southeast Asian relations, see J. Robert Kerrey and Robert A. Manning, *The United States and Southeast Asia: A Policy Agenda for the New Administration* (New York: Council on Foreign Relations Press, 2001); Rizal Sukma, "US–Southeast Asia Relations After the Crisis: The Security Dimension," Background Paper prepared for the Asia Foundation's Workshop on America's Role in Asia, Bangkok, March 22–24, 2000.
16 John Gershman, "Is Southeast Asia the Second Front?" *Foreign Affairs*, Vol. 81, No. 4 (2002), pp. 60–74.
17 David Capie and Amitav Acharya, "A Fine Balance: US Relations With Southeast Asia Since September 11," paper presented to the Colloquium on US–Asia Relations Today: A New "New World Order," Centre d'Etudes et de Recherches Internationales (CERI), Paris, December 2–4, 2002, available online at www.ceri-sciences-po.org/archive/jan03/artca.pdf.
18 White House, "Joint Statement between the United States of America and the Republic of the Philippines," November 20, 2001, online at www.whitehouse.gov/news/releases/2001/11/20011120-13.html.
19 Ibid.; "US Trip Yields $4.6B Investments, Trade, Aid," *Philippines Daily Inquirer*, November 22, 2001.
20 "The Bush Administration's New Strategy in the War Against Terrorism," *The New Yorker*, December 23, 2002, p. 66.

21 "Philippine Troops Eagerly Await US Help and Arms," *New York Times*, February 12, 2002.
22 "US Mission in Philippines Too Little?" MSNBC News Online, 2002, at www.msnbc.com/news/720731.asp?cp1=1.
23 "Philippine Vice President Cautions United States Against Pre-emptive Strikes in War on Terror," Associated Press Worldstream, August 8, 2002.
24 Within a year, five American carriers and around 100 naval vessels berthed at the base. Chin Kin Wah, "Singapore's Perspective in the Regional Security Architecture," in See Seng Tan and Amitav Acharya, eds., *Asia-Pacific Security Cooperation: National Interests and Regional Regional Order* (Armonk, NY: M.E. Sharpe, 2004).
25 See at http://usinfo.state.gov/topical/pol/terror/texts/03102107.htm.
26 "Moderate Muslims know goal in Iraq: PM Goh," *The Straits Times*, March 29, 2003, online at http://straitstimes.asia1.com.sg/iraqwar/story/0,4395,179932,00.html.
27 Ibid.
28 Online at www.iht.com/articles/98398.html.
29 Abdullah Badawi, Keynote Address to the Asia-Pacific Roundtable Conference, Kuala Lumpur, June 3, 2002.
30 "At Least 183 Dead in Bali Bombings," *CNN.com*, October 13, 2002, online at www.cnn.com/2002/WORLD/asiapcf/southeast/10/13/bali.blast/.
31 "Australia Chooses Pre-Emptive Strike Against Threat," *Xinhua News Agency* (Beijing), June 20, 2002.
32 "Ralph Cossa, "Multilateral Solutions to Bilateral Problems Help Contain Unilateralist Tendencies," *Comparative Connections*, 4th Quarter (2002).
33 Amitav Acharya, "Enemies and Neighbors: Howard's Call and SE Asia's Anger," *Today*, December 20, 2002.
34 Dan Murphy, "Terror-Preemption Talk Roils Asia," *Christian Science Monitor*, December 5, 2002.
35 "Aussie PM's Strike Threat a Warning to Asia" online at http://straitstimes.asia1.com.sg/latest/story/0,4390,159916-1039557540,00.html.
36 "Pre-emptive Strikes Overseas 'Would be Act of War,'" *Sydney Morning Herald*, December 4, 2002; "PM Blasts Crean for Backing Asia Apology Demand," *Courier Mail* (Queensland, Australia), December 6, 2002; "Australian Government Invokes First-Strike Doctrine in Asia," World Socialist Web Site, December 7, 2002, online at www.wsws.org/articles/2002/dec2-2/howa-d07_pm/shtml.
37 "Japan Backs PM Howard's Pre-Emptive Strike," *Channel NewsAsia*, December 10, 2002.
38 Amitav Acharya, "Enemies and Neighbors."
39 "Paranoia Has Gripped The World, Says Mahathir," *The Straits Times*, February 24, 2003.
40 Cited in Dan Murphy, "Terror-Preemption Talk Roils Asia," *Christian Science Monitor*, December 5, 2002.
41 "Terrorism—Reactions to John Howard's Statement," *MITA-MEDIA_ANALYSIS, Daily*, December 3, 2002.
42 "Malaysia Widens Terror Spat with Australia to Japan, United States," *Associated Press Worldstream*, December 10, 2002.
43 "Malaysia Urged To Also Demand Right To Pre-Emptive Strikes" *New Straits Times*, December 17, 2002.
44 "Terrorism—Reactions To John Howard's Statement."
45 "Asian Condemnation Grows Over Australia's Call for Pre-Emptive Anti Terror Strikes; Howard Unrepentant," *Associated Press Worldstream*, December 2, 2002.
46 "Indonesia VP, Foreign Minister Rap Howard Over Pre-Emptive Strikes," *Agence France Presse*, December 2, 2002.
47 "Pre-emptive Strikes Overseas 'Would be Act of War,'" *Sydney Morning Herald*, December 4, 2002; "PM Blasts Crean for Backing Asia Apology Demand," *Courier Mail* (Queensland, Australia), December 6, 2002; "Australian Government Invokes First-Strike Doctrine in Asia," World Socialist Web Site, December 7, 2002, online at www.wsws.org/articles/2002/dec2-2/howa-d07_pm.shtml.

48 "Asian Condemnation Grows Over Australia's Call For Pre-Emptive Anti Terror Strikes; Howard Unrepentant," *Associated Press Worldstream*, December 2, 2002.
49 "Asia Anger Grows At Defiant PM," *The Age* (Melbourne), December 3, 2002.
50 "Howard: I Didn't Mean You," *The Nation* (Thailand), December 3, 2002.
51 "Howard Stands by First Strike Talk," *ABC Online*, December 3, 2002, online at www.abc.net.au/news/politics/2002/12/item20021202164150_1.html.
52 "Howard: I Didn't Mean You," *The Nation* (Thailand), December 3, 2002.
53 Ibid.
54 "More Condemn Aussie Proposal as Howard Sticks to His Guns," *New Straits Times*, December 4, 2002.
55 Amitav Acharya, "Second Gulf War: Why Asia and US are Gulf Apart," *Straits Times*, January 16, 2003; Amitav Acharya, "Security Lessons: Ripples from Iraq Will Rock Asia," *International Herald Tribune*, April 25, 2003.
56 *Straits Times*, April 12, 2003.
57 "Preemption is Dangerous," *Global News Wire*, April 10, 2003; "Indian Minister Ignores US Remarks, Says Pakistan Fit For Pre-Emptive Strike," *BBC Worldwide Monitoring*, April 11, 2003.
58 "Pak Opposed to Pre-Emptive Strikes, War on Iraq," *Press Trust of India*, March 30, 2003.
59 "Pakistan Warns India of Grave Consequences of Pre-Emptive Strikes," *Xinhua News Agency*, April 3, 2003; "India's Threat of 'Preemption' Stirs Alarm," *Inter Press Service*, April 8, 2003.
60 "Preemption Not Permissible for India Against Pak: White House," *Indian Express*, May 23, 2003.
61 "China Opposes Indian Threat of Pre-Emptive Strikes," *Pakistan Newswire*, April 8, 2003; "China–India," *Press Trust of India*, April 8, 2003.
62 "Mulling Action, India Equates Iraq, Pakistan; Preemption Cited in Kashmir Conflict," *Washington Post*, April 11, 2003.
63 "Indian DM Downplays Remarks on Pre-Emptive Strikes on Pakistan," *Xinhua News Agency*, April 12, 2003.
64 "FM Spokesman on Australia's Pre-Emptive Strike Proposal," *Xinhua News Agency*, December 3, 2002; "China Joins in Criticism of Howard's Pre-Emptive Strike Policy," *Channel NewsAsia*, December 4, 2002.
65 Rob Radtke, "Iraq Effect on US Role in Asia," *Christian Science Monitor*, May 8, 2003, online at www.csmonitor.com/2003/0508/p11s02-coop.html.
66 Lee Kyong-hee, "Sunshine Policy in Shambles," *Korea Herald*, June 18, 2003.
67 "US Keeps Preemption Doctrine 'Open'; Rebuffs Roh's Call To Exempt North Korea," *Washington Times*, May 13, 2003.
68 "South Korean Wary About 'Bush Doctrine,'" *Associated Press Online*, May 14, 2003.
69 "North Korea Tests Bush's Policy of Preemption; Strategy Seems To Target Weaker Nations," *Washington Post*, January 6, 2003.
70 Philip Bowring, "Asia is Waiting To See How America Handles Victory," *International Herald Tribune*, April 17, 2003.
71 Robert A. Levine, "Preemption Didn't Win," *International Herald Tribune*, April 22, 2003.
72 William Safire, "Preemption Proves Itself," *International Herald Tribune*, April 15, 2003.
73 "Japan Strike Threat to Korea," *Sydney Morning Herald*, February 15, 2003; see, also, "Japan Threatens Force Against North Korea," *BBC News*, February 14, 2003; "Japan Studied Strike Against North Korea To Prevent Missile Attack: Report," *Agence France Press*, May 8, 2003; "Japan Flexes Military Muscle Over Korea," *The Times* (London), May 22, 2003; "Japan Debates a First-Strike Defense," *The Age* (Melbourne), May 22, 2003.
74 "Japan to Consider First Strike Strategy," *Guardian* (London), February 26, 2003.
75 "Japan Wants Pre-Emptive Policy," *Australian Financial Review*, May 22, 2003.
76 "Chinese paper says Japan's legislative pretext for overseas military action," *Global News Wire (BBC Monitoring International Reports)*, May 25, 2003.
77 Excerpted from "'Emergencies Legislation' is Legislation that Serves War Preparation," *Renmin Ribao* (People's Daily, Beijing) web site, May 23, 2003, p. 3.
78 Personal Notes of the Shangri-la Dialogue, May 31–June 1, 2003, Singapore.
79 *CIA World Factbook*.

80 Ibid.
81 *AP Wire Service* story; *National Post* (Canada). The US Government has not released a definitive list of who has contributed what to "Operation Iraqi Freedom," so the table is based largely on press articles for these figures.
82 *Reuters*, March 10, 2003; *CanWest News Service*, 2003.
83 Raymond Bonner, "Thais Give US Secret Help in War on Terror," *International Herald Tribune*, June 9, 2003.
84 Lee Kuan Yew, "US Needs to Nurture Its Relations with the World," *Straits Times*, May 31, 2003, p. 30.
85 Amitav Acharya, "Coping with American Power," *Japan Times*, May 3, 2003.
86 Amitav Acharya, "Security Lessons; Ripples from Iraq Will Rock Asia," *International Herald Tribune*, April 25, 2003.

10 Australia and the Bush Doctrine
Punching above our weight?

Owen Harries[1]

Viewed from the standpoint of classical Realism, the United States under George W. Bush is a revisionist power bent on transforming the world rather than maintaining the status quo. It is questionable whether such an agenda fits with Australia's more conservative national interests.

Taking on Utopia

End of a "holiday"

According to the neoconservative *Washington Post* columnist Charles Krauthammer, from the end of the cold war until the terrorist attacks of September 11, 2001, the United States took a ten-year "holiday from history."

On the face of it, this seems a strange way to characterize American behavior during the decade. United States military forces were more active during these years than at any time since the Vietnam War. The American economy enjoyed a sustained six-year boom, easily outperforming both the Japanese and European economies. On Washington's initiative, the North Atlantic Treaty Organization (NATO) expanded eastward toward the Russian border. The North American Free Trade Agreement (NAFTA) was negotiated and the World Trade Organization (WTO) established.

Far from thinking that the United States was on vacation during these years, other countries were increasingly aware of its dominant presence. Already during the Clinton administration, the German chancellor, Gerhard Schröder, was expressing the view: "That there is danger of unilateralism, not by just anybody but by the United States, is undeniable." And the French Foreign Minister, Hubert Vedrine, reflected that "American globalism ... dominates everything. Not in a harsh, repressive, military form, but in people's heads."

Given all this, what did it mean to say that the United States had taken a "holiday from history"? What Krauthammer meant was that during these years, the United States, having become the sole remaining superpower and an authentic global hegemon, had failed to define and activate a grand purpose or mission commensurate with that status and the opportunity it presented. Now, most countries and peoples might not feel the need for such a thing. But Americans do. They have a great taste for doctrines that set out the principles and objectives that are to determine policy, as in the Monroe Doctrine of 1823, the Truman Doctrine of 1947, and the Reagan Doctrine of the 1980s. They expect their leaders to have a "vision," a much-used word in American politics.

Well, no such thing was evident during the last decade of the twentieth century. True, George Bush the elder did have a shot at it. But as he himself confessed, he wasn't very good at what he called "the vision thing," and his concept of a "new world order" was still-born.

His successor, William Jefferson Clinton, was a brilliant intuitive politician, an improviser with little taste for doctrines or vision. Clinton was a pragmatist, a compromiser, a deal-maker, a triangulator of differences. A connoisseur of opinion polls and focus groups, he knew that in the post-war period Americans consistently gave foreign policy a very low priority. Clinton acted accordingly, taking a limited interest in foreign policy. When he did act abroad, he lived largely by improvisation. He came to office describing his policy as "assertive multilateralism," but it was usually more reactive than assertive, more responsive to the pressure exerted by others—as in the case of the Bosnia crisis—than self-initiating. Those who looked for a grand, unifying design for American foreign policy were left frustrated and unhappy by Clinton's eight years in office.

In January 2001, George W. Bush succeeded Clinton. When a new president comes to office, especially when he is of a different party, there is a settling-in period that takes months. This process had barely finished when the terrorist attack occurred on September 11. How the Bush administration's foreign policy would have developed in the absence of that attack, we shall never know, and what evidence we have is ambiguous.

In his election campaign, Bush had talked about the need for America to be more "humble" and expressed a lack of enthusiasm for nation building. But the first few months were notable mainly for some peremptory announcements that the United States was disassociating itself from a number of multilateral agreements, including the Kyoto Protocol, the setting up of an International Criminal Court, and a treaty banning land mines. In each case, it should be said, Washington had a good case, in terms either of flaws in the agreement or of the special responsibilities of the United States (as, for example, in protecting South Korea along the 38th parallel). But the decisions were made and announced in a way that certainly did not suggest humility.

In any case, with the attack of September 11, America's alleged "holiday from history" came to an abrupt end. In an instant the terrorists had given the country the clear purpose, the central organizing principle, that it had previously lacked, and that some had been strenuously demanding.

That organizing principle came under the name of "a war on terrorism." It was adopted not as a result of cool calculation or choice, but out of necessity and in a mood of understandable outrage at the unprecedented violation and insult that had been visited on the United States.

The concept of a "war on terror" is general enough to support more than one meaning. It can be interpreted precisely, in terms of destroying the organizations and instruments of terror, and protecting the homeland against theft efforts. But it can also be defined much more broadly to encompass changing the conditions that give rise to terrorism, and creating an international order that would be inimical to its existence—not only "draining the swamp," as the phrase goes, but creating a fertile liberal and democratic pasture in its place.

Initially, the stress was on the former, the destruction of terrorism. But there were many in Washington's foreign policy establishment who saw things in much more sweeping terms, and one of the effects of September 11 was that it shifted the political balance in their favor—away from prudence and moderation toward conceptual boldness and an ambitious, assertive use of American power. Within a year the "war on terror" had metastasized into something much grander and more radical, something that would give full expression to one of the strongest strands in the history of the American people: the profound belief that they and their country are destined to reshape the world.

It is a conviction that resounds through the generations: America's "cause is the cause of all mankind," said Benjamin Franklin; "We have the power to begin the world over again," insisted Tom Paine; "God has predestined, mankind expects, great things from our race ... We are pioneers of the world," declared the author of *Moby Dick*, Herman Melville; "I cannot be deprived of the hope that we are chosen, and prominently chosen, to show the nations of the world how they shall walk in the paths of liberty," said the twenty-eighth president, Woodrow Wilson—and it would be easy to extend this list of quotations many times over.

There were many in and around the Bush administration who shared this sense of America's destiny. They now saw in September 11 not merely a disaster to be avenged but an opportunity to reawaken America and redirect it to its true historic mission.

This is what Robert Kagan, who is one of the ablest articulators of this belief, means when he insists in his best-selling book, *Of Paradise and Power*, that "America did not change on September 11. It only became more itself." As he explains, the national ideology has always insisted that "The proof of the transcendent importance of the American experiment would be found not only in the continual perfection of American institutions at home but also [in] the spread of American influence in the world ... That is why it was always so easy for so many Americans to believe, as so many still believe today, that by advancing their own interests, they advance the interests of humanity." And he goes on to advise that the American people's "conviction that their interests and the world's interests are one, may be welcomed, ridiculed, or lamented. But it should not be doubted."[2]

The Bush Doctrine

In the aftermath of September 11, those who thought in these terms came into their own. The result became fully evident with the publication a year later of a thirty-one page statement by the President titled *The National Security Strategy of the United States of America*.[3] In my judgment, this document is, without a doubt, the most important statement about American foreign policy, not just since the terrorist attack, and not just since the end of the cold war, but since the enunciation of the Truman Doctrine in 1947, which committed the United States to resisting further communist expansion. For in it is spelled out how the United States intends to use its hegemonic power. There are four features of this statement that stand out.

First, for a document concerned with strategy, it puts an extremely heavy emphasis on ideology, on "values," in defining America's purpose. In the first three pages alone, the President uses the words "liberty" and "freedom," or some variation of them, twenty-eight times, while the word "interest" occurs only twice.

The document declares that the national strategy will be based on "a distinctly American internationalism." It not only will be concerned to defend freedom where it already exists but will "use this moment of opportunity to extend the benefits of freedom across the globe ... [and] will actively work to bring the hope of democracy, development, free markets, and free trade to every corner of the world." To that end, the United States will seek "to create a balance of power that favors human freedom: conditions in which all nations and all societies can choose for themselves the rewards and challenges of political and economic liberty." The assumption is that given a free choice, these are the values that all people will choose. It cannot be otherwise, for, echoing Francis Fukuyama's "End of History" thesis, the President asserts that "the twentieth century ended with a single surviving model of human progress" and that "the values of freedom are right and true for every person, in every society."

As well as reordering the internal conditions of countries in this way, the United States will be concerned to reorder relations among states, for, as the document asserts, "the international community has the best chance since the rise of the nation-state in the seventeenth century to build a world where great powers compete in peace instead of continually prepare for war."

The President ends his introduction by declaring that "[t]he United States has responsibility to lead this great mission." But if that is to be the mission, how is it to be carried out? The other three features of the document that I wish to emphasize bear on this question of means.

It is made unambiguously clear that the United States military will be an indispensable instrument for the creation of the new order that President Bush proclaims as his country's great mission, and that the United States intends to maintain indefinitely the enormous military superiority it now enjoys. It is time, the President says:

> to reaffirm the essential role of American military strength. We must build and maintain our defenses beyond challenge ... Our forces will be strong enough to discourage potential adversaries from pursuing a military build-up in hopes of surpassing, or equalizing, the power of the United States.

The military will be used actively and assertively, not just passively or defensively ("our best defense is a good offense," the document asserts). The American military is envisaged as being deployed even more widely than it was during the cold war, as a kind of global gendarmerie maintaining order.

And while it intends to maintain, if not increase, America's own military power, it is concerned to discourage others from building up theirs. Thus, two pages before the statement declares the essential role of American military strength, the Chinese are advised that:

> In pursuing advanced military capabilities that can threaten its neighbors in the Asia-Pacific region, China is following an outdated path that, in the end, will hamper its own pursuit of national greatness.

This might strike one as a clear example of double standards—good for me, bad for you. The defenders of the new doctrine do not deny this but justify it in terms of the special responsibilities of the United States for world order. As Robert Kagan puts it, because of those responsibilities, America "must refuse to abide by certain international conventions that may constrain its ability to fight effectively ... It must support arms control, but not always for itself. It must live by a double standard." Which, of course, raises the important question of whether other countries will ever be willing to accept that double standard. The whole history of international politics suggests that they will not.

The third feature of the new doctrine is its abandonment of deterrence, the policy that had served so well throughout the cold war, as the central strategy for dealing with enemies. While deterrence was effective in dealing with a rational and cautious adversary like the Soviet Union, the document maintains that it is less so in dealing with risk-taking rogue states. Instead of deterrence, a policy of preemptive action must now be adopted. The document rightly asserts that international law has long recognized the right of preemption when an imminent danger of attack exists. But it maintains that, given the threats posed by terrorism and weapons of mass destruction, the concept of "imminent threat" is no longer sufficient and that the right of preemption must now be extended beyond that:

> The greater the threat, the greater is the risk of inaction—and the more compelling the case for taking anticipatory action to defend ourselves, even if uncertainty remains as to the time and place of the enemy's attack. To forestall or prevent such hostile acts by our adversaries, the United States will, if necessary, act preemptively.[4]

The document goes on to recognize the danger of preemption's being misused as a pretext for aggression, and stresses that it will only be used deliberately, after close consultation with allies. But again there is the question of the precedent being set and the danger of its misuse in future.

The last feature of the Bush doctrine that I draw attention to is its unilateralism. In a sense the very genesis of the document testifies to this, since its intention to alter the international system fundamentally was conceived, formulated and announced with little or no prior consultation with other states, not even other democracies and allies. It is an American enterprise, representing American assumptions and values. And it is made clear that America will proceed to implement the new doctrine on its own if it has to: "While the United States will constantly strive to enlist the support of the international community, we will not hesitate to act alone, if necessary, to exercise our right of self-defense."

Evaluating the doctrine

What can we say about this strategic doctrine? Well, the first thing to be recognized is its breathtaking scope, its huge ambition to do no less than to effect a transformation of the political universe—according to some of its language, to stamp out evil and war between states, to create a benign world. Students of international politics who belong to the Realist school—as I do—tend to see such goals as utopian, beyond even the reach of a country with the enormous power of the United States. The English journalist Frank Johnson once wittily remarked that, "In politics, Utopia is always an important country, always one of the Great Powers." While America has enough strength to defeat all other adversaries and rivals, it remains to be seen whether she can take on and conquer Utopia.

Second, in emphasizing and insisting upon the dominant role of the United States and the assertive use of American power, the doctrine makes very questionable assumptions about what other states will accept and live with. They are asked to take its stated good intentions and respect for their interests on trust. States have never been prepared to do this in the past with other would-be hegemons. When Britain was riding high in the eighteenth century, after defeating the French in the Seven Years War and acquiring much of North America and India, the great political philosopher Edmund Burke warned his fellow countrymen that:

> Among precautions against ambition, it may not be amiss to take precaution against our own. I must fairly say, I dread our own power and our own ambition. I dread our being too much dreaded ... We may say that we shall not abuse this astonishing and hitherto unheard of power. But every other nation will think we shall abuse it. It is impossible but that, sooner or later, this state of things must produce a combination against us which may end in our ruin.[5]

Will the United States be the exception? Does the fact that it is a democratic and liberal state make a decisive difference? Will other states accept the concept of a benign hegemon or regard it as a contradiction in terms? Indeed, do they have a choice?

The thrust and tone of the doctrine reject the advice given by most pundits on the best way to play a hegemonic role in order to prolong its duration—which is to be restrained and prudent in the use of its power, to disguise it, to strive to act as far as possible by persuasion and consensus in order to coopt others. Dr Coral Bell of the Australian National University sums up that advice by saying, "the unipolar world should be run as if it were a concert of powers"[6]—as if, that is, it were really multipolar. Professor John Ikenberry of Georgetown University has the same thing in mind when he talks about a "stake-holder" hegemony, whereby the hegemon encourages others to associate with it, to climb on its bandwagon, rather than form coalitions to try to balance and oppose it. As he says: "The implication of my argument is that the more America's brute power capabilities emerge from behind mutually acceptable rules and institutions, the more that power will provoke reaction and resistance."[7]

In the 1940s, when the United States was already the dominant power within the Western Alliance, it acted on this advice. It went out of its way to act multilaterally, to create a network of rule-making institutions—the UN system, the International Monetary Fund (IMF), the World Bank, the General Agreements on Tariffs and Trade (GATT)—that allowed it to act cooperatively with others, as *primus inter pares*—the first among equals. There is little of this to be found in the current doctrine, no talk of creating institutions to run the new order. The emphasis is overwhelmingly on the mission, and the prevailing view in Washington, as famously enunciated by US Secretary of Defense Donald Rumsfeld, has been that "the worst thing you can do is allow a coalition to determine what your mission is."[8]

The Bush Doctrine should be taken very seriously, and any inclination to treat it as mere rhetoric would be a serious error. It has already been put into effect in Iraq. All four of the features that I have drawn attention to have been evident there: the use of American military force as the main instrument; preemptive action; a clear indication that the United States was prepared to act without a great-power consensus, and unilaterally if necessary; and the avowed intention to replace a tyrannical regime with a liberal representative government.

That is why the Iraq commitment has an importance that goes way beyond the fate of Iraq itself. If, in the end, it turns out successfully, it is likely that the setbacks that have occurred since the end of the heavy fighting will be seen as part of a learning experience, a breaking-in period for a new, revolutionary strategic doctrine. If, on the other hand, it fails at the first hurdle—if, that is, the United States finds that bringing about security, stability, a decent political order, and an improvement in the living standards of the Iraqi people, is beyond its capacity; if the whole thing becomes a "quagmire," or, indeed, if it has to internationalize the whole project by giving the United Nations a preeminent role—then not only will there have to be a reconsideration of the whole global strategy, but the limits of the United States' capacity will have been made evident, and the inclination to resist it greatly strengthened.

All this is fully understood by the advocates and supporters of the policy. The editors of the influential neoconservative magazine *The Weekly Standard*, for example, insist: "The future course of American foreign policy, American world leadership, and American security is at stake. Failure in Iraq would be a devastating blow to everything the United States hopes to accomplish, and must accomplish, in the decades ahead."[9]

As for the skeptics and critics, some of them will conclude that having committed itself so far, the United States now has no option but to go on and see it through—an argument that prevailed for a long time during the Vietnam War. Others will argue that even at this late stage, it is preferable to cut one's losses than to proceed further with a deeply flawed policy, citing the old saw, "If you're in a hole, stop digging."

Punching above our weight?

A couple of years ago, Walter Russell Mead, a Fellow of the Council on Foreign Relations in New York, wrote a book identifying four traditions of American foreign policy, each one represented by a leading American statesman.[10]

- The Hamiltonian tradition consists of a combination of commercialism and realism.
- The Jeffersonian tradition is apprehensive of the corrupting influence of the outside world and therefore skeptical about international commitments and what Thomas Jefferson referred to as "entangling alliances."
- The Jacksonian tradition is populist, patriotic, pugnacious, and ultra-sensitive concerning any slight to the country's honor.
- And last there is the Wilsonian tradition of crusading liberal internationalism.[11]

Throughout the country's history, Mead maintains, these four traditions have interacted: sometimes mutually supporting each other, sometimes competing and conflicting, always overlapping, the mix changing as both domestic and international circumstance change.

Reading Mead's book encourages reflection as to what a similar exercise concerning Australia's foreign policy traditions would yield. It seems to me that here there have been three main traditions.

Three traditions in Australian foreign policy

First, there is the Menzies tradition. This is a thoroughly Realist, power- and interest-based tradition, though in Menzies' own case it was sometimes obscured by his taste for sentimental declarations of attachment to Britain and the Queen, which misled some into thinking that he was merely a romantic loyalist.

As a Realist and a conservative, Menzies was skeptical of abstract, general schemes. He looked to interest rather than principle as the motive for action, to history and experience rather than abstract reasoning for the basis of sound judgment.

Menzies' central assumption was that in an international environment that was inherently dangerous—one that in his day contained predators like Nazi Germany, a militarized Japan, and later the Soviet Union—it was vital for a large, sparsely populated, and geographically isolated Western country like Australia that the global balance of power should favor the leading democratic powers. And it was also vital that Australia should have close, friendly relations with those powers.

In order to ensure that state of affairs, Australia must be prepared to support the United States and Britain politically and, when necessary militarily. Such support was our insurance policy. It was also highly congenial to Menzies personally, since it was a policy that enabled Australia—and Menzies himself—to be wired in to the main game of global power politics in a way that was otherwise impossible.

National interest and personal ambition, then, were both served by such a policy. But inherent in it was the risk of losing sight of a distinctive Australian identity and of exaggerating the cohesion and solidarity represented by the larger concept, whether it be the British Commonwealth, "the West," or the "Free World."

The Menzies tradition is skeptical of most international institutions, including the United Nations, which it claims should be seen not as an alternative to power politics, but as power politics with a different facade—a different way for sovereign states to play essentially the same game. The Security Council is in reality no more than a kind of permanent conference of the great powers, where important and contentious issues can be discussed. Every member votes according to how it sees its own interests. To think otherwise, Menzies once argued, was to see the organization as a "house fully constructed which in due course, by some miracle, would be able to build its own foundations." The United Nations reflects the realities of international politics, but it does not and cannot change them significantly. The United Nations has no particular moral authority, and to make one's response to a course of action depend on whether or not it is sanctioned by the UN is more a way of evading than of making a moral choice.

The Menzies tradition is, of course, strongest on the conservative side of politics, though it has its representatives across the spectrum. John Howard is probably the tradition's purest representative since Menzies himself.

The second tradition is, I think, best identified as the Evatt tradition. It is both strongly nationalist and internationalist. No contradiction is involved here, since internationalism is favored, not only on principle, but because international organizations are regarded as the most congenial and effective forums for a middle power like Australia to register its presence and extend its influence.

This tradition is assertive and energetic. It is concerned to give Australia a high profile as a country capable of making a distinctive contribution to international affairs. Sometimes it leads to hyperactivity and attention-seeking. At the Paris Peace Conference of 1946, to take an extreme example, Dr. Evatt, as leader of the Australian delegation, managed to propose no fewer than 400 amendments. Sadly, only one of them was adopted.

The Evatt tradition is concerned to establish Australia's independence, is sensitive to slights, and is concerned with status. It is suspicious of great powers, and will go out of its way to assert its independence of them, in order both to preserve its freedom of action and to strengthen its own sense of identity. It is inclined to believe that lesser powers like itself, being more detached, are better able than great powers to assess the morality and justice of an issue objectively. Power politics tends to be seen as a chosen mode of behavior, rather than something inherent in a system of sovereign states and necessary for survival.

One of Evatt's favorite words was "machinery," by which he meant organizational and institutional frameworks, procedures and rules. In his view, getting the machinery right was the secret of progress, for he believed that, to a great extent, form determines substance. Those of this persuasion tend to subscribe to the dictum "build and they will come."

They also attach great importance to international law. Thus, in Evatt's first ministerial statement to Parliament, only a few days before Pearl Harbor and in an atmosphere of impending crisis, he found time to express concern that Australia was not legally at war with Finland, Hungary, and Romania, explaining that if this was not rectified the consequences "might well be disastrous to Russian morale." In somewhat the same spirit, three decades later, another eminent representative of the tradition, Gough Whitlam, was to feel compelled to recognize formally the incorporation of the Baltic States into the Soviet Union, in order to clarify the legal situation. Realists, on the other hand, tend to be skeptical about the claims made for a system of law that lacks any coercive power to enforce itself.

Unlike the Menzies tradition, the Evatt tradition draws a sharp distinction between power politics and the United Nations, seeing the latter as laying a foundation for an entirely different international order and norms of behavior. Action that is sanctioned by the UN has a legitimacy and moral quality that is otherwise lacking. For, whatever its shortcomings, the organization represents an ideal to be striven for. A typical Realist reaction to the stress on machinery and forms is that of Nicholas Mansergh in his magisterial *Survey of Commonwealth Affairs*: "Dr Evatt did not appear to understand ... that no elaboration of machinery could sensibly modify a relationship determined by relative power."[12]

This is a tradition represented most clearly on the Labor side of politics; as well as Evatt himself, Gough Whitlam and Gareth Evans have embodied much of what it stands for.

The distinguishing mark of the third tradition—call it the Spender-Casey tradition, or, if you prefer, the Keating tradition—is the importance it attaches to regional affairs. The nature and content of that concern has varied over the decades: strategic and security matters during and immediately after World War II; support for Indonesian independence by the Chifley government in the late 1940s; the Colombo Plan[13] and other aid to the newly independent states of the region in the 1950s; concern over the increasing instability, violence, and radicalization of the region in the 1960s, leading to military involvement in Malaya and Vietnam; and, increasingly from then on, a concern to develop relations, and to integrate, with a region that had become economically dynamic and significant.

As ministers for external affairs, both Percy Spender and Richard Gardiner Casey represented this tradition early on, creating and extending the Colombo Plan, and developing diplomatic relations with the region's new states. All this in the face of considerable indifference on Menzies' part. According to Spender, Menzies viewed his preoccupation with the region as a "hobby horse" and was given to saying patronizingly, "Come on Percy, let's have your thesis about South East Asia."

Menzies' power-centered outlook made him a big-picture man, inclined to play down a regional approach. "Regionalism," he once reflected, "is open to the view that it may involve nothing more than a slightly enlarged form of isolationism—a collective form of isolationism, if I may use a curious phrase." He tended to regard the parochial affairs of weak, inexperienced, regional states as low on the agenda. Like many conservative Realists, he was slow to identify, and to react to, significant forces of change. As time passed, such an attitude toward the region became increasingly unsustainable. By the 1990s, Paul Keating was giving priority to regional relationships.

In contemplating these three traditions, the question is not which one of them is the right one for Australia to adopt in perpetuity, but what balance or mix of them is appropriate at any given time, as circumstances, and the priorities of our interests, change.

Australia's policies

Against this background, what can be said about the policy of the Howard government since 2002? That it has been a policy of unhesitating, unqualified, and—given the attitude of many other states—conspicuous support for the United States in its wars against terrorism and against Iraq. As such, it is a policy that can be and has been defended both on Menzian grounds—that is, protecting one's own security and paying one's insurance premium to a great and powerful friend—and in terms of our values, given that it was tyranny and terror that were being combated.

Many people whom I respect have found this combination of arguments a compelling one, demanding support for the policy of the Howard government. I would like to explain why, on Realist grounds, I have not.

First, a bit of self-protective ground-clearing. As things have not exactly gone according to plan in Iraq since Saddam Hussein was overthrown, and as a favorable outcome seems less than certain, it might seem that I'm simply being wise after the event and second-guessing the government. This isn't so. As it happens, I published a relevant piece on Australian–US relations in the *Australian Financial Review* on September 10, 2001: that is, precisely one day *before* the terrorist attack on New York and Washington. In it, I argued that:

> Australia should proceed carefully and without illusion in dealing with its powerful ally. For one thing, post-cold-war American foreign policy is still, in some respects, a work in progress, and those who get too close to it run the risk that a piece of the scaffolding might fall off and hit them ... Even more important, while the United States is by historical standards a benevolent hegemon, a hegemon is what it is. Not only is its power vast, but it is concerned to use that power ... to create a world in its own image with institutions and rules determined by Washington ... While such a world would have many attractions, the attempt to bring it into being will inevitably generate serious opposition and a great deal of strife and conflict. It would be inappropriate and dangerous for a country of Australia's limited means and interests to associate itself closely with such an enterprise.

I went on to maintain that "however sweet the rhetoric and however warm the hugging, the priorities of the two countries are likely to differ at least as often as they coincide."

I believe that while these arguments had validity before September 11 and the Iraq War, they, and some additional ones, have even more validity today. Let me enumerate.

First, concerning terrorism, the first and overriding responsibility of an Australian government is not to combat global terrorism generally but to protect this country from terrorism. The two ends are not necessarily identical. By being an early, unqualified, and high-profile supporter of American policy, when so many others—including longstanding allies of the United States and some of our neighbors—were expressing serious reservations about both the legitimacy and the effectiveness of that policy, Australia may well have increased rather than decreased its chances of becoming a terrorist target.

Second, the course Australia has followed since September 11 is open to the charge that it has got the balance between alliance policy and regional policy wrong. We are living in the same region as the most populous Muslim state in the world, a state that, being less than a model of stability and order, is a breeding ground for terror. As well, we are in close proximity to some failed or failing states that are potential hosts for terrorists.

Looking ahead, by the year 2050—that is, by the time someone born now will be entering middle age—the population of the nine countries extending from Pakistan to China will have increased by something on the order of 1.4 billion. That of Indonesia alone is projected to increase by 120 million in that period. While all this does not mean that the region is inevitably going to be more unstable or threatening than it is now, it does suggest that its importance is going to loom larger rather than smaller in our strategic calculations, and that anything that can justify distracting our attention and resources from it must be of a compelling nature.

But, third, the case made by the Bush administration for the Iraq war was not compelling. Indeed, it was inconsistent and surprisingly incompetent, with dubious and shifting rationales being offered: one day, weapons of mass destruction; the next day, links with al-Qaeda; after that, the cruelty of the regime and the need for liberation of the Iraqi people; and then Saddam's alleged reckless, unpredictable nature, which, it was claimed, ruled out deterrence and required preemption. As well as all that, the case for overthrowing Saddam Hussein was made against the background of a proclaimed new strategic doctrine aimed at nothing less than remaking the world in America's image.

Given all this, restraint, some deep reflection, and a request for clarification, rather than eager and unqualified support, would have been an appropriate Australian response; appropriate in terms not only of Australia's own interests but of those of its great ally. And it could have been accompanied by a clear statement of our need to give priority to dealing with terror where it was most likely to impinge on us, that is, not in the Middle East but in Southeast Asia.

Supporters of the policy might respond to such criticism by saying that, however things turn out in Iraq, Australia has built up a lot of credit in Washington and with the American people, and that this on its own justifies the policy followed by Prime Minister Howard. Perhaps so. But—and this is my fourth point—in international politics, expectations of gratitude rest on shaky foundations. As Charles de Gaulle once remarked, great powers are "cold monsters," and gratitude is not one of their stronger motivators. When, in 1848, Czarist Russia intervened to put down an insurrection in Hungary, thus saving the Habsburg Empire, which was then in deep trouble, the Habsburg prime minister commented: "We shall astonish the world with our ingratitude." Sure enough, half a dozen years later, when Britain and France went to war with Russia in the Crimea, the Habsburgs studiously stayed on the sidelines. But the world was not very astonished.

Now you may think that this example, like de Gaulle's remark, represents the cynicism of Old Europe. However, it was not de Gaulle but George Washington who observed that "no nation can be entrusted further than it is bound by its interests" and that "there can be no greater error than to expect or calculate on real favors from nation to nation."

Fifth, these words of Washington's are just as relevant and carry just as much weight in considering another assumption that many Australians, including John Howard, make concerning our American connection, which is that a great deal of weight should be attached to cultural affinity. Listen to Mr. Howard in a radio interview, expressing a conviction about Australian–US relations that he has repeated many times: "they do have a lot of values and attitudes that we share, and I'm a great believer that you should have close relations with the countries whose way of life is closest to your own."[14]

Mr. Howard is not alone in this belief. In recent years there has been renewed support for an old idea—that English-speaking nations with cultural affinities should draw together and form some kind of political and economic union, what has been termed an "Anglosphere."

The whole notion that cultural affinity can be the solid foundation of a relationship needs to be treated very warily. Consider this: Great Britain and the United States fought World War II together in an extraordinarily close alliance. One million American troops were stationed in Britain before D-Day. British soldiers fought under American generals, and American soldiers under British generals. President Roosevelt and Prime Minister Churchill were in constant touch, and there was extraordinary intimacy between the top people on both sides. The American establishment at the time was very Anglophile and much more WASP (White, Anglo-Saxon, Protestant) than it is now.

Yet as soon as the war was over, the United States cut off Lend-Lease[15] aid to a virtually bankrupt Britain and imposed very harsh terms on the loan it negotiated with the Attlee government.

And only a decade after that close partnership, when Dwight D. Eisenhower and Anthony Eden, two wartime colleagues, were leading their respective governments, the United States publicly humiliated its British and French allies at the time of the Suez Crisis, forcing them to climb down and leave the Canal in Egyptian President Nasser's hands. From this episode the British and the French drew opposite conclusions: the British, that they should never again cross the United States; the French, that they should never again depend on the United States.

Closer to home, all Australian prime ministers should bear in mind the American handling of the Dutch New Guinea question in the early 1960s. Despite the

ANZUS alliance, and despite the fact that Robert Menzies was a great "Western values" man whose standing in Washington was high, the Kennedy administration chose to try to placate a radical, anti-Western Sukarno over the issue, rather than support either Australia or America's NATO ally, the Netherlands.

None of this is meant as a criticism of the United States, which just behaved as great powers normally behave—quite properly putting their own interests ahead of everything else, and giving less weight to the views of those whose support can be taken for granted than to those whose support they wish to gain.

Most people who follow international politics are familiar with a version of Lord Palmerston's dictum: "We have no eternal allies, and we have no perpetual enemies. Our interests are eternal and perpetual, and those interests it is our duty to follow."[16] But again, George Washington had said it more crisply fifty years earlier: "Permanent, inveterate antipathies against particular nations, and passionate attachments to others, should be avoided."

Sixth, for the internationalists of the Evatt tradition, one of the drawbacks of this policy followed by the Australian government is that it has weakened Australia's position in the UN, through the conspicuous association with a course of action that, in the eyes of most members, lacked UN authority. Normally, this would be a matter of little concern to Realists, but at a time when much of the serious diplomatic power game is likely to be played in the UN, as the other permanent members of the Security Council use it to try to restrain the United States, this has more significance than it would normally have.

My seventh and last point concerns ends and means. Australia is a large continent to defend. It exists in a region characterized by a great deal of turbulence. As by far the most populous, powerful, and wealthy country in the southwest Pacific, it properly assumes responsibility for stability in some of the smaller countries of the region that have serious problems.

To meet these commitments, Australia spends under 2 percent of its Gross National Product on defense. It has an army of only 25,000 personnel. In these circumstances, for it to engage in serious military campaigns beyond its region, and to do so preemptively and when it is not directly threatened, is to leave itself open to the charge of being a cheap hawk, which is a dangerous and irresponsible thing to be. Punching above one's weight may be a source of pride, but it is also hazardous and a form of activity best avoided.

Back in the 1940s, Walter Lippmann wrote a sentence that has a claim to be one of the most important ever written about foreign policy. It reads as follows:

> Without the controlling principle that the nation must maintain its objectives and its power in equilibrium, its purposes within its means and its means equal to its purposes, its commitments related to its resources and its resources adequate to its commitments, it is impossible to think at all about foreign affairs.[17]

Those responsible for Australian foreign policy could do worse than have that sentence framed and hung prominently on their office walls.

Notes

1. This chapter, which brings together parts of the Boyer Lectures for 2003, originally appeared in Owen Harries, *Benign or Imperial? Reflections on American Hegemony* (Sydney: ABC Books, 2004). It is reprinted here with minor editorial changes.
2. Robert Kagan, *Paradise and Power: America and Europe in the New World Order*, (London: Atlantic Books, 2003), p. 88.
3. Unless otherwise indicated, all quotations in this chapter are from that document.
4. Robert Kagan, p. 88.
5. "Remarks on the Policy of the Allies with Respect to France," *The Works of Edmund Burke* (Boston: Little Brown, 1901), Vol. IV, p. 457.
6. Coral Bell, "American Ascendancy and the Pretense of Concert," *The National Interest*, No. 57 (Fall, 1999), p. 60.
7. G. John Ikenberry, "Getting Hegemony Right," *The National Interest*, No. 63 (Spring, 2001), p. 22.
8. Television interview with Larry King.
9. *The Weekly Standard*, August 2003.
10. Walter Russell Mead, *Special Providence: American Foreign Policy and How it Changed the World* (New York: Knopf, 1991).
11. Alexander Hamilton (1757–1804) was one of the authors of the highly influential *Federalist Papers*. He served as Washington's first Secretary of the Treasury and as his principal adviser.
12. Nicholas Mansergh, *Survey of British Commonwealth Affairs—Volume 2: Problems of Wartime Cooperation and Post-War Change, 1939–52* (Oxford: Oxford University Press, 1958), p. 139.
13. The Colombo Plan was conceived during a 1951 meeting of British Commonwealth Foreign Ministers in Ceylon (now Sri Lanka). It was an economic aid program specifically focusing on such areas as agriculture, health, and education in, mainly, Asian nations.
14. Interview with Ray Hadley, Radio 2GB, October 2, 2002.
15. President Roosevelt instituted the Lend-Lease Act in 1941 to allow the United States to provide war materials to its World War II allies for payment "in kind." By the end of the war over forty nations had benefited from Lend-Lease aid.
16. Viscount Palmerston served as British Foreign Secretary three times, and then as Prime Minister (1855–65).
17. Walter Lippmann, *US Foreign Policy* (London: Hamish Hamilton, 1943), p. 3.

11 The North Korean nuclear crisis

Four-plus-two—an idea whose time has come

Peter Van Ness

The confrontation between North Korea and the Bush administration over North Korea's nuclear programs threatens to plunge Northeast Asia, one of the most strategically volatile regions in the world, into chaos and to ignite a nuclear arms race. But there is a way to achieve a peaceful resolution to this crisis that would be minimally acceptable to all parties, including both North Korea and the United States. It would be a four-plus-two security consortium, composed of the four major powers in Northeast Asia (China, Japan, Russia, and the United States) plus the two Korean states. They would guarantee the security of the region and assure that the Koreas remained non-nuclear. This is a "cooperative security" design, the idea being to achieve security by working out mutually beneficial arrangements with or among likely adversaries, rather than constructing alliances against them.

Competing paradigms in the North Korean nuclear negotiations

The second session of the six-party negotiations on North Korea's nuclear programs, held in Beijing in February 2004, concluded with nothing more than the expectation that the six participating nations would meet again before July 2004, and that working groups would meet in the interim to set an agenda for the next session. Meanwhile, North Korea threatened to escalate tensions further by testing a nuclear device, while the United States remained undecided about how to proceed. Washington continued to insist on what it called CVID (complete, verifiable, and irreversible dismantlement of North Korea's nuclear programs), and pointed to Libya as a model of a "rogue state" that agreed under pressure to give up its weapons of mass destruction.

Had anything been achieved in the first two sessions of the six-party negotiations? Is a peaceful solution to the North Korean nuclear crisis possible? If so, what is most needed to produce a mutually acceptable conclusion to the crisis?

For starters, to have any hope for a successful multilateral negotiation, especially on a topic as sensitive as nuclear weapons, it is vitally important to have the right parties at the table: not too many, not too few. All of those states whose core interests are most directly involved must be included, but, at the same time, it is equally important to include as few parties as possible, because each additional state creates one more hurdle to achieving a viable consensus among the participants. This important first step was accomplished in Beijing in August 2003. The first session of the six-party talks brought together what has been labeled the "four-plus-two" (the four major powers—the United States, China, Russia, and Japan—plus North and South Korea), a formula that has been widely discussed in the region ever since Nakayama Taro was Japan's Foreign Minister, in the early 1990s.

Among the six countries, however, there are deep disagreements about what a solution to the North Korean nuclear problem might be and how it could best be achieved. Both the United States and the North Korean regime have taken such extreme positions that a peaceful resolution of the standoff is not possible without outside pressure to convince both governments to modify their irreconcilable positions.

But the conceptual divisions among the six are not what one might expect. Strangely enough, North Korea and the United States tend to understand security issues in a similarly "Realist" way, while the other four, especially South Korea and China, are arguing for a very different "cooperative security" design. Both the United States and the Democratic People's Republic of Korea (DPRK, North Korea) see the world as anarchy, self-help as the only reliable strategy, and negotiated outcomes as inevitably zero-sum (i.e., I can gain only at your expense). By contrast, the other four are proposing an "everybody benefits," win–win solution. They emphasize the importance of avoiding military conflict, and stress the need to maintain existing trade, aid, and investment ties—a network of mutual benefit that the DPRK would be invited to join.

Yet North Korea seems far from considering such an attractive proposal. The DPRK has become convinced that it is now target number one on the Bush administration hit list, after having been marked as a member of the "axis of evil" in the President's 2002 State of the Union Address, and identified by name in the US Nuclear Posture Review as a potential target for US nuclear attack. The US declaration of a right to engage in preemptive war, plus its invasions of Afghanistan and Iraq, have only confirmed the DPRK in its strategic judgments.[1] As a result, the DPRK leadership has determined that a nuclear capability is its best and perhaps only defense against a possible US attack.[2] Some analysts believe that the DPRK would not willingly give up its nuclear capability under any conditions.

Within the Bush administration, there is a parallel, Realist debate on what to do about the North Korean nuclear programs and the continuing DPRK escalation of the confrontation. Should Bush opt for preemption, coercive diplomacy, or engagement?[3]

At present, US policy is a combination of the latter two, focused on what is called the Proliferation Security Initiative (PSI), a strategy designed to pressure North Korea by cutting off any exports of missile components or nuclear materials to other countries. Ten other countries signed up in support of the PSI after two meetings, first in Madrid and then in Australia, hosted by the John Howard government.[4] The problem with PSI is that none of the three countries that border the DPRK (South Korea, China, and Russia) has agreed to join, and the operational difficulties and international legal implications of trying to intercept DPRK flights and to stop North Korea ships in international waters are very serious. Nuclear material, which is the greatest concern, could easily be transported in a backpack and walked across North Korea's 800-kilometer border with China, as a Japanese diplomat described to me recently in Tokyo. That kind of material would be virtually impossible to interdict by US and allied military forces without close Chinese cooperation.

A further problem on the US side that must be resolved is that, despite occasional assurances given by officials that the United States would not invade North Korea, at least some of the Bush hardliners are as committed to "regime change" in North Korea as they are to dismantling the DPRK nuclear programs. If there is to be a peaceful resolution of this confrontation, the United States cannot have both regime change *and* a non-nuclear North Korea. As long as North Korea is convinced that Bush is determined to overthrow the DPRK government, its leaders will see their nuclear capability as their best deterrent.

The task of finding a peaceful solution is further complicated by the fact that some US leaders conceive of the confrontation with North Korea as a struggle between good and evil, and continue to make personal attacks on Kim Jong-il. The US President's personal contempt for Kim Jong-il is well known: "I loathe Kim Jong-il," he told Bob Woodward during interviews for his book on the invasion of Afghanistan.[5] More recently, the US Under Secretary of State for Arms Control, John Bolton, denounced Kim Jong-il by name 41 times in a 25-minute speech in Seoul in July 2003, just when other diplomats were working overtime to bring the six countries together for the first six-party negotiations.[6] Clearly, strong emotions like these, on both sides, contribute to the danger of misperception and miscalculation.

This is where multilateral diplomacy becomes essential. To achieve a peaceful outcome, both the United States and the DPRK have got to be moved away from their extreme positions. China and Russia must convince North Korea that they are prepared, together with the United States, to provide the DPRK with credible security commitments to guarantee the DPRK regime against foreign military attack and to help in the economic modernization of the country, in return for a verified dismantling of its nuclear programs. At the same time, Japan and South Korea, as America's closest allies in the region, will have to convince the Bush administration that it must leave regime change to the Korean people.

Nonetheless, there will also be myriad bilateral problems to overcome. Somehow these issues in dispute between two countries must be put aside while the six parties seek agreement on how to deal with the Korean crisis. For one example, China and Japan disagree about a whole range of problems: how to interpret their World War II history, territorial claims over islands in the East China Sea, which side will win a pipeline agreement with Moscow to bring much-needed Russian energy exports their way, US–Japanese cooperation on missile defense, Japanese sex tourism in South China, compensation for Chinese workers injured when they unearthed Japanese wartime chemical weapons left in

China, and more. Meanwhile, however, they enjoy a close and cooperative relationship with respect to trade, investment, and foreign aid.

Each of the six participating countries also has domestic problems that might prove to be obstacles to a successful negotiation. One of the most serious has been the situation facing South Korean President Roh Moo Hyun, who was suspended from office following an unprecedented impeachment motion passed by the opposition-controlled National Assembly in March 2004. The nine-justice Constitutional Court decided in May not to endorse the impeachment, which was based on allegations of election law violations, corruption, and incompetence; and President Roh's party won majority control of the National Assembly in the most recent election. Nevertheless, the uproar over this incident could have a big impact on Seoul's role in the six-party negotiations.

Another serious problem that may have a direct impact on the negotiations is the abduction of Japanese citizens in the past by North Korea. With respect to this issue, however, China, which has taken the lead in hosting the multilateral meetings, has perhaps already set an important precedent. During summit meetings of the Asia-Pacific Economic Cooperation (APEC) forum in October 2003, People's Republic of China President Hu Jintao reportedly told Japanese Prime Minister Koizumi that the kidnap issue was a bilateral matter that should be resolved separately by Japan and North Korea.[7] If China, as convener and host of six-party negotiations, can insist on keeping bilateral problems off the agenda at these meetings, that should increase the chances for their success by a wide margin.

Despite the many difficulties facing the six participants, a four-plus-two security consortium would be the best way both to resolve the current crisis and to provide a long-term institutional structure to support the strategic stability of Northeast Asia. The participants have an opportunity to take advantage of the immediate crisis to create new security institutions capable of providing long-term security for a historically volatile region.

The four-plus-two concept

Four-plus-two is a cooperative security concept that has been discussed by analysts in Asia and implemented in so-called Track II dialogues for over a decade. The idea is that *the four* major powers of Northeast Asia (China, Japan, Russia, and the United States) should commit themselves jointly to guarantee the security of the region and to support a peaceful reconciliation between *the two* (North and South Korea). Four-plus-two is particularly appropriate today, both as a basis for peacefully resolving the current crisis over the DPRK's nuclear programs, and as a foundation for building mutually beneficial economic and political cooperation in the future.

The idea of "cooperative security" arrangements among major powers is not new. The US arms-control agreements with the former Soviet Union are the best example to date of cooperative security in practice. The Nuclear Age created new imperatives for the major nuclear-weapons adversaries to cooperate in order to enhance their own security and, most importantly, to avoid a suicidal nuclear war. Once the governments of both superpowers realized that their combined nuclear arsenals constituted a ticking time bomb capable of destroying human civilization, a new way of thinking became essential. That realization, sharpened by dangerous confrontations like the Cuban missile crisis of 1962, led both governments to conclude that it was in their fundamental interest to cooperate across their many ideological and material differences to reach agreements to control the nuclear arms race and to minimize the probability of military confrontations between the two nuclear superpowers.

The "cooperative security" design of a consortium like this is unfamiliar to many of the decision makers who presumably would have to be involved to make a four-plus-two institution work. Nevertheless, they should be able to identify the very substantial mutual benefits to be had for all parties from such an arrangement. The history of Northeast Asia shows just how necessary it is to build new security institutions in the region.

The geopolitics of this area (where China, Russia, Korea, and Japan come together) has been one of the most volatile in the world. For more than one hundred years, the countries of the region have been in conflict with each other. Today, more than fifty years after the end of World War II, Russia and Japan still have not concluded a peace agreement, and the Korean peninsula remains divided into two states that confront each other across the demilitarized zone (DMZ) that marks the 1953 truce at the end of the Korean War. It is the most militarized frontier in the world.

The current crisis began with North Korea's reported admission in October 2002 to US Assistant Secretary of State James Kelly that it did indeed have a program for enriching uranium that might be used to make nuclear weapons. This, in turn, threw Bush administration plans for dealing with the "axis of evil" into a tailspin. Ever since Pyongyang's revelation became public, Washington has been on the defensive, trying to explain why it insisted on making war with Iraq, where no evidence to date has been brought forward to show that Saddam Hussein had any weapons of mass destruction, while insisting that diplomacy is the right way to deal with North Korea. The US Central Intelligence Agency estimated that North Korea probably already had one or two nuclear weapons, and at the trilateral meeting (US, DPRK, and China) in Beijing in April 2003, the DPRK representative reportedly told the United States that indeed it did have nuclear weapons. Subsequently, Pyongyang denied making both admissions.

The United States has demanded that the DPRK give up its nuclear programs and accept international inspection, while Pyongyang has declared that it first wants to negotiate a bilateral security pact with the United States. While the United States refused to negotiate before there was evidence that North Korea had moved toward denuclearization, the DPRK increased the pressure through a series of unilateral escalations, including the expulsion of International Atomic Energy Agency (IAEA) inspectors and withdrawal from the Nuclear Non-Proliferation Treaty.

Eighteen months later, however, it appeared that pressure from the other four parties had begun to work on both the DPRK and the United States. Pyongyang, having earlier refused to meet in a multilateral setting, later agreed, first, to participate in the three-party meeting in Beijing in April 2003, and then, more importantly, to join the first six-party negotiation in Beijing in August. For its part, the United States won its point about insisting on a multilateral meeting, but also began to change its position to meet the North Korean demand for a security guarantee in return for giving up its nuclear-weapons programs. At the APEC summit meetings in Bangkok in October 2003, President Bush still rejected the idea of a bilateral security treaty with the DPRK, but proposed to the DPRK instead a five-nation security commitment.[8]

To describe the four-plus-two idea in more detail, I will discuss first *the four* powers and then *the two* Koreas.

The four major powers

The first steps toward constructing a four-plus-two consortium might be the most difficult. Each of the four powers is very different: two Asian states, one communist and one capitalist; a former communist superpower; and the US hegemon. Each has its own vital national priorities, and no previous experience in working together in a foursome like this. In the region, their previous relationships have typically been confrontational, not cooperative. Most often, they have fought wars against each other rather than sought opportunities to work together for mutual benefit.

Yet, what is not widely understood is the fact that the four major powers of Northeast Asia (China, Japan, Russia, and the United States), despite their many differences, actually agree on a number of key strategic priorities in the region. Moreover, they are now more in agreement on these fundamental issues than they have ever been before.

First, all four have a substantial stake in maintaining the strategic stability of the region. None would benefit from a major destabilizing crisis. For example, it would not serve any of their interests if military conflict broke out again in the region, as it did during the Korean War, 1950–53. Moreover, all four major powers especially value their relations with South Korea, based mainly on commercial ties. More important, all four have an even more substantial interest in maintaining and developing mutually beneficial relationships with each other. They therefore do not want a Korean problem to pit them against each other.

With regard to relations between North and South Korea, all four powers would probably prefer that Korea remain divided (the status quo), because of a variety of different concerns about what a reunified Korea might become—for example, for China, a concern that Korea might become a US ally; and for Japan, that Korea might become a nuclear-armed, independent state harboring hostile memories of its colonial past under Japanese rule. But a gradually reunifying Korea within a regional strategic consortium dominated by the four powers would potentially alleviate many of those fears. Moreover, the status quo that the four preferred was the one *before* North Korea revealed its nuclear programs to James Kelly. Now, they have a potential nuclear-weapons power to deal with.

Second, all four are strongly opposed to either Korean state (North or South) becoming a nuclear-weapons power. Three of the four powers (the United States, China, and Russia) are of course already established nuclear-weapons powers. None of the three favors nuclear proliferation in Northeast Asia, nor would any of them like to see a nuclear DPRK ignite a nuclear arms race. Most particularly, if Japan were to respond by deciding to arm itself with nuclear weapons, many analysts believe that South Korea, Taiwan, and perhaps other Asian countries would follow suit. Such a regional nuclear arms race would be likely to destroy the global nuclear nonproliferation regime.

Finally, apart from those important issues about which they all agree, only three of the four major powers (all except the United States) are opposed to a collapse of the North Korean regime. This is principally because it might undermine the strategic stability of the region. But another reason is that neighboring countries fear that tens of thousands of refugees might want to seek protection in their countries. Although the United States has spoken of favoring "regime change" in North Korea, once Washington realized what strategic instability a collapse might bring, perhaps the United States would also prefer to maintain regime stability in the North as part of a transitional arrangement for the peninsula.

One of the major obstacles for the four powers in identifying their common interests and acting upon them is the history of the region. Northeast Asia has been the cockpit of battles among the powers and the two Koreas, time and time again. The cold war in particular divided the region into two competing camps. Moreover, there is a long list of earlier conflicts, beginning with the Sino-Japanese War of 1894–5, the Russo-Japanese War of 1904–5, the Japanese occupation of Korea from 1910 to 1945, the Manchurian Incident of 1931 and the Japanese occupation of Manchuria, war between Japan and China from 1937 to 1945, the Japanese attack on Pearl Harbor in 1941 and war with the United States (and in the final days of the war with the Soviet Union as well), the Korean War, the Sino-Soviet dispute (1963–76), and the cold war (1950–89). The Korean peninsula today remains divided along cold war lines, half a century after the end of the Korean War, in which more than 3 million Koreans died.

The two Korean states

The design here proposes that the two existing Korean states would be full participants in the process of establishing a security consortium, and that upon reunification, the united Korea would become a fifth member of a Northeast Asia five-power consortium. Divided since the end of World War II, when American and Soviet Union forces occupied separate parts of the peninsula, the two Korean states have developed in markedly different ways.

The DPRK, the last truly Stalinist state, has less than half the population of the democratic Republic of Korea in the South; its per capita GDP is only about 7 percent that of South Korea. But North Korea maintains the third-largest standing army in the world.

The truce negotiated to end the Korean War in 1953 still marks the dividing line between the two Korean states. China withdrew its "volunteers" from the North years ago, but 37,000 American troops remain in the South. US Defense Secretary Donald Rumsfeld wants to relocate US troops further south on the peninsula, or possibly entirely out of Korea. The reasons presumably are two: to limit US casualties in the event of a North Korean military response to a US attack on North Korean nuclear facilities, and to increase the pressure on President Roh Moo Hyun to agree to a hardline US position on the DPRK.

The United States and North Korea blame each other for violating commitments made under the so-called Agreed Framework, the bilateral agreement concluded in 1994 with the Clinton administration to halt the DPRK's nuclear program and to keep North Korea within the Nuclear Non-Proliferation Treaty. The Agreed Framework called for the IAEA to verify the shutting down of the DPRK's plutonium-producing Yongbyon reactor, in exchange for shipments to the North of 500,000 metric tons of fuel oil per year until two light-water power reactors, to be built by Japan and South Korea, came on line to replace the energy that could be produced by the Yongbyon facility. Economic and political relations were also to be formalized, and the United States pledged itself to "provide formal assurances to the DPRK against the threat or use of nuclear weapons by the United States."[9]

During the last months of the Clinton administration, accommodation with the DPRK had reached new levels. The South's former president Kim Dae Jung's "sunshine policy" of engaging Pyongyang had led to a historic summit meeting with Kim Jong-il in June 2000, and US Secretary of State Madeleine Albright had visited Pyongyang, opening the possibility that President Clinton might also visit North Korea. But all of this came to an end in March 2001, when President Kim Dae Jung met the newly-elected President George W. Bush, who indicated his deep distrust of engaging with the DPRK.[10] President Bush's State of the Union speech the following January included the infamous "axis of evil" charge against Iraq, Iran, and North Korea; and the administration's Nuclear Posture Review, leaked to the press two months later, listed North Korea by name as a potential target for US nuclear attack. The administration's declaration of its strategic doctrine in September 2002, and most importantly its commitment to preemptive war against "rogue states," explicitly detailed Washington's hostile intent.[11]

North Korea, however, remained in engagement mode, inviting Japanese Prime Minister Koizumi for an unprecedented meeting in Pyongyang in September 2002, at which both sides made new concessions in what appeared to be a major step toward DPRK–Japanese reconciliation and normalization of relations.[12] From North Korea's perspective, the visit by James Kelly the following month appeared to be planned within a similar frame of mind. However, when Kelly provided evidence to his hosts of a DPRK uranium enrichment program (quite separate from the plutonium facility secured by the IAEA) and the North Koreans reportedly acknowledged its existence, charges and counter-charges began to fly, each government attacking the other with allegations of violations of their earlier agreements.

The DPRK then escalated the tension while Washington prepared to make preemptive war against Iraq, another member of the "axis of evil." North Korea expelled the IAEA inspectors and restarted its Yongbyon reactor; it withdrew from the NPT and even threatened to withdraw from the 1953 Korean War truce agreement; and it confronted a US spy plane in international airspace and tested short-range missiles, firing them into the Sea of Japan.

Following US military success in overthrowing the Saddam Hussein regime in Iraq, North Korea apparently then believed, as mentioned earlier, that it was the next target for US preemptive war, and that having nuclear weapons (unlike Iraq) was its best deterrent. At a second meeting with James Kelly under Chinese auspices in April 2003, North Korea reportedly told Kelly that it had nuclear weapons; but in the same meeting, the North Koreans surprisingly offered to do all of the things of greatest concern to the United States: abandon its nuclear weapons programs and accept independent verification, stop missile exports, and work within a multilateral framework to reach an accommodation. North Korea put all of the key issues on the negotiating table. In return, Pyongyang wanted a formal nonaggression treaty with the United States, and other substantial economic and political concessions.[13]

The Bush administration has said time and again that the DPRK has violated the Agreed Framework, and that it will not reward "bad behavior" with concessions. It insists that it will not give in to "nuclear blackmail" or "appease" North Korea, as it charges Clinton did. The administration says that it seeks a peaceful, diplomatic solution to the nuclear crisis, but at the same time it is keeping the military option open. The administration is conflicted: triumphant in its military victory over Saddam Hussein, but mindful of the potential pitfalls of its being a presidential election year—and especially of the failure in 1992 of the senior Bush to win reelection after his own success in the first Gulf War.

Negotiating a multilateral solution to the Korean crisis would benefit the administration by showing the world that preemptive war is not its only strategic alternative, and that Washington is capable of negotiating peace with as well as making war against its adversaries. This might be especially important as events in Afghanistan and Iraq play back into the North Korean negotiations. The failure of the United States to consolidate its victories in either country means that the military option for the United States against North Korea has become increasingly untenable. The aircraft that the United States would need to make air strikes against the DPRK's nuclear facilities have long been in place, but the United States is now unable to move sufficient troops into the region to deal with the kind of counter-attack that Pyongyang might launch in response.

Moreover, the failure to find any weapons of mass destruction in Iraq or evidence of a pre-war operational link between al-Qaeda and Saddam Hussein; the body bags coming home from the continuing chaos in Iraq; the sabotage of Iraqi oil pipelines, power systems, and water supplies; and the unwillingness of most other powers to provide troops or major financial contributions without UN control, taken together, put the Bush administration on the defensive with respect to considering any new military adventures.[14] In addition, escalating costs for both the troops in Iraq and the rebuilding of the country have contributed to unprecedented government budget deficits, and John Kerry, the Democratic Party candidate for the presidency in the 2004 election, has begun to challenge the administration's wisdom in the "war on terror." Revelations about torture techniques used against detained Iraqis have only made a bad situation worse.[15]

A security consortium for Northeast Asia

What would a security consortium for Northeast Asia actually do, and how would it work?

Four key commitments

To begin, the member-states of the consortium would have to commit to four key points. Indeed, their agreement on just these four would suffice to meet the crucial external needs of the two Korean states and the region.

First, the four major powers would individually and jointly agree not to commit aggression against the existing states of North and South Korea (and a reunified Korea once that has been achieved).[16] There is no model for such an agreement that I am aware of, but the four-power commitments would provide the security that has been so lacking for both Korean states since the end of World War II. It would also meet the highest priority concern of the DPRK, as reflected in the demands that it has been making on the United States, for more than a decade, for a formal nonaggression pact.

Second, in return, the four major powers would insist on international verification to affirm and to sustain the 1992 Joint South–North Declaration of the Denuclearization of the Korean Peninsula, i.e., the joint pledge by North and South Korea to maintain themselves nuclear weapons-free. Assurances that both Korean states remain non-nuclear is the highest shared priority among the four major powers. This would require an institutionalized inspection regime, to be operated by an international organization like the IAEA. Rose Gottemoeller, an architect of the arrangement with the Ukraine by which it gave up 1,900 nuclear warheads after the collapse of the Soviet Union, has suggested that the Ukrainian experience might serve as a model for how to denuclearize the DPRK.[17]

Third, the member-states of the consortium would commit themselves jointly to maintain the strategic stability of the Northeast Asian region, in a way similar to how the United States has served as guarantor of stability in East Asia since the end of the cold war. In turn, this strategic cooperation could serve as a foundation for joint development projects in the region, such as the exploitation of Russian natural gas and its transmission through the region.

Fourth, the four major powers would agree to assist in the economic development of North Korea and to support a process of gradual reconciliation between North and South as determined by those two states.

How would the consortium operate?

In order adequately to guarantee the security of the two Korean states, formal institutions would be required: four-plus-two must be much more than just "a talking shop." For the first time in the history of the region, multilateral security institutions would have to be constructed for Northeast Asia—a security consortium or a formal concert of powers. The new arrangement would have one feature in common with the idea of a post-cold-war NATO: the objective of using a security agreement to stabilize a potentially volatile region. But a key difference would be that all the major powers in the region would be included. This would not be a pact against any other state. It would help to stabilize a region that has been traumatized repeatedly by military conflict. A dialogue mechanism alone would not suffice.

Agreement would first be sought among the four major powers, with both South and North Korea invited to participate in the institution building. Presumably, South Korea would support the idea with enthusiasm. Former president Kim Dae Jung officially endorsed such strategic thinking as a part of his "sunshine policy" to the North, and new President Roh Moo Hyun has himself called for a "structure of peace" in the region. Moon Hayong, Director-General for Policy Planning in the ROK Ministry of Foreign Affairs and Trade, also emphasized the importance of a multilateral approach, in a paper presented to a Berkeley meeting of the Council for Security Cooperation in the Asia Pacific (CSCAP) on March 13, 2003.[18]

North Korea may at first oppose the idea, but its opposition should not stand as an obstacle to continued negotiations among the four major powers. North Korea should at every stage be invited to participate, but its possible boycott should not stop forward progress. The DPRK should not be permitted to sabotage the process. Once the consortium is in place, North Korea would not really have an option to oppose the arrangement, for two main reasons: first, because the consortium would include as members all of its outside supporters, and, second, because the commitments made by the consortium would meet the principal security and developmental objectives declared by Pyongyang.

The United States is currently trying to pressure each of the other powers, especially China, to force North Korea to agree to the US unilateral demands. But a cooperative-security consortium of all of the relevant powers is much more likely to win Pyongyang's compliance. As Hendrik Hertzberg writes in the *New Yorker*, Washington's only viable option is to rely on the help of the other powers.[19] China has emerged as the key player in shaping a multilateral solution.[20]

Even if North Korea were to comply with the present US demands, which I think is most unlikely, what about the next time? Because of the deep distrust on both sides, it would be very difficult to conclude a bilateral US–DPRK agreement to resolve the currrent crisis. Equally important, even if such a deal were concluded, it is very unlikely that it would be honored, because of the continuing mutual distrust. In the end, such a bilateral agreement probably would once again come unstuck, like the 1994 Agreed Framework before it.

What if the four powers disagree?

Of course, they will often disagree, but once the four states decide to join together to build a security institution that can provide substantial benefits for all parties, it is very likely that the bases for agreement listed above (plus others that they may become aware of in the future) will serve as a solid foundation for sustained cooperation. Meanwhile, quite separately from their common interests in Northeast Asia, all of the four major powers are becoming increasingly interdependent in their worldwide economic and political relationships with each other.

Meetings of the four focused directly on identifying areas of mutual agreement also could help to dispel mutual mistrust. For example, Japanese distrust of China's willingness to participate in such a cooperative venture should prove unwarranted, because the Chinese know that a nuclear-armed North Korea would sharply increase the domestic pressure in Japan to go nuclear. As a result, China is likely to be more helpful in working for a nuclear-free Korea than many analysts in Japan expect.[21]

In attempting to design a successful multilateral arrangement, especially on sensitive security issues, it is vital, as I have argued, to include all of those states whose interests are most directly involved, because if you leave one of them out, that state will almost inevitably view the multilateral agreement as a pact against it. At the same time, however, it is important to include as few states as possible, because each additional state creates one more hurdle to achieving consensus among the member-states of the consortium. Therefore, all six (four-plus-two) should be parties to the consortium, but probably no others.

Some commentators, for example, have suggested that Russia could be left out. But Russian participation is essential to the success of the consortium for several reasons.[22] If Moscow were excluded, not only might the Russians begin to think that the consortium was somehow being designed contrary to their interests and therefore try to sabotage it, but also the DPRK might try to play Russia against the others to obstruct the formation of a working consensus within the consortium. On the other hand, if a four-plus-two solution is reached, the consortium members will probably want to obtain United Nations sanction, and Russia could help facilitate that endorsement by means of its role as a permanent member of the UN Security Council. Finally, Russian participation is central to achieving multilateral cooperation for the development and transmission of energy resources in the region. This kind of economic cooperation can benefit all parties and could serve as a major foundation stone for political and strategic cooperation in Northeast Asia.

A role for the United Nations?

The United Nations would *not* be an ideal site for constructing a four-plus-two consortium. Trying to achieve consensus in the context of the UN Security Council would be likely to make things more, rather than less, difficult: Japan is not a permanent member, and Britain and France, which are, would want to put their particular stamp on the outcome. It would be difficult enough to achieve agreement among the six parties without including the two European UN Security Council permanent members whose interests in Northeast Asia are relatively remote. However, UN Security Council endorsement of the consortium should be sought *after it is formed and tested*, in order to affirm and strengthen its legitimacy. It will be vital that the six participants remain focused on those key objectives and interests about which they agree, and not be diverted into tangential disputes about their disagreements.

This raises the question whether an independent facilitator might help in the search for consensus among the six parties. UN Secretary-General Kofi Annan is probably the only person in the world who might have both the stature and independence needed to perform such a facilitating role. Without some sort of independent convener, the initial meetings to build consensus among the four, let alone the six, might easily deteriorate into arguments about their disagreements rather than their common interests. Also, the United States as the only superpower might attempt to intimidate the others into accepting its particular unilateral view, which simply would not work. Maurice Strong, the Secretary-General's personal representative, has already made trips to Pyongyang to assist in the effort to find a peaceful solution.[23]

Initially Pyongyang said that it only wanted to talk to the United States, while Bush insisted on a multilateral approach. Yet both a bilateral US–DPRK agreement and a multilateral arrangement might serve together as component parts of a four-plus-two solution. The DPRK–US nonaggression pact that Pyongyang has demanded might turn out to be a necessary (but by no means a sufficient) condition for achieving a successful four-plus-two arrangement for the region. At best, however, a bilateral US–North Korean agreement alone is unlikely to provide a durable resolution to the problems of strategic volatility in Northeast Asia, because of the deep distrust between the two governments and the history of conflict in the region.

Economic agreements among the six countries for the exploitation and delivery of energy resources could provide another foundation stone for a successful Northeast Asian security consortium. Selig Harrison shows how "American encouragement of regional cooperation could make a difference" in helping the countries of the region conclude mutually beneficial deals to exploit natural gas resources in Russia and to deliver it through pipelines to markets in China, Korea, Japan, and beyond. Russia has the world's largest gas reserves, but it needs capital to develop them. Constructing gas pipelines through the DPRK and extending the Trans-Siberian Railroad from Russia through to South Korea would help to bind the countries of Northeast Asia together in ties of mutual benefit and common interests.[24]

The importance of a multilateral solution

Bilateral approaches to resolving strategic differences with the DPRK to date have failed. The Agreed Framework, which was essentially a US–DPRK arrangement (although other countries were involved), has collapsed, and that precedent is now explicitly rejected by the Bush administration in its own approach to North Korea. Earlier initiatives by both South Korea and Japan have also backfired. Kim Dae Jung's "sunshine policy," and his courageous attempt to resolve North–South differences through personal diplomacy with Kim Jong-il, failed after their first meeting in Pyongyang in June 2000, the victim of charges that Seoul had to pay the North $500 million up front to convince Kim Jong-il to meet. Two years later, in September 2002, Japan's Prime Minister Koizumi made another attempt to resolve historical differences with the DPRK through summit diplomacy, but his effort also failed when the problem of Japanese who had been kidnapped years before by North Korea to serve Pyongyang's spying operation became an explosive domestic issue in Japan.

Kim Jong-il may well have made the admission to Koizumi about the kidnapped Japanese citizens as one way to reciprocate the Japanese Prime Minister's good will in making the visit; but subsequent charges and counter-charges about how many Japanese had actually been kidnapped, what had happened to those few that Pyongyang acknowledged having taken, and a tug-of-war over the five Japanese who returned to Japan from North Korea, all poisoned the earlier good will. (At this writing in May 2004, however, it appears that Koizumi will visit Pyongyang again to bring back the children of the returned abductees.) It is very likely that Pyongyang's acknowledgment about a uranium enrichment program to James Kelly the following month, during Kelly's visit to North Korea (and before the kidnapping problem had become a huge issue in Japan), was also made by the North Korean leaders in a similar spirit of good will; but this also failed, as we have seen.

In light of the failure of these bilateral attempts to resolve strategic issues with Pyongyang, there are three main reasons why a multilateral solution is essential. First, as mentioned earlier, both the United States and the North Korean regime have taken such extreme positions that a peaceful resolution of the standoff is not possible without outside pressure to convince both governments to modify their irreconcilable positions—to bring the two "Realist" states into the "cooperative security" solution. If they were left to themselves, their "zero-sum" perspectives would be most likely to lead them to confrontation and possibly to military conflict.

Second, four-plus-two includes all of the countries with the most important relationships with the DPRK. If any one country were left out, North Korea could still try to play that country against the others, but with all of the most interested and influential countries included, the circle of influence on the DPRK is truly closed. However, the United States wants to use the multilateral forum for a different purpose: to close the circle coercively on the DPRK and to force it to accept its terms. These are all "sticks."

By "closing the circle," I mean something quite different. The key point here is to demonstrate unequivocally to North Korea that there is a consensus among the five other states *both* that the DPRK must give up its nuclear-weapons capability and accept verification, *and* that, in return, the group accepts North Korea's concerns about security and development as legitimate, and is prepared to make appropriate commitments to achieve them. The solution requires the right combination of both "carrots" and "sticks."

Finally, a multilateral approach can provide a much higher probability that once an agreement is concluded, it can be successfully sustained. As already discussed, both the United States and the DPRK accuse the other of failing to fulfill the commitments they made before under the earlier Agreed Framework. Moreover, the Bush administration has earned a reputation during its brief time in office for playing what is called "bait and switch": making a commitment to another party in order to gain something in return, but then failing to fulfill one's own promise.[25] In a multilateral arrangement such as the one proposed here, it is assumed that all parties have a substantial interest in assuring that the others honor the commitments that they have made. Multilateral pressure can help to ensure that no consortium member plays bait and switch.

Conclusion

All of the US bilateral options have serious problems. The use of military force could result in a horrific retaliatory attack by the North on Seoul, on US military forces, and possibly on Japan.[26] Heavy economic sanctions are opposed by Japan, South Korea, and China, and they could result in the economic collapse of the North, flooding the region with tens of thousands of refugees.[27] And to negotiate bilaterally an offer of aid in return for a promised denuclearization deal with Pyongyang would be criticized by American hardliners as repeating Clinton's earlier "appeasement" of North Korea. Moreover, the Bush administration is seeking some sort of face-saving multilateral format for resolving the crisis to avoid being charged with caving in to North Korean "nuclear blackmail."

Why would four-plus-two be preferable for the United States? It would be the multilateral solution demanded by Washington and would thereby help defend the administration from its domestic critics. More significant for the United States, four-plus-two would not only deal with the immediate DPRK nuclear issue but also put in place a long-term arrangement that has the potential to bring peace and stability to a volatile region in which the United States has important interests. Four-plus-two would not be simply a strategic Band-Aid like the earlier Agreed Framework. Finally, it could provide a precedent for multilateral security cooperation more broadly in the East Asian region, which could help to alleviate the widespread concerns there about possible unilateral US actions either to intervene in or to withdraw from the region.

An additional benefit for all parties would be that participation in such a security consortium would allow Japan (the only non-nuclear-weapons power of the four) to become a much more active and influential player—to be a major power in its geographical region of highest priority *without going nuclear*.[28] Such a security consortium might well assist Japan to participate strategically as what Ozawa Ichiro would call a "normal nation."[29] A further benefit for Japan would be that four-plus-two could set a precedent for strategic cooperation in the region, which might facilitate, for example, the completion of Russo-Japanese negotiations for a peace treaty to formally end the hostilities of World War II.

In its negotiations with the DPRK, the United States needs a firm commitment of support by all four of the other countries in order to achieve a peaceful solution. A bilateral US–DPRK agreement is most unlikely to work, because of the absolute distrust between the two governments. Just as North Korean commitments to the United States are not credible because of past violations by the DPRK,[30] American promises to the DPRK are not believed for the same reason. They are two "Realist" governments playing a "zero-sum" game.

Moreover, unrelenting pressure will be needed to convince the DPRK to do what it fundamentally does not want to do: give up the nuclear programs that Pyongyang believes, in its "self-help" security strategy, to be the best deterrent to a possible military attack by the United States. That pressure can only be imposed by closing the circle of influence on the DPRK through inclusion of all of its major sources of outside support.

At the same time, however, China, Russia, and South Korea will not commit to a unilaterally imposed solution by the United States (as we have seen in their unwillingness to join Washington's Proliferation Security Initiative) that fails to include sufficient incentives to meet Pyongyang's minimum security and development requirements. Coercive diplomacy alone will not suffice. The other parties insist that there must be both "carrots" and "sticks" to achieve a peaceful solution to the North Korean nuclear crisis.

Finally, in the proposed Northeast Asian security consortium, the other four parties would in effect serve as guarantors to both the DPRK and the United States that the deal, once made, will stick—because it will be in their collective interest to make it work. In that sense, the four in combination have the power to frustrate either side from prevailing. They know that they cannot let either the United States or North Korea have its own way, or there will be no peaceful solution to the crisis. Earlier, the Bush administration might not have been willing to agree to a cooperative-security solution to the crisis, but as the coalition in Iraq continues to fail even to maintain security in that country, and the United States becomes militarily and financially more overextended, the Bush leadership has begun to appear more willing to listen to its five four-plus-two negotiating partners.

Notes

1 Long before the US invasion of Iraq, David Hendrickson argued that what the United States was proposing to do was not preemption but "preventive war." The United Nations Charter does provide for war-making in self-defense, but only in the face of an imminent threat. However, the Bush administration had explicitly shifted US strategic calculations, as articulated by Donald Rumsfeld, from a "threat-based" concept to a "capabilities-based" understanding of threat. Rumsfeld's argument was that the United States should be prepared to make war against any state with the capabilities to do it serious harm. This would be "preventive war," however, not "preemption." David C. Hendrickson, "Toward Universal Empire: The Dangerous Quest for Absolute Security," *World Policy Journal* (Fall, 2002), pp. 1–10. Noam Chomsky later entered the debate, arguing that what the Bush administration was doing should not be understood as either

"preemption" or "preventive war," but rather as what he calls "preventative war"—"the use of force to eliminate a contrived threat." *Sydney Morning Herald*, March 29–30, 2003.

2   See, for example, Don Kirk, "North Korea Says Publicly It Needs a 'Nuclear Deterrent,'" *International Herald Tribune*, June 10, 2003. Presumably, Iran is making similar calculations. See Anatol Lieven, "Dangers of an Aggressive US Approach to Iran," *Financial Times*, June 8, 2003; Ray Takeyh, "Iran's Nuclear Calculations," *World Policy Journal*, Vol. 20, No. 2 (Summer, 2003), pp. 21–8; and David Albright and Corey Hinderstein, "Iran, Player or Rogue?" *Bulletin of the Atomic Scientists* (September–October, 2003), pp. 52–8.

3   Robert J. Art and Patrick M. Cronin, eds., *The United States and Coercive Diplomacy* (Washington, DC: US Institute of Peace, 2003).

4   Paul O'Sullivan, "Chairman's Statement: From Proliferation Security Initiative (PSI) meeting in Brisbane on 9–10 July," July 16, 2003, Northeast Asia Peace and Security Network Special Report, from The Nautilus Institute, at napsnet@nautilus.org. For the Bush Administration's assessment of PSI, see Carnegie Endowment for International Peace, "John Bolton on the Proliferation Security Initiative," *Proliferation Brief*, Vol. 6, No. 21 (December 3, 2003), at the Carnegie Non-Proliferation Project (nnp@ceip.org).

5   Bob Woodward, *Bush at War* (New York: Simon & Schuster, 2002), p. 340. Bush described his responsibility to Woodward as being to "rid the world of evil" (p. 67).

6   James Brooke, "Kim Jong-il Called a Tyrant by US," *International Herald Tribune*, August 1, 2003.

7   "China Rejects Helping Japan on Kidnappings," *International Herald Tribune*, October 21, 2003.

8   John Aglionby, "Bush Offers Deal to End N Korea Crisis," *Guardian Weekly*, October 23–29, 2003.

9   Quoted in "North Korea's Nuclear Program, 2003," *Bulletin of the Atomic Scientists* (March–April, 2003), p. 74. See also Bruce Cumings, "Wrong Again," *London Review of Books*, Vol. 25, No. 23 (December 4, 2003).

10 Spurgeon M. Keeny, Jr., "Preserving the North Korean Threat," *Arms Control Today*, Vol. 31, No. 3 (April, 2001), p. 2.

11 Excerpts from the version of the Nuclear Posture Review that was leaked to the press on March 15, 2002, can be found at www.globalsecurity.org/wmd/library/policy/dod/npr.htm. The full text of "The National Security Strategy of the United States" is available at www.nytimes.com, September 20, 2002.

12 At this writing in May 2004, Prime Minister Koizumi is planning a second visit to Pyongyang for the same objectives.

13 Julian Borger and Jonathan Watts, "North Korea Offers to Lift Nuclear Threat," *The Guardian Weekly*, May 1–7, 2003.

14 Amin Saikal, "US Policy Has Isolated Only One Extremist Group—Its Own," *Sydney Morning Herald*, October 31, 2003; and Thomas Powers, "The Vanishing Case for War," *New York Review of Books*, Vol. 50, No. 19 (December 4, 2003), pp. 12–17. See also Maureen Dowd, "A Front Here, A Front There: Bush Is Scaring Up Votes," *International Herald Tribune*, November 27, 2003.

15 James Risen and David Johnson, "Photos Give Further Sign of Violence at Prison: Dead Iraqi Detainees Lead to Questions," *International Herald Tribune*, May 8–9, 2004, p. 2.

16 Reuters, October 30, 2003, quoted North Korean defector Hwang Jang Yop as saying: "I don't understand how we can guarantee the continued existence of a dictator that abuses human rights." It is important to note that the security guarantees proposed here would not guarantee Kim Jong-il's power or any regime's overall security. The commitments to be made by the four major powers would be explicitly restricted to guaranteeing the Korean regimes against foreign military attack, nothing more.

17 Rose Gottemoeller, "North Korean Nuclear Arms: Take Ukraine as a Model," *International Herald Tribune*, April 28, 2003.

18 Moon Hayong, "Korean Nuclear Crisis: Benefits of a Multilateral Approach," March 20, 2003, Northeast Asia Peace and Security Network Special Report, from Nautilus, at napsnet@nautilus.org.

19 *New Yorker*, January 13, 2003.

20 It is important to note that in addition to taking initiatives with respect to North Korea, China has taken a number of "cooperative security" initiatives in its relations with Russia, Central Asia, Southeast Asia, and even India. This cooperative-security strategic response to the Bush

administration's unilateralism is likely to have a significant influence in shaping the future of the Sino-American bilateral relationship and even of global international relations. See my concluding chapter in this book.
21 Robert Madsen, "China Holds the Key to North Korea," *International Herald Tribune*, November 27, 2003.
22 Cristina Chuen, "Russian Responses to the North Korean Crisis," North Korea Special Collection, Center for Nonproliferation Studies, Monterey Institute of International Studies, online at www.cns.miis.edu/research/korea/rusdprk.htm. See also Alexander Zhebin's analysis in Chapter 6.
23 The European Union has also offered to facilitate a multilateral arrangement, but it is unlikely that the EU could maintain a united position on the North Korean crisis when, for example, it is so divided on Iraq. "3-Country Defense Initiative Further Divides the EU," *International Herald Tribune*, March 22–3, 2003.
24 Selig S. Harrison, "Gas and Geopolitics in Northeast Asia: Pipelines, Regional Stability, and the Korean Nuclear Crisis," *World Policy Journal* (Winter, 2002/03), pp. 23–36. See also the Northeast Asia Regional Grid Project, at the Nautilus Institute in Berkeley: napsnet@nautilus.org.
25 For example, Paul Krugman describes Bush's post-9/11 economic policies as "the largest bait-and-switch operation in history." Quoted in Russell Baker, "The Awful Truth," *New York Review of Books*, November 6, 2003, p. 8.
26 Phillip C. Saunders, "Military Options for Dealing with North Korea's Nuclear Program," North Korea Special Collection, Center for Nonproliferation Studies, Monterey Institute of International Studies, online at www.cns.miis.edu/research/korea/dprkmil.htm.
27 For an analysis of existing US sanctions on the DPRK, see Dianne E. Rennack, "North Korea: Economic Sanctions," Report for Congress, Congressional Research Service, Library of Congress, January 24, 2003; and for analysis of the likely impact of economic sanctions, see Kimberly Ann Elliott, "The Role of Economic Leverage in Negotiations with North Korea," April 1, 2003, Northeast Asia Peace and Security Network, Special Report, online at www.nautilus.org/fora/security/0326A_Elliot.html.
28 See Richard Tanter's analysis in Chapter 7.
29 Ozawa Ichiro, *Blueprint for a New Japan: The Rethinking of a Nation* (Tokyo: Kodansha International, 1994).
30 Nicholas Eberstadt, "Diplomatic Fantasyland: The Illusion of a Negotiated Solution to the North Korean Nuclear Crisis," September 23, 2003, Northeast Asia Peace and Security Network, Special Report, at www.nautilus.org/fora/security/0342_Eberstadt.html.

12 Conclusion

Peter Van Ness

In this project, we have examined the strategic implications of the Bush Doctrine and the multiple responses of governments to Washington's radical initiatives. Each author has examined a separate dimension of that story. Our investigations, focused on the Asia-Pacific region, have been undertaken in the full awareness of the global range of US power and the importance of the continuing conflicts in Afghanistan and Iraq as test cases of the Bush Doctrine in practice. What have we learned from this research?

In this brief conclusion, I focus on two topics: some general strategic lessons, and the Chinese response to the Bush Doctrine. The Sino-American relationship is arguably the most important one in the Asia-Pacific region, and Beijing has now begun to lay down step by step an alternative strategic design to the Bush Doctrine. How the relationship between the United States and China evolves will probably be decisive in determining whether there is peace or war in the region. For example, Mike Lampton has characterized the relationship as one of *tong chuang yi meng* ("same bed, different dreams"): America and China are viewed as two lovers in bed, with very different understandings about why they are there and what the future may hold.[1] Faced with a series of security initiatives that potentially threaten its own national security, how has China responded to the Bush Doctrine?

Lessons from the Bush Doctrine

From the presidential election campaign of 2000 through Bush's first months in office before the attacks of 9/11, there were strong indications of what was to come. Bush had staffed his administration with conservative Republicans, who, especially on defense and security issues, had articulated a hardline, unilateralist position. Their strategic priorities included: missile defense; withdrawal from the ABM Treaty; creation of a high-tech, rapid-reaction military with overwhelming scope and power; and a revitalizing of the US nuclear weapons industry. Their worldview was a combination of a Manichean ideology about pitting good against evil, and a Realist commitment to the construction of such overwhelming capabilities (military, economic, and technological) that no other state or coalition of states would dare to confront the United States.

Shortly after Bush took office, and several months before 9/11, I was invited to lecture on missile defense at Singapore's Institute of Defence and Strategic Studies at Nanyang Technological University. I was critical of the Bush plans for missile defense, arguing that the upper-tier, "hit-to-kill" technology was unlikely to be successful; that deployment might well prompt a nuclear arms race, especially with China; and that because of the adverse strategic implications, America would as a result probably be less secure, rather than more secure. To my surprise, most of the audience seemed to agree, and during the question-and-answer period, we began to speculate about why the Bush leadership was so committed to missile defense if it was indeed such a bad idea.

I suggested that perhaps the administration really did not understand the dynamic of what in international relations theory is called the "security dilemma," the idea that when one country builds up its military capability to enhance its defense, often an adversary will understand that buildup as an offensive threat and increase its own military capability as a result, thereby igniting a vicious circle of arms racing in which both countries become less secure. Some in the audience thought that was probably right: The Bush people simply did not understand the security dilemma.

After leaving Singapore, I flew to Beijing, where I spent a week interviewing PRC strategic analysts. Among the most prominent is Professor Yan Xuetong, Director of the Institute of International Studies at Qinghua University. Yan and I discussed the Bush administration, and I put forward this same argument, that perhaps they did not understand the security dilemma. Yan disagreed. No, he said, they understand it better than you and I do. He explained: When the power capabilities of two states are roughly equal, the security dilemma is likely to have the outcome that I had suggested, namely, that neither side benefits and everyone is likely to lose. But when one state is much stronger than the others, that state might deliberately create a security dilemma between it and its perceived adversaries in order to intimidate and to dominate them. That, he argued, is what the Bush administration was trying to do.

After 9/11 but before the invasion of Iraq, analysts like David Hendrickson began to spell out the serious strategic implications of Yan Xuetong's insight. Writing in *World Policy Journal*, Hendrickson characterized the Bush Doctrine as a "quest for absolute security." Unilateralism and a strategic doctrine of preventive war were the key elements of this futile search. Hendrickson argued that these were "momentous steps," standing in "direct antagonism to fundamental values in our political tradition," which threaten "to wreck an international order that has been patiently built up for 50 years, inviting a fundamental de-legitimation of American power."[2] Hendrickson concluded his essay with a quote from Kissinger that sums up the basic flaw in a search for absolute security: "the desire of one power for absolute security means absolute insecurity for all the others."[3]

The invasion of Iraq, for the Bush leadership, became the prototype of this search for absolute security: "regime change" by military force to punish any adversary that dared to stand up to American power. The overthrow of the Saddam Hussein regime in Iraq was intended to show the world that opposition to the Bush grand design was futile. Washington would have its way, through the use of overwhelming military force if necessary, regardless of the opposition of some of its major allies. On the other side of the same coin, Libya later became a model for the Bush administration of the "rogue state" that saw the light, in the face of US intimidation, and agreed to give up its "weapons of mass destruction" and submit to the hegemon. UK Prime Minister Tony Blair played his part in the coalition with the United States by welcoming Libya's Colonel Muammar al-Qaddafi into the community of nations, illustrating the point that the Bush Doctrine effort to transform world politics was capable of using both carrots and sticks. But meanwhile, the deteriorating security situation in Iraq and Afghanistan and the continued bloodletting in the Israel–Palestine conflict demonstrated that there were limits to what even the most powerful state in the world could do in imposing its will on other nations.[4]

So what strategic lessons does the Bush Doctrine teach? From our investigations together in this project, and informed by the insights of other colleagues like Yan Xuetong and David Hendrickson, it seems to me that we can infer four general propositions that are amply illustrated by the efforts of the Bush administration to date. They are:

1. *There is no such thing as absolute security*—it is simply unattainable for any country, including the United States, the most powerful state the world has ever seen.
2. *The world today is confounded by a unique and complex range of insecurities: military, political, economic, environmental, and public health insecurities that we are only beginning to comprehend.* For example, some scientists cogently argue that climate change, all by itself, is the greatest threat to our existence, and specialists on Islam are convinced that if we do not treat the global problems of human security seriously, terrorism will be with us forever. More obviously, the 1997 financial crisis in Asia showed how vulnerable even some of the most highly reputed countries are to the whims of the global market.
3. *No individual state, no matter how powerful, can adequately manage this range of insecurities alone. Self-help strategies are not adequate to the task.* An effective response to the broad range of threats to national security requires a shared, multilateral response. Obviously, the leaders of every independent state will attempt to advance their own interests as best they can, but the Realist assumption that strategies based on narrow self-interest might be adequate to protect the security of a country are utopian in today's world. Security, and even survival, require a search for "win–win" solutions, rather than the playing out of zero-sum games with potential adversaries.[5]
4. *The more that the most powerful states seek to achieve absolute security by building up their economic and military power and operating with impunity to advance their perceived "national interests," the more insecure the world becomes—including themselves.*[6]

These are the general lessons that I have learned from our work together. In turn, these propositions have prompted me to think more deeply about the real meaning of the much-used and much-abused term "national security"—and how it can most successfully be enhanced.[7]

Several pioneering projects in re-thinking national security provide excellent examples about what must be done. Jeffrey Record in his essay "Bounding the Global War on Terrorism" concludes that the administration's goals are "politically, fiscally, and militarily unsustainable"; he analyzes the *real* terrorist threat to the United States and offers pragmatic advice on how to defend against it.[8] The Non-Proliferation Project at the Carnegie Endowment for International Peace, led by Joseph Cirincione, has produced an independent analysis of the immensely controversial issue of weapons of mass destruction and the Iraq war, complete with a list of key findings and recommendations for the future.[9] And Mohamed ElBaradei, Director-General of the International Atomic Energy Agency, has begun the important work of redesigning the nuclear nonproliferation regime based on his service as head of the IAEA, making specific proposals for strengthening the regime.[10] The questions raised by the Bush Doctrine urgently demand answers. These studies begin to show us the way.

It is often remarked that, since the collapse of the Soviet Union, there is no longer any state or group of states with the capabilities and will to balance US power; and following the delegitimation of socialism as a developmental alternative to capitalism, there is no longer any global, ideological alternative to market economics and representative political democracy. Where does one stand intellectually, people ask, to respond to the Bush Doctrine, other than to argue that the neoconservatives are not really practicing what they preach when they say that all they are really trying to do is to bring freedom and democracy to the world?

On what substantive basis can a systematic alternative to the Bush Doctrine be built? The Bush Doctrine has prompted a variety of responses, as the studies in this volume clearly demonstrate. Often, the official, governmental response has been quite different from public opinion, especially with regard to approval of the US-led invasion of Iraq. Reacting to the American initiatives, the Japanese and Australian governments, as the Richard Tanter and Owen Harries chapters point out, have chosen to move even more tightly into their security alliances with the United States, while much of the rest of East Asia has remained ambivalent.[11] The most substantive and promising international reaction to date, however, has been Beijing's response.

The Chinese response

The Chinese leadership was aware of the hardline political views of many of the people chosen for top positions in the new administration when George W. Bush was inaugurated in January 2001. Typical of right-wing opinion in the United

States had been an argument both that China was the most likely challenger of the US position as unipolar power and that the "China threat" should be a priority concern for the new administration. Although President Bush chose to identify "rogue states" as the main danger in his early speeches on national security, many analysts inferred that the main rogue that the administration had in mind was China. When the classified Nuclear Posture Review of 2002 was leaked to the press, it specifically identified China as one of seven possible targets for nuclear attack by the United States, and a PRC–Taiwan confrontation as one of three likely scenarios in which nuclear weapons might be used.[12] Administration commitments to both missile defense and preemption or preventive war further elevated Chinese concerns.[13]

Official Chinese reaction to the Bush Doctrine has gone through three distinct stages that might be called *avoidance, collaboration*, and *strategic response*. Jing-dong Yuan in Chapter 5 discusses the first two at length. At first, Chinese policy seemed designed to *avoid confrontation* with the new president. As the administration set about putting its foreign and security policies in place, Beijing could see that many of the Bush initiatives clashed with PRC interests. But rather than confront the new president, the Chinese appeared determined to stand aside from the hardline bulldozer if possible, hoping, for example, that the early enthusiasms for missile defense and preventive wars against "rogue states" would pass in time.

Then, as Jing-dong Yuan shows, 9/11 changed all that. The terrorist attacks in the United States provided China with an opportunity to find common ground with the new administration—to *collaborate* in the new "war on terror." This second stage began almost immediately after the attacks, when President Jiang Zemin telephoned Bush to offer his sympathy and support. In effect, Beijing's message was: We have terrorists, too (among China's 100 million Muslims), and we want to work together in the struggle against terrorism.[14] When it came to invading Iraq, however, China joined France and Russia in opposition. If the United Nations Security Council had put a second resolution on Iraq to a vote, one that proposed to endorse a US-led invasion, it was unclear whether China would have joined France and Russia in vetoing that resolution. But China clearly opposed the invasion, and did not join in other US undertakings such as the Proliferation Security Initiative, the multilateral attempt to interdict shipments of weapons of mass destruction and missile delivery systems.

Meanwhile, however, the PRC began to take its own initiatives, step by step implementing a full-blown third stage, *a strategic response* to the Bush Doctrine. The focus was on Asia. The core of the Chinese alternative was a cooperative-security response to Bush's unilateralist, preventive war strategy. In contrast to the American determination to reshape the world by force, China proposed to build cooperation among different groupings of states to create new international institutions by achieving win–win solutions to common problems.

For Beijing, these initiatives were unprecedented. From dynastic times to the present, China's leaders had adopted a largely Realist view of the world, and, like the United States, they had preferred to bilateralize their foreign relations: to play "the barbarians" off against each other in the Chinese version, or to build security ties like "spokes" in an American "wheel" in the US version. Moreover, in both its dynastic past and communist present, China had been no more benevolent toward its neighbors or more hesitant to use military force in its international relations than most major powers.[15] For China now to found its foreign relations on a multilateral, cooperative-security design was something new and important.

By the mid-1990s, some analysts had begun to identify China as a so-called responsible power, pointing to Beijing's increasing participation in international institutions like APEC, the ASEAN Regional Forum, and then the World Trade Organization. China won the opportunity to host the Olympics in 2008, and in many different ways, Beijing began to signal that it was aware of its growing stake in the status quo, and was prepared to help in maintaining the strategic stability that was such an important prerequisite for the continued economic prosperity of East Asia.

From this beginning emerged the strategic response to the Bush Doctrine. Some called it "China's new diplomacy,"[16] but it was much more than that. Beijing followed the establishment of "ASEAN+3" (yearly meetings between the ten member-countries of ASEAN with China, Japan, and South Korea) with the establishment of "ASEAN+1," just China and the ASEAN countries. China took the lead in creating the first multilateral institution in Central Asia, the six-member Shanghai Cooperation Organization (China, Russia, Kazakhstan, Tajikistan, Uzbekistan, and Kyrgyzstan),[17] and worked to demonstrate to its neighbors that both economic and security cooperation could be based on a win-win design.

In the name of "non-traditional" security cooperation to deal with terrorism and other transnational crime, Beijing even normalized its relations with its former adversary India,[18] and conducted unprecedented, joint naval exercises with both India and Pakistan in the East China Sea near Shanghai in late 2003. Chinese commentators emphasized the cooperative-security theoretical basis for these initiatives: "China has been a proponent of mutual understanding and trust through international security cooperation and opposed any military alliance directed at any other countries," and "China won't accept any military cooperation that is directed at other countries."[19]

In October 2003, China signed the ASEAN Treaty of Amity and Cooperation (the first non-ASEAN country to do so), and negotiated a "strategic partnership for peace and prosperity" with the ten ASEAN member-countries. The objective is to build an East Asian Community founded on economic, social, and security cooperation.[20] And, finally, Beijing's offer to host the six-party negotiations to find a peaceful solution to the North Korean nuclear crisis is the classic example of China's cooperative-security strategic response to date. Chapters in this volume by Moon and Bae, Zhebin, and Van Ness analyze this initiative in detail.

The key distinguishing features of the two very different approaches to dealing with the post-cold-war world are the following:

Bush	PRC
• absolute security for the US	• cooperative security (seeking to work *with* potential adversaries, rather than to make war against them)
• unilateral	• multilateral
• preventive war and regime change	• rules-based collective action, and conflict-resolution diplomacy
• zero-sum strategic games	• positive-sum strategic games, designed to achieve win–win outcomes
• disdain for international law, treaties, and institutions	• international institution-building

China's is by no means a pacifist design. For example, there is absolutely no question but that China is seeking to modernize its military capability, and giving very serious thought to exactly what kind of military would be most effective in dealing with the dangers of today's world, including a potential US threat. Paul Godwin notes that "a primary objective of the PLA is to exploit perceived US vulnerabilities."[21] But I think it would be a mistake to understand the Chinese modernization project as predicated on launching an arms race with the United States—at least not yet.

To date, Chinese nuclear doctrine has focused on maintaining a "minimum nuclear deterrent" capable of launching a retaliatory strike after surviving an initial nuclear attack, rather than building huge arsenals of more and more powerful nuclear weapons.[22] The Chinese are well aware of the great disparity in military capabilities between China and the United States, as well as the disparity in financial and technological capacities to sustain them. They are also aware of the argument, popular in some circles, that one of the key factors that finally broke the back of the former Soviet Union was its inability to sustain the arms race with the United States. They don't want to fall into that kind of trap.

Chinese analysts have described this strategy as a design for *heping jueqi*, or "peaceful rise," contrary to charges that a more powerful China should be seen as a threat. Zheng Bijian, former vice president of the Central Chinese Communist Party School, says that the "peaceful rise" initiative is prompted by the conviction that "China must seek a peaceful global environment to develop its economy even as it tries to safeguard world peace through development."[23] Building win–win relations with all of its neighbors is a central objective of this strategy. Beijing wants to demonstrate that closer trade, investment, and even security relations with China can be beneficial to its neighbors.

Eric Teo Chu Cheow has suggested that this new strategy resembles the ancient Chinese tributary system. He writes: "China's Ming/Qing tributary system was based on three cardinal points: first, China considered itself the 'central heart' of the region; this tributary system assured China of its overall security environment.

Second, to ensure its internal stability and prosperity, China needed a stable environment immediately surrounding the Middle Kingdom. Third, the Chinese emperor would in principle give more favors to tributary states or kingdoms than he received from them; for this generosity, the emperor obtained their respect and goodwill."[24]

Obviously, the international relations of the 21st century are very different from China's imperial relations during the Ming and Qing dynasties, but the idea of establishing relations with neighboring states in terms of mutually beneficial economic and security ties makes sense for everyone in Asia. Meanwhile, if successful, such a concert of power (in this case, among states that are formally equals rather than dependents of China) would help to maintain the strategic stability that China needs for its economic modernization. Critics, like Cao Siyuan, argue that to be successful, the "peaceful rise" strategy must be accompanied by substantial domestic political liberalization and greater transparency with respect to China's military posture: "Diplomacy is often the extension of domestic policy. A leadership's commitment to global fraternity and solidarity will be called into doubt if it is so reluctant to give its own people adequate human rights."[25] Can China practice what it has begun to preach?

Beijing's new strategy has yet to be tested. How well will Beijing's commitment to cooperative security hold up when disputes with neighbors over territory or political differences reemerge? As Chih-yu Shih in his analysis of the Taiwan problem in Chapter 4 might ask, will it also apply to cross-strait relations? Yet when compared with Bush's record of making war to achieve peace in Afghanistan and Iraq, the Chinese response has a substantial appeal, especially among the ASEAN countries where ideas on cooperative security have long been popular.

Clearly, China wants to avoid a conflict with the United States. The Japanese journalist Funabashi Yoichi quotes one Chinese think-tank researcher as saying: "We are studying the origin of the US–Soviet cold war. Why did it happen? Was there no way to prevent it? Some see that a US–China cold war is inevitable, but what can we do to prevent it?"[26] China's strategic response to the Bush Doctrine does not confront the United States, and does not require China's Asian neighbors to choose between Beijing and Washington, something none of them wants to have to do.[27] It is not actually a design for what Realists would call "balancing" the United States, yet it challenges Washington to think and to act in a very different way when trying to resolve differences in international relations.

Notes

1 David M. Lampton, *Same Bed, Different Dreams: Managing US–China Relations, 1989–2000* (Berkeley, Calif.: University of California Press, 2001).
2 David C. Hendrickson, "Toward Universal Empire: The Dangerous Quest for Absolute Security," *World Policy Journal* (Fall, 2002), pp. 1–2.
3 Ibid., p. 7. See, also, Nick Wheeler's Chapter 8 and his analysis of American exceptionalism.
4 See, for example, Ahmed Rashid, "The Mess in Afghanistan," *New York Review of Books*, Vol. 51, No. 2 (February 12, 2004), pp. 24–7. The inability to maintain security in Iraq has obstructed the rebuilding of the country, while charges that US intelligence agents tortured detained Iraqis

have further undermined the legitimacy of the US occupation. See Jamie Wilson, "Attacks Halt Rebuilding Work in Iraq," *The Guardian Weekly*, April 29–May 5, 2004, p 1; Seymour M. Hersh, writing in *The New Yorker* in May 2004, reprinted in *Sydney Morning Herald*, May 8–9, 2004, "News Review," p. 28; and Scott Wilson, "US Abuse Worse Than Saddam's, Say Inmates," *Sydney Morning Herald*, May 4, 2004, p. 9.

5 Peter Van Ness, "Hegemony, Not Anarchy: Why China and Japan Are Not Balancing US Unipolar Power," *International Relations of the Asia-Pacific*, Vol. 2, No. 1 (2002), pp. 131–50.

6 For example, Richard Clarke, former head of counterterrorism in the White House during both the Clinton and George W. Bush administrations, found that for Bush and his neoconservative advisers: "Iraq was portrayed as the most dangerous thing in national security. It was an idee fixe, a rigid belief, received wisdom, a decision already made and one that no fact or event could derail." Invading Iraq constituted "a rejection of analysis in favor of received wisdom. It has left us less secure. We will pay the price for a long time." Richard Clarke, *Against All Enemies: Inside America's War on Terror* (New York: Free Press, 2004), pp. 265 and 287.

7 Mel Gurtov's earlier work set out an agenda for such a reevaluation. See his *Global Politics in the Human Interest*, 4th ed. (Boulder, Colo.: Lynne Rienner, 1999).

8 Jeffrey Record, *Bounding the Global War on Terrorism* (Carlisle, Penna.: Strategic Studies Institute, US Army War College, December 2003).

9 Joseph Cirincione, Jessica T. Mathews, and George Perkovich, *WMD in Iraq: Evidence and Implications* (Washington, DC: Carnegie Endowment for International Peace, January 2004).

10 Mohamed ElBaradei, "Towards a Safer World," *The Economist*, October 18, 2003, pp. 51–2.

11 Tokyo and Canberra both sent troops to Iraq, joined the US Proliferation Security Initiative (PSI), and committed their governments to participate in the controversial American missile defense program.

12 See Tim Savage's Chapter 3 and David S. McDonough, *The 2002 Nuclear Posture Review: The "New Triad," Counterproliferation, and US Grand Strategy* (Vancouver, B.C.: Centre of International Relations, University of British Columbia, Working Paper No. 38, August 2003).

13 Li Bin, "China: Weighing the Costs," *Bulletin of the Atomic Scientists*, Vol. 60, No. 2 (March/April, 2004), pp. 21–3. Paul Godwin argues that "assuring a reliable second-strike capability in the shadow of US ballistic missile defense programs is unquestionably China's highest priority." Paul H. B. Godwin, "The PLA's Leap into the 21st Century: Implications for the US," The Jamestown Foundation, *China Brief*, Vol. 4, No. 9 (April 29, 2004).

14 You Ji, "China's Post 9/11 Terrorism Strategy," The Jamestown Foundation, *China Brief*, Vol. 4, No. 8 (April 15, 2004).

15 See, for example, Alastair Iain Johnston, *Cultural Realism: Strategic Culture and Grand Strategy in Chinese History* (Princeton: Princeton University Press, 1995); Allen S. Whiting, "The Use of Force in Foreign Policy by the People's Republic of China," *Annals of the American Academy of Political and Social Science*, No. 402 (1972), pp. 55–65; and Allen S. Whiting, *The Chinese Calculus of Deterrence* (Ann Arbor, Mich.: University of Michigan Press, 1975).

16 Evan S. Medeiros and M. Taylor Fravel, "China's New Diplomacy," *Foreign Affairs*, Vol. 82, No. 6 (November–December, 2003), pp. 22–35.

17 For the Shanghai Cooperation Organization statement on terrorism, see *Beijing Review*, January 17, 2002, p. 5.

18 For agreements signed and a chronology of Sino-Indian contacts, April–June 2003, see *China Report* (New Delhi), Vol. 39, No. 4 (October–December 2003).

19 Xiao Zhou, "China's Untraditional Thoughts on Security," *Beijing Review*, November 27, 2003, pp. 40–41.

20 "East Asian Community Now Possible," *Beijing Review*, October 30, 2003, pp. 40–41. *China: An International Journal*, published by the East Asia Institute, National University of Singapore, has taken a special interest in China's relations with ASEAN. In each issue of this new journal, there is a final section in which a chronology of events and documents on the relationship is published.

21 Godwin, "The PLA's Leap into the 21st Century." See also William S. Murray III and Robert Antonellis, "China's Space Program: The Dragon Eyes the Moon (and Us)," *Orbis*, Vol. 47, No. 4 (Fall, 2003), pp. 645–52.

22 Joseph Cirincione et al., *Deadly Arsenals: Tracking Weapons of Mass Destruction* (Washington, DC: Carnegie Endowment for International Peace, 2002), pp. 141–64.
23 Willy Wo-Lap Lam, "China Aiming for 'Peaceful Rise,'" *CNN.com*, February 2, 2004.
24 Teo Chu Cheow, Eric, "An Ancient Model for China's New Power: Paying Tribute to Beijing," *International Herald Tribune*, January 21, 2004, online at www.iht.com.
25 Quoted in Lam, "China Aiming for 'Peaceful Rise.'"
26 Funabashi Yoichi, "China's 'Peaceful Ascendancy,'" December 2003, YaleGlobal Online, at yaleglobal.yale.edu.
27 See Amitav Acharya's Chapter 9 and his "Will Asia's Past Be Its Future?" *International Security*, Vol. 28, No. 3 (Winter, 2003/4), pp.149–64.

Index

9/11 terrorism attacks 6, 9–10

ABC (Anything But Clinton) policy 43, 45
Abdullah II, King of Jordan 22
ABM (Anti-Ballistic Missile) Treaty 140
Abrams, Elliot 9
absolute security 261, 262
Abu Sayyaf guerrillas 15, 208
accountability 206
Acharya, Amitav xi
Afghanistan 11, 16, 26–7, 262
Agreed Framework *see* Geneva Agreed Framework (1994)
Albright, Madeleine 8, 249
Albright–Cho joint communiqué (2000) 42, 49
Algeria 15
alliance structure: Northeast Asia 77–80
Allison, Graham 205
al-Qaeda 15–16, 18, 19, 26–7, 182, 208; motives 6–7
American nuclear umbrella 77–80
'American way of life' 7–8
Annan, Kofi 12, 20, 187, 189, 191, 197–8, 254
Anti-Ballistic Missile (ABM) Treaty 67, 110, 115, 140, 207
anticipatory attack 197, *see also* preemption
anticipatory self-defense 184
ANZUS (Australia–New Zealand–US alliance) 80
APEC (Asia-Pacific Economic Cooperation) 44
Arafat, Yasser 13
Armitage, Richard 162, 213
arms control agreements 64, 131; China 76
arms race 248, 261

arms reduction 76
arms sales 13–14, 207
Arroyo, Gloria Macapagal 208
Article 51: UN Charter 184, 190
ASEAN (Association of Southeast Asian Nations) 210, 265
Ashcroft, John 10
Asia: National Security Strategy (NSS) 204; response to Bush doctrine 203–22; security 220–2, *see also* Central Asia; Northeast Asia; Southeast Asia; individual countries
Asia-Pacific Economic Cooperation (APEC) 44
Association of Southeast Asian Nations (ASEAN) *see* ASEAN
Australia 211–13; foreign policy 234–40
Australia–New Zealand–US alliance (ANZUS) 80
'axis of evil' 10, 13, 46, 110, 183, 194, 206
Ayatollah Khomeini 11
Azerbaijan 24

Badawi, Abdullah Ahmad 211
Bae Jong-Yun xi
Baker, James A. 48
Bali bombings 15–16, 207, 212
Ball, George 3
Bankok summit (2003) 44
Barber, Benjamin R. 183
Barnet, Richard A. 5
Bell, Coral 232
bilateralism: Asia 220–1
bilateral security treaty: DPRK 246–7
bilateral talks: North Korea 50
bin Laden, Osama 18, 211
Biological and Toxic Weapons Convention 110

Blair, Tony 22, 262
Blix, Hans 192, 194
'Blue Team' 120
Bolton, John xv, 53, 65; opinion of Kim Jong-il 71, 244
Bosnia 23
Bowring, Philip 217
Britain 22, 162, 232, 239
Brookings Institute analysis: National Security Strategy (NSS) 205–6
Brzezinski, Zbigniew 217
Burke, Edmund 232
Burma *see* Myanmar
Bush, George H. W. 8, 10, 63, 228
Bush, George W. 6, 9, 195, 228; alliances 47–8; North Korea 44; NSS 229–32
Bush, Jeb 9
Byrd, Robert 48

Cambodia 210
campaign contributions 75–6
Cao Siyuan 267
capital punishment 13
Caroline case 184–5
Carter, Ashton 55
Carter, Jimmy 91
Casey, Richard Gardiner 236
Castro, Fidel 11
Central Asia 24
Chechnya 23
Cheney, Dick xv, 9, 10, 65, 172, 186, 195
Chen Shui-bian 92, 93–4, 98–9, 100–2
Chiang Ching-kuo 96
Chiang Kai-shek 89, 96
Chih-yu Shih xii
China: arms issues 113–15; Bush doctrine: analysis of 112–13; response to 263–7; containment of 75–7; four-plus-two consortium 247; international order 117, 119–20; international terrorism 117–18; Japan 121–2; national interests 118–25; North Korea 56, 116–17; NSS 231; preemption 216; security interests 117–18; US relations 4, 17, 120–5; US–Taiwan relations 122–3
'China Fever' 92, 95, 96–8
Chirac, Jacques 22
Churchill, Winston 239
Cirincione, Joseph 263
civil liberties 27
Clarke, Richard A. 18
Clinton, Bill 8, 228; China 75
Clinton administration: policy on North Korea 45

'coalition of the willing' 219, 220
Cohen, William 172
cold war: legacies 2–3; practices 22–3
collective security 2
Collective Security Treaty Organization (CSTO) 136
Colombo Plan 236
communism: war on 23
Comprehensive Test Ban Treaty (CTBT): China 76; ratification failure 65, 140
conflict prevention 25
Congress: authority of 3
Congressional hearings: on Iraq 18–19
containment 4–5, 10–12, 204; China 75–7
contingency plans 14
cooperative security 245–6; China 265; consortium 251–4
Coser, Lewis 56
counterfeit currencies 52
counterinsurgency training 15
counter-proliferation strategy 110
CSTO (Collective Security Treaty Organization) 136
CTBT (Comprehensive Test Ban Treaty): China 76; ratification failure 65, 140
Cuba 11
cultural affinity 239

Defense Planning Guidance draft paper (1992) 9, 206
de Gaulle, Charles 238–9
democracy 263
Democratic People's Republic of Korea (DPRK) 71–5, 243–4, 248–50; and Russia 136–50
Democratic Progressive Party (DPP) 96, 100
democratization 16, 24, 206; Taiwan 90
Deng, Francis M. 187
deterrence 10–12, 13, 182, 204, 231
disarmament: nuclear 14, 63–5, 69
Djibouti 15
doctrines: American 227–34
Dominican Republic 11
DPP (Democratic Progressive Party) 96
DPRK (Democratic People's Republic of Korea) 71–5, 243–4, 248–50; and Russia 136–50
drug eradication 15
drug trafficking 52
Dutch New Guinea 239–40

Eagleburger, Lawrence 48
earth penetrating weapons *see* RNEP (robust nuclear earth penetrator)

economic development: Northeast Asia 251
Eden, Anthony 239
Eisenhower, Dwight 6, 185, 239
El Baradei, Mohamed 263
Endriartono Starto 214
energy dependence 27
engagement: North Korea 58–9
Europe 221
European Union (EU) 22
Evans, Gareth 236
Evatt, H.V. 235
Evatt tradition 235–6
exceptionalism 1–8, 9, 193–7

family reunion policy 96; Taiwan 90
Fernandes, George 215, 216
Fleischer, Ari 213, 216
foreign policy 7–8; American 227–34 *see also* National Security Strategy (2002); Australian 234–40; Bush administration 110; post-9/11 14–18; post-Vietnam 3–4; redefining 25–8; Russian 133–6; unilateralism 1–2
former Soviet republics 15
four-plus-two concept 245–51
France 22; Suez crisis 239
Franck, Thomas 193, 198
Franklin, Benjamin 229
freedoms 6–7, 27, 47, 230, 263
Fukuda Yasuo 161, 171
Fukuyama, Francis 4, 230
Funabashi Yoichi 267

Gaddis, John Lewis 204, 206
Galbraith, John Kenneth 3
Garwin, Richard 68
GATT (General Agreement on Tariffs and Trade) 233
Geneva Agreed Framework (1994) 41, 42, 49, 56, 138–9, 249, 250
Germany 22, 221
global engagement 22–8
globalism 227
Globalist interests 7–8, 10
global leadership 26
global warming 13
Global War on Terror (GWOT) 161–2, 169–70
Godwin, Paul 266
Goh Chok Tong 209, 210
Golez, Roilo 214
Gotoda Masaharu 153
Gottemoeller, Rose 251
graduation speech: West Point 10, 181

Grenada 11
Guantanamo Bay xv–xvi
Guingona, Teofisto 209
Gurtov, Mel xi
GWOT (Global War on Terror) 161–2, 169–70

Haass, Richard 11, 187–9
Habsburg Empire 239
Hagel, Chuck 48
Hamiltonian tradition 234
hardliners xv
Harries, Owen xi
Harrison, Selig 254
Hassan Wirayuda 214
Hassner, Pierre 196
hegemonic unilateralism 47–50
hegemony 5, 206, 232–3
Heisei militarization 155, 162–4, 175
Hendrickson, David 196, 261
Hertzberg, Hendrik 252
HEU (highly enriched uranium) program 17, 39, 41, 48, 255
home-visit policy *see* family reunion policy
hostile neglect: North Korea 55–6
Howard, John 212, 215, 235, 239
Howard government policy 237–40
Hu Jintao 245
human development 26
humanitarian crises 23
humanitarian intervention 115–16
human rights 16, 24, 47, 207
human security 26–7
Huntley, Wade 56
Hussein, Saddam 11, 12, 18, 19
Hu Xiaodi 115

IAEA (International Atomic Energy Agency) 82
ideology 230
Ikenberry, John 48, 232
IMF (International Monetary Fund) 233
India: Afghanistan war 16; NPT 65; and Pakistan 23, 190; preemption 215–16; US military relations 15, 17, 80–1
Indonesia: anti-American feeling 211; arms sales 207; and Australia 214; terrorism 209; US military relations 15–16
interdictions: North Korea 73
International Atomic Energy Agency (IAEA) 82
International Convention on Land Mines 140, 228

International Criminal Court 23, 140, 207, 228
internationalism 9
international law 212
international legal order 131
International Monetary Fund (IMF) 233
international order 119–20
International Peace Cooperation Law 164
international relationships 14–18
international security 25
International Thermonuclear Reactor (ITER) 174
intervention 4, 7; justification for 187–8; legitimacy 190–3
Iran 11, 25, 183
Iraq 11, 12, 183; legitimacy 192; nuclear reactor: Osirak 186
Iraq war 18–22, 261–2; Asian attitudes 215–19; case for 238; China 115, 264; consequences of 233; influence on Asia 207; Japan 153–4, 158–9; legacy of 24, 250–1; Southeast Asian attitudes 210–11; Taiwan 93–4
Ishiba Shigeru 161, 218
Ishihara Shintaro 155, 168
isolationism 23, 193; avoidance of 4
Israel 13, 24, 211; attack on Osirak 186; protection of 4
Israeli–Palestine issues 24
Israeli–Palestinian issues 211, 213, 262
ITER (International Thermonuclear Reactor) 174
Ivanov, Igor 131–2

Jacksonian tradition 234
Jamali, Zafarullah Khan 215
Japan 153–76; Australia 213; China 121–2, 173; 'coalition of the willing' 219; four-plus-two consortium 247; kidnap issues 159, 245, 255; NDPO (National Defense Program Outline) 167–8; North Korea 172, 245; nuclear weapons 78–9, 170–5; preemption 218; security legislation 164–6; security policy 154–6; support for Bush doctrine 157–61; TMD (Theater Missile Defense) 77; US–Japan Mutual Security Treaty 164–5
Jefferson tradition 234
Jemaah Islamiyah 16, 208
Jiang Jemin 264
Johnson, Chalmers 28
Johnson, Frank 232
Johnson, Lyndon B. 3, 6

Jordan 22, 211

Kagan, Robert 190, 229
Kang, Sokjoo 41, 48
Kaplan, Lawrence F. 186–7
Karaganov, S. 132–3
Kasuri, Khurshid Mahmood 215
Kazakhstan 15, 24
Keating, Paul 212, 237
Keating tradition 236–7
KEDO (Korean Peninsula Energy Development Organization) 41, 138
Kelly, James 41, 246, 249, 250, 255
Kennan, George 27
Kennedy, Edward M. 48, 186
Khan, A. Q. 81
Khomeini, Ayatollah 11
kidnapping issues: Iraq 159; North Korea 245, 255
Kim Dae Jung 217, 249, 252, 255
Kim Il-Sung 11
Kim Jong-il 11, 44, 150, 244, 249, 255; Bush's opinion 46, 71
Kim Myong Chol 150
Kissinger, Henry 7, 91, 189, 196, 261
Klare, Michael 13
Koizumi Junichiro 158, 165, 167–8, 169–70, 171, 218, 245, 249, 255
Korea 11, see also North Korea; South Korea
Korean Peninsula Energy Development Organization (KEDO) 41, 138
Korean War 146
Kosovo 23, 191–2
Krauthammer, Charles 8, 172, 227
Krystol, William 186–7
Kyoto Protocol 13, 23, 110, 140, 207, 228
Kyrgyzstan 15

Lampton, Mike 260
land mine treaty 140, 228
Laos 210
Latin America 23
Layne, Christopher 3–4
leadership 47; global 26
Leahy, Patrick J. 20
Lebanon 11
Lee Kuan Yew 219–20
Lee Tenghui 91, 96, 100, 101
legitimacy: for anticipatory action 190–3; of 'war on terror' xv–xvi
Lend-Lease aid 239
Leunig, Michael xi
liberty 6, 230

Libya 11, 25, 262
Lieber, Robert J. 5
limited sovereignty 11
limits of sovereignty thesis 187
Lippmann, Walter 240
Liu Jianchao 216
Losyukov, A. 146
low-yield nuclear weapons 70
Lumumba, Patrice 11

Madrid bombings 23
Mahathir, bin Mohamad 135, 213, 214
Malaysia: and Australia 213
malign neglect: North Korea 55–6
Mansergh, Nicholas 236
Mao Zedong 89
Mathews, Jessica Tuchman 25
McCain, John 172
McNamara, Robert S. 28
MD (missile defense): China 76
Mead, Walter Russell 234
Megawati Sukarnoputri 135
Melville, Herman 229
Menzies, Robert 240
Menzies tradition 234–5
Mexico 23
Middle East 22, 24; bases 15
Middle East policy 13
militarization 162–4
military aid 15, 207, 208
military bases 15, 207, 209
military expenditure 9, 13–14
military options: North Korea 53–5
military power 51, 230–1
mini-nukes 69–70
missile defense (MD) 68–9, 114–15, 261; China 76; Japan 159–61
MLSA (Mutual Logistics Support Agreement) 208
Mongolia: 'coalition of the willing' 219
Monroe Doctrine 195, 228
Moon Chung-in xii
Moon Hayong 252
moral absolutism 45–7
moral clarity 6, 9, 45–7
Morocco 211
Moscow Treaty (2002) 14
multilateral approach: Korean crisis 254–6
multilateral cooperation 131
multilateral diplomacy 25
multilateralism 12–13, 207, 233
Musharraf, Pervez 16, 17, 81
Mutual Logistics Support Agreement (MLSA) 208

Myanmar 210

Najib, Datuk Sri 213–14
Nakasone Yasuhiro 168–9
Nakayama Taro 165
National Defense Program Outline (NDPO): Japan 167–8
nationalism: Japan 168–70
National Missile Defense (NMD) 77, 141
national security 5, 9–10, 263; redefining 25–8
National Security Strategy (NSS: 2002) 10–11, 12, 110, 183–5, 184, 204, 229–32; Brookings Institute analysis 205–6; evaluation 232–3
National Strategy for Combating Terrorism 50
NATO 71, 115–16
NATO allies 12–13, 23
NCND (neither confirm nor deny) policy 80
NDPO (National Defense Program Outline): Japan 167–8
negotiated settlement option: North Korea 57–9
neoconservatism 112
neoconservatives xv, 8–9, 42–3, 55, 66–7, 263; North Korea 53
neo-Globalists 4
neo-Realists 4
Nepal 15
Netanyahu, Benjamin 186
'New Triad': offensive strike systems 68, 69
New Zealand 80
Nikolaev, A. 134
Nishimura Shingo 171
NMD (National Missile Defense) 77, 141
Nonaka Hiromu 154
noninterference 51
nonintervention principle: exceptions 187–8
nonproliferation 64–5, 81–2, 131
Non-Proliferation Project 263
Northeast Asia: economic development 251
North Korea 39–59; 'axis of evil' 216–17; nuclear crisis 242–57; Pakistan 17, 24; preemption 190; 'rogue state' 183; Russia 136–50; US confrontation 25; US relations 71–5
NPR (Nuclear Posture Review) *see* Nuclear Posture Review (NPR)
NPT (Nuclear Non-Proliferation Treaty) 64–5, 81–2, 139

nuclear arms race 248, 261
nuclear arms reduction 76
nuclear crisis: North Korea 39–59
nuclear disarmament 63–5; Korea 251
Nuclear Non-Proliferation Treaty (NPT) 64–5, 81–2, 139
Nuclear Policy Review 76
Nuclear Posture Review (NPR) 14, 50–1, 52, 67–8, 69–70, 78, 114, 264
nuclear proliferation 248
nuclear tests 65
nuclear weapons 14, 24, 25, 69–70; Bush policy 65–7; Japan 170–5; reduction 26; tactical use of 51; US defense policy 63–4
nuclear weapons testing 13
Nye, Joseph 48, 193

offensive realism 50–3
offensive strike systems: 'New Triad' 68, 69
Of Paradise and Power 229
oil 27; protection of 4
'One China' 91, 92–3, 122, 123
one-side-one-country (OSOC) 92–3, 101
Ople, Blas 214
OP Plan 5030: strategy for North Korea 72
Osama bin Laden *see* bin Laden, Osama
Osirak attack 186
OSOC (one-side-one-country) 92–3, 101
Ozawa Ichiro 155, 171

Paine, Tom 229
Pakistan: anti-American feeling 211; nuclear proliferation 80–1; nuclear tests 65; preemption 215–16; US relations 16–17, 24
Palestinian Authority 211
Palestinian–Israeli issues 211, 213, 262
Palmerston, Lord 240
Panama 11
Paris Peace Conference (1946) 235
'peaceful rise' initiative 266–7
Peace Keeping Operations Law 164
Pearl Harbor 205
Pena, Charles 172
Pentagon 9, 13; use of budget 16
Perle, Richard xv, 12, 18, 53, 72, 195
Perry, William 72, 145
Philippines: Australia 214; 'coalition of the willing' 210, 219; terrorism 208–9; US advisors 15; US military bases 207
post-post-cold-war era 2, 22
Powell, Colin 4, 9, 11, 12, 13, 16, 44

power xv–xvi, 206
preemption 73, 87, 111, 113, 184–90, 204–5, 207, 218, 231–2; Australia 211–13; China 216; India 215–16; legitimacy 190–3, 203–4
preemptive action 10–12, 50, 110, 184; Japan 161; North Korea 52
preventive war 11, 27, 205
primacy 5; America's 1–2
programs: military funding 15
Project for the New American Century 9, 66–7
Proliferation Security Initiative (PSI) 73, 243–4, 264
Putin, Vladimir 130, 135–6, 137–8
Putin–Bush summit meetings 132, 133
Putin–Kim Jong-il summit 147

al Qaddafi, Muammar 11, 262
Quemoy crisis (1958) 89

radicals xv
radioactive fallout 70
Rafidah Aziz 214
Ratthakit Manathat 215
Reagan, Ronald 9, 64, 91, 169; presidency 3
Reagan Doctrine 228
Realist interests 7–8, 10
Record, Jeffrey 161–2, 205, 263
'Red Team' 120
regime change 194; Asian response 206; Iraq 18, 20, 261–2; North Korea 244; preempting 111
regime stability: North Korea 248
regionalism: Australia 236–7
Republic of Korea (ROK) 140–1
reunification: Korea 247–8; Taiwan 89–90, 98
revolution in military affairs (RMA) 13
Rice, Condoleezza 8, 50, 51, 185, 189, 194, 195
RNEP (robust nuclear earth penetrator) 51, 52, 69
'road map': Israeli–Palestine settlement 24
'rogue states' 183, 194, 262, 264
Rohingyas Muslims 210
Roh Moo Hyun 217, 245, 252
ROK (Republic of Korea) 140–1
Roosevelt, Franklin D. 239
Rosati, Jerel A. 6
Rostow, Walt W. 2, 3
Ruggie, John 23
Rumsfeld, Donald xv, 9, 12, 13, 19, 46, 48, 49, 53, 65, 72, 195, 233

Russell, James 111
Russia 130–50; Asia 135–6; foreign policy 133–6; four-plus-two consortium 247; Kosovo 191–2; Moscow Treaty (2002) 14; North Korea 56; and North Korea 136–50; US relations 17
Russia–NATO council 134
Rwanda 23

Saddam Hussein *see* Hussein, Saddam
Safire, William 217
Saigon regime 3, 7
SALT (Strategic Arms Limitations Talks) 64
sanctions: North Korea 39–40, 72
Saudi Arabia 22, 27
Savage, Timothy xii
Schmitt, Carl 195
Schröder, Gerhard 18, 22, 227
SCO (Shanghai Cooperation Organization) 136, 265
Scowcroft, Brent 48
security consortium: for Northeast Asia 251–4
Security Council: preemption 191–2
'security dilemma' 261
security legislation: Japan 164–6
'selective engagement' 4
self-defense 184–5
self-image: America's 6
September 11 terrorism attacks 6, 9–10
Shanghai Cooperation Organization (SCO) 136, 265
Shangri-la Dialogue (2003) 218
Shebarshin, L. 134, 141–2
Shigeta Hiroshi 213
Sibal, Kanwal 80, 216
Singapore 208, 209, 210; 'coalition of the willing' 219
Singh, Jaswant 190
Sinha, Yashwant 215
Sino-Russian relationship 119
Sino-US relations 120–5, 260
six-party talks 44, 45, 57–9, 72, 74–5, 143–7, 242–3, 265
Slouka, Mark 6
South Asia 80
Southeast Asia 16, 207–11
South Korea: 'coalition of the willing' 219; North Korea relations 140–1; preemption 216–17; sanctions on North Korea 56; TMD (Theater Missile Defense) 77; US military bases 53; US relations 54, 66, 78–9

sovereignty 115, 188; limited 11; limits of 187; Westphalian 51
Soviet republics: former 15
Spain 23
speeches: State of the Union address (2002) 110, 249; West Point 10, 181, 206
Spender, Percy 236
Spender-Casey tradition 236–7
stability: Northeast Asia 251
START (Strategic Arms Reduction Talks) 64
State Department 9
State of the Union address (2002) 110, 249
state sovereignty 115
STRATCOM (US Strategic Command): China 75
Strategic Arms Limitations Talks (SALT) 64
Strategic Arms Reduction Talks (START) 64
strategic overextension 14–18
Sudan 11
Suez crisis 239
Sukarnoputri, Megawati *see* Megawati Sukarnoputri
Sun City Extended Study: China 75
'sunshine policy' 249, 252, 255
Surakiart Sathirathai 215

tactical nuclear weapons 51
Taiwan 86–103; China 122–3, 216; TMD (Theater Missile Defense) 77; US relations 75
Tajikistan 15
Taliban 16
talks: North Korea 44, 45, 57–9, 72, 74–5, 143–7, 242–3
Tanter, Richard xii
Teo Chu Cheow, Eric 266
terrorism: Australia 238; Indonesia 209; North Korea 46–7; Southeast Asia 208; Vietnam 209–10
terrorism threats 10, 182–3
terrorist threats 263
Thailand: Australia 214–15; 'coalition of the willing' 210
Thaksin Shinawatra 214–15
Theater Missile Defense (TMD) 77, 78, 141, 159
Third World trade 13
training: counterinsurgency 15
triangular relations game theory: Taiwan 88
Truman, Harry S. 185–6

Truman Doctrine 228, 230
Turkey 22

Ukraine 251
UN (United Nations) 12, 23, 115–16, 131, 233; Iraq war 20
UN Charter 212; Article 51: 184, 190
unilateral action 10–12
unilateralism 1–2, 5, 8, 12, 14–18, 23, 47–50, 110, 206–7, 219–20, 227; costs of 24
United Nations (UN) *see* UN (United Nations)
UN Security Council 82, 117, 197, 235; Australia 240; four-plus-two consortium 253–4
UN weapons inspectors 194
uranium enrichment program *see* HEU (highly enriched uranium) program
US–German relations 221
US Military Academy: Bush's speech *see* West Point
US nuclear umbrella 77–80
US Strategic Command (STRATCOM): China 75
US–Taiwan relations: Chinese view 122–3
US–Japan Mutual Security Treaty: guidelines 164–5
US–Philippines cooperation 208–9
US–Singapore security ties 209
Uzbekistan 15

values: American 193–4
Van Ness, Peter xii, 162
Vedrine, Hubert 227
Viet Cong 2–3
Vietnam 11; terrorism 209–10
Vietnamese communists 7

Vietnam War 233
Vietnam War era 2–3
violations: allegations 250; of principles xv–xvi

Walzer, Michael 184, 185
war on communism 23
'war on terrorism' 10, 228–9; globalization of 14–18; manipulation of 15–18; Southeast Asia 210–11; Taiwan 99–100
War Powers Resolution (1993) 3
Washington, George 239, 240
'way of life' 7–8
weapons of mass destruction *see* WMD
Webster, Daniel 205
Westphalian sovereignty 51
West Point: Bush's graduation speech 10, 181, 206
Wheeler, Nicholas J. xii
Whitlam, Gough 236
Williams, William A. 5
Wilson, Woodrow 193, 229
Wilsonian tradition 234
Wirtz, James 111
WMD (weapons of mass destruction) 4, 263; evidence for 19
Wolfowitz, Paul xv, 9, 13, 19, 65, 195, 206, 218
Woodward, Bob 244
World Bank 233

Yan Xuetong 261
Yemen 15, 24
Yoshida Doctrine 155
Yuan Jing-dong xii–xiii, 264

Zhebin, Alexander xiii
Zheng Bijian 266

eBooks – at www.eBookstore.tandf.co.uk

A library at your fingertips!

eBooks are electronic versions of printed books. You can store them on your PC/laptop or browse them online.

They have advantages for anyone needing rapid access to a wide variety of published, copyright information.

eBooks can help your research by enabling you to bookmark chapters, annotate text and use instant searches to find specific words or phrases. Several eBook files would fit on even a small laptop or PDA.

NEW: Save money by eSubscribing: cheap, online access to any eBook for as long as you need it.

Annual subscription packages

We now offer special low-cost bulk subscriptions to packages of eBooks in certain subject areas. These are available to libraries or to individuals.

For more information please contact webmaster.ebooks@tandf.co.uk

We're continually developing the eBook concept, so keep up to date by visiting the website.

www.eBookstore.tandf.co.uk